EMS MANIFESTO

		PRINCIPLES OF DATA COMMUNICATION (second edition)	SECURITY, ACCURACY, AND PRIVACY IN COMPUTER SYSTEMS
AN END USER'S GUIDE TO DATABASE			A BREAKTHROUGH IN MAKING COMPUTERS FRIENDLY: THE MACINTOSH COMPUTER

Books On Data Base	Books On Telecommunications	Books On Teleprocessing	Books On Systems In General
PRINCIPLES OF DATABASE MANAGEMENT (second edition)	COMPUTER NETWORKS AND DISTRIBUTED PROCESSING	TELEPROCESSING NETWORK ORGANIZATION	DESIGN OF MAN-COMPUTER DIALOGUES
COMPUTER DATABASE ORGANIZATION (third edition)	DESIGN AND STRATEGY FOR DISTRIBUTED DATA PROCESSING	SYSTEMS ANALYSIS FOR DATA TRANSMISSION	DESIGN OF REAL-TIME COMPUTER SYSTEMS
MANAGING THE DATABASE ENVIRONMENT (second edition)	Books On Distributed Processing	DATA COMMUNICATION TECHNOLOGY	STRATEGIC DATA-PLANNING METHODOLOGIES (second edition)
DATABASE ANALYSIS AND DESIGN	TELECOMMUNICATIONS AND THE COMPUTER (third edition)	DATA COMMUNICATION DESIGN TECHNIQUES	INFORMATION ENGINEERING (Volume I: Introduction and Strategy)
VSAM: ACCESS METHOD SERVICES AND PROGRAMMING TECHNIQUES	FUTURE DEVELOPMENTS IN TELECOMMUNICATIONS (third edition)	SNA: IBM's NETWORKING SOLUTION	INFORMATION ENGINEERING (Volume II: Analysis, Design, and Construction)
DB2: CONCEPTS, DESIGN, AND PROGRAMMING	COMMUNICATIONS SATELLITE SYSTEMS	LOCAL AREA NETWORKS	WORLD INFORMATION ECONOMY
IDMS/R: CONCEPTS, DESIGN, AND PROGRAMMING	ISDN	OFFICE AUTOMATION STANDARDS	
STRATEGIC DATA-PLANNING METHODOLOGIES (second edition)	WORLD INFORMATION ECONOMY	CORPORATE COMMUNICATIONS NETWORKS	
		NETWORK STANDARDS	

successful author of computer books. He has been a high-level advisor to several governments. He was a member of the first joint American-Russian committee to study possible exchanges of computer expertise. James Martin has signed what is probably the largest contract in the history of television, to make 280 video and computer-based training course modules with Deltak's Advanced Technology Library.

James Martin's World Seminar is the most highly attended in the computer industry. More than 10,000 people have attended. A new edition of this seminar is created every six months to accommodate the rapid changes of computers, software, and telecommunications.

About the authors:

JAMES MARTIN is the chairman of James Martin Associates, a worldwide consulting group based in Reston, Virginia. His work includes consulting with the top management of many of the large computer industry corporations about their corporate product strategies. He advises many organizations on their implementation of new DP methods. He received an honorary degree from Salford University for his work in the field of Information Engineering.

James Martin was with IBM for 19 years, in both the field and development laboratories. He is the world's most

STEVEN OXMAN is president and chief scientist of the OXKO Corporation, a knowledge engineering consulting firm located in Annapolis, Maryland. Mr. Oxman lectures on expert system technology and the knowledge engineering discipline, and has been consultant to many commercial concerns such as Ingersoll-Rand, Armco Steel, and Monsanto, as well as government agencies including the Netherlands Ministry of Education and Science, and the United States National Bureau of Standards.

Mr. Oxman has been researching commercial expert systems since 1983 and developing them since 1985.

BUILDING EXPERT SYSTEMS

A ~~*James Martin*~~ ——— **BOOK**

Steven Oxman

THE JAMES MARTIN BOOKS

- Application Development Without Programmers
- Communications Satellite Systems
- Computer Data-Base Organization, Second Edition
- Computer Networks and Distributed Processing: Software, Techniques, and Architecture
- Design and Strategy of Distributed Data Processing
- Design of Man-Computer Dialogues
- Design of Real Time Computer Systems
- An End User's Guide to Data Base
- Fourth-Generation Languages, Volume I: Principles
- Future Developments in Telecommunications, Second Edition
- Information Engineering
- An Information Systems Manifesto
- Introduction to Teleprocessing
- Managing the Data-Base Environment
- Principles of Data-Base Management
- Recommended Diagramming Standards for Analysts and Programmers
- Security, Accuracy, and Privacy in Computer Systems
- Strategic Data Planning Methodologies
- Systems Analysis for Data Transmission
- System Design from Provably Correct Constructs
- Technology's Crucible
- Telecommunications and the Computer, Second Edition
- Telematic Society: A Challenge for Tomorrow
- Teleprocessing Network Organization

with Carma McClure

- Action Diagrams: Clearly Structured Specifications, Programs, and Procedures, Second Edition
- Diagramming Techniques for Analysts and Programmers
- Software Maintenance: The Problem and Its Solutions
- Structured Techniques: The Basis for CASE, Revised Edition

with The ARBEN Group, Inc.

- A Breakthrough in Making Computers Friendly: The Macintosh Computer
- Data Communication Technology
- DB2: A Practical Guide
- Fourth-Generation Languages, Volume II: Representative Fourth-Generation Languages
- Fourth-Generation Languages, Volume III: 4GLs from IBM
- Local Area Networks: Architectures and Implementations
- Principles of Data Communication
- SNA: IBM's Networking Solution
- VSAM: Access Method Services and Programming Techniques

with Adrian Norman

- The Computerized Society

with Steven Oxman

- Building Expert Systems: A Tutorial

BUILDING EXPERT SYSTEMS

A Tutorial

JAMES MARTIN

STEVEN OXMAN

 PRENTICE HALL Englewood Cliffs, New Jersey 07632

Library of Congress Cataloging-in-Publication Data

MARTIN, JAMES (date)
    Building expert systems.

    "The James Martin books."
    Bibliography: p.
    Includes index.
      1. Expert systems (Computer science) I. Oxman,
Steven W.   II. Title.
QA76.76E95M37 1988   006.3'3   88-5797
ISBN 0-13-086240-1

Editorial/production supervision: Kathryn Gollin Marshak
Cover design: Bruce Kenselaar
Manufacturing buyer: Mary Ann Gloriande

Selection on p. 13 from 2001: A SPACE ODYSSEY by Arthur C. Clarke. Copyright © 1968 by Arthur C. Clarke and Polaris Productions. Reprinted by arrangement with NAL Penguin Inc., New York, and by permission of the author and the author's agents, Scott Meredith Literary Agency, Inc., 845 Third Avenue, New York, New York 10022.

Printed in the United States of America

10 9 8 7 6 5 4 3 2 1

ISBN   0-13-086240-1

PRENTICE-HALL INTERNATIONAL (UK) LIMITED, *London*
PRENTICE-HALL OF AUSTRALIA PTY. LIMITED, *Sydney*
PRENTICE-HALL CANADA INC., *Toronto*
PRENTICE-HALL HISPANOAMERICANA, S.A., *Mexico*
PRENTICE-HALL OF INDIA PRIVATE LIMITED, *New Delhi*
PRENTICE-HALL OF JAPAN, INC., *Tokyo*
SIMON & SCHUSTER ASIA PTE. LTD., *Singapore*
EDITORA PRENTICE-HALL DO BRASIL, LTDA., *Rio de Janeiro*

**TO
CORINTHIA
AND
JUDITH**

CONTENTS

PREFACE

The demand for expert systems in business is beginning to outstrip the supply of expert system developers. To continue the introduction of expert systems technology into business environments, more people capable of developing expert systems are needed. Demand for expert systems in business has been increasing because the technology is proving itself a valuable tool that, when used properly, provides reasonable returns on the investments it requires.

Expert system technology is a valid alternative computer-based tool. It can be used to solve certain problems more effectively than other computer-based tools. Although the technology cannot do everything, expert systems have been built to solve previously unsolved problems.

What are expert systems? What does the future hold for this technology? What business situations have generated interest in expert systems? What opportunities become available through the use of expert systems? Part I, which contains the first four chapters in this tutorial, answers these questions, and the Prologue provides a comprehensive glossary. The goal of Part I, along with the Prologue, is to introduce the expert system technology. No background in expert systems or artificial intelligence is required for comprehension of this material.

Part II moves on to the subject of expert system construction. We start by helping the reader determine whether a particular task is suitable for expert system support. We then explore the specifics of building expert systems, including the consideration of architectural issues, design issues, the expert system life cycle, and expert system construction requirements.

Part III presents discussion on tools needed to build expert systems. Alternative tool usage, like programming languages versus shells, is presented. Although keeping a textbook current on commercial expert system-related products is not possible, we supply some product and vendor information to give the reader an idea of what is available. More up-to-date product and vendor information can be obtained through the James Martin Reports (36 Bessom Street, Marblehead, Massachusetts 01945). We conclude this part with a discussion of computer hardware specially designed for artificial intelligence software, such as expert systems. This discussion deals with LISP machines. We note in the introduction of this discussion that more and more vendors are offering products for use on conventional computing machinery, including minicomputers, work-stations, and personal computers.

Part IV presents expert system construction strategies. The first chapter in this part provides a great deal of material concerning the building of a large, commercial expert system, XSEL. The second chapter in this part provides a complete description of the development of a small, personal computer-based expert system. This chapter shows that such systems can be built with modest investments and can provide organizations with effective and useful aids that save manpower and reduce operational expenses. The next chapter provides information on how to select the right tools with which to develop an expert system, including pertinent selection criteria and a useful discussion on the selection process itself.

The final chapter tells what to expect from this technology and this industry in the future. Since the technology has proved itself useful, organizations are investing in it. Since organizations are investing in it, capital is available to expand it. Consequently, vendors will continue to offer new capabilities for their existing products and will develop new, more capable products as well.

We hope that this book will acquaint many more people with the expert system technology, both people in the computer field and those in other areas who would like to use computer-based tools to make their job tasks more efficient or to assist people around them. This book should provide computer science students with a good introduction to this new and exciting technology. Students in many other fields in which experts pass on knowledge and expertise to others should also be able to see where expert systems might be of benefit to them and their peers.

Expert system technology is multidisciplinary. Expert system tools have helped professionals in scientific fields, engineering, and business and management, as well as laborers in many traditional industries, including heavy machinery and steel production, and they should therefore be of interest to people in numerous fields.

Corporate decision makers who already use or would like to use computer-based tools and aids should find this tutorial of value. Expert system technology will support more and more decision makers by providing additional decision-making power with less training and in less time than at present.

People who have expertise that they wish to pass on to others should find this technology exciting. For the first time, expertise can be represented in forms that more closely approximate thinking than classical, mathematical models and computer programs do. This book will help experts learn what expert systems are, how they can help experts, and just how capable the systems are.

As we said at the beginning of this preface, there is a demand for people who are capable of building effective expert systems. We hope that this book will help many of those people become familiar with the basics. Our goal was to develop a book that could be used as a first tutorial on the subject. Most of the readers of this tutorial will be people who have read either few or no textbooks on the expert system technology.

Although expert system technology is not the ultimate technology, it is an exciting one. We believe that it will provide valuable tools and aids to get work done more quickly and more easily, at reduced costs.

James Martin
Steven Oxman

BUILDING EXPERT SYSTEMS

PROLOGUE: THE VOCABULARY USED WITH EXPERT SYSTEMS

Artificial Intelligence

The study of mental faculties through the use of computational models by attempting to duplicate (or simulate) the mental faculties and thought processes of an individual, as in speech and vision. A field of inquiry with many real-world applications. Covers a multitude of disciplines including cognitive psychology, linguistics, electrical engineering, operations research, decision theory, computer science, information science, and computer programming. The study of ideas that enable computers to do the things that make people seem intelligent. The study of ways in which to make computers do things that people do better through the use of techniques for solving exponentially difficult problems by exploiting knowledge about a problem domain. The underlying assumption of artificial intelligence is supplementing and extending human capabilities by means of computer computational programs. The science concentrates on making machines intelligent so that they become more useful and are able to understand intelligence, not just act in response to commands, and is concerned with concepts and methods of symbolic inferencing by computers and the symbolic representations of the knowledge that is used in deriving inferences. This field pursues the possibility that a computer can be designed to behave in ways that people perceive as "intelligent." Artificial intelligence may be concerned with the collection, assembly, selection, understanding, and perception of knowledge by an artifact, the computer. Artificial intelligence may also be referred to as machine intelligence or heuristic programming.

Knowledge

Cognizance; the fact or condition of knowing something with familiarity gained through experience or association; the fact or condition of being aware of something; the range of one's information or understanding; the fact or condition of having information; the sum of what is known, an accumulation of the body of truth, information, and principles acquired by an individual or by humanity. Encoding of facts affording the knower the ability of using these encoded facts in practical interactions. The ability to form a mental model that accurately describes the object and represents the actions that can be performed by and on that object. Facts, beliefs, and heuristic rules. The integration of a collection of facts and relationships.

Knowledge Engineering

A subfield of artificial intelligence addressing the design and development of knowledge systems; concerned with the acquisition, representation, and application of knowledge. The process of reducing a large body of knowledge to a definitive set of rules and facts through both the construction of a knowledge-base and the inference procedures required for interpreting that knowledge. The task of knowledge engineering is to identify pertinent information (knowledge), develop a knowledge framework through a combination of representation and inference, and then execute this framework using the necessary tools. Knowledge engineering can take the form of systems analysis of some aspect of the world to determine meaningful premises. As an engineering discipline, knowledge engineering integrates knowledge into computer systems so that they can solve complex problems that normally require a high level of human expertise. It is concerned with the task of building knowledge-based systems like expert systems and the tools and methods used to design and develop them. The goal of knowledge engineering is to plan, design, construct, and manage knowledge-based systems for the transfer, application, and extension of knowledge.

Knowledge-based Systems

Computer programs using knowledge and inference procedures for solving problems that are difficult enough normally to require a significant amount of human expertise to arrive at their solution. They structure data and reasoning rules that link the evidence about a problem to derived conclusions. Such systems, which contain the knowledge of a particular expert on a specific subject, may be used as a substitute for an expert human consultant who is unavailable at the time needed and may incorporate knowledge acquired from human experts and apply it in novel ways. Knowledge-based systems components include a knowledge base (consisting of facts and rules of thumb about the domain), a database of current dynamically changing data, and control mechanisms for finding and using the knowledge.

Knowledge Engineer

An individual who designs and builds knowledge-based systems like expert systems by helping problem domain experts map information into a form suitable from which to build a system that other individuals may later use to get advice. The knowledge engineer's specialty is to assess problems, acquire knowledge relating to the problems, and build knowledge systems using the information gathered. He or she is concerned with identifying the specific knowledge that is used by an expert in solving a given problem, determining the inference strategy that the expert would use, and developing a system that uses similar knowledge and inferencing to simulate the expert's behavior and solutions. The knowledge engineer concentrates on the meaning of the data gathered, the logical interdependencies between the facts, and the schemas and inference rules that apply to the data. To fulfill this function, the knowledge engineer must interview experts to extract knowledge, abstract the main characteristics of the problem, and then undertake the building of a computer system that represents the knowledge garnered, thereby serving as an intermediary between the knowledge-base and its author.

Knowledge Representation

Analysis of the knowledge of an expert, including facts and rules of thumb he uses, the determination of how this knowledge should be delineated in the software that comprises a knowledge-based system, and the method used to encode and store facts and relationships in a knowledge-base. The knowledge, which can be represented symbolically in various forms of logic, is then formalized, structured, and programmed into a computer so that it can be manipulated by the knowledge-base management system in order to determine the validity of a statement by referring to knowledge previously received and to rules for manipulating that data. The representation consists of a vocabulary of symbols and some prescribed methods for arranging the symbols in order to describe things. The knowledge representation can be seen as a set of objects, each having a collection of attributes and a set of relationships to other objects.

Data

Factual information. Facts or figures from which conclusions may be drawn. Data is composed of raw material that may be refined, shaped, interpreted, selected, and transformed in order to produce information.

Information

Aggregate of data that is acquired, derived, or obtained from investigation, study, or instruction; something that justifies change in a construct (such as a plan or theory) that represents physical or mental experience or another construct.

Fuzzy Information

Unreliable data, soft data, or inexact data from which assumptions may be drawn. Probabilistic. Concepts that provide a continuous range of variability and possibilities. Vagueness that results from the imprecision of natural language. Arises from deficiencies in the ability to represent a concept within crisp, finite boundaries, but rather represents the concept by gradual progression (or along a continuum) without a definitive point of demarcation.

Common Sense

Sound and prudent, often unsophisticated judgment. The unreflective opinions of ordinary men. Reasoning based on naive physics and naive psychology and composed of everyday knowledge. Often involves rapid sensing in order to understand a situation.

Experience

Facts or events or the totality of facts or events observed; knowledge, skill, or practice derived from direct observation of or participation in events; the conscious events that make up an individual life; the events that comprise the conscious past of a community or nation or humankind generally; something personally encountered, undergone, or lived through. Knowledge or skill derived from actual participation or training. The totality of judgments or reactions. Accumulated variety of things in which one has been engaged.

Heuristics

Rules of thumb. Techniques that provide aid or direction in solving a problem that would be otherwise unjustified or incapable of justification, or that involve exploratory problem-solving strategies that rely on self-educating techniques to improve performance. The many forms of rules of thumb used in problem solving. The most common is the if-then rule, through which a program is activated by a control structure only when certain conditions are met. Such activation is based on knowledge about a specific problem to be solved. Heuristics also takes the form of a systematic guessing structure in which the best option is selected for consideration, options that are not feasible are eliminated, or the current condition is tested against the end goals (criteria); in this way, heuristics that reduce or limit searches in large problem spaces, thereby improving the efficiency of the search process. These search limitations may make a trade-off between time and thoroughness in obtaining problem solutions. Heuristics may also be described as rules of good judgment. A heuristic may be anything that serves as a guide in problem solving and usually achieves the desired results. Heuristics are often used with problems whose outcomes cannot be guaranteed to be successful or whose solutions cannot be guaranteed to be correct.

Cognition

The act or process of knowing, including both awareness and judgment; the product of the act or process of knowing. The process involved in intelligent reasoning.

Objects

Anything physical or mental, of which a person is cognitively aware. Physical or conceptual entities that have attributes and constitute part or all of the subject matter of an investigation or science. An object is static if it only describes the generic relationship of a group of attributes and their possible values. An object is dynamic if precise values are associated with a specific example or form of the object.

Concepts

Things conceived in the mind; thoughts, notions; abstract or generic ideas generalized from particular instances. Descriptive outlines of classes of things or a specific instance of an outline with general characteristics differentiated in order to define a specific subcategory or element that instantiates the class description. May represent any entity, action, or state that can be described by language. Used for the nodes (basic units representing knowledge) that encode information in networks or graphs. Concepts are discrete.

Facts

Actual occurrences or events. Pieces of information presented as having objective reality. Data structures that give information about actual data values obtained. Specific knowledge relevant to a particular case. Propositions or statements having accepted validity. In most knowledge systems, facts take the form of logical expressions that consist of predicates or attributes and values specifically associated with them.

Perception

A mental image; a concept; awareness of the elements of environment through physical sensation; physical sensation, often in the form of vision or speech, interpreted in the light of experience; quick, acute, and intuitive cognition; a capacity for comprehension.

Intuition

The power or faculty of obtaining direct knowledge or cognition without evident rational thought and inference; quick and ready insight.

Rules

Customary guides for conduct or action; the implications derived from the descriptions of these guides. Representation of knowledge as conditional statements consisting of "IF . . . THEN . . . clauses. Knowledge used as criteria for drawing conclusions; single units of information. Composed of antecedent conditions and consequent propositions used to support deductive processes. Rules form the basis of knowledge formation in human short-term memory; they are the basic building blocks of human knowledge structures. Rules have become the dominant form of symbolic knowledge in first-generation expert systems. Rules represent a formal means of encoding knowledge. Rules may represent a quick guide to be used for determining actions.

Metarules

Rules about rules. A special class of rules that represent control knowledge and prescribe the manner in which rules are to be applied. Also help to break down a knowledge base into segments that apply to classes of situations. May provide strategies for the selection of paths of reasoning that may be useful. May be used for ordering of rules.

Rule-based Systems

Reasoning systems built around set rules and not concerned with the underlying causal knowledge that comprises the rules. Rule-based systems encode the knowledge critical for decision making in the form of individualized reasoning rules. Storage of the knowledge is in the form of simple if-then or condition-action rules. Computer programs or systems that use rules to represent knowledge and consist of collections of antecedent-consequent rules. Rule-based systems are a general programming technique used for deriving structures for large systems in order to allow small additions to be made incrementally without the necessity of understanding the entire control structure. Such systems can be used to manage large programs that require frequent local changes. These systems are effective for use in the performance of tasks that require expertise but do not require great insight or common sense.

Decisions

Judgments reached after a great deal of thought and consideration; conclusions. Determinations arrived at through a selection process from a finite number of previously designated alternatives. Decisions use inputs from two sources: human judgment (experience, expertise, feelings, and knowledge) and information (a processed set of data). Decisions are the result of the integration of rule development and the exercise of control.

Beliefs

Uncertain knowledge; hypotheses derived about unobservable situations; tenets held in common by a group. The certainty of the truth of something when based on an examination of available evidence; it may intimate mental acceptance of something without directly implying certainty on the part of the believer. Measures of a believer's confidence in uncertain premises. Represented in expert systems by means of certainty factors.

Routine Tasks

Actions, often repetitive, that require task knowledge and specific dexterity but no high-level or specialized skills.

Planning Tasks

Actions that break a complex task into a series of primitive actions (or routine tasks) that when performed in sequence will produce the desired result. Can also encompass advance analyses of sequences of steps to determine where they lead before actually undertaking the first step. May be compared with the interpretation of problems.

Domain Expert

An individual who is widely recognized as having the knowledge and know-how necessary to solve a particular type or class of problem. This person has learned to focus quickly on the important facets of the problem. This individual contributes expertise, in collaboration with the knowledge engineer, for the creation of a system that can function as an expert in a given field, solving problems efficiently and effectively.

Expert System User

A person who requires greater expertise than he or she already possesses to complete a task. A professional who requires expertise in an associated field of knowledge in order to upgrade his or her performance in a specialized field. Expert system users require information in such areas as disease diagnosis, ore deposit probabilities, performance analysis of electronic circuits, mathematical formula manipulation, and advice on how to use other computer systems.

State-Space Searches

Seeking a solution by systematically probing through the valid conditions of the question in the hope of attaining the ends. State-space, also called a state graph or a tree, is the set of all possible states that may occur in a dynamic model, where any change in a state is defined as a function of the preceding state. State-space searches can be quite useful in solving problems that are well formed (meaning that the initial state, the goal state, and the required operators are definitive). An ill-formed problem will lack at least one of the features that make up a well-formed problem and will turn up so many possible choices as to be unsolvable. State-space searches may be either backward-chaining, in which a number of attributes are connected via rules to particular solutions, or forward-chaining, in which the goal states may not be known. In addition, the search may be either depth-first, where subgoals are sought from each piece of information considered, or breadth-first, in which all premises in a rule are considered before additional detail is sought. Both depth-first and breadth-first searches have advantages. Depth-first searches, which expand trees along a single path until a goal, a dead end, or a duplicate path is reached, eliminate backtracking. Breadth-first searches, which expand trees one level at a time, require redundant operations but eliminate the possibility of reaching a dead end.

Graph Searches

Use of a graphing technique to represent facts to uncover relationships. If Venn diagrams, involving overlapping circles, are used, each circle would represent one logical expression of knowledge that is either true or false. Graph searches keep track of the effects of several sequences of rules simultaneously and use various kinds of graph structures and graph-searching procedures. They are an effective means of finding a path in a graph from a node that represents the initial database to another node that represents a database that satisfies the termination condition of the system. Each node represents a problem state, and each arc represents a relationship between the problem states of the nodes it connects. Backtracking strategies in use in graph searches effectively forget any trial paths that result in failures; only the path currently being extended is stored explicitly.

Domain-specific Searches

Searches restricted to a topical area or region of knowledge from which to gather relevant information, build prototype solutions, and revise hypotheses based on the domain-imposed restraints, thereby ignoring a multitude of irrelevant details.

Instantiation

The procedure for deciding on a specific value for attributes stored in a knowledge-base. Specification of particular values. Representation of an abstraction by concrete examples. An object fitting the general characteristics of some class or pending process that associates definitive data objects with the conditions of a general procedure.

Unification

A pattern-matching method in which two patterns or literals are compared to discover whether or not there exists a set of substitutions whereby an assignment of values to the variables of the two patterns will cause the patterns to become identical. This common assignment of values produces a common instance of each pattern, which is the most general common instance. Finding ways of replacing variables by other expressions so that all the equations being considered have identical left and right sides. Unification is the PROLOG equivalent of instantiation.

Inference Engine

The portion of an expert system that contains the strategies for controlling the selection and application of knowledge and facts in the knowledge-base. The part of the expert system where the reasoning actually takes place. The inference engine considers the form of the problem, the theorem to be proved or the question to be answered, and the relevant portions of the knowledge-base. The inference engine also supports various knowledge acquisition, explanation, and user interface subsystems. Inference engines are described by the types of inference and control strategies that they employ.

PART I   WHY EXPERT SYSTEMS?

1 WHAT IS AN EXPERT SYSTEM?

Computer technology has provided many new and innovative products over the past 30 years, perhaps none so exciting as the new computer-based products that are coming out of the artificial intelligence laboratories. Witness the following conversation. It has an interesting twist to it that is related to these new technologies.

"Sorry to interrupt, . . . but we have a problem."
"What is it?" . . .
"I am having difficulty in maintaining contact with Earth. The trouble is in the AE-35 unit. My Fault Prediction Center reports that it may fail within seventy-two hours."
"We'll take care of it. . . . Let's see the optical alignment."
"Here it is. . . . It's still O.K. at the moment." . . .
"Do you know where the trouble is?" . . .
"It's intermittent and I can't localize it. But it appears to be in the AE-35 unit."
"What procedure do you suggest?"
"The best thing would be to replace the unit with a spare, so that we can check it over."
"O.K.—let us have the hard copy." . . .
A sheet of paper slid out of the slot . . . .
"You might have told us . . . . This means going outside the ship."
"I'm sorry. . . . I assumed you knew that the AE-35 unit was on the antenna mounting."
"I probably did, a year ago. But there are eight thousand subsystems aboard. Anyway, it looks a straightforward job. We only have to unlock a panel and put in a new unit."

A technical discussion like this might occur at any time among scientists or engineers. However, what makes this conversation a bit special is that one of the people involved in this conversation is not a person at all; the first person to speak is, in fact, a computer. Actually, the conversation is an exerpt from Arthur C. Clarke's science fiction novel, *2001: A Space Odyssey*. The computer involved in the conversation is the HAL 9000.

Clarke's HAL 9000 computer had the ability to receive commands and information through various means including the spoken word and video cameras. HAL provided information and advice to his human colleagues mostly through the spoken word. HAL could calculate algorithms and develop intelligent inferences from heuristic knowledge. It would be fair to say that the HAL 9000 computer was comprised of numerous subsystems, each representing a different computer technology. HAL's technologies included traditional data processing, voice recognition, signal processing, pattern recognition, voice synthesis, and expert systems. The technology that provided HAL with his human-like inferencing capabilities was that of knowledge-based expert systems. But, you say, HAL did not really exist; HAL was only something Clarke developed in his mind. True as this may be, with today's technologies, HAL is feasible. Voice recognition, signal processing, pattern recognition, voice synthesis, and expert systems do exist today and are rapidly getting better. These systems should be able to support a limited version of HAL 9000 by the early 1990s.

Expert systems have been in development since the 1960s, and the first appeared in the early 1970s. Commercial interest increased in the early 1980s, and as a result, so have efforts to design expert systems and the tools used to build them. The most significant development of the mid-1980s has been the introduction of expert system–building tools and environments that do not require artificial intelligence scientists. These tools and environments can often be used by subject domain experts. Most of the tools can be used by software engineers with minimal training and exposure. It will be important for all software engineers to learn about expert systems and how to build them in the 1990s just as it was important to learn about database management systems and fourth-generation languages in the 1970s and 1980s.

DEFINITION   An expert system is a computer-based system that uses knowledge, facts, and reasoning techniques to solve problems that normally require the abilities of human experts.

Expert systems can be designed for specific hardware and software configurations, or they can be software systems that are designed to run on a general-purpose computer.

The knowledge the expert system uses is made up of either rules or experience information about the behavior of the elements of a particular subject domain. Rules generally give descriptions of a condition, followed by implications of that condition. Here is an example of a rule: "If employee X is a very hard worker and employee X is well liked in the local industry and employee X is being paid under the regional salary level, then there is a high likelihood that employee X will leave the company.'' Experience information is a collection of experiences on a particular subject. A successful venture capitalist who specializes in providing venture capital to high-technology startups might not be able to capture his or her expertise in a set of rules, but he or she can articulate that knowledge in such a way that the experience can be used by an expert system.

An expert system *subject domain* might be cost accounting, the *elements* might be the cost categories, and the *rules* might have to do with the placement of account entries under specific cost accounting categories. Facts provide the expert system with information specific to the problem at hand. An accounting record stating that Mr. Brown made a long-distance telephone call to client A for a period of 20 minutes at a cost of $10.00 concerning the Alpha project is an example of a fact. The reasoning technique often used by expert systems is *inferencing*. An answer to a question posed to the expert system is inferred from the knowledge and facts presented to the expert system.

EXPERT SYSTEM GOALS

The goals sought by expert system builders in the development of expert systems include substituting for an unavailable human expert, assimilating the knowledge and experiences of several human experts, training new experts, providing requisite expertise on projects that do not attract or retain experts, and providing expertise to projects that cannot afford experts.

Sometimes there exists a valuable expert on a particular subject in an organization. It would be desirable to have a substitute expert in case the expert is not available. In ICI, for example, an expert on problems in a chemical plant was not available on the second and third shifts. It might not be possible to use a substitute human expert. A substitute human expert might be prohibitively expensive for the organization, or perhaps this expert is unique in his or her knowledge and experience, or perhaps a substitute human expert cannot be found. In ICI an expert system was built to provide the substitute expert function for the organization. The expert system was developed in such a manner that it incorporated the knowledge of the expert as well as the expert's decision-making attributes. The solutions provided by the expert system in ICI were good substitutes for the unavailable human expert.

Assimilating the knowledge and experience of several experts is no easy task, particularly if the experts are experts in more than one subject domain. Expert systems can be built to store and use more knowledge and facts than any single human expert. Expert systems built with a large amount of knowledge, having more information than the human experts, can develop inferences that would not be available to the human experts. The knowledge information provided to the expert system could be from one specific subject or from a few, closely related subjects. In any case, the amount of information available to the expert system is greater than any one of the contributing experts. These expert systems could then be used to assist human experts in carrying out their work. An example of this application would be building an expert system that incorporates the knowledge and experiences of a tax expert and a real estate investment expert. The expert system would be able to develop real estate investment schemes that fit well with the tax laws and the tax position of the potential investor.

Future experts need training and experience. In a subject area in which an organization requires more useful experts, expert systems could prove to be valuable intelligent instruction systems. If an expert system existed in the subject domain, a future expert could present the expert system with a problem and request a solution. The expert system would then supply the solution. If the student understands the solution, the student could then present a new problem. If the student does not understand the solution, the student can make a request to the expert system to explain the line of reasoning used to develop the solution. The expert system would then articulate the rules and facts it used in developing the solution. Tying an expert system and a simulation system together might provide for a very interesting instruction system. A system of this type might be beneficial where knowledge and speed are necessary skills of the expert, as, for example, in a brokerage house.

There are work tasks that experts usually do not perform. For example, system development experts typically leave system development projects as they are finishing. These experts do not stay on a project into the operations phase. Even though many large operational systems may have benefited from the expertise of the development expert, these experts tend to move on to new projects. Expert systems could be developed to include the expert's knowledge about the construction of a particular system. This knowledge could include information about the internal system design, the data flows, reasons why certain designs were used, and specific system dependencies that are often not documented. Even when documented, the dependencies of a particular system are not always understood by the user. Documentation for large systems tends to be extensive and a challenge for anyone to grasp. Expert systems developed with the knowledge about large systems could advise operations and maintenance personnel on operational and maintenance actions. An operator who is trying to get a system to perform a particular action and cannot figure out how could query the expert system. Software maintenance of a large computer system often involves modification and extension of the software. These acts can involve more of the software than was intended and can in the process of fixing the intended problem introduce new problems that might not be found for some period of time. An expert system to assist the maintenance team could be built by the development team during the original construction of the system. This expert system could then advise the maintenance team during maintenance actions so that the fixing of one system problem does not introduce new problems.

It could also update its knowledge base with system modification data after each maintenance action. In this way, the expert system stays current with the system about which it is providing advice.

Large international corporations often develop new products at one location and then manufacture the products at another location. The development location is often chosen for its proximity to the requisite development talent. The manufacturing location is often chosen for purely economic reasons. Thus sometimes the development talent, often the expert, is not working at the manufacturing location. If problems arise in the manufacturing process, delays might occur while contact with the expert is attempted. An expert system could be developed in parallel with the development of the new product and could be installed at the manufacturing plant location during the installation of the new manufacturing process for the new product. Problems with the new manufacturing process could then be referred to the expert system. The expert system should be able to solve many of the problems presented to it and thereby decrease delays incurred while attempting to contact the human expert.

Organizational priorities and goals sometimes require a project to function without the benefit of certain expertise. The organization has determined that the project is important enough for funding but not for hiring or reassigning experts to make the project's goals easier to attain. Expert systems can help projects that are in this predicament. There are many examples of organizations using an expert system in place of human workers for financial reasons.

Expert systems already working provide many examples of the above goals.

A FEW EXAMPLES

Expert systems have been developed in research laboratories for many years. Commercial application of expert systems, however, is a fairly new development. For this reason, many of the expert systems discussed in the literature today have been developed in commercial research and university laboratories.

TAXADVISOR

The TAXADVISOR expert system is a university research product. It was developed by Dr. Robert Michaelsen, now of the University of Nebraska. TAXADVISOR is a good expert system example because it is representative of what can be expected to be implemented in the business marketplace in the near future. TAXADVISOR clearly shows the transition path of expert systems from the research laboratory to the business world.

TAXADVISOR is an expert system that assists in solving problems concerning personal finance and transfer tax planning. TAXADVISOR is designed to make tax planning recommendations that will maximize the wealth that an individual will bequeath. It looks at important financial matters including health, accident, casuality, disability, and life insurance; retirement issues; lifetime planning elements such as short-term trusts and tax shelters; gifts to charity and family members; and wealth transfer at death to family, charity, and other beneficiaries. The goal in developing TAXADVISOR was to support a human finance and tax adviser who often is not a tax expert but rather a professional, such as a lawyer, to whom a client looks for advice. In an interactive interchange between the expert system and the user, the person using the system and who will provide the advice is asked questions about the client, the person who wishes to be advised. When the system has the requisite information, the system will develop recommendations for the client through the use of the information provided by the user and by using heuristics the system contains in its knowledge-base. An example of a recommendation might be: ''I recommend that the client explore permanent *inter vivos* gifts.''

A short dialogue with TAXADVISOR should illustrate how the system works. However, since TAXADVISOR is a model of the future, we will modify the dialogue slightly to provide an idea of how a commercially developed and supported version might appear. The person who will provide the advice to the client and who wishes assistance would sign on to use a computer system that has the expert system on it. Figure 1.1 depicts a possible dialogue between the expert system and the financial and tax planning adviser.

The expert system also has the facility for the user to query the system as to why a particular question is being asked. If, for example, the user responded ''why'' to the fifth question, the system would have responded with an explanation as follows:

> This will aid in determining whether the client should make permanent gifts.
>
> It has already been established that the client has an estate that is substantial enough, given his present age and health, that the client can afford to forgo the income from gifted assets and to pay the expenses associated with making gifts.
>
> Therefore, if
>
> 1. a. Client is willing to relinquish possession and enjoyment of assets and power to alter, amend, revoke, or terminate any trust in which the assets are placed, or
>   b. Client is willing to transfer term life insurance, or whole life that is borrowed up, to an irrevocable trust, and
>
> 2. a. Gift will produce a net increase in family wealth by saving income and/or transfer taxes,
>   b. Particular beneficiaries need the help,
>   c. Client desires to shield assets from future business risk,
>   d. Client desires to be relieved of asset management responsibilities,

THE TAXADVISOR II EXPERT SYSTEM

Hello, I am the TAXADVISOR II expert system. I am ready to assist you. I will ask you questions about your client. Please provide answers to each question. When you do not know an answer, please respond with "unknown." If you want an explanation as to why I am asking a question, ask "why." I will be providing you with my recommendations. Let us begin.

What is your client's name or account number?
> ****Mr. Baker**

What is the age of the client (in years)?
> ****unknown**

What is sex of your client?
> ****male**

Does the client have an estate that is substantial enough, given the client's present age and health, that he can afford to forgo the income from gifted assets and to pay the expenses associated with making gifts?
> ****yes**

Is the client willing to relinquish possession and enjoyment of assets and power to alter, amend, revoke, or terminate any trust in which the assets are placed?
> ****yes**

Will gifts produce a net increase in family wealth by saving income and/or transfer taxes?
> ****yes**

Are gifts likely to cause family disharmony, and does client wish to avoid this?
> ****no**

I recommend that the client explore permanent inter vivos gifts. This is an intermediate recommendation; would you like me to continue?
> ****yes**

Is the client expected to live at least three years?
> ****no**

Does the client own assets that are expected to appreciate substantially during the period before his death?
> ****yes**

Is this client's tax motivation to get future appreciation out of his estate?
> ****yes**

I recommend that this client transfer as gifts those assets expected to appreciate in value. This is an intermediate recommendation; would you like me to continue?
> ****no**

Consultation is closed.

Figure 1.1 Consultation session example

    e. Client desires to avoid probate on particular assets, or

    f. Client desires to experience personally the gratitude of the benefi-
       ciaries, and

3. Gifts are unlikely to cause family disharmony or the client is uncon-
   cerned,

then
    Client should explore permanent inter vivos gifts.

The TAXADVISOR expert system can advise financial and tax planning consultants who are advising corporate executives and passive investors. The TAXADVISOR II expert system could be designed to support other groups of clients as well. This type of expert system is often referred to as a consultation system. It provides expert consultation services to its user. This type of system can be helpful to many professionals. Many professionals are experts in some but not all aspects of their professions. Many professions are too large to have experts in the complete field. Expert consultation systems can be built to provide expert-level knowledge to professionals in the areas of their professions in which they are not experts. A lawyer who specializes in contract law might use the TAXADVISOR expert system to assist in advising an executive on a personal finance problem. Although the client could have sought out a lawyer who is an expert in this financial area, the client has worked with the present lawyer for a long time and feels more comfortable discussing this personal matter with this lawyer. A general practitioner might use an expert system to perform a top-level diagnosis of a patient's problem prior to referring the patient to a specialist. The expert system might aid the GP in determining the type of medical specialist the patient should see. Expert systems are well suited to perform this kind of consultation service; we should be seeing many commercial expert consultation systems in the near future.

ISIS

ISIS is a knowledge-based scheduling system capable of incorporating relevant constraints (such as required completion dates) in the development of job shop schedules. In this capacity, the ISIS system personifies the creator of the job shop schedule, the creator of the shop's leadership, in much the same way that the Egyptian goddess Isis was the creator of the king of Egypt. ISIS was developed by a team of researchers from the Robotics Institute at Carnegie-Mellon University and the Westinghouse Turbine Component Plant.

ISIS is a decision support system for job shop scheduling. Job shop scheduling involves the selection of shop operations and their sequencing and the assignment of resources and times to perform the operations. The desired goal of this activity is to make efficient use of the facility and to produce the products ordered. The Westinghouse Turbine Component Plant was chosen as a practical test application for the system. This plant produces many styles of steam turbine blades for new and existing turbines.

ISIS can run in one of two modes. In the first mode, ISIS automatically develops the schedules that govern the production of the orders in the job shop. In the second mode, ISIS runs interactively with a user, assuming the role of intelligent assistant. Most expert systems that have been built to date are designed to operate in a single-user environment. ISIS, however, was designed to operate in a multiuser environment. More than one user can interact with ISIS on parts of the same schedule at the same time.

The usefulness of a schedule for a job shop depends on many organizational, technical, and personnel constraints. These constraints originate in various parts of the plant. Examples of organizational constraints include cost, quality, and completion dates. Machine setup time, processing time, and equipment requirements are examples of technical constraints. Personnel requirements and preference of machine use are examples of personnel constraints. The development of a schedule should consider these constraints. It should make a best-efforts attempt to satisfy most, if not all, of the constraints. The design of the knowledge representation and the control structure of ISIS is focused on this issue.

The ISIS system models all the knowledge, at various levels of detail, needed to plan and schedule work in the job shop. This knowledge includes descriptions of orders, groups of orders (known as lots), plant and equipment, processes, cost centers, departments, and personnel resources. The system uses this knowledge to make intelligent shop schedules.

ISIS contains knowledge on all of the constraints that will influence the development of a shop schedule. The design of the knowledge representation scheme was an important part of the system's design. ISIS knowledge representations include constraint relaxation, importance, relevance, interaction, and generation.

The control structure of ISIS is very interesting. It is based on a constraint-directed, hierarchical search scheme. Being constraint-directed means that ISIS considers and incorporates a wide range of constraints that normally would influence the job shop scheduling process. ISIS is able to identify which constraints need to be satisfied for a particular order. Control flows downward through a four-level hierarchy: order selection, capacity analysis, resource analysis, and reservation selection. The *top level* selects an order to be scheduled for production in the shop according to a prioritization scheme that is based on order category and required completion date. The *second level* determines the availability of machine resources required by the order selected in the first level. The second level employs a critical path analysis method to analyze the operations involved in production. This level also attempts to detect potential bottlenecks in the shop. The *resource analysis level* produces detailed schedules of all requisite resources to fulfill the selected order and then proceeds to use a rule-based search analysis technique to select a detailed schedule for the order.

The *bottom level* finalizes the schedule for the order by selecting and assigning reservations for the shop resources required.

The interactive scheduling facility of ISIS provides the abilities to group orders into lots, schedule shop resources by reserving them for a particular use at a specified time, partially specify schedules in the hierarchy and let ISIS fill in the levels not filled in by the user, resolve assignment conflicts that the user inadvertently specified, and check for constraint satisfaction while the user is specifying resource reservations.

ISIS supports the complete development of job shop production schedules. Independent of plant design, ISIS can provide plant production management and control either automatically or in the role of intelligent assistant.

EDAAS

The EDAAS expert system was developed for the Environmental Protection Agency (EPA) by Booz, Allen & Hamilton, Inc. The EPA is a regulatory agency involved in actions that are directed by rules and procedures. It would seem to be a viable candidate for expert system application and support.

The Expert Disclosure Analysis and Avoidance System (EDAAS) is used by the EPA to assist in the screening of Freedom of Information Act (FOIA) requests. EDAAS is a public information specialist intelligent assistant. The system is used to determine what information concerning toxic chemical manufacture, distribution, and disposition may be released to a FOIA requester without compromising confidential business information (CBI), which the EPA is obligated to protect pursuant to section 14 of the Toxic Substances Control Act (TSCA).

The EPA has procedures to protect CBI from improper release. Prevention of release of sensitive information is handled by a set of routine procedures that have proved to be effective. However, there was a problem. Sometimes a request for a specific piece of information that of itself was not sensitive could be used with other information that was available to the requester to ultimately provide the requester with CBI or something very close to it. This indirect information can be used, just like the CBI itself, to determine sensitive corporate planning and strategy information that is protected by federal nondisclosure policy and law. Because of budget constraints, the EPA did not have the wherewithal to perform manual reviews of all information requests for potential indirect disclosure.

EDAAS manages the problem of determining whether the release of a specific piece of FOIA-requested information could directly or indirectly disclose CBI. The EPA is using EDAAS to help answer FOIA requests relating to information stored in large federal chemical databases. EPA management believes that the use of EDAAS helps to guard against both indirect and direct disclosure of CBI by the EPA.

EDAAS automates the work tasks of and the decisions made by the agency's public information specialists and legal advisers. The system assembles the information that would be released if the FOIA request is satisfied. Using this information and industry knowledge, the system emulates an industrial espionage agent and tries to identify sensitive information. This is passed on to another component of EDAAS that emulates the legal adviser. This module evaluates the information and, in terms of the relevant federal rules, makes determinations in favor of or against the information release as requested by the FOIA requester and provides reasons to support its decision. The system also has the ability, at the option of the system's user, to make the information to be released less precise so as not to violate the law but to provide some relevant information to the requester.

To assemble the information manually and go through the motions of an industrial espionage agent for each FOIA request would be a tedious and labor-intensive exercise. The tasks of an industrial espionage agent are well understood; therefore, it is possible to build an expert system to emulate the agent's actions. The use of an expert system to assist in this task saves time, effort, and money. The information release procedures are numerous, but they are rule-oriented. This means that the person making the information release decisions could be assisted or emulated by a rule-based expert system. By emulating the espionage agent and the legal adviser, EDAAS has provided the EPA with a service the agency could not afford to support manually.

The system includes a user interface module, a control module, an editor, two knowledge-bases, numerous databases, and a justifier (see Figure 1.2).

The user interface is an interactive, natural-language interface that allows the user to communicate with the system in a conversational English dialogue.

The control module coordinates system activities, interacts with the user interface, and includes two inference engines. One inference engine supports the public information specialist's tasks, including the assembly of information. This inference engine employs a constraint propagation inferencing technique. The second inference engine is a production rule inference engine and supports the legal adviser's tasks.

The editor allows the user to modify the dominance rules, the release criteria, and the constraint relationships between the confidential business information and the freely available information.

The system employs two knowledge-bases. These knowledge-bases are set up to support the two inference engines. One knowledge-base provides knowledge information to the constraint propagation inference engine. This knowledge-base is a network of relationships between the CBI and the information that is generally available to anyone or any business. The relationships in this knowledge-base constrain the inferencing process; as more knowledge is included, the reasoning is more and more constrained, which has the ultimate effect of narrowing down the CBI estimates. The second knowledge-base contains if-then rules that follow the EPA rules on information release as provided for in the TSCA and required by the FOIA. There are dominance rules and

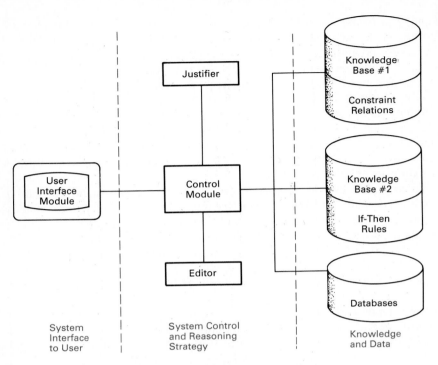

Figure 1.2   The EDAAS expert system

release criteria rules in this knowledge-base. The dominance rules are used to make a first determination as to the releasability of the requested information. If this first determination does not provide for release, the release criteria rules are consulted. This knowledge-base provides the second inference engine with the knowledge it needs to emulate the agency's legal advisers in the role of information release determination.

Approximately 60,000 chemicals are cataloged in the EPA databases. These chemicals are broken into classes, with about 100 chemicals belonging to each class. The databases contain approximately 30 data categories of chemical data.

The last component of EDAAS is the justifier. The justifier develops justification in all no-release decision cases. The law requires that specific legal reasons be provided to the FOIA requester. The justifier meets this FOIA requirement.

The EDAAS expert system is a good example of an operational expert system that is providing a service an organization could not otherwise afford. It demonstrates what expert systems can do to provide economical and effective assistance to government and business organizations today in the course of their normal business activities. The technology of expert systems is ready to serve the business community.

EXPERT SYSTEM COMPONENTS

Expert systems have been structured in many ways. The various expert system architectures include different components. However, certain components are common to most expert systems: a user interface, a database, a knowledge acquisition facility, and an inference mechanism.

The *user interface* is software that provides for the communication exchange between the system user and the system. Through the user interface, the user can enter facts about a specific situation that are relevant to the system's subject domain and can ask the expert system questions within the system's subject area. Many expert systems also accept new knowledge through the user interface. The user interface also provides the expert system with the requisite facilities to proffer responses.

The *expert system database* contains expert-level knowledge on a particular subject. This knowledge is obtained from one or more human experts and is stored in a knowledge-representational form that is inherent to the expert system design. Expert systems are often referred to as knowledge-based systems because they always include a knowledge database.

The *knowledge acquisition facility* (KAF) is software that provides a dialogue between the expert system and the human experts for the purpose of acquiring knowledge from the human experts. The KAF places this acquired knowledge in the system's database. The interface between the expert and the expert system is sometimes the user interface and at other times specific to the task of knowledge acquisition.

The *inference mechanism* is software that performs the inference reasoning tasks for the expert system. The inference mechanism is often called the *inference engine*. The inference engine uses the knowledge in the expert system's database and information provided by the user to infer new knowledge.

These basic expert system components have been designed and implemented in a variety of ways. Sometimes design-specific components have been developed. Different integrations of these components have led to various expert system architectures.

REPRESENTATIVE ARCHITECTURE

The architectures of expert systems today reflect knowledge engineers' present understanding of how to represent knowledge and how to perform intelligent decision-making tasks with the support of a computer-based system. As the participants in this engineering discipline have learned and developed, so have the systems that they have built and rebuilt. This discipline is still in its infancy.

Through experimentation in the laboratories and practical experience in the field, more is being learned about how to represent knowledge and use this knowledge. Basic architectural principles are starting to become apparent.

Figure 1.3 shows the architecture of a simple expert system. This software architecture is independent of specific computer hardware. Determinants for computer hardware selection would include the size of the knowledge database, the desired speed of the system's responses, the development environment, and the level of sophistication for the user interface.

The user interface allows the system user to enter rules and facts about a particular situation and ask questions of the system, provides responses to user requests, and supports all other communication between the system and the user.

The knowledge-base contains the knowledge of a human expert on a particular subject in a codified form. Usually the codification is easy to read and understand. Although knowledge-bases are developed by experts, their contents ought to be understandable by anyone who knows the subject matter.

The inference engine uses the information provided to it by the knowledge-base and the user to infer new facts. In so doing, it is simulating the deductive thought processes of an expert. The new facts that are generated by the system might be the advice the system user is seeking.

The architecture of our simple expert system could be extended. One common extension is to expand the knowledge base into a knowledge database and a domain database. These two databases could be managed by a database management system (DBMS). Figure 1.4 depicts this extension.

The knowledge database contains *rules* about the behavior of the elements

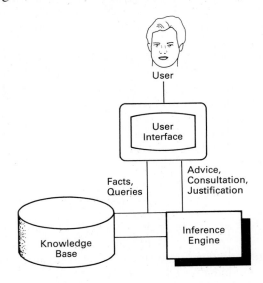

Figure 1.3   Architecture of a simple expert system

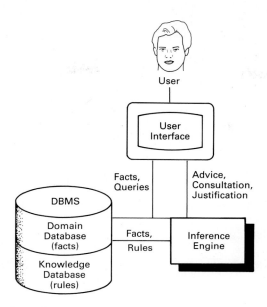

Figure 1.4 Extending the knowledge base into a knowledge database and a
domain database and adding a database management system

of a particular subject. These rules would be formatted in such a manner to be
usable by the expert system. Here is an example of a rule: "An accounting item
is a current asset if it is an asset and if it is liquid within one year." Expert
systems that represent their knowledge in this rule format are often referred to
as rule-based systems.

The domain database contains *facts* about the expert system's subject. The
domain database also uses formatting conventions to manage and use the data
efficiently. Here is an example of a fact: "Cash is a current asset."

The knowledge information in most expert systems will be updated and
expanded over the lifetime of the system. This is done to assure the user that
the system is providing the most complete and current assistance possible. Many
expert systems have a module dedicated to this updating process. This module
or set of modules is often called a *knowledge acquisition facility* (KAF). The
KAF is most often used by the domain expert to ease the transfer of knowledge
from the human expert to the computer-based expert system. Figure 1.5 shows
our expert system with the knowledge acquisition facility added on.

The *knowledge acquisition facility* provides a dialogue with the human
expert for the purpose of acquiring knowledge in the form of rules and facts.
This facility then places the rules in the knowledge database and the facts in the
domain database.

One of the functions most expert systems will include is *justification*. The
justification function allows users to ask the expert system to justify the answer

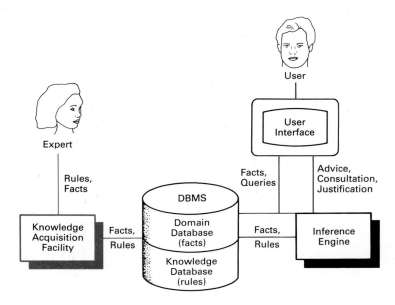

Figure 1.5   Adding the knowledge acquisition facility

or the advice the system has provided. Expert systems justify their answers or advice by explaining their reasoning. If the system is rule-based, it provides an ordered list of the rules and facts it used to formulate its answer. This function of explaining reasoning is important enough that some expert system designers have developed a separate *explanation facility* within their expert systems. Figure 1.6 extends the expert system architecture of Figure 1.5 with the addition of an explanation facility.

The *explanation facility* keeps track of the advice and consultations provided as well as the reasoning paths the inference engine used to produce the advice. At any time during an interactive session with the expert system, the user can ask the system how it arrived at a given conclusion, and the explanation facility will respond with a quick, well-formatted explanation.

Human experts are constantly updating and upgrading their expertise. A lot of the expertise improvement comes as a by-product of acting out the role of an expert. The expert is asked to look at new, difficult situations. The expert studies the situation, provides advice, observes the product of his or her advice, and stores this information in his or her memory. The new advice developed and the new knowledge ascertained enhance the expert's expertise. The expert has converted experience into self-training. Self-training is another goal for expert systems. When an expert system derives a new fact through its inference procedure, this new fact could be added to its knowledge-base as well as presented to the user. Figure 1.7 shows our expert system architecture with the addition of a *self-training facility*.

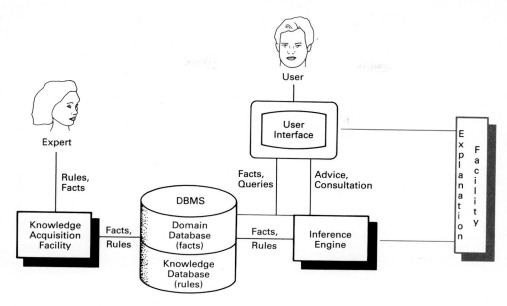

Figure 1.6   Adding the explanation facility

The *self-training facility* accepts facts that the expert system's inference engine has developed and compares these derived facts with the facts stored in the domain database. If a new derived fact is not in the domain database, it is a candidate to be added to the database. Whether the fact is added to the domain database might be contigent on agreement by the user to add the fact to the database or on some consistency check the self-training facility might perform to assure that the derived fact does not conflict with another fact that is already in the domain database. The self-training facility will also try to ascertain if the fact is specific to the problem at hand or general to the expert system's subject.

The expert system architectures presented in this discussion are examples of how expert systems are being developed today. Variations of these architectural examples are also being developed. As an example, the database management system might be extended to include a data dictionary. The data dictionary is helpful when the expert system supports several data types that are used by various inference techniques within one expert system.

Most of our expert system architecture examples presented knowledge representation in the form of rules. Going back to Figure 1.3, the knowledge-base could represent its stored knowledge in another form, and the inference engine could be designed to infer new information and knowledge from this knowledge. As an example, the CENTAUR expert system uses a knowledge representation known as *frames* for the representation of its medical knowledge. A *frame* is a collection of related *slots*. *Slots* are storage devices for objects, their names, their relationships with other objects, rules, numeric procedures, and any other

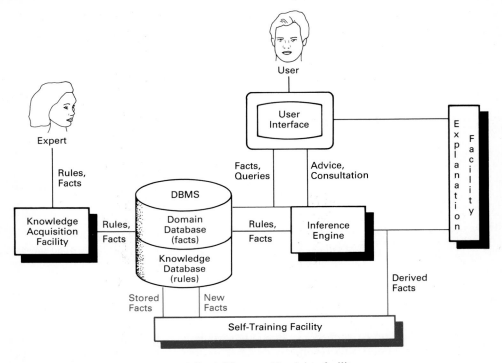

Figure 1.7   Adding a self-training facility

information the expert system designer deems important. Frames are usually ordered hierarchically and inherit properties from the frames above them in the hierarchy.

Each component of an expert system can be designed in a variety of ways. The user interface, for example, could employ menus, dialogues, graphics, or another appropriate communication vehicle. There are, however, certain characteristics that would qualify a computer program to be called an expert system.

QUALIFYING CHARACTERISTICS

Expert systems are computer-based systems that use knowledge and reasoning techniques to solve problems that would normally require the expertise and ability of human experts. Expert systems are used to collect, represent, and store the knowledge of human experts in a computer and allow access to this knowledge by others. Although expert system technology has been in the university laboratories for some time, commercial products based on expert systems are relatively new.

When a scientific discovery is converted into new commercial products by several economic groups simultaneously, differences of opinion often exist as to what the scientific discovery is exactly and what commercial products are based on the new science. This is true of the commercialization of expert systems.

Regardless of the differences of definition, we suggest four characteristics that qualify a system as an expert system. The first is that *the system should perform at an expert's level of competence*. Expert systems should have special knowledge derived from the system's knowledge-base and the ability to use this special knowledge to develop inferences. The special knowledge in the system's knowledge-base was derived from one or more human experts in the particular domain in which the expert system is working. The expert system should be able to deduce conclusions from this special knowledge. These deductions will provide information the user did not possess. More important, only an expert in the particular field would be able to develop the equivalent deductions. The expert system is therefore considered to possess expertise in the system's subject area. The next two characteristics are natural consequences of this first one.

An expert system uses an inference mechanism to produce its deductions. This inference mechanism is often referred to as an inference engine or the control structure of the expert system. An expert system should have an inference control structure that can reason judgmentally and be able to justify the deductions it develops and presents.

The expertise an expert system possesses is based on the special knowledge it has acquired. Expert systems make use of the knowledge and the experience information that human experts provide. This information includes facts and heuristics about the subject domain. The codification of this domain knowledge is known as knowledge representation. There are various forms of knowledge representation. Examples include production rules, frames, and semantic networks (explained later). The expert system knowledge that is manipulated by the inference engine is stored in a knowledge-base. A knowledge-base is a characteristic of expert systems. A knowledge-base can have many forms, but its purpose is to store and manipulate symbolic data structures. These symbolic data structures tend to represent the knowledge as independent packets. As a result, the knowledge data is easy to examine, change, or extend.

Programming expert systems involves describing and presenting expert-level knowledge to the system. This knowledge will be stored in the knowledge-base for future use. A characteristic of expert systems is that *there is no programming for how the system uses the knowledge that is presented to it*. The system's inference control mechanism will make the determination of how and when to use the knowledge that is provided to it.

These four characteristics should help differentiate expert systems from other computer-based systems. Additional attributes are characteristic of the majority of the expert systems developed thus far. It might be helpful to go over some of them to obtain a clearer idea of just what an expert system is. These attributes may or may not be part of future expert system designs, and they do not apply to all present expert systems. However, these attributes are common enough in the field to make them interesting and informative.

Like human experts, many expert systems deal with uncertain or incomplete information. Human experts must often deal with problems for which some information is vague or unavailable. Different expert systems handle uncertain and incomplete information in various ways.

An expert system often accepts *uncertain information* with an associated certainty factor. The certainty factor is an informal measure of the extent to which the expert believes the information is true. Certainty factors are propagated with the inferences. Expert systems that accept certainty factors have rules for combining and managing them. These certainty factors are presented with the conclusions.

Incomplete information is handled very simply by most expert systems. When an expert system is missing a fact or a premise that it needs to derive a conclusion, it will first ask the user for the requisite information. If the user provides the information, the expert system continues. If the user does not have the information, the inference mechanism of the expert system fails to derive the conclusion it was trying to develop and continues along a different line of reasoning. If too much information is missing, the expert system will be unable to derive a conclusion for the problem at hand and will go on to the next problem that is presented to it.

Another attribute that is often associated with expert systems is the ability to search for a problem solution. The ability to search among many possibilities for a solution or goal in a nonrandom fashion is considered a characteristic of intelligent problem solving. Expert systems use a variety of search techniques. The heuristic search technique, for example, guides the search with domain-specific knowledge. Instead of blindly searching all possibilities, an expert system that employs heuristic search reduces the possibilities to be searched by applying rules of thumb that would typically be used by a human expert trying to solve a problem in the particular subject domain. If an expert system was developed to assist real estate agents in finding homes for clients, the system should not have to search through all the "homes for sale" listings for each client. The expert system should use client information like work location, salary level, and number of family members to reduce the number of candidates for a particular client. Here is an example of a rule of thumb for this system: "If a home for sale is more than 50 miles from the client's work location, do not consider the home a candidate for this client."

We stated that a knowledge-base is one characteristic of an expert system. Many expert system knowledge-bases are readable and understandable. A person who understands the subject being supported by an expert system can often read and understand the information that is stored in the knowledge-base. For example, here are two rules from an investment expert system:

IF   the time scale of the investment is long-term,
          the desired return on the investment is greater than 10%, and
          the risk class of the investment is speculative,
THEN   there is evidence (0.6) that the area of investment could be high
          technology.

IF   the desired return of the investment is greater than 10%,
          the time scale of the investment is long-term,
          the number of dependents of the client is less than 3, and
          the age (in years) of the client is less than or equal to 35,
THEN   there is evidence (0.4) that the area of investment could be high
          technology.

A user request for an explanation from an expert system in the middle of a consultation is not an unusual event. Expert systems are typically interactive and can provide justification for all their results, even intermediate results in the middle of a run. These intermediate results can often provide valuable information. The ability of a computer-based system to provide intermediate results in the middle of its execution is an attribute of many expert systems.

PROBLEM-SOLVING ACTIVITIES

Expert systems today support many problem-solving activities. Future expert systems will support even more. Expert systems have been built to model the problem-solving strategies of human experts. Because different human experts use different problem-solving techniques, the expert systems modeled after the strategies of the human experts use a variety of problem-solving approaches.

Depending on an expert's intentions and preferences in problem-solving strategies, the expert will perform one or more of the activities listed in Table 1.1. This list may not be all-inclusive, but it does feature activities that experts have been known to use and can be supported by expert systems. In fact, such systems are already performing all the activities in the table. Some perform only one of the activities (such as interpreting), and some perform more than one (such as diagnosing and prescribing).

Decision making involves solving unstructured problems. Decision making often involves processes that are difficult to define in advance. It is also often difficult to determine which data is relevant to a given problem. LDS is an experimental expert system that models the decision-making processes of lawyers and claims adjusters involved in product liability legislation.

The fusing of knowledge sources is an activity that is just starting to be supported with expert systems. Two experts in different but related fields often need to cooperate to reach a goal. An accountant and a computer specialist might need to cooperate to develop a new automated accounting system that their organization requires. A tax lawyer and an accountant might need to work together to determine how to invest or account for valuable assets of an individual or an organization. A data management expert and a data communications expert might have to work together to develop a new distributed information system. Besides fusing the knowledge of two or more domain experts, an expert system could fuse knowledge from numerous knowledge sources in a manner similar to an encyclopedia. KNOESPHERE is an encyclopedia knowledge system.

Designing is the mental task of creating, fashioning, or constructing according to a developed plan. The mental exercise is usually translated into a drawing, a descriptive document, or some other symbolic material. The activity of designing is often bounded by practical or required constraints. The product of the design activity might have to cost less than a specified amount of money. The design activity itself might be financially bounded. The goal of the design activity often further restrains the design activity. If the product of the design activity is a computer program to assist bookkeepers in performing their bookkeeping function, the program must be understandable and usable by the bookkeepers and must be able to perform the desired bookkeeping functions. The KBVLSI expert system is a design aid for very large scale integration microelectronics development.

Planning is the activity of establishing goals, plans, policies, and proce-

Table 1.1 Problem-solving activities

Activity	Example
Decision making	Making product liability decisions
Knowledge fusing	Linking real-estate knowledge and financial knowledge
Designing	Designing a microprocessor chip
Planning	Planning a large construction project
Forecasting	Forecasting economic conditions
Regulating	Regulating a nuclear power plant
Controlling	Controlling a blast furnace
Monitoring	Monitoring patients in intensive care
Identifying	Identifying ships from sonar data
Diagnosing	Diagnosing a computer network failure
Prescribing	Prescribing a network reconfiguration
Interpreting	Interpreting oil well logs
Explaining	Explaining investment options
Training	Teaching programmers new languages

dures to achieve some end. Planning involves specifying what is desired and developing a scheme for achieving it. Planning involves organizing actions as well as determining the modes of the actions. In large projects, planning also includes the development of standardized policies and procedures so that the actors involved with the project will know what to do or how to act when the explicit plan fails to direct them. For example, the construction of a new high-rise office building requires a lot of planning. The organization of the actions in a large construction project is often referred to as the project schedule. The project schedule must specify the order of actions in the project. For example, the schedule must specify that a particular item must be installed prior to the construction of the walls around it if the entrance to the walled-in area is smaller than the item. There are expert systems under development to assist in large construction projects. The ISIS expert system schedules job shop activities.

Forecasting involves the examination of information of a given situation and predicting future situations. The forecasting activity could also be looked at as inferring future consequences of current decisions. Forecasting usually includes the activities of observing situations and correlating common aspects of a situation with other situations that have been experienced previously. Forecasting is often the act of presenting predictions after study and analysis of all available pertinent information. The PROSPECTOR expert system predicted a molybdenum mineral deposit that was valued at $100 million. PROSPECTOR developed this prediction through the study and analysis of geologic data. Geologic data is presented to the expert system; the system interprets the data and advises as to the probability of finding a mineral deposit.

Regulating systems are used to assure uniformity of some rate, degree, or amount of some process. This regulation is often dependent on time, in some cases on events, and occasionally on both. A thermostat is a regulating system. Expert systems that regulate some process or environment are integrated with some real-world system. Regulating expert systems must operate in a real-time mode. One or more sensors feed real-time, real-world data to the expert system, and the system provides direction back to maintain the desired regulation. Regulating expert systems could either be directly connected to the feedback loop of the regulation system or provide the regulation to a human operator in the form of regulation advice. In the latter case, the actual regulation actions would be performed by the human operator. There is an expert system under development that will assist in the regulation of nuclear power reactors.

Controlling activities include direction, regulation, and coordination of systems, machines, or apparatus. Controlling includes regulating activities plus directing and coordinating activities. The directing activities include planning activities such as establishing goals and procedures, forecasting activities such as observing the present environment and condition of a system and correlating this with past data, and activities that show or point out what is to be done or what should be done. Putting things into the same or required order is an example of a coordinating activity. Organizing things into a common movement or condition is another example. Organizing, energizing, and supervising are all controlling activities. The Blast Furnace Control System is an example of an expert control system.

Monitoring involves observing and checking for some specific purpose. To monitor a system means to keep track of the system, to observe the behavior of the system and compare the observations with planned or designed behaviors. Monitoring systems usually have set limits within which the behavior of the system being monitored can vary without any action on the part of the monitoring system. However, if observed system behaviors exceed these limits, the monitoring system is usually designed to notify some system or operator. The VM expert system monitors patients in hospital intensive care units.

Identifying an object involves establishing its identity or distinguishing character. Identification starts with some form of information from some sensor. During World War II, identification of enemy aircraft or ships was done by human observers sighting the aircraft or ship. The next identification step is to note any distinguishing characteristic. The observers would note the silhouette features of the particular aircraft or ships that they were observing. The last step in identification is to establish the identity of the object. The observers would compare the silhouette observed with silhouette pictures in their field intelligence manuals and determine the aircraft type or ship class of the observed object. Medical laboratories routinely identify objects in blood and other samples. Expert identification systems could be integrated into the laboratory equipment. Identification of ships using sonar equipment used to mean having a human sonar expert listen to sonar signals or look at sonar graphs presented on a video data terminal and determine the class of ship creating the sonar noise signals. The HASP/SIAP expert system analyzes sonar signals for the identification and tracking of ships.

Diagnosing activities include investigating and analyzing the cause or nature of a problem or condition. Diagnosing often involves the act of identifying a cause or problem (such as a disease) from observable signs or symptoms. Expert diagnostic systems infer what the problem is from the observable signs and symptoms that are presented to them. The Caduceus expert system combines its disease entity and manifestation knowledge with patient data presented to it in the diagnosis of medical problems.

Prescribing is the activity of recommending or designating the use of some agent as a remedy for a problem. Prescribing activities are very often related to diagnosing activities. When a doctor diagnoses a patient as having some illness, he or she will often prescribe some medicine as a remedy to correct the problem. Doctors can describe patient symptoms to the MYCIN expert system, and the system will diagnose bacterial infections and prescribe treatment for the infections. In this scenario, the expert system is actually playing the role of expert assistant, which can be very helpful to busy experts in many fields.

Interpreting systems form concepts or notions in light of information supplied to them from system users or sensors. These systems sometimes convey the meaning of something through some representation. The DENDRAL expert system interprets data produced by mass spectrometers and determines molecular structure and atomic composition.

Explaining activities attempt to give reasons for something, clarify or account for something, or assign a meaning to something. Explaining how to fit a particular situation into the standard operating procedures of an organization is a task that must be accomplished often in many companies but is not always easy to do. Supervisors find themselves doing work that their subordinates should be doing because the supervisors feel they can complete the task in less time than it would take to explain to subordinates how to do the work. This situation is especially likely where there is a high turnover in personnel. A company might have standard operating procedures and guidelines on how to ship merchandise to customers. These procedures and guidelines might explain how to pack the merchandise, how to mark the shipping containers, and how to determine the most economical shipping method. How to pack the merchandise and how to mark the shipping container can easily be handled by procedure and guideline documents. Determining the most economical shipping method might be able to be handled in this way also; however, with the variety of shipping methods and the competition between shippers, this task might need additional support for the organization to realize savings through the constant use of the most economical means. Adding another dimension to the task, that of shipping to foreign countries, makes the shipping task even more complex. Export licensing, import licensing, customs labels and inspection requirements, port of entry locations versus customer locations, and the like, require a lot more knowledge to assure that the merchandise will get to the customer on time and economically. An expert system could be designed to explain to the shipping personnel the specifics of each foreign shipment. The shipping personnel could give the expert system information about the shipment (item, size, weight, destination), and the expert system could then explain shipping requirements (required customs forms) and procedures (how to fill the forms out) as well as the most economical shipping method for this shipment.

Training involves the imparting of knowledge or skill by some systematic means or method. This knowledge might include precepts or rules. The goal of training is to increase the knowledge or skill level of a student in some subject domain. Training often starts with some investigation of what the student already knows about the subject of interest. Analysis of what the student already knows versus what the student should know (the goal of the training) determines what needs to be taught. Once the material to be taught has been identified, the trainer will plan the student's lessons and will proceed with the lessons. The GUIDON expert system is an intelligent instruction system that trains a student by asking questions to technical subjects, receiving answers to its questions, and then either telling the student that the response is correct or correcting the student's response.

Experts use these problem-solving activities in their work. They can also be used by less knowledgeable or less skilled workers in an organization. Expert systems modeling the problem-solving strategies of experts that include the domain knowledge of the experts can be used to support the nonexpert workers in an organization. These problem-solving activities have already been supported by expert systems in many subject domains.

SUPPORTED DOMAINS

The first expert systems to be developed were in the chemical and scientific domains. DENDRAL interprets data produced by mass spectrometers and determines the structure of molecules. HEARSAY is a speech-understanding system, and MACSYMA manipulates algebraic symbols. In the early 1970s, the second wave of expert systems appeared. Three expert systems, MYCIN, INTERNIST, and CASNET, dealt with problems in the medical domain. Later in the decade, the PROSPECTOR system, a natural resources system that evaluates geographic sites for potential mineral deposits of commercial interest, appeared. At this time, some of the original expert systems were redesigned and extended; the HEARSAY II system is an example of this. The SOPHIE expert system was the first in the education domain. SOPHIE teaches electronic circuit troubleshooting. By the end of the 1970s, expert systems were operating in the chemical, education, natural resources, and science domains.

Expert systems started to gain in popularity in the early 1980s. With the announcements of successful operational systems like the molybdenum deposit find by the PROSPECTOR system came commercial interest and funding, followed by the creation and commercialization of expert system development tools. The availability of powerful development tools has permitted many more expert systems to be built. Operational and experimental expert systems today support many subject domains. Business domains like manufacturing, sales, management, and finance are represented. The defense community has taken a strong interest in the development of expert systems and is already testing some in the field. Other systems are being tried in the bioengineering, computing, engineering, legal, operations, and social domains. Table 1.2 provides a list of these subject domains and expert systems supporting them.

With the increasing interest in expert systems and the availability of more powerful development tools, many more domains will be represented within the next few years.

With the increased development of expert systems, knowledge engineers will learn better knowledge representations and control strategies. This will translate into the development of more powerful systems.

With the increased presence and use of expert systems, the integration of expert systems with other business systems will occur.

Table 1.2 Domains currently supported by expert systems

Bioengineering

MOLGEN designs experiments to determine the nature of a particular DNA molecule.

POL-I analyzes the action of DNA polymerase 1 on various DNA structures.

SEQ is a nucleic acid sequence analysis and manipulation tool.

Chemical

DENDRAL interprets data produced by mass spectrometers and determines a molecule's structure and atomic constituents.

GA1 infers molecular structure from measurements of molecular pieces.

GENOA identifies unknown compounds such as impurities and pollutants.

SECS assists chemists in organic synthesis planning.

Computing

BIMBO is a speaker-independent, continuous speech recognition system for the Italian language.

CHI creates and modifies software and provides for a supported environment including project management assistance.

CHOICE assists in the development of high-quality graphics presentations.

EDD designs databases.

EXSYS develops software from entity-attribute relationship information provided by systems analysts (not to be confused with the EXSYS expert system development shell).

KM-I is an experimental knowledge management system that attempts to integrate the capabilities of the data management system and the knowledge base system.

PQCC develops compilers from supplied language and target machine specifications.

Computing *(Continued)*

PROGRAMMER'S APPRENTICE assists programmers with software construction and debugging.

PSI composes computer programs based on descriptions of the tasks to be performed.

QUEST is a database search and retrieval system.

PROUST analyzes Pascal programs written by novice programmers.

RABBIT is an experimental system that assists the user to formulate queries to a database.

RUBRIC is an information retrieval system.

Defense

AALPS advises on the loading of cargo on military transport aircraft.

ADVISOR is a decision aid for air traffic controllers and pilots returning from missions.

AIRPLAN plans air traffic movements on an aircraft carrier.

AMUID identifies hostile forces from sensor and intelligence reports and provides battlefield analysis.

BACH accepts multisensor message data and provides fused interpretations of intelligence reports.

HASP/SIAP identifies and tracks ships using ocean sonar signals.

SAMPL plans missions in the area of air command and control.

SPAM semiautomatically interprets high-resolution aerial photographs.

TATR supports tactical air targeting.

Education

EMD diagnoses children's multiplication errors.

GCA advises graduate students on which courses to take.

(Continued)

Table 1.2 *(Continued)*

Education *(Continued)*

GUIDON is an experimental intelligent computer-aided instruction system that teaches the student by eliciting and correcting answers to a series of technical questions.

KNOESPHERE is an encyclopedia knowledge system.

RESEDA is an intelligent biographical information retrieval system that presently has medieval French history knowledge incorporated.

SOPHIE teaches electronic circuit troubleshooting.

STEAMER teaches naval officers about problems of running a steam propulsion plant.

Engineering

AIR-CYL designs air cylinders according to user requirements.

DESTINY is an integrated structural design tool.

EL performs steady-state analysis of resistor-diode-transistor circuits.

EURISKO is an experimental system that learns by discovery; applied to designing new kinds of three-dimensional microelectronic circuits.

HI-RISE aids in the preliminary structural design of high-rise buildings.

KBVLSI is an experimental system to aid in the development of VLSI designs.

MAPLE assists in the design of microprocessor systems.

SACON assists structural engineers in identifying the best analysis strategy for each problem.

SCC predicts stress corrosion cracking in stainless steel material.

SMECI is a civil engineering design tool currently being applied to ocean harbor design.

VEXED assists in the top-down refinement of converting a high-level functional specification into a digital VLSI circuit.

Engineering *(Continued)*

WRIGHT assists designers in analyzing and synthesizing designs and has been applied to the domain of kitchen designs.

Finance

AUDITOR is an experimental system that recommends procedures to be used by an independent auditor.

FOLIO is a portfolio management system.

LE COURTIER suggests stocks to bank customers based on various financial criteria such as price-earnings ratios and revenue growth.

LOAN RISK ADVISOR offers advice on loan management decisions to small and medium-size companies.

TAXADVISOR recommends tax and estate plans that will maximize the wealth an individual transfers at death.

Legal

LDS is an experimental system that models the decision-making processes of lawyers and claims adjusters involved in product liability legislation.

TAXMAN is an experimental system that deals with rules implicit in tax laws and suggests a sequence of contractual arrangements that a company can use to attain its financial objectives.

Management

CALLISTO models and monitors large projects and serves as a project manager's assistant.

CORP aids in the strategic management of technology in an enterprise through technology planning, resource allocation, and analysis of technology for its impact on business.

ODYSSEY plans business travel itineraries under various task requirements and timing constraints.

PTRANS assists with management tasks in manufacturing.

Table 1.2   *(Continued)*

Manufacturing

GREASE aids in the selection or design of parts that should extend the life of manufacturing machinery.

IN-ATE is an electronics troubleshooting system.

ISIS schedules workloads in a job shop of a turbine blade plant.

OCEAN specifies the correct combination of computer components to configure an NCR computer to meet customer needs.

OPGEN plans the sequence of instructions for technicians to follow to assemble printed circuit boards.

ORDER EDIT configures computer communications systems.

XCON configures DEC computer systems.

XSITE assists engineers in determining computer site requirements (such as power) and making site selections.

Medical

ABEL diagnoses acid-base and electrolyte disorders.

ALVEN assesses the performance of the human heart's left ventricle after corrective surgery and incorporates computer vision technology.

ATTENDING critiques a physician's plans for anesthetic management.

BSM is a medical assistant for victims of disasters (such as earthquakes) and people needing medical care where none is available (as on a ship at sea).

CAA recognizes and describes arrhythmias, a cardiac rhythm disorder, with input data coming from an electrocardiogram device.

CADUCEUS performs differential diagnosis in internal medicine.

CANSEARCH aids doctors in searching for cancer therapy literature.

CASNET is a causal network that associates treatments with various diagnostic hypotheses (such as the

Medical   *(Continued)*

severity or progression of a disease) and is used in treatment of glaucoma.

CLINISCAN interprets blood tests.

GALEN is a system for the diagnosis of congenital heart disease in children.

HELP provides medical expert advice to hospital doctors and nurses.

MDX is a system for medical diagnosis.

MYCIN diagnoses meningitis and blood infections.

NEOMYCIN is a medical consultation system with strong explanation capabilities.

ONCOCIN is an oncology protocol management system for cancer chemotherapy treatment.

PIP simulates an expert nephrologist in taking patient history of the present illness with underlying renal disease.

PUFF analyzes patient data to identify possible lung disorders.

RED identifies red-cell antibodies in blood.

VM monitors patients in intensive care and advises about respiratory therapy.

Natural Resources

CONE interprets geotechnical data from a field exploration device known as a cone penetrometer.

DIPMETER ADVISOR is an expert system that analyzes information from oil well logs.

DRILLING ADVISOR diagnoses oil well drilling problems and recommends corrective and preventive measures.

HYDRO is a consultation system for solving water resource problems.

LITHO interprets oil well logs.

PROSPECTOR evaluates sites for potential mineral deposits.

SITECHAR infers the structural material of a potential construction site on the basis of observations made on recovered soil samples and prior site experience.

(Continued)

Table 1.2   *(Concluded)*

Natural Resources   *(Continued)*

WAVES advises engineers on the use of a seismic data analysis program.

Operations

ABSTRIPS devises plans for a robot to move objects between rooms.

ACE identifies and diagnoses communications cable problems and provides advice on repairs.

AUTO-MECH diagnoses fuel problems in automobile engines.

CRIB diagnoses computer hardware and software faults.

DIAG8100 assists in problem determination with IBM 8100 computer systems.

DART is an experimental system for diagnosing computer system faults in the field.

DELTA helps railroad maintenance personnel maintain diesel-electric locomotives.

EARL analyzes the condition of large electrical transformers.

EPISTLE reads mail and informs recipients of important material.

NDS is a network diagnostics system.

NOAH is a robot planning system.

PA is a pilot adviser to oversee and control aircraft monitoring and alerting functions.

PDS is a system for real-time diagnosis of machine processes.

PERITUS is a system for automobile engine fault diagnosis.

PSDM identifies and diagnoses in-flight anomalies in aircraft propulsion systems.

SPEAR analyzes computer error logs in the field.

YES monitors a number of MVS operating system functions and assists the computer operators by performing some operator functions.

Sales

REAL ESTATE AGENT consults on the selection of an apartment.

SELECTMICRO assists potential purchasers of microcomputers in selecting an appropriate configuration.

XSEL assists salespeople in selecting appropriate computer system components.

Science

AM assists in the discovery of mathematical concepts.

CRYSALIS interprets protein electron density maps.

GENESIS helps scientists plan and simulate gene-splicing experiments.

HEARSAY II is a speech understanding system.

MACSYMA manipulates algebraic symbols.

NAVEX assists with the plotting of the positions of satellites and the course of the space shuttle.

SIMULAB models the interactions between planets and the sun.

SMP manipulates algebraic and other symbolic expressions and reduces complex expressions to simpler ones.

WILLARD forecasts the likelihood of severe thunderstorms in the central part of the United States.

Social

NEIGHBORHOOD ADVISOR assists local social services officers in determining the nature of neighborhood problems such as housing and provides guidance on relevant regulations, rulings, and actions that can be taken.

SUMMARY   Computer technology has introduced many new and innovative products. Perhaps the most exciting is expert system technology, from the artificial intelligence domain. Expert system technology will most likely affect everyone in the computer and software engineering fields, and most software engineers should learn about it.

An expert system is a computer-based system that uses knowledge, facts, and reasoning techniques to solve problems that normally require the expertise, abilities, and experiences of human experts.

The goals sought by expert system builders in the development of expert systems include substituting for an unavailable expert, assimilating the knowledge of multiple experts, training new experts, and providing requisite expertise on projects that fail to attract, retain, or afford experts.

Many expert systems were developed in commercial and university laboratories. Some of these systems provided us with basic expert system technology. Many of the more recent systems can easily be transformed into viable commercial systems that can provide organizations with financial and operational benefits. The TAXADVISOR expert system is an example. Some of the expert system research projects are working toward systems that will find commercial utility as soon as the technology and the particular domains under study are better understood and production of the systems is completed. The ISIS expert system is an example of this. Finally, ad hoc expert systems are actively supporting the mission and goals of the organizations that purchased them. The EDAAS expert system is an example of such a system.

Expert systems have been designed in many ways, but they share certain basic components. The components common to most expert systems are a user interface module, a knowledge acquisition facility, an inference mechanism, and a database. The database is the repository for the system's fundamental knowledge, the system's knowledge of a particular domain, and the facts on particular cases that are presented to the system. Often the database is managed by a data manager and is segmented in some logical scheme to support data management, system efficiency, or both. Separate explanation facilities are found in some expert system architectures, while others rely on explanation capabilities of the system's inference mechanism. Future architectures will also include self-training facilities.

Expert systems are used to collect, represent, and store the knowledge of experts in a computer and allow access to this knowledge. Expert systems share four main characteristics:

1. Expert systems perform at an expert's level of competence in a particular problem domain.

2. Expert systems have inference mechanisms that can reason judgmentally and justify their deductions.

3. Expert systems have databases of expert knowledge, codified and stored for use by the systems' inference mechanisms.

4. Expert system programming involves describing and presenting knowledge to the system; there is usually no programming for using the knowledge, as this is part of the task of the inference mechanism.

Other characteristics that many expert systems share include the ability to deal with uncertain or incomplete information, the ability to search efficiently through a problem space for a solution, the readability of the system's database, and the ability to provide intermediate results while the system is executing.

Expert systems are already supporting many problem-solving activities, such as decision making, designing, planning, monitoring, diagnosing, and training activities, to name only a few. Subject domains that are supported by expert systems include bioengineering, defense, education, engineering, finance, and medicine. The commercialization of expert systems is in its infancy. The future should see more systems working in new areas on more diverse problems.

REFERENCES

1. E. A. Feigenbaum and P. McCorduck, *The Fifth Generation* (Reading, MA: Addison-Wesley, 1983).

2. P. Harmon and D. King, *Expert Systems: Artificial Intelligence in Business* (New York: Wiley, 1985).

3. F. Hayes-Roth, D. A. Waterman, and D. B. Lenat (eds.), *Building Expert Systems* (Reading, MA: Addison-Wesley, 1983).

4. P. H. Winston and K. A. Prendergast, *The AI Business: The Commercial Uses of Artificial Intelligence* (Cambridge, MA: M.I.T. Press, 1984).

2 KNOWLEDGE-BASE MANAGEMENT AND SYSTEM EVOLUTION

The building of basic expert systems is fundamentally different from conventional programming.

When an implementor writes a conventional program he enters statements that must be executed in a precise sequence. The program may be difficult to debug and to modify, hence the delays and costs associated with maintenance of programs. A seemingly trivial change to a complex program can trigger a crop of new bugs that are difficult to find.

When an implementor builds an expert system he fills up a shell with knowledge, using the software as a guide in entering facts and rules into the shell. He does not necessarily write programs. The facts and rules can be stated in any sequence. Any fact or rule can be changed at any time, and in most cases the changes can be made independently of one another. When users put the system to work the inference engine finds the rules and facts which are appropriate at any moment and employs them to come to conclusions and give advice. The implementor can change the system's behavior merely by changing the facts and rules. He does not have to modify a program; the inference engine does the work. When the knowledge is changed the inference engine comes to different conclusions.

The facts and rules that an expert system uses are stored in a knowledge-base and managed with a knowledge-base management system. A knowledge-base management system might be thought of as an extension of the idea of a database management system. A database management system stores data and makes it independent of the programs that use it. A knowledge-base management system stores facts and rules in a manner independent of the programs that use them. The knowledge-base is used by an inference engine which may access many rules and use them to create inferences (Figure 2.1). The facts and rules may be stored in a conventional database management system which is, in effect, a subset of the knowledge-base management system.

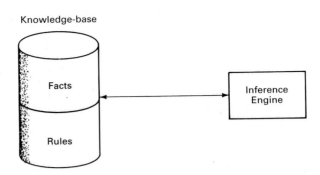

Figure 2.1   Knowledge-base management system

DEVELOPING SYSTEMS IN CONSTANT EVOLUTION

Some computer systems are designed to meet a well-defined need that is constant. Such systems require little, if any, modification once they are functioning properly. A word processing system is an example.

Others are designed to meet a well-defined, constant need, but events modify exactly what the computer system must do. In general, these events do not occur with great frequency. A payroll system is a good example. The requirement to calculate payroll amounts is constant, but new tax laws, for example, change some of the calculations required of the computerized payroll system.

Some computer systems are being designed to support activities that are not well defined. Often these activities are also very fluid by their nature. The needs and requirements of these activities are constantly changing. The computer systems that support these activities must evolve with the changes in the requirements. Decision support systems are examples of constantly evolving computer systems.

Developing computer-based systems that are in constant evolution has been difficult using traditional computer technology and methods.

It has long been accepted that computer programs are made up of algorithms and data. The first computer programs written included both the algorithms and the data needed to run. The introduction of database management systems made possible the disconnection of the data from the algorithms. The data is specified, both logically and physically, and is stored in the DBMS. The algorithms and logical data names are used by the programs. If the data specifications changed (for example, if a data field was extended from 2 bytes in length to 4 bytes), the algorithms did not necessarily have to be modified. If the algorithms changed (for example, if the number of times a program loop is executed was changed), the data specifications did not necessarily have to change. The introduction of DBMS did make the modification of computer programs easier, quicker, and less error-prone.

However, even with the use of a DBMS, the development and continued modification of a computer system that is in constant evolution is still difficult.

Most computer programs today provide two specifications:

1. Exactly what data to use
2. Exactly what procedures to perform on the data

These specifications must be communicated to the computer via a computer programming language. Each time there is a change in requirements, these specifications must be modified. The specifications are often interrelated and dependent on each other. The change of one operation in a computer program can potentially affect the function of one or more other operations in that program or another related program.

The use of an expert system changes what has to be specified and what is affected by system specification modifications. To understand why, let us look at the example of an expert system architecture in Figure 2.2.

The user interface is a component that accepts facts and queries from a user and provides advice, consultation, and explanation information to the user. This component provides the user's queries to the inference engine and the facts to the inference engine and the domain database. It accepts the advice and consultation information from the inference engine and the explanation information from the explanation facility. If new methods of interfacing with the user are

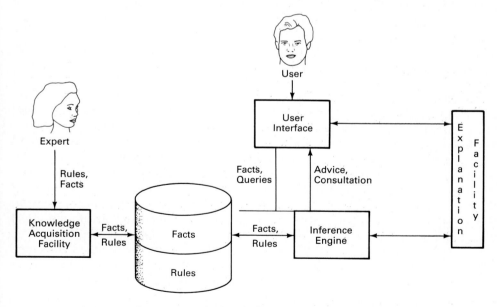

Figure 2.2   Knowledge-base architecture of a rule-based expert system

desired, this component could be modified. This modification should not affect the other expert system components. This component would continue to provide user facts and queries and would still accept advice, consultation, and explanation information. However, once an expert system is operational, there will most likely be little call for modification of the user interface. And as already stated, modification to this component should not have any effect on the other components.

The knowledge acquisition facility provides the means for acquiring knowledge from human experts. Modification of this component would only occur if one of these circumstances should arise:

1. If the method of knowledge acquisition was to be changed
2. If the knowledge representation was to be changed
3. If a new knowledge representation scheme was to be added

Once an expert system is in use, these types of changes are not likely. The knowledge acquisition facility accepts facts and rules from the expert and provides this knowledge to the system's knowledge base. Throughout the lifetime of the system, this facility will most likely accept and provide new knowledge to the knowledge base. If changes are desired, modifications to this component would not affect the other system components.

The explanation facility provides explanations to system users in response to user requests for explanations. This facility gets support from the inference engine to provide this service and passes the explanations to the user interface facility. This is another component that should not require any modifications once the system is up and running. Also, any modifications to this component should not affect the other system components.

The inference engine is the central control mechanism for the expert system. How the system develops inferences is determined by the inference engine. The inference engine determines how the system will act on the knowledge (what procedures the system will use). The choice of inference mechanism used for a particular expert system implementation is dependent on the domain, the expert's working manner, and the knowledge representation scheme. For a particular application, an inference mechanism should be selected and should not need to be changed. If changes are made to a particular inference mechanism, these changes should be localized to the inference engine and should not affect the other components.

The expert system DBMS component manages the knowledge data stored in the knowledge and domain databases. It provides the services needed by the other expert system components to store and retrieve the system's knowledge. This component manages three basic types of knowledge data:

1. Case-independent static facts
2. Case-dependent dynamic facts
3. Case-independent rules

The expert system DBMS manages the logical and physical definitions of the knowledge data formats. This component is separate and should not be affected by changes in other components. Similarly, changes to this component should not affect other components. The services this component provides are very basic and should not need redefinition.

The knowledge data stored in the expert system DBMS component are the entities that give a particular expert system its knowledge and personality. This knowledge data will require modification as the needs and requirements of a particular expert system change. More on this will be provided later in this discussion.

So far we have discussed five expert system components:

1. User interface
2. Knowledge acquisition facility
3. Explanation facility
4. Inference engine
5. Database management facility

Expert systems in the future will include additional facilities such as a self-training facility.

The first expert systems were handicrafted. That is to say, all of the necessary software components were coded by their developers, as was the development of the knowledge base. Examples of such expert systems are DENDRAL, SAINT, MYCIN, and HEARSAY I. These systems required a lot of development resources, including both human and computer resources.

Researchers wanted to develop more expert systems, but they wanted to do so using fewer development resources. They decided to try to use some of the previously built expert systems by removing the domain-specific knowledge and adding new knowledge that dealt with a different subject domain. For example, the MYCIN expert system was stripped of its domain knowledge, and the result was the EMYCIN (Essential MYCIN) expert system shell. If you remove the knowledge from an expert system you are left with an empty *shell*. The shell has the mechanisms for knowledge representation inferencing and use, but contains no knowledge about a given area of expertise. The *shell* is a framework that a knowledge engineer can fill with knowledge.

The PUFF expert system provides diagnostic consultations in the domain of pulmonary function disease. PUFF was developed by populating the empty EMYCIN knowledge-base with expertise in pulmonary function disease and using the expert system functions that are available from EMYCIN.

Expert systems are now being built using expert system shells. These expert systems are taking less time to develop because the basic expert system components are already in place.

The builders of today's expert systems perform three essential steps in the development of a system:

1. Study the domain to be supported by an expert system.
2. Determine which expert system shell best fits the domain.
3. Develop the expert system by filling the shell with knowledge.

The construction of one of these systems can be closely compared with the development of a corporate database using a database management system product. When building a database using a DBMS, the DBMS is the database framework, and it provides the functions required to enter, change, delete, and retrieve data from the database.

Most future expert systems will be developed using an expert system shell. The system developers will not hand-code the basic system components. The system developers will rely on the expert system shell vendors to develop, enhance, and maintain these shell products.

Summarizing the discussions so far, expert system components are, for the most part, highly modularized and independent, and most future expert systems will be built on (commercially available) expert system shells. This has two corollaries:

1. If an expert system component needs to be built or modified, it should not affect the other components.
2. The major task of building an expert system will be the development of the knowledge-base.

The first statement tells us that there is independence in the system components; this attribute is beneficial to a system that is being built with constant evolution in mind. If this evolution requires that a component be modified or exchanged, there is an excellent chance that the other components will not be affected. This reduces the modification task and also reduces the chance of introducing unintentional side effects. This is true regardless of the mechanisms used in the various components or the knowledge representation scheme used in the knowledge base.

The second statement tells us that the attributes of the knowledge base are key to the appropriateness of the application of expert system technology to systems that will be in constant evolution. The important question to answer about the attributes of knowledge-bases is, can the elements of a knowledge-base be sufficiently isolated that any addition, modification, or deletion of one element will not affect any other element?

Expert systems that use a rule knowledge representation scheme, for instance, have rules and facts as knowledge-base elements. Which rules and facts to use is determined by the current content of the knowledge-base. The elements are used as a logical consequence of their presence in the knowledge-base and their logical connection to the inferencing at any given point in the operation of the system. Rules and facts are not directly linked. There is no direct-call function by the inference engine to rules or facts. Expert system control mechanisms do not "know" what rules and facts should be or could be in the knowledge-base. For any given inference step, the inference engine uses all the relevant rules and facts that are available to it at the time.

The addition of a rule or fact would be reflected in that the inference engine would avail itself of the new rule or fact if it fit an upcoming inference. The deletion of a rule or fact would be reflected in that the deleted rule or fact would no longer be available to the inference engine. It is important to note here that the inference engine would not "know" that a rule or fact was added or deleted. The inference engine would not stop because of the addition or deletion of a rule or a fact. The inference engine would simply take the most appropriate rules and facts that are available to it and develop the best inferences it can, given the present state of the knowledge-base.

Let's take a look at using these operations by building a small accounting knowledge base. We start with an empty knowledge-base. We add our first three knowledge-base entities, in this case, three facts about the accounting domain (Figure 2.3).

With this knowledge-base, we can ask a few basic questions about the accounting domain. For instance, we could ask the expert system that includes this knowledge-base if cash is an asset. The system would correctly respond in the affirmative. We could then ask it if inventory is an asset and again the system would provide a correct, affirmative response. However, if we ask the system if goodwill is an asset, the system would respond incorrectly with a negative response. Looking at our knowledge-base, we would see that the reason for this incorrect response is that a fact is missing from the knowledge-base.

cash is an asset.
accounts receivable are assets.
inventory is an asset.

Figure 2.3 Beginning of an accounting knowledge-base

Using an addition operation, we add a new fact to our knowledge-base (Figure 2.4).

Now if we ask the system if goodwill is an asset, the system would respond with the correct, affirmative answer. Also notice that if we ask the system if cash is an asset, the system will still respond with a correct, affirmative response. The addition of a fact did not affect the other fact entities. Each entity is an independent actor.

cash is an asset.
accounts receivable are assets.
inventory is an asset.
goodwill is an asset.

Figure 2.4 Accounting knowledge-base II

We would now like to ask questions about the liquidity of our assets. By inspecting our knowledge-base, we see that we do not have any knowledge about asset liquidity in our knowledge-base. We therefore decide to add four new facts (Figure 2.5).

If we ask the system if cash is an asset and if cash is liquid, it will provide a correct, affirmative response. If we ask this version of our expert system if goodwill is liquid, it will tell us yes. However, after checking with an accounting text or an accounting expert, we learn that goodwill is not, in fact, liquid. We had previously believed that goodwill was liquid, but we have learned through experience or further investigation that it is not. Whenever we learn that a knowledge-base entity is incorrect, we delete it from the knowledge-base. In this case, we will delete the fact that goodwill is liquid (Figure 2.6).

cash is an asset.
accounts receivable are assets.
inventory is an asset.
goodwill is an asset.

cash is liquid.
accounts receivable are liquid.
inventory is liquid.
goodwill is liquid.

Figure 2.5 Accounting knowledge-base III

cash is an asset.
accounts receivable are assets.
inventory is an asset.
goodwill is an asset.

cash is liquid.
accounts receivable are liquid.
inventory is liquid.

Figure 2.6   Accounting knowledge-base IV

Now if we ask the system if goodwill is liquid, it will correctly respond in the negative. If we ask if goodwill is an asset, the system will respond correctly in the affirmative. The deletion of the incorrect fact corrected the knowledge-base but did not affect other facts in the knowledge-base about goodwill or any other item.

Figure 2.7 shows an updated version of our knowledge-base that was built by adding new facts to our previous version. This time we are adding facts about liability accounts.

We may have stated that "tax payable is a liability." This fact could more accurately be stated as "income tax payable is a liability." We therefore decide to modify this fact. Applying a modification operation to this fact, we arrive at the version of our knowledge-base in Figure 2.7.

Notice that this modification operation did not affect any knowledge-base entity except the particular fact that was the object of the modification operation.

The addition, deletion, and modification examples presented so far have used case-independent *static* fact data. This data is dependent on the subject

cash is an asset.
accounts receivable are assets.
inventory is an asset.
goodwill is an asset.

cash is liquid.
accounts receivable are liquid.
inventory is liquid.

accounts payable are liabilities.
salaries payable are liabilities.
income tax payable is a liability.

Figure 2.7   Accounting knowledge-base V

domain but independent of the particular run of the system. In other words, it is independent of the case on which the system is presently working. This data is called *static* data because it does not change between runs or during a run. The only time this data is changed is when the knowledge-base is being built or modified, operations to the knowledge-base that occur when the system is not in productive use.

The same operation and knowledge-base entity independence prevails when case-dependent *dynamic* fact data is being added, deleted, or modified. For example, during a run, a fact might be added to the knowledge-base stating that the current cash balance of the business is $10,000.00 (Figure 2.8). Later this figure might be changed by the system or by a user during a specific run.

The last type of entity that we would want to put in our knowledge-base is case-independent *rule* data. Figure 2.9 shows the addition of a rule to our knowledge-base. (Two syntactic conventions have been followed in this example rule: Reserved words such as IF, AND, and THEN are capitalized, and variables such as *Accounting-item* are continuous strings, the first character of which is a capitalized alphabetic character.)

Our expert system can now provide correct answers for some questions in the accounting domain. Here are some examples of the questions to which our system can provide answers:

Is cash an asset?

Is cash liquid?

Is cash a current asset?

Is inventory an asset?

Is income tax payable a liability?

```
cash is an asset.
accounts receivable are assets.
inventory is an asset.
goodwill is an asset.

cash is liquid.
accounts receivable are liquid.
inventory is liquid.

accounts payable are liabilities.
salaries payable are liabilities.
income tax payable is a liability.

cash equals $10,000.00.
```

Figure 2.8   Accounting knowledge-base VI

cash is an asset.
accounts receivable are assets.
inventory is an asset.
goodwill is an asset.

cash is liquid.
accounts receivable are liquid.
inventory is liquid.

accounts payable are liabilities.
salaries payable are liabilities.
income tax payable is a liability.

cash equals $10,000.00.

IF   Accounting-item is an asset
          AND Accounting-item is liquid,
THEN   Accounting-item is a current asset.

Figure 2.9   Accounting knowledge-base VII

Notice that the addition of this rule to the knowledge-base did not affect the facts that were already in the knowledge-base. Also notice that the system could answer the question "Is cash a current asset?" To answer this question, the system used our rule plus two facts (cash is an asset; cash is liquid). Rules and facts are not connected in the knowledge-base. However, the inference engine can use them together to derive from them a fact that it is seeking.

The addition of more rules will make this knowledge-base more helpful to the intended user. Let us add another rule to our knowledge-base, about the currency of liabilities (Figure 2.10).

The addition of the new rule did not affect the other entities in the knowledge-base, including the other rule. However, if we ask if accounts payable are current liabilities, the system will respond with a negative answer, and we know that this answer is incorrect. After some investigation of our knowledge-base, we note that our newest rule will never find the IF part of the rule true. The reason for this is that there are no facts in the knowledge-base that state that any accounting item will be satisfied within one business cycle. Therefore, the THEN part of the rule will never apply. We fix this situation with the addition of some facts to the knowledge-base (Figure 2.11).

We can now ask if accounts payable are current liabilities, and the system will correctly provide an affirmative response.

Notice that each time our system did not provide us with the correct an-

cash is an asset.
accounts receivable are assets.
inventory is an asset.
goodwill is an asset.

cash is liquid.
accounts receivable are liquid.
inventory is liquid.

accounts payable are liabilities.
salaries payable are liabilities.
income tax payable is a liability.

cash equals $10,000.00.

IF   Accounting-item is an asset
          AND Accounting-item is liquid,
THEN   Accounting-item is a current asset.

IF   Accounting-item is a liability
          AND Accounting-item will be satisfied within one business operating
          cycle,
THEN   Accounting-item is a current liability.

Figure 2.10   Accounting knowledge-base VIII

swer, we were able to add, delete, or modify one fact or rule at a time in order to update our system so that the system could provide us with correct responses. In our examples, we sometimes showed more than one operation at a time; this was done to save time and space. In the development and maintenance of an expert system, facts and rules can be operated upon singly or in groups. Whichever way the knowledge engineer wishes to perform these tasks, the resulting knowledge-base will be the same.

The facts and rules of the above knowledge-base are isolated elements. The addition, deletion, and modification operations involving one fact or rule do not affect any other facts or rules in the knowledge-base. Each fact and each rule is an independent piece of knowledge. They can be isolated sufficiently that any addition, modification, or deletion of one element will not affect any other element. This is not always the case.

It is not generally desirable that an expert system developer should have to tell the system about accounting principles. Such textbook knowledge ought to be available for purchase with appropriate expert system shells. It is likely that shells for specific applications will become more common and will bring

cash is an asset.
accounts receivable are assets.
inventory is an asset.
goodwill is an asset.

cash is liquid.
accounts receivable are liquid.
inventory is liquid.

accounts payable are liabilities.
salaries payable are liabilities.
income tax payable is a liability.

accounts payable will be satisfied within one business operating cycle.
salaries payable will be satisfied within one business operating cycle.
income tax payable will be satisfied within one business operating cycle.

cash equals $10,000.00.

IF   Accounting-item is an asset
          AND Accounting-item is liquid,
THEN   Accounting-item is a current asset.

IF   Accounting-item is a liability
          AND Accounting-item will be satisfied within one business operating
          cycle,
THEN   Accounting-item is a current liability.

Figure 2.11   Accounting knowledge-base IX

with them static knowledge that is applicable to all systems in a given domain.

The knowledge-base entities of the frames knowledge representation (described in detail later) scheme could also be independent elements. The elements of the frames scheme are called slots. Slots are used to store basic knowledge units. One slot might contain the name of the frame. Another slot might contain the name of the expert who provided the knowledge that is contained in the particular frame. Domain knowledge can be inserted into various slots. Often the domain knowledge inserted into a slot is represented using one of the other knowledge representation schemes. For example, CENTAUR uses the frames scheme and represents its knowledge using the rule scheme. Other slots could be used to store help information and the answers to why and how questions. If nothing else is stored in the slots, the frames are independent elements.

The entities of a frames-based knowledge-base are often not independent. Slots in frames are often used to provide inheritance knowledge. For example, using our accounting knowledge-base, there might be a frame called *assets*. This frame would provide the basic knowledge of what assets are. Another frame might be called *current assets*. The *current assets* frame could totally represent the current assets concept and thereby retain independence. However, to save time and space and to be able to use certain inheritance properties, the *current assets* frame could have a slot that points to the *assets* frame. This slot-to-frame reference would provide the *current assets* frame with the knowledge representation of the *assets* frame. The *current assets* frame would then have only enough additional slots to provide the conceptual knowledge necessary to extend the *assets* concept to the *current assets* concept (the concept of liquidity).

Although the elements of a frames knowledge representation scheme are not necessarily independent, it is possible to develop an automated tool that can make updating less error-prone and more efficient. The TEIRESIAS expert system is an example of this. TEIRESIAS is an expert system that was developed to provide knowledge-base construction and updating for expert systems. Therefore, although the knowledge-base entities of some frames-based knowledge-bases are not independent, it is still relatively easy to develop systems that are in constant evolution.

The semantic network knowledge representation scheme (discussed later) seems to lend itself the least to the constant evolution requirement. The semantic network representation, one of the oldest in the artificial intelligence field, is the most general knowledge representation scheme.

In summary, the components that make up an expert system are highly modular and independent. The modification or replacement of one should not affect other components. Commercially available expert system shells are being developed along these lines. Knowledge-bases that are developed using the rule or first-order logic knowledge representation scheme are composed of highly independent modular elements. The addition, modification, or deletion of one element will not affect other elements in the knowledge-base. Knowledge-bases that use the frames scheme might be composed of independent modular elements. However, if they are not, their architecture lends itself to the use of automatic tools to support update operations.

Expert systems that use rule, first-order logic, or frame-based knowledge-bases should make the development of constantly evolving computer-based systems easier and less error-prone.

THE INCREMENTAL CONSTRUCTION OF LARGE SYSTEMS

The incremental development of a large computer-based system could be viewed as the nonincremental development of a small system followed by constant evolution. In this case, the constant evolution is the follow-on incremental development of the system.

The construction of small expert systems is usually an easy task. Using an appropriate expert system shell, small expert systems can often be developed at the rate of one fact or rule per hour of effort. Small developments incorporating 25 to 50 facts and rules often are useful and can be considered legitimate operational systems.

We have established that expert system technology can be effectively applied to the development of systems that are in constant evolution. The evolution of a large expert system from a small system through a process of constant updates to the knowledge-base should present no problems with this technology. Therefore, when a problem is to be supported by an automated system and expert system technology is determined to be appropriate and the resulting system will be large, it is advisable to build a small system first and then to expand the system incrementally.

It is suggested that the construction of all large computer-based systems that might use expert system technology as the base technology follow a development path that includes the following steps:

1. Define the problem to be supported or solved.

2. Determine if expert system technology seems to be appropriate. If not, stop the development of an expert system–based approach and search for a more appropriate technology on which to base the system; otherwise, proceed.

3. Determine the appropriate knowledge representation scheme and inference mechanism for the problem.

4. Determine the form of the user system interface.

5. Determine the knowledge acquisition requirements for the system.

6. Determine the level of explanation that will be required by the system.

7. Decide, using the information gathered in steps 1 through 6, if there exists an expert system shell that is appropriate to this project. If there is, buy it; if there is not, determine what compromise can be achieved with existing shells or stop the project.

8. Build a small version of the system to be built; this small system should have approximately 25 to 50 entities in the knowledge-base.

9. Have the domain expert run the system and determine if the small system has been started correctly. If so, proceed; if not, determine whether the project must go back to step 3 or step 8 and then return to the appropriate step.

10. Obtain comments about the system from the expert.

11. Delete or modify entities in the knowledge-base that are in error.

12. Add new knowledge entities as suggested by the domain expert or as derived by the knowledge engineer.

13. Make any system component modifications that might be needed.

14. Have the domain expert run the system.

15. Determine if the system is accurate and ready to be fielded. If it is, stop the initial development project and field the system; if it is not, go back to step 10.

This development path has 15 steps. These 15 steps can be placed into four logical groups. The first group would consist of the first two steps. The objective of this group of tasks is to define the problem and determine if expert system technology is appropriate.

The second group would comprise steps 3 through 7. The objective of this group of tasks is to obtain the basic expert system for the project, either through purchase or development. Unless the company has the monetary and personnel resources to develop an expert system shell, it is strongly recommended that a commercially available shell be used.

Group three contains steps 8 and 9. Here, a small expert system is developed and is experimented with by the domain expert. The objective of this work is to see if the project is on track. Does the system have all the facilities that are perceived as necessary? Does the system provide an appropriate level of service? Does the system provide support in a manner that is appropriate to the targeted tasks? Does the system correctly handle the set of situations addressed by the small knowledge-base?

If there is a problem with the basic system—for instance, if the explanation facility is not sufficient—the project must iterate back through the second group of tasks to rectify the basic system problems. Perhaps a different expert system shell needs to be used for the project.

If the basic system seems to be fine but the problem seems to be with the knowledge in the knowledge-base, step 8 in this group needs to be done again. Totally rebuilding the knowledge-base at this point should not be costly. The development of the knowledge-base should not have taken more than a few weeks.

The first three groups of tasks lay down the foundation for the development of the system. By the time these task groups are completed, the problem has been defined, the technology has been determined to be appropriate, the basic expert system skeleton (shell) has been acquired, and a small knowledge-base has been developed, tested, and approved by the domain expert. The remaining work involves the incremental development of the full system.

The fourth group consists of steps 10 through 15. The objective of this group is incrementally to enhance the small expert system that was produced in the first nine steps until the system provides all the services it is initially intended to provide.

This group of tasks should be reiterated many times until the system is completed. More iterations will mean more interactions with the expert, but the interactions should be more effective. Any deviations from the desired goals will be small if the reviews with the expert are frequent. The time required to fix the errors in the knowledge-base should therefore be small. This technique should ensure the efficient use of both the domain expert and the knowledge engineer.

If building on a commercially obtained expert system shell, the work performed in steps 1 through 9 should normally take between one and three months. Part of this time will require the assistance of the domain expert, and all of it will require a knowledge engineer. Developing the basic expert system components independently could take a year or more.

The time needed to perform steps 10 through 15 will be proportional to the size of the system being developed, the tools being used, and the availability of the domain expert or experts. Large systems, like MYCIN, have taken teams of developers many years to develop. However, tools like the TEIRESIAS expert system should help to decrease the development resources required to develop large systems.

TEIRESIAS has been elaborated to assist in the development of large MYCIN knowledge bases. TEIRESIAS is an expert system with knowledge about the knowledge that is to be acquired for and used by the MYCIN expert system. TEIRESIAS assists with the task of transferring expertise from the experts to the MYCIN knowledge-base.

The KAS expert system provides similar knowledge acquisition services for the PROSPECTOR expert system.

This technology provides numerous benefits to developers of large systems, among them these:

1. The ability to build the systems incrementally
2. The ability to run systems that are incomplete
3. The ability to tell if the incomplete systems are functioning properly relative to their stage of completion
4. The ability to change a system component without affecting other components
5. The ability to alter one entity in the knowledge-base without affecting other entities in the knowledge-base

KNOWLEDGE CLASSIFICATION AND CONTROL STRATEGIES

Two key issues of expert system technology are the classification of knowledge and the use of control strategies that are appropriate to the various classes of knowledge in relation to the requirements of the subject and tasks to be supported. The way knowledge is represented and used can vary by subject and task and sometimes by the personal preference of the domain expert.

It is important to represent and use subject domain knowledge in a way that approximates the way in which the domain expert represents and uses it. There are several reasons for this. The first is to show the expert what you are using to build the expert system and that you are truly attempting to build a model of his or her expertise and not just some general expertise model.

The second reason is of a practical nature. The closer the expert system approximates the expert's representation and uses of knowledge, the easier it will be for the expert to tell you if the expert system you are building is accurate.

People who regularly use human experts have come to learn how to present a problem to an expert and how the expert will format the advice. These people have learned how the expert represents and uses expert-level knowledge. These people will also expect an expert system to accept problems and present advice in a similar manner. Therefore, the third reason to approximate the expert's knowledge representation and control schemes is to assist in getting user acceptance of the system since the people who go to human experts for advice are potential users of the expert system.

Another reason is based on the fact that the human experts are acclaimed as such because of their abilities to perform effectively in the particular subject domain, and part of their abilities are based on their subject knowledge. The manner in which they represent and control their knowledge seems to be important to their success. Therefore, it is logical to accept their knowledge as is, unless further research justifies something more effective.

The task that the expert system is to perform is also important. Let us take the example of the XCON expert system. XCON is used by the Digital Equipment Corporation (DEC) to design the configuration of the VAX minicomputers DEC is selling. The task is to take the ordering information from the customer-salesman meeting and design a VAX product that satisfies the customer's request and will function properly.

It is XCON's job to assure that the ordered components have their requisite facilities. If a peripheral device is ordered, XCON must make sure that a requisite controller card is ordered. Then XCON must make sure that the equipment racks ordered have the physical room, electrical power, and bus connections for the controller card. XCON makes use of a database that describes the properties of the VAX system components. The work of designing a VAX computer system to meet a customer's requirements, using the predesigned DEC components, is a matter of seeing if each item ordered is available, is properly supported by other items ordered, and is reasonable—in other words, making sure that the components are not mismatched.

VAX system configuration experts deal with heuristics like this: "If a VAX 11/750 is ordered and the customer's intent is to connect 20 terminals to it, then the order must include enough terminal multiplexers for at least 20 terminals." (Most DEC terminal multiplexers support either 8 or 16 terminals; therefore, more than one multiplexer will be required.) With the configuration heuristic knowledge of this form, the if-then rule form of knowledge representation fits the task.

It is also important to choose the right control strategy. The configuration experts always deal with initial order information. They do not start with a preconceived notion of the final design. The configuration experts take the customer's order and go through it one component at a time. For each component ordered, the expert infers the other components required and then checks to see if the requisite components are on the order. If they are all there, the expert moves on to the next item. If a requisite component is missing, the expert adds the component. Support for the added component is also checked. The configuration moves forward, one component at a time, until the design task is completed. The expert system control strategy that supports this type of work task is called forward chaining. This strategy is driven by the data supplied by the system user. In this case, the user provides the system with the VAX system order data. The system uses this data to provide the user with a complete VAX configuration that will meet the customer's needs.

To illustrate the importance of the proper selection of the control strategy for an expert system in relation to the task at hand, let us look at the XCON example again. If the expert system builder decided that the control strategy of XCON should have been the backward-chaining technique, the system would first ask the configuration designer for a hypothesis of the final VAX computer system configuration design, and the expert system would start with this design goal and go back through its knowledge-base to see if it could validate the hypothesis. Because a great many DEC components are available, the number of possible VAX configurations is very large. This means that the configuration designer would have to do a lot of work prior to being able to have the expert system assist the designer, and the expert system would have to search through a very large search space. The goal of XCON was to assist the configuration designer with as much of the total configuration task as possible. Therefore, the backward-chaining technique would not provide DEC with as effective a configuration assistant system as XCON.

KNOWLEDGE REPRESENTATION SCHEMES

The current state of the art for knowledge representation and expert system control strategies is analogous to the state of the art for data modeling and database management strategies around the late 1960s. Basic techniques for system development are in place, but research on more efficient and more effective methods continues, seeking a better understanding of knowledge representation schemes and control strategies and ways of matching these technical issues to particular tasks.

Four basic knowledge representation schemes are in use today and are described in chapter 10:

- Rules
- Frames
- Semantic networks
- First-order logic

New knowledge representation ideas are being prototyped and tested, and the results are being documented in papers. Some of these new representations are enhancements to the knowledge representation schemes.

INFERENCING STRATEGIES

Many expert system control strategies are in use today. One or more of these strategies are incorporated into the inference engine of each expert system. Here are some of the more popular control strategies:

- Backward chaining
- Forward chaining
- Breadth-first search
- Depth-first search
- Heuristic search
- Problem reduction
- Pattern matching
- Hierarchical control
- Unification
- Event-driven control

Matching the task to the correct combination of knowledge representation and control strategy is still an art form. There are some combinations that seem to work well together. For example, small diagnostic expert systems seem to work well when the rules knowledge representation scheme is matched with the backward chaining control strategy. However, this architecture might be beneficially modified in a few ways. First, the frames knowledge representation might augment the rules representation. In this combination, each rule would be a slot (a frame component) in a particular frame. The frames concept would allow more information to be included in the expert system. An example would be a help slot. Any time a user needs assistance with the operation of the expert system, the user could request help information. The help information provided would come from these help slots. With this architecture, the help information would be pertinent to the user's current point in the operation of the expert system. Numeric or heuristic control strategies might augment the backward chaining strategy in order to be able to consider and rank competing hypotheses. We will go into these technical details later; the point here is that the selection of knowledge representation schemes and control strategies is important, and more research is needed so that we will be able to match expert system technology with work and task requirements more precisely.

Knowledge engineering is the new discipline that is responsible for matching task requirements with knowledge representation scheme and control strategy selections. The knowledge engineer has to study the task to be supported and infer which representations and control mechanisms are appropriate. Perhaps expert systems could be built to assist in this work.

As knowledge engineering matures, techniques for task analysis, technology matching, and knowledge acquisition will emerge. Knowledge engineers will need techniques to analyze tasks identified as needing expert system support. These analysis techniques will have to be comprehensive enough to determine whether the expert system technology can be effectively applied to the task and provide requisite inputs to the technology-matching work. Technology-matching techniques will be needed to assure that the most effective combination of knowledge representations and control mechanisms is used for a given task and that the effort required for the knowledge acquisition work is minimized.

Acquisition of expert knowledge has been a costly and lengthy process. The acquisition of knowledge for some of the larger expert systems has taken many years. The use of domain experts for long periods of time is difficult and expensive. Knowledge acquisition techniques that allow the knowledge engineer to acquire the expert-level knowledge quickly and with less direct participation of the human expert are needed.

The future for knowledge engineering holds the promise of new knowledge representation schemes and control strategies on the one hand and standardization of these issues on the other. Standard knowledge representation schemes and control strategies will result as we gain a greater understanding of this technology. Further, we will be able to classify tasks by the knowledge representation and control that support them best. Standard techniques to build expert systems need to be developed and taught, and tools must be developed to support these standard expert-system-building techniques. These steps are necessary if we wish to see a greater commercialization of expert system technology.

3 BUSINESS OPPORTUNITIES OFFERED BY EXPERT SYSTEMS

BUSINESS INTEREST IN EXPERT SYSTEMS

Expert systems seem promising in many ways from a business standpoint. Some examples of how organizations might use expert system technology should illustrate why.

The ability of businesses and other organizations to hire and retain experts to produce, deliver, and maintain their products is often a problem. Expert systems appear to be possible substitutes for some of these experts. Take the CATS-1 expert system. A manufacturer of locomotives had a locomotive expert in its employ for many years. The company relied heavily on this expert in the diagnosis of difficult maintenance problems associated with their locomotive products. The expert was approaching retirement age. The company knew it had to do something about retaining the knowledge and expertise this expert possessed. Being a forward-thinking company, it authorized the study of an expert system approach. The result was a very effective locomotive maintenance expert system, CATS, also referred to as the DELTA system. CATS is a very innovative system that integrates an expert system with audiovisual aids. A locomotive repair engineer can use the expert system component to seek advice on what is most likely wrong with a particular locomotive. The repair engineer provides the expert system with problem information, and the system provides repair assistance by suggesting repair actions. If the repair personnel do not know how to perform the recommended actions, the system will provide instant audiovisual material right at the repair site. CATS is an example of an expert system substituting for a domain expert who is no longer available to the organization. In this case, retirement is the reason that the expert is no longer available; vacation, illness, and business travel could also place an expert out of reach just at the moment that the expert is needed.

The BSM expert system was developed to assist when expertise is not available for another reason. The BSM system is a medical assistant for disaster victims and people in need of medical care who are in a location that does not have the requisite medical care. Often after a disaster like an earthquake or a hurricane, people need medical attention. Sometimes medical care is available, but if the disaster is big enough, there might not be enough for all who need it. Sometimes medical care people cannot reach the disaster victims. Other circumstances can produce a need for medical help where the help is not available. A medical emergency on a ship at sea is an example. In many cases, the only hope for a victim is immediate action. In the absence of qualified medical personnel, it is less risky for the victim to be treated by partially trained people, such as paramedics, firemen, search and rescue personnel, and police officers, than not to be treated at all. The BSM expert system could provide medical knowledge to assist these people. The future might even see computers designed for rugged environments mounted on fire engines and ambulances. Expert systems supporting the domains of burn treatment and smoke inhalation could be very helpful on fire apparatus.

Some organizations are developing expert systems in order to make their back-office operations more effective. Other organizations are developing expert systems to assist their sales people in the development of competitive proposals for potential clients. One organization developed an expert system to do both. A large firm that deals in the production and sales of reciprocating pumps developed an expert system that assists with the administrative and technical aspects of developing a proposal for the potential sale of a reciprocating pump. In the past proposal generation incurred a great amount of time by both the sales force and the back-office personnel. The sales force would provide potential clients with information about the product line, including information on what kinds of pumps might help the client. The sales force would obtain information from the client on specific application requirements. They would bring this information back, and company experts in the area of generating proposals would work on the proposal. The proposal-generation work included the use of multiple experts, some of whom were technical experts in the area of pump development and some experts in the area of the business of this particular company. As a team, they would decide what particular pump product would be offered to the client, what options would fit the client's particular needs, and they would then develop a proposal for the client. An expert system was developed to assist in all phases of this process. The goals of this expert system included developing an accurate and consistant technical proposal and being able to deliver the proposal to the client in a very timely fashion. It was further hoped that this expert proposal-generation system would decrease requisite manpower requirements. The system is capable of meeting its intended goals.

Organizations sometimes have several experts in a particular field, each having special domain knowledge. These experts' knowledge often overlaps, but each individual expert also has knowledge that the other experts do not have. Organizations have been interested for many years in developing composite knowledge pools of their experts' knowledge to be able to provide this resource to other members of the organization. PROSPECTOR is an example of an expert system knowledge base developed by several experts. PROSPEC-TOR provides consultations to geologists during the investigations of a site when looking for ore-grade deposits. The geologists interact with the expert system, providing the system with earth surface geologic observation data. The system provides the geologists with potential interpretations of the observations and suggests additional observations that might assist the geologists in developing conclusions. The knowledge required to perform this investigation is different for different mineral deposits. The team that developed PROSPECTOR worked with different mineral experts to develop the various mineral knowledge bases. When the system is running, it decides which mineral knowledge base best fits the situation and proceeds with its investigative consultation. The geologist in the field using the system gains the benefit of all of the experts' knowledge that is represented in the system.

Future expert systems could be constructed with knowledge from numerous experts in the same subject area, such as medicine, or related subject areas, like finance and insurance. With the tendency to specialize, medical doctors tend to know more about a specific medical area, such as cardiology, and less about the general medical field. Expert systems that fuse the knowledge of a variety of medical specialists could be of help to both the medical profession and society. These systems could assist doctors who must work in an area in which they are not specialists during an emergency. These medical expert systems could also benefit the general practitioner who is trying to determine what is wrong with a patient before referring the patient to a medical specialist.

Subjects like finance and insurance are often studied by different specialists. However, there are people who need someone who can balance the two subjects properly. A person might be trying to develop a personal finance plan that covers investments and family security. Investments might come from the financial domain, like stocks and bonds, or they might come from some specialized insurance package. Security might come from insurance policies, like life insurance and mortgage payment insurance, or they might come from a financial device, like a savings account. Many financial experts offer insurance options, and many insurance agents offer financial options. However, neither offer all that is available from the two domains. Firms could use an expert system that includes knowledge about both domains when trying to develop a plan for a client that provides balance of investment and security instruments.

Training equipment operators and engineers is a requirement of many organizations. Sometimes the actual equipment is not available for training purposes. Sometimes it is too dangerous to train new personnel on the actual equipment. The operation of a nuclear power plant is an example. However, the organization still has the requirement to train new personnel. Expert systems and systems incorporating expert system technology in support of these training requirements have begun to appear. STEAMER is an example. STEAMER assists in the training of naval officers in the operation of complex steam propulsion plants that power naval ships. STEAMER can present normal operational training as well as challenge the student with problems in the operations. The student then has the opportunity to train on problem resolution without endangering equipment or personnel. Training with STEAMER is very realistic. A STEAMER training system costs a lot less than a naval ship and is available for training at all times. Also, the system can be located at the Navy's training site, which is more convenient for the instructors.

In the future, expert training systems should appear in other industries that have similar training requirements and similar operational constraints, such as the chemical industry and the metals processing industry.

Many businesses rely on the effective operation of machines and equipment in order to produce their products or offer their services to the marketplace. Equipment breakdowns and inefficient equipment operations can be very costly to a firm. Expert systems can be built to assist businesses and other organizations in solving their problems. The ACE expert system, for example, identifies and diagnoses communications cable problems for a telephone company. ACE analyzes the communications network in the late evening hours when there is little customer demand for communications services. When the system finds potential or actual problems with a communications cable, it notifies the responsible maintenance team and presents recommendations on repair actions.

The operation of certain large machinery, including large computer systems, is complicated. Many factors must be considered to use some computer systems efficiently. The IBM Corporation has developed the YES expert system to assist computer operators of large IBM computer systems. The YES system monitors a number of MVS operating system functions and assists the operators by performing some of the operator functions.

Large operations and maintenance manuals for industries' equipment and machinery will be replaced by computer-based expert systems. These systems will be easier and quicker to use. The user will simply ask an operational or maintenance question, and the system will provide advice and, if requested, explanations of the advice offered. The knowledge-base of expert operations systems can be configured to reflect the current configuration of a particular machine and therefore be able to provide advice in line with the exact requirements of the machine. These systems will sometimes be integrated into the equipment. In this configuration, the machinery will be able to sense its state and advise the operator on the best courses of action. These expert systems will be able to be located alongside the operational machinery.

Expert system technology can help organizations realize one or more of the following benefits:

- More effective operation (because employees are better informed)
- More cost-effective operation (because the average worker will be able to do more)

- Safer operation (because a computer-based expert system could constantly monitor the manufacturing processes)

- More productive operation (because the expert system can relieve the human worker of certain routine tasks, freeing the worker for more important tasks)

- More independent operation (because the knowledge of key employees can be retained by the expert system)

Because of these potential benefits, businesses will be developing more expert systems in more domains in the near future. Domains already being supported have been mentioned. Let us now look at some of the domains to be supported by expert system technology in the future.

DOMAINS TO BE SUPPORTED IN THE FUTURE

Expert systems will support totally new domains in the future and will provide support to new subject areas within domains that expert systems are already supporting. An example of a totally new domain is consumer products. The science domain is already supported in some areas by expert systems. Weather, however, is not yet supported and is a good candidate for expert system support in the future.

Let us explore the consumer product domain. Some consumer products have so many options that they are becoming too complex for the average consumer. Some of the new microwave cooking products fit into this category. An expert system could be integrated into the microwave oven. The cook would provide the oven with a description of what is being placed in the oven and a description of the desired final product. The oven expert system would then advise the cook of any necessary attachments to be used, such as a probe. Once all is ready, the oven expert system would take control of the oven and cook the food. The control might include the sequencing of different cooking methods if the oven incorporates several cooking appliances, such as microwave and convection. The control would include the amount of time the food is cooked and the intensity of energy applied to the food. This control would take into account the type of food being cooked, the amount of food being cooked, and the results desired.

The automobile is another consumer product that might incorporate an expert system. A diagnostic expert system could be installed in automobiles. The system could include sensors that would be used to monitor fuel and air flow, exhaust gas temperature, exhaust gas composition, oil temperature, and the like. The diagnostic system could monitor and record this operational data. From this data, the system could infer the operational condition of the automobile and advise the driver of potential impending failures. The system could also be of assistance to the automotive mechanic when the car is in for routine or corrective maintenance.

Industries that rely on knowledge workers should certainly be looking toward expert system technology to improve their productivity and maintain a specific level of customer support, regardless of the status of their knowledge workers. These industries would include banking, insurance, stockbroking, and accounting.

Anyone who has ever taken an accounting course or has ever maintained the accounting books of a firm knows that there are a lot of heuristics involved in maintaining the books. Consistency and traceability are more important than operating via some natural law. Accounting is an art structured by guidelines, practices, and laws that have developed through the years. When a bookkeeper or an accountant tries to decide which accounts to place paid bills under, some of the bills naturally fall into certain accounts. An example would be the placing of memo tablets under the office supply account. However, there are also items that are not categorized so easily. A software firm might purchase floppy diskettes. If the diskettes are to be used for word processing, they would be office supplies. However, if the diskettes are to be used to transfer software products to customers, they might be part of the goods-in-process inventory. An expert system could be set up for the organization's accountant or bookkeeper to assist in determining in which account each entry belongs. This system would be especially useful in large organizations, where it would assist in assuring consistency in account determination. Account determination is only one example where expert systems could support the accounting department.

A successful stockbroker must assimilate a great deal of information. A large proportion of this information is heuristic in content. First the broker must know both his or her personal goals and the goals of the brokerage house. Next the broker must know the goals, aspirations, limits, and constraints of the clients. Finally, the broker must know the technical and financial aspects of the stock market and of stock buying and selling. An expert system could be built that included knowledge of the mechanics of the stock market and stock trading, knowledge about the policies of the brokerage house, heuristics about the typical clients the house serves, connectivity to stock activity databases, and so on. The broker could then use this expert system as an assistant. Certain types of stocks have trading patterns that a skilled broker can observe. The broker might convey this knowledge to a computer so that the computer could alert him when trades should be made. The expert system could query the broker about the client as to qualities that will help decide what type of stocks to buy. The expert system should be able to infer whether the client wants and can afford to purchase high-risk, potentially high-payoff stocks or low-risk stocks. The system would then use this client knowledge, with knowledge about the goals of the house and information from various stock activity databases, to assist the broker in advising the client on a stock-trading strategy.

Financial expert systems do not have to be limited to stock-trading strategies. The systems' knowledge bases could include knowledge about other financial investment instruments like bonds. The systems could then advise on the types of investment instruments as well as specific choices. The system could be designed to provide heterogeneous suggestions that contain a mixture of investment instruments.

Financial expert systems could also assist people in the banking and insurance industries. Today there are infinite combinations of personal finance options. Depending on a customer's financial picture, there are many ways to manage money. The two, often conflicting, goals that most customers are trying to maximize are liquidity and earnings. Expert systems could look at the customer's income level, tax bracket, current financial status, estimated short-term financial status changes, and financial goals and offer advice on what checking and savings plans the customer should select. The system's explanation capability should also be helpful to the customer. Expert systems could be developed to provide assistance in selecting the most beneficial insurance plan for a client at a particular time in the client's life. The expert system could look at the client's income and spending levels, tax bracket, current financial position, family status, and present insurance portfolio. The system could ask some questions to infer the amount of protection the client wishes to provide his or her family. This insurance advisory system would then provide its recommendations on the type of insurance instruments and financial levels of coverage that would make sense for this client. One further step would be, as mentioned before, the integration of the banking and insurance advisory systems. The resultant expert system would be able to offer the same individual banking and insurance advice and would also be able to offer advice on a balanced financial program of banking and insurance.

The piloting of large oceangoing ships involves many important tasks that must be constantly monitored while the ships are underway. Ship avoidance radar systems, depth-reading sonar systems, weather-monitoring radar systems, and ship propulsion status systems must all be monitored on a frequent basis. Oceangoing ships can be at sea for long periods of time. They progress to their destination port around the clock. The operational workstation for the people running these ships can be pitching and rolling for days, given certain weather patterns. Clearly, this job requires the monitoring of important operational systems to assure the safety of crews, the ships, cargoes, and passengers in a work environment that is demanding and tiring.

A ship management and monitoring expert system could provide valuable assistance to the crew. The expert system could monitor all the operational systems and alert the crew to potentially dangerous future situations given the real-time operational situation and heuristics about ship operations that ships' captains have employed for many generations. Rather than individual systems presenting their data, algorithmic results, and alerts, the expert system could monitor all the ship's systems and provide information and alerts to the crew from inferences developed from the composition and integration of the data from all the systems as well as from the heuristics of ship management. This expert system would not tire on long trips and would not be fatigued during extended periods of bad weather. The expert system could have a link to the radio room. In emergency situations, the expert system could broadcast distress messages. These messages could contain the nature of the emergency, the identification of the ship, and the ship's position obtained from the ship's navigation system. With today's technology, these radio broadcasts could be key-coded or voice-synthesized; the choice would be made to support the mode of operation desired. The expert system would provide a cost-effective assistant to the person who is monitoring the operational systems. The system would provide redundancy for the important ship management tasks that relate to ship safety.

Some tasks related to the operation of aircraft are already being supported by expert systems, and more systems are under consideration. The military aerospace industry is especially interested in expert systems to support pilots in high-pressure situations such as emergencies and combat. Expert piloting assistants have not yet been developed for commercial aircraft. The duties of flying today's commercial aircraft are complex. The pilot must understand many complicated systems and laws as well as know how to fly the aircraft. A piloting assistant could be integrated with the flight computer that most commercial and military aircraft have today. A piloting assistant could also receive real-time data from aircraft radios and instruments. Together with heuristics about flying aircraft, the assistant could support the pilot in the performance of piloting duties. An unexpected instrument or switch setting could be sensed by the expert system and reported to the pilot via a voice synthesizer, a warning indicator, or both. The expert system could also provide system monitoring assistance and warn of impending equipment failures.

Commercial aircraft on long transoceanic flights are also candidates for medical assistance expert systems. The typical medical emergencies that airlines deal with could be loaded into a medical expert system that would be available to the crew. The subjects might include childbirth, heart attacks, and severe allergic reactions.

Beyond the aircraft, the commercial airline industry might benefit from the use of expert systems on the ground. Rescheduling and rerouting of aircraft could be assisted by an expert system. Rescheduling is a fact of life for the airlines. Events within their control, such as aircraft maintenance, might create a rescheduling requirement. However, other events that create schedule changes are beyond the airlines' control; examples include extreme weather conditions and the closing of airports. The system could include in its knowledge-base facts and rules like these:

Flight 001 (from Washington, DC, to New York) is a high-priority flight.
Flight 111 (from Washington, DC, to Norfolk) is a low-priority flight.
Flight 222 (from Washington, DC, to Boston) is a medium-priority flight.
Flight 333 (from Boston to Pittsburgh) is a medium-priority flight.
Flight 333 uses the aircraft from Flight 222.

IF   a high-priority-flight aircraft becomes unavailable
            AND there is a low-priority-flight aircraft
            available at the same origination airport,
THEN   use the low-priority-flight aircraft for the high-priority flight
            AND find alternative aircraft or alternative travel means for the
            low-priority flight.

The knowledge-base might have even more basic facts and rules, like these:

To drive between Washington, DC, and Norfolk would take 3 hours.
To drive between Washington, DC, and New York would take 6 hours.
Flight 001 is almost always 100% full.
Flight 111 is usually 70% full.

IF   the driving time between the origination airport
            and the destination airport is less than 4 hours
            AND the flight is usually not more than 75% full,
THEN   the flight is a low-priority flight.

This rescheduling expert system would be able to advise the airline scheduler of the best options available, given the situation that caused the need for rescheduling. The expert system could include rules that, under conditions of a rescheduling requirement, would maximize profit, maximize public relations, or both, with rules for reconciliation when rules from the two objectives conflict. This expert system would help the airline scheduler develop crisis situation schedule modifications more quickly and more easily. Use of the expert system by the airlines might also permit them to have fewer personnel standing by for schedule changes.

   The automobile club industry is also travel-related. One of the services automobile clubs provide is information on how to drive between an origination point and a destination. Some of the clubs will even alter their advice depending on what kind of trip the driver wishes. The fastest method and the most scenic method are two options these clubs might offer. Expert systems could be developed to help with these tasks. Here are a few facts and rules that might be in the knowledge-base for an automobile trip adviser system:

The quickest route between Boston and New York is I-95.
The quickest route between New York and Washington, DC, is I-95.
The most scenic route between Boston and New York is Route 20.
The quickest route between New York and Baltimore is I-95.
The most scenic route between New York and Baltimore is US-1.
The quickest route between Baltimore and Annapolis is Route 2.
The most scenic route between Baltimore and Annapolis is Route 301 plus
   Route 50.

IF   trip route request is for going between city A and city B
         AND there is no A-to-B route,
THEN   find a city Z such that there is an A-to-Z route
         AND a Z-to-B route.

IF   trip information request is for fastest route,
THEN   link quickest routes together.

IF   trip information request is for most scenic route,
THEN   link most scenic routes together.

This expert system would help the automobile clubs service their membership more quickly. The expert system should be a labor-saving device and could possibly allow the clubs to service more trip requests with fewer trip advisers.

The federal government is experimenting with expert system technology a bit, particularly in the Department of Defense, NASA, and the Department of Health and Human Services. But there are many more opportunities for the government to benefit from the introduction of expert systems. Let us look at two, specifically, the income tax function of the Internal Revenue Service and the procurement function that all government agencies perform.

The IRS receives millions of income tax returns from individuals and businesses every year. The people sending in the tax returns, for the most part, are honest people who try to follow the laws and try not to cheat the government. The tax rules and regulations are all specified in some manual or publication. Not all people sending in their tax returns know where to get all the information they need. Not all people know where to get help or have the time or ability to get to where tax help might be found.

The IRS could develop sets of small expert systems that would run on a variety of personal computers to help taxpayers fill out their tax forms correctly. The IRS would benefit because the knowledge in the tax adviser systems would be from the IRS and the advice the taxpayers are using would be consistent and accurate. Filers would benefit because they could receive accurate assistance quickly. For people who have no access to a personal computer, the IRS, the public libraries, and the public schools could make PCs available.

Different expert tax adviser systems could be developed for different groups. There could be an expert system for individual taxpayers and different systems for businesses, for example. The systems could be broken down into finer detail if need be. There could be one system for singles and another one for married taxpayers. Special advisory systems could be developed separately for special tax returns that fewer taxpayers need. An example of this would be the form for declaring tax deductions as a result of moving to a foreign country for a period of time. By keeping the special cases and different categories of advisory systems separate, the resultant expert tax advisory systems would be small enough to fit on small personal computers and operate at reasonable speeds.

Taxpayers could continue to prepare their tax returns as they do now, or they could use the advisory systems and thereby spend less time filling out their tax forms. The advisory systems could be distributed by a government agency like the National Technical Information Service (NTIS) for the cost of the distribution media and postage. The software should be in the public domain, meaning that it would carry no copyright and should be free to duplicate. Business taxpayers should benefit from this type of program. Firms that fill out tax forms for taxpayers should also benefit.

The next logical step the IRS could take is the acceptance of magnetic-media tax returns from taxpayers. The tax advisory system could ask questions of the taxpayer, and instead of only providing advice, the system could also record the information and actually prepare the taxpayer's return data for the IRS. After an interactive session with the system, all the taxpayer would have to do is submit the magnetic medium to the IRS. The IRS would then have computer-readable returns, which would save the IRS the time and money involved in keyboarding the tax return data.

The federal government procures a large amount of goods and services from private enterprises each fiscal year. Most individual departments and agencies have their own procurement section. These procurement groups can purchase the majority of items needed by the agency of which they are a part. These noncentralized procurement groups must follow some centralized and some noncentralized policies and procedures. The procurement policies and procedures of the federal government are copious and complex. They are difficult to learn. Most procurement specialists have trained and worked under other procurement specialists for many years. These policies and procedures could easily be transferred into a knowledge-base because they are rule-like in format. Here are some examples of possible rules in a procurement expert system:

> IF   the item to be procured costs less than $25,000,
> THEN   procure under the small purchase procurement regulations.

> IF   the item to be procured costs more than $25,000,
> THEN   procure under the major purchase procurement regulations.

> IF   the item to be procured costs more than $350,000,
>   AND the item is ADPE (automatic data processing equipment),
> THEN   send the procurement request to GSA.

Procurement expert systems could be developed to assist the procurement specialists with their work. These systems would allow the specialists to review all the rules and regulations that apply to a particular procurement action. The federal government would benefit in that the federal procurement activities would be more consistent. Another benefit is that the procurement activities would be more auditable because of the consistency of the procurement documents.

Scientists interested in natural phenomena like earthquakes, volcanic eruptions, hurricanes, and tornadoes and specialists working in government agencies like the National Weather Service could develop expert systems to assist them with their work. These expert systems would be most effective if interconnected with traditional computer systems that are receiving natural phenomenon data in real-time. Scientists still do not understand enough about natural phenomena to allow them to develop purely algorithmic models that would assist in predicting these phenomena. Some of the knowledge that scientists and weather specialists have is heuristic rather than algorithmic.

This knowledge could be represented in an expert system knowledge base and used to assist these scientists and specialists in predicting the natural phenomena they are interested in.

In this application, expert system technology allows the worker to use more knowledge by means of automated support tools. In this case, the tools are the research computer facilities these people typically use.

Without this technology, the scientists would use the computers to receive real-time data and perform calculations like average movement speed of a hurricane.

With the integration of expert system technology and scientific computers, the computers can receive the data, perform calculations, and develop inferences of prediction. The knowledge used to develop these inferences could be the composition of knowledge of several experts, each providing knowledge of a particular segment of the total knowledge-base on the subject of natural phenomena.

The legal profession has already experimented a little with expert system technology. Expert systems have been built to deal with tax laws and product liability legislation. New legal expert systems should appear in the near future. The legal domain is a good candidate for expert system support from a technical standpoint. This domain requires experts to possess a great deal of heuristic knowledge and be able to retrieve this knowledge together with factual knowledge that supports the heuristics historically. Furthermore, the domain is heavily rule-oriented. The legal system is made up of rules and regulations. These rules and regulations are often substantiated by their application in the past or through inferences of other events in the past and how these rules and regulations would have supported these historical events. Lawyers must often perform searches in law libraries, looking for historical data that might support their cases. Past decisions often create precedents that judges will accept. Often the lawyer with the most appropriate historical data to support his or her side of the case will win. Expert systems could be developed to assist a lawyer search through the large online legal databases and could be an extension of today's database services such as LEXIS. This expert system would provide the lawyer with more pertinent information with less of the lawyer's own valuable time being spent.

Consumer-oriented legal expert systems could also be developed. These systems could provide consumers with basic legal advice on matters like the writing of a will. These systems would ask questions, accept responses from the user, and provide advice. These systems could be developed with the innate capability to know their limits. When the user asks a question that goes beyond the limits of the knowledge base, the expert system could inform the user of this and recommend seeing a lawyer. These systems could save the consumer the cost of a legal consultation as well as the time it would normally take to go to the lawyer's office for the consultation.

Many businesses deal at one time or another with some form of crisis management. Typically, the business managers have planned a sequence of events. If all goes well, each event will occur on time or within some acceptable tolerance. The desired result of each event will occur, and the project will proceed.

Sometimes all does not go well. Something happens that causes a delay or an unsatisfactory result. Sometimes such events create large problems for businesses. If many other events are dependent on the problem event and the project is very important to the organization, management has a crisis to deal with.

If the project is very large, this crisis management task can become very complex. The managers might have to assimilate many pieces of information on the status of the project and a lot of knowledge about what can and cannot be done. What events can be rescheduled, what events can occur while the problem is being resolved, what events can be designed to work around the problem, and what events have to be designed and introduced into the schedule to rectify the problem are examples of what the managers might have to deal with in a crisis situation.

The construction industry is a good example of an industry that must deal with crisis management. The construction of a 1000-house development and the construction of a very large commercial building are examples of projects that might develop crises before they are completed. Expert systems could be developed specifically to assist in the management of crises. The project plan could be input into the system's knowledge base at the beginning of the project. The expert system might be designed even to offer advice on the design of the project plan, given planning knowledge of the particular domain. Knowledge of dependencies in the events and possible alternative plan designs could also be loaded into the system's knowledge-base at the beginning of the project. This work might also serve as a plan audit. As the project progresses, the status could be input into the expert system. The system could then look for potential problems and provide warnings where appropriate. This support constitutes secondary benefits the system will be able to provide because of the knowledge that the expert system has been provided.

The crisis management expert system would really be helpful in a crisis. By providing the information on what led to the crisis along with the information and knowledge already provided to the system, the system can quickly search through the alternatives that are evident from the knowledge in the knowledge-base plus alternatives that it can infer from this knowledge. This system would therefore assist the managers in restoring the project plan or in developing an effective modification.

If a particular company did many similar projects, the knowledge-base could be used on future projects. As crises occur and are rectified, this knowledge could be placed in the system's knowledge-base. When similar crises occur at different projects with different site managers, the total knowledge wealth of the organization would be available to each site manager. This would provide all company managers with the total corporate knowledge, regardless of how long they have been with the company. The result is that all crises are resolved according to the best available information and knowledge independent of the people involved.

Good people with good tools will get the job done. The company will be able to be more flexible with its personnel resources and will be able to apply all available knowledge to all the company's projects.

With the introduction of expert systems into these new domains and new areas of the domains already partially supported by expert systems, the expert system technology will be stretched to its present limits. New forms of knowledge will possibly need to be represented and new control strategies will be needed to deal with these new knowledge representations.

TOWARDS GREATER COMMERCIALIZATION

Expert system research and development began in the early 1960s. The first systems to show commercial promise appeared in the early 1970s. Expert system technology started to gain attention from the general computer science community during the early 1980s and from the commercial data-processing community in the late 1980s. Commercial interest in expert system technology is new, manifested in the interest to study and experiment with the new technology, seeing where it is applicable in normal business operations. The business community is also exhibiting interest through investments in firms that are creating products based on expert system technology.

Greater commercialization of expert system technology will result from the development of five classes of commercial products:

1. Applications based on expert system technology
2. Software tools to help build expert systems
3. Software to link expert systems to other software
4. Expert system products that will support other new high-technology products
5. Computer hardware products

Computer products based on expert system technology is the most obvious commercial product class. Expert systems will first be built to monitor, diagnose, and identify specific commercial operations, situations, and status. Expert systems will then be built to fuse and distill knowledge from various sources. These systems will be extended to assist operational experts through interpreting, explaining, and advising actions. Soon more complicated and more important operational actions, such as prescribing remedies, forecasting future operational conditions and states, regulating and controlling equipment, and training new experts, will be supported with these systems. The last step in the evolution of these systems will be their assisting in designing, planning, and decision-making activities.

Prototype systems have already been built to support all of these activities; thus the feasibility of constructing these types of systems has already been proved.

Companies desiring venture capital to develop commercial products based on expert system technology have reasonable examples of the viability of the technology to show potential investors. Companies that want to interest potential customers in an expert system product can also use these examples to show what has already been accomplished. It is up to these companies to draw reasonable analogies between the available examples and the needs of their potential clients.

Expert systems are also being built as part of database management system query packages. These query packages will be given knowledge of the user's work tasks and subject domain. This tailoring will assist the query package with context and semantic knowledge. For example, the query ''Give me all Smiths'' would provide the user with a list of people with the last name Smith in a personnel context like a payroll search and a list of all people with the occupation of Smith in a job context like skilled worker search. Expert system technology could also assist with the natural-language requirement of the user-system interface of the query package.

The running of large computer systems today is the responsibility of computer systems operators. These operators have two key tasks, the operational requirements of the machinery (such as loading and unloading magnetic tape) and commanding the system to function. The latter task is accomplished through operator-system communications. These communications on the system side are handled by large software systems often referred to as operating systems. The tasks related to communicating with the operating system in such a manner as to use the computer system's resources most efficiently are becoming increasingly complex. Expert systems are already being developed to assist the operators with their work.

IBM Corporation has developed a prototype expert system to assist computer operators with the MVS operating system environment. It is called YES (Yorktown Expert System); it was developed at an IBM research center in Yorktown Heights, New York. The YES expert system is a real-time interactive monitor of the MVS operating system. This operating system is used on IBM's large mainframe computers, some of which are multiple-CPU configurations. This system was designed to assist the human operators. IBM believes that this system might ease the workload on the operators as well as decrease the experience and training required to operate these systems. IBM also hopes that YES will assist in providing better management of large computer operations. The YES system is presently not a product that an IBM computer system customer can purchase or lease from IBM; it is a prototype. What is learned and developed from this prototype will most likely be integrated into the MVS operating system rather than offered as a separate product. The integration of expert system technology should enhance IBM's MVS product.

Intelligent Instruction Systems (IIS) will be developed using expert system technology. These expert-system-based instructors will be self-paced, just like the computer-assisted instruction (CAI) systems available today. CAI systems present information to the student and periodically quiz the student before going on to new material. CAI systems have no understanding or knowledge of the subject domain or the teaching function. The teaching function in CAI systems is a product of the CAI system designer and is nonadaptive to the different needs of different students. CAI systems also lack interactive explanation capabilities.

Expert-system-based instruction systems will possess knowledge of the subject domain and teaching. The system should be able to infer why a student is having difficulties and reformat the instruction material in such a manner as to overcome the student's problems. These systems will also have the capability to explain themselves interactively at any point in the training session. The knowledge-base of these systems should include knowledge about various categories of students, and the system should be able to infer which category a particular student belongs to and present the training material accordingly. A simpler version of this could be developed where the category of the student is provided to the system by a human instructor prior to the student's using an IIS. The system would not have to be able to determine the category for itself but would still be able to present the training material appropriately for the needs of the particular student.

Computer products will be developed to support expert system technology. Some of these types of products are starting to appear on the market. However, the products to come will be more functional and easier to use. They will not require a long apprenticeship in knowledge engineering. They will assist in the true commercial introduction of knowledge engineering concepts, tools, and systems.

These products will generally fit into one of the following categories:

- Programming languages
- Programming environments
- Basic expert-system-building tools
- Expert system shells
- Knowledge acquisition tools

The LISP (list processing) and PROLOG (programming in logic) programming languages are the most popular expert system development languages. Both are able to manipulate symbols well. Each has its strong points. These languages will be discussed in more detail later. Improvements to these languages as well as movements to provide standard specifications of the two languages will be seen in the future.

A comprehensive programming environment is one strong point of the LISP programming language. There exist many comprehensive programming environments for the LISP language. These environments include facilities to assist programmers with tasks related to graphics, data manipulation and management, and mouse (pointing device) use. Many of the software tools required to develop prototype systems quickly are included in these LISP environments. The LISP environments need standardization specifications so that software can be more portable and LISP programmers can be more mobile between systems.

The PROLOG language repertoire includes a lot of the required programming facilities inside the language interpreters and compilers. However, the PROLOG language still requires a programming environment.

Programming environments need to assist the programmer with tools to provide basic functions, user-system interface functions, and data management functions. These environments need to provide the programmer with the capability to specify a function but must not actually program the function until that level of detail is needed in the development. Rapid prototyping tools need to be offered to the programmer. These capabilities will be built by various vendors. Each vendor will try to develop these tools in a way that differentiates its products from the rest of the market. This is healthy for competition. However, certain terminology and interface specifications should be standardized so that everyone will understand what is available and to provide interoperability.

National and international standardization groups will support this standardization work. Already there is a move afoot to standardize the LISP language in the COMMON LISP dialect. This standardization activity will also occur in the area of programming environments.

Programming environments designed for expert system development will also include tools to port developed systems to hardware environments that do not support expert system developments like microprocessor-based process control systems where the expert system logic will be loaded onto a read-only memory (ROM) device. These environments will also provide the capability to port the developed expert system to a procedural language like C or Ada. The underlying language of the environment will most likely be LISP or PROLOG. However, some of these environments will most likely be programmed in procedural languages like C or Ada or system development languages like SPL (Systems Programming Language).

Basic expert-system-building tools like knowledge editors and knowledge consistency checkers will appear on the market. These tools should be generalized enough so that they will be able to support many expert system projects. Even if the resultant expert system is going to be large, these tools should be able to run on convenient microcomputer systems that can be moved around and should be inexpensive enough that they can be purchased in quantity. These tools will provide support in areas where the work is repetitive yet well defined to a small number of procedures.

Expert system shells are products that include one or more inference mechanisms integrated into a complete inference engine subsystem, a skeleton knowledge-base with the knowledge management facilities needed to manage the developed knowledge-bases in relation to the needs of the inference engine, a user-system interface subsystem, a knowledge acquisition subsystem, and an explanation subsystem. Sometimes these products also have facilities to attach programming logic via some specific set of computer languages and facilities.

Some expert system shell products are in the marketplace now. The future will see these products becoming more powerful and providing more functionality. Most shell products on the market today either provide strong inference mechanisms with basic user-system interfaces or easy-to-use, well-designed user-system interfaces with weak inference mechanisms. These products will be improved; their individual weaknesses will be addressed by the vendors. Future shells will provide interfaces to commercial databases, particularly those designed around the relational database model. When self-training technology becomes available, these shells will integrate a self-training facility into their products. A key to the shells is that they should be modular and extensible and should allow for tight integration of new shell subsystems.

Current expert system shells have been developed with a particular computer hardware system in mind. These shells are developed and run on the hardware that the shell designers had in mind from the beginning. There are shells available to run on microcomputers, minicomputers, and mainframe computers. However, the more powerful shells run on computers that are optimized for the LISP programming language and are known as LISP machines. These are relatively expensive minicomputers designed with the LISP language in mind. Future expert system shell products will allow the development of the expert systems on one or more hardware configurations and will assist in porting the developed expert systems to other hardware configurations.

All expert system shells run on centralized, conventional, von Neumann computer architectures. Future shells will be developed to run in distributed configurations and on the new parallel computer systems.

Knowledge acquisition tools will be the most important contribution to the furtherance of knowledge-based system use in the commercial world. The largest task in the development of significant expert systems like MYCIN and PROSPECTOR is the development of the knowledge-base. The knowledge, information, and data that are applied to the systems' knowledge-bases are captured from literature and human experts. The capturing, codifying, and application of knowledge to a knowledge-base has proved to be a difficult and labor-intensive job.

The Knowledge Acquisition System (KAS) is the skeletal system of the PROSPECTOR expert system. KAS was developed with knowledge acquisition in mind. The knowledge-based editor of KAS can operate directly with the knowledge representation of the system. It uses knowledge about knowledge representation formalisms to assist the knowledge engineer, and it facilitates the development of the knowledge-base by providing the engineer with immediate feedback on the consequences of the changes the engineer is making.

Future knowledge acquisition systems will assist the knowledge engineer and, in some cases, the domain expert directly with the acquisition of the knowledge. These systems will in their own right be expert systems that maintain knowledge on knowledge acquisition and representation. These systems will be able to discern the different knowledge representation formalisms and advise the knowledge engineer on the benefits of the different representation schemes. The engineer will be able to work interactively with the system. By providing the system with information about the particular domain knowledge and the desired functionality of the resultant expert system, the knowledge acquisition system of the future will be able to advise the knowledge engineer as to which knowledge representation scheme is appropriate. Once the knowledge representation scheme is determined, the system will assist with the actual acquisition of the knowledge. Knowledge editing and consistency checking are examples of the assistance that will be available from these systems.

Some expert system applications will not require the expert system to be connected to any other system. An example of this might be a small expert diagnostic system that assists a maintenance team with a machine that has malfunctioned and connection to this machine will provide no information because of its present state. However, once the machine is in a state other than the inoperative state, connection to it might make the expert diagnostic system more effective. Interfacing expert systems with other systems will be more the rule rather than the exception in the future.

Computer products that interface the expert system technology with other systems will appear on the market, including these:

1. Hardware to connect LISP machine-based expert systems to traditional computer systems

2. Hardware that will accept LISP machine-based software and software that is based on traditional computer systems simultaneously

3. Software that will port LISP machine-based expert systems over to traditional computer systems

4. Software that will port expert systems to special-purpose hardware like ROM-based microprocessor systems, industrial controllers, and military systems

5. Software to allow intercommunication between expert systems and other computer-based systems

6. Software to allow expert systems the ability to receive real-world data and information and also the ability for expert systems to send their results to other systems and machines

Expert system technology has great applicability to other new high-technology products such as robotics, machine vision, and speech recognition. Expert-system-based products will be designed and built to support these other high-technology products.

Intelligent robots will get their inferencing capabilities from expert system technology. An example of such an application is robot navigation in a manufacturing plant. The expert system would assist the robot in determining the proper path to take in navigating between two points, for instance, a work area and a parts pickup area. Expert-system-based techniques will be used to assist machine vision systems determine what the machine is looking at. Expert systems will be built along the idea of the HEARSAY II speech-understanding expert system. These systems will assist future speech recognition products. In these applications, the expert system will be an important subsystem of a larger system. The ultimate product user will not necessarily even know that there is an expert system within the product.

The expert subsystem will be integrated into the product to provide more functionality and a more understandable user-system interface. In many ways, future expert system products will be analogous to many of today's data management products. These products influence the system's use, but often their presence is not realized or understood by the user. These systems are providing the user with increased functionality or ease of system use without being involved in the operation of a separate subsystem.

New computer hardware products will be designed and marketed as a result of the commercialization of expert systems. LISP machines are an example of this trend. Current research projects will result in LISP and PROLOG machines the size and price of personal computers (sometimes called personal sequential inference machines). A logical conclusion from these developments is the introduction of expert-system-based machines into the consumer market.

As an example of new expert-system-based consumer markets, look at encyclopedias. Instead of purchasing an encyclopedia in book form, consumers will be given the option of purchasing a microcomputer version. This product will hook up to the family's television and provide the encyclopedia information interactively. Such products will incorporate user models and information retrieval models, as well as the knowledge, information, and data typically found in encyclopedia books. The incorporation of these models will mean that the resultant system will understand what levels of information are appropriate to a particular user (at the beginning of an interactive session, the system will query the user as to age and educational level) and will understand the goals associated with information search and retrieval. With this understanding the system will be able to assist the user intelligently in finding the information that the user seeks.

With the commercialization of current expert system technology, the next logical steps will be the development of new expert system technology, a second-generation expert system technology, and the integration of expert system technology into present mainline computer technology systems like management information systems and decision support systems.

NEXT GENERATION OF EXPERT SYSTEMS

All expert system products that are currently available are based on what we will call first-generation expert system technology. The products built with this technology have proved that the concept is important and useful. Some systems developed with this technology have proved to be useful. However, with use, the weaknesses of the technology are becoming apparent. Knowledge engineers and users want greater functionality. Knowledge engineers want more flexibility to represent and use knowledge and are looking for products that make the knowledge acquisition and expert-system-building tasks easier and quicker. Users are looking for expert systems that are less stylized to the technology and are more oriented to the way they perform their tasks.

To understand the issues, let us look at some of the weaknesses and the problems that can be associated with the technology as it presently exists. First-generation expert system technology limitations can be characterized as follows:

1. The knowledge representation languages tend to be limited in their ability to handle and represent knowledge from the many domains in which knowledge engineers would like to work.

2. Knowledge representation schemes in use today support only shallow or surface knowledge.

3. The knowledge representation techniques and tools available today leave knowledge engineers handcrafting the knowledge, and the knowledge is manually acquired and entered into the systems' knowledge-bases.

4. Explanations provided by expert systems as to how they came to a particular line of advice or reasoning tend to be stylized and weak in the amount of new information provided to users.

5. Present systems degrade in a nongraceful manner; they do not know or understand when a problem is beyond their capabilities.

6. Present systems are not able to cope with knowledge inconsistencies and cannot effectively resolve conflicts among pieces of knowledge.

7. There are no systems today that can learn automatically from operational experiences to which they are subjected.

8. The construction of an expert system is very time-consuming.

The limitations of the first generation of expert systems need to be addressed. Many universities and research laboratories are already performing research that is aimed at removing these limitations from expert system technology. The second generation of expert systems should address some or all of these issues. Let us take a closer look at these issues and propose some of the goals future planners and second-generation expert system builders should be considering.

Knowledge representation is an important issue. Future knowledge representation schemes need to be able to provide representation methods for more subject domains. The knowledge of some domains does not seem to fit into any of the knowledge representation paradigms that are available today; therefore, either new paradigms are needed for these domains, or we will have to learn how to represent this knowledge with the present knowledge presentation paradigms. Both involve learning more about how to represent knowledge.

New knowledge base structures could include knowledge about the complete search space. This way, the expert system could fall back on very weak search methods when all else fails. This suggestion falls at one end of the knowledge complexity continuum. Here we are suggesting a simple scheme that is supplemented by a large amount of knowledge. Intellectually, this technique should be relatively easy to develop. However, the intensive labor requirement to develop knowledge-bases this way might be prohibitive unless good knowledge acquisition tools are developed to support this effort. Also, knowledge consistency might be a more significant problem with this technique. More research needs to be performed in this area.

Knowledge representation schemes also need to support deeper knowledge and reasoning. Causal knowledge models need to be supported instead of just the surface rule type of knowledge models that are supported today. This requires more complex knowledge representation paradigms than those in use today. Although more complex knowledge representations might be more difficult to develop, they should offer more complete domain knowledge and would allow knowledge-bases to be built with fewer knowledge elements. This would decrease the possibility of knowledge inconsistencies between knowledge elements. Knowledge acquisition tools could be developed to support acquisition of complex knowledge in an efficient manner.

Future knowledge representation and acquisition techniques and tools need to be developed so that the knowledge engineer does not have to handcraft knowledge-bases. Many of the engineering practices that are being developed in the software engineering domain are directly applicable to the knowledge engineering domain. Future knowledge representation schemes and knowledge acquisition tools should do the following:

1. Support modularity (develop knowledge in logical units),
2. Support abstraction (common elements are grouped in higher-level units as in a data hierarchy),
3. Provide the knowledge engineer with a variety of formalism choices (examples could include property, role, relation; function, procedure, rule; and single elements, sets, sequences),
4. Support typical automated computer programming tasks (bookkeeping, documentation, day and time stamping, knowledge version management, knowledge display, graphics support, and graphical data management),
5. Support as many control structures as possible, and
6. Provide the knowledge engineer with assistance in the effective use of all features.

Explanations provided by the second-generation expert systems should be deeper and less stylized. Most explanation functions are developed as a secondary benefit to the format of the stored knowledge. Since the knowledge in the knowledge-base is readable, many expert systems provide explanations by presenting appropriate pieces of the knowledge-base to the user, sometimes with some additional formatting. If the user requests an explanation of why the system is asking a particular question, many systems will respond with the particular rule the system is currently working on. An example of this is presented in Figure 3.1.

Similarly, if a user asks an expert system how it developed a particular conclusion, a rule-based system would provide the user with an ordered list of the rules and facts it used to develop its conclusion. Figure 3.2 provides a simple example of a user asking a system how it developed its conclusion.

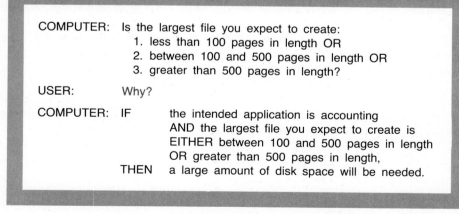

```
COMPUTER:   Is the largest file you expect to create:
              1. less than 100 pages in length OR
              2. between 100 and 500 pages in length OR
              3. greater than 500 pages in length?

USER:       Why?

COMPUTER:   IF      the intended application is accounting
                    AND the largest file you expect to create is
                    EITHER between 100 and 500 pages in length
                    OR greater than 500 pages in length,
            THEN    a large amount of disk space will be needed.
```

Figure 3.1   Explanation example for a ''why'' question

COMPUTER: RECOMMEND 40 megabytes of disk space for the intended application.

USER: How?

COMPUTER: IF   a large amount of disk space will be needed,
          THEN RECOMMEND 40 megabytes of disk space for the intended application.

          IF   the intended application is accounting
                    AND the largest file you expect to create is EITHER between 100 and 500 pages in length OR greater than 500 pages in length,
          THEN a large amount of disk space will be needed.

          IF   (any) file created will be greater than 500 in length,
          THEN the largest file you expect to create is greater than 500 pages in length.

          IF   the inventory cost file contains more than 10,000 inventory items,
          THEN file created will be greater than 500 pages in length.

          FACT The intended application is accounting.

          FACT The inventory cost file contains more than 10,000 inventory items.

Figure 3.2   Explanation example for a "how" question

Explanations presented by second-generation expert systems will contain more information and will be less stylized. Future expert systems will use deeper knowledge in their knowledge-bases. This will provide them with the foundation to explain their actions with more in-depth information. With more effective knowledge acquisition facilities, future expert systems should employ more domain knowledge. This will also assist them in providing more information during an explanation. The explanation function was originally developed as an engineer's tool. However, it has become evident that the explanation function is very helpful to expert system users.

The explanation function is often cited as one of the advantages of expert system technology. Future expert systems will be developed with separate, more functional explanation facilities. Explanation facilities will be designed to provide the user with the best explanation possible. Better explanation facilities will result because more effort will go into their development and because better knowledge representation and acquisition will make better explanations possible. Advances in natural-language research will also assist in providing better explanations.

The ability of expert systems to explain themselves instills trust in some users. This ability makes expert systems effective in certain applications like instruction. The value of the explanation function is generating a sufficient level of interest that future expert system developers will invest the time and effort to provide full-function explanation facilities.

As we learn more about representing knowledge, the expert system explanation function should improve. One of the goals of improving knowledge representation is to be able to provide users with explanations that are more instructive and less stylized. Natural-language research should also assist in meeting these goals. The "why" and "how" user explanation requests are important expert system features. Future expert systems will improve on these features. Figure 3.3 is an example of a very simple improvement to the explanation example for the "why" query presented in Figure 3.1.

First-generation expert systems work well when problems presented to them are within the boundaries of their knowledge-base. When problems presented to a first-generation system can be solved using only the knowledge that is in the knowledge-base, the expert system has little or no difficulty in providing assistance to the user.

COMPUTER: Is the largest file you expect to create:
             1. less than 100 pages in length OR
             2. between 100 and 500 pages in length OR
             3. greater than 500 pages in length?

USER: Why?

COMPUTER: Presently trying to satisfy the rule:
      IF   the intended application is accounting AND the largest file you expect to create is EITHER between 100 and 500 pages in length OR greater than 500 pages in length,
      THEN   a large amount of disk space will be needed.

It has already been determined that:
the intended application is accounting.

Therefore, by answering this question, we can determine if: a large amount of disk space will be needed.

Figure 3.3   Improved explanation example for a "why" question

When problems presented to a first-generation expert system require knowledge that is not in the system's knowledge-base, the system tends to degrade rapidly. The system does not know how to continue. Often the system cannot offer the user any advice as to what to do next. Often the system also does not understand that the problem it is having is related to the fact that it is missing requisite knowledge in order to handle the user's problem. In situations like this, the system degrades nongracefully to an unusable state.

Second-generation expert systems will contain knowledge about the boundaries of their knowledge and will know when a problem submitted to them is beyond these boundaries. A second-generation system will be able to advise the user of the situation and present possible options. The system will be able to continue operating, although it might have to skip a problem that it has determined it cannot work on without additional data, information, or knowledge. These systems will degrade in a graceful manner in situations that are beyond their capabilities; that is, they will be aware of their problem and help the user determine an alternative course of action.

Knowledge needed to assist a user with a particular problem might be missing for many reasons. The knowledge might not be available. In many cases, the knowledge is available but is not in the knowledge-base for one of many practical reasons. Figure 3.4 lists some of the reasons why the requisite knowledge might not be in the knowledge-base.

There will be cases where some knowledge a particular user would like to have in an expert system knowledge-base will be lacking. The user would like the knowledge to be in the knowledge-base so that the expert system can support the user in some particular activity. The user reasons that since the knowledge requirements of the activity are closely related to the knowledge already incor-

1. The knowledge was not available earlier but is available now.

2. The knowledge engineer did not know about the existence or importance of the particular piece of knowledge, but the user does know.

3. At the time of the knowledge-base's development, the knowledge, information, or data was available but was thought to be unnecessary for the operation of the particular application for which the expert system was designed.

4. At the time of development, the knowledge was available but was not installed in the knowledge base for important nontechnical reasons like cost or schedule constraints.

Figure 3.4 Possible reasons why a knowledge-base might not include certain requisite knowledge

porated in the particular expert system's knowledge-base, it would be appropriate to add the requisite knowledge.

Second-generation expert systems will be able to assist this user. If the user has the requisite knowledge, the system will provide the user with the tools necessary to incorporate the new knowledge into the knowledge-base. These knowledge application tools will include knowledge editors and knowledge-base configuration managers. These tools would help the user in applying the new knowledge to the knowledge-base in such a manner as to assure that the knowledge-base is not corrupted. These tools might also classify new knowledge by user and provide a knowledge-base update audit trail that is indexed by day and time.

If the user does not have the knowledge and does not know where to find it, the user has another problem. The system could be told of the location of certain classes of knowledge that the knowledge engineer knew existed but did not include in the knowledge-base. This way, the expert system could advise the user that certain requisite knowledge is not in the knowledge-base but could tell the user where the knowledge could be obtained. Once the user has obtained the knowledge, the system could assist the user in applying the knowledge to the knowledge-base.

These system capabilities would assist the user when the expert system is not able to support a particular request. The goal is graceful degradation of operation. When an expert system cannot do something, it should be able to continue to run and assist the user with alternative actions.

Present expert systems are not able to cope effectively with knowledge inconsistencies. They cannot resolve conflicts between pieces of knowledge, and they handle inconsistencies either very crudely or not at all. Some systems cannot even detect inconsistencies in their knowledge-bases. Second-generation expert systems will address these issues.

One effective tool to manage knowledge inconsistency would be an intelligent knowledge editor. An intelligent editor could be designed to detect inconsistencies between knowledge already in the knowledge-base and knowledge a user or knowledge engineer is attempting to add to the knowledge-base. This editor could first alert the user or knowledge engineer to the potential problem and then offer alternative courses of action (for example, not input the new, inconsistent knowledge or remove the older knowledge that is inconsistent with the new knowledge and then apply the new, more up-to-date knowledge). In cases where the knowledge is being provided to the expert system via an automated method (such as real-time data being input to an expert monitoring system), rules could be developed to specify how to resolve knowledge conflicts. Future expert systems will be designed with at least conflict detection and warning facilities. The better systems will also be able to resolve the detected conflicts either in a totally automated manner or in a cooperative user-machine scenario.

First-generation expert systems do not learn automatically from operational experiences and appropriately modify their knowledge-bases while they are running. Machine learning is being researched extensively today. One of the goals of machine learning research is to optimize the time and costs associated with the problem-solving process. In the case of expert systems, the goal is to decrease the time and costs associated with the development of the expert system knowledge-bases and the problem-solving activities for which the expert systems were built. Factual knowledge and system control knowledge are two of the types of knowledge machine learning researchers are examining. The architecture of certain first-generation expert systems in university and research laboratories already includes experimental learning modules.

Second-generation expert systems will benefit from this research. Future systems should be able to learn from their experiences and be able to modify their knowledge-bases appropriately. This learning capability will assist in the knowledge acquisition tasks that are so labor-intensive today.

Expert systems today learn via the manual inputting of domain knowledge. This domain knowledge comes mostly from human experts. Another source of basic knowledge for most domains is books, journals, and magazines. This source is being used a little today. More work needs to be done in the area of automated machine knowledge acquisition from printed matter. Basic domain knowledge can be loaded into the expert system under development prior to obtaining knowledge from the human expert. This would provide three benefits:

1. Basic knowledge would be acquired more quickly.
2. The expert system would start out with the ability to understand the expert to a certain extent rather than being totally ignorant of the domain.
3. The time required of the domain expert during the development of the expert system would be reduced.

Second-generation systems with machine-learning capabilities should be able to assist significantly with knowledge acquisition tasks.

The construction of an expert system can be very time-consuming. Many of the successful first-generation expert systems were entirely home-grown. The developers of systems like MYCIN developed all the components of the expert system (inference engine, knowledge database, user interface), methods for acquiring the knowledge, and the subject domain knowledge-base. Today, effective products are available to assist in the construction of expert systems, with varying levels of system structure and flexibility. Some provide the knowledge engineer with a functional inference engine, a knowledge acquisition tool, a knowledge database, a user-system interface (sometimes with sophisticated graphics presentations), and an explanation facility in an integrated package. With these tools, the bulk of the work in developing a specific expert system involves the creation of the domain-specific knowledge-base. This greatly decreases the time required to develop an expert system.

Although a knowledge engineer who uses an expert-system-building package does not have to develop the system components, the engineer still has an important task, that of elaborating the subject knowledge-base. Often the development of the knowledge-base is the most time-consuming task in the construction of an expert system. In the future, new knowledge acquisition methods and tools will be available to assist the knowledge engineer in the creation of the knowledge-base.

Second-generation expert systems will also be specifically designed to interface with other computer-based systems. The first of these are database management systems. The interfacing of DBMS with expert systems is a synergistic situation. The DBMS will provide the expert systems with well-defined, rigorous management mechanisms for the knowledge-bases. The expert systems will provide the DBMS with new, innovative techniques and tools for data design and data retrieval.

EXPERT SYSTEMS IN BUSINESS SITUATIONS

What business situations have generated interest in expert system technology? Figure 3.5 provides a list of some. The retirement of a key expert in an organization can be a disruptive event. Any event or activity that would normally require consultations with this retiring expert would

1. Retirement of a key business expert
2. Inability to develop a solution using the tools available to the organization
3. Nonavailability of highly skilled people in specific areas of expertise
4. Demands and importance of certain tasks
5. Desire to develop more cost-efficient tools
6. Desire to distribute specific knowledge to an organization's operational sites
7. Desire to have a computer-based system that uses the same kind of rules and reasoning that the organization's experts use
8. Need for expertise where it is not feasible to have a human expert
9. Need to reach a decision that requires several human experts
10. Desire to allow experts to return to more important tasks and still be able to maintain the routine business activities

Figure 3.5   Business situations that generate interest in expert system technology

potentially be difficult for the organization to handle. Often retiring experts have developed their expertise through many experiences that have occurred over many years. It is difficult to replace such people, and the knowledge they have acquired is very valuable to the organization.

It is logical for the organization to want to acquire, codify, and preserve this knowledge. In the past, this could not be done; the technology simply did not exist. Expert system technology, along with the knowledge engineering discipline, has changed this situation. The acquisition, codification, storage, and utilization of expert knowledge is now possible thanks to this new technology.

Expert system technology is a solution to the retiring expert problem. The CATS-1 (Computer-Aided Troubleshooting System 1) or DELTA (Diesel-Electric Locomotive Troubleshooting Aid) expert system is an example. CATS-1 was developed by General Electric. Its purpose was to retain the expertise of a highly skilled locomotive engineer who was about to retire. This engineer had worked for General Electric for many years and was an expert in diagnosing faults in locomotives. The loss of his expertise would have been disruptive to the General Electric group responsible for this work. The resulting system is an innovative integration of expert system technology with computer-aided instruction technology. When the system diagnoses a problem and suggests a remedy, it is also able to instruct the user in the actions required.

The inability to develop a solution using the tools available to an organization has traditionally led organizations to search out new tools and methods. Sometimes this has led to the investigation of the applicability of expert system technology. The XCON (expert configurator) expert system is a case in point.

The XCON expert system was developed by the Digital Equipment Corporation (DEC) with the assistance of John McDermott of Carnegie-Mellon University. XCON (originally called R1) was developed to solve a problem that DEC was unsuccessful at solving with other computer-based tools and programming techniques. The purpose of XCON is to configure the DEC VAX computer systems from the hundreds of possible VAX components that DEC offers. The input to XCON is a customer order, and the output is a set of configuration diagrams that are used by DEC technicians who assemble the VAX computer systems.

The nonavailability of highly skilled people in specific areas of expertise is a problem common to many organizations today. It is especially prevalent in organizations involved in technology-driven activities. The oil-drilling industry is an example. One of the oil-drilling activities that requires an expert is freeing a stuck drill bit. Inoperative oil drilling platforms are very costly. Oil-drilling companies do not have enough people with expertise in this area.

The DRILLING ADVISOR expert system assists the oil rig crew with stuck-drill-bit problems. The system walks the crew through each problem and recommends remedial actions. The system also provides some advice on preventive measures. This expert system is being used experimentally as it is being incrementally enhanced. To date, the system has made positive suggestions in a number of stuck-bit situations. In the future, the system will be fielded to many drilling platforms. This should decrease the requirement for people who are highly skilled in the area of solving stuck-drill-bit problems.

The demands and importance of certain tasks have generated interest in expert system technology. Take the example of monitoring the operation of a nuclear-powered electrical power plant. The monitoring function is only one of many management functions that are required at the plant. It is needed on a constant basis, 24 hours a day, 365 days a year. The monitoring of the plant's processes cannot stop because of holidays, illness, fatigue, or any other reason.

An expert system could be developed to oversee the monitoring function and to provide alerts as problems develop. An expert system could be developed with heuristics that would enable it to infer potential future problems and appropriate levels of urgency. These inferences might be based on the interrelationship of various sensor values, the relationship of one or more sensor values with a time function, or the relationship of certain sensor values with certain historical facts about the particular plant or a similar plant. Unlike traditional automated monitoring systems, an expert monitoring system would also employ expert-level heuristics about the operation and potential problems of operation of the plant. The system would develop an inference of a future problem and its urgency and would then present an appropriate alert or alarm. Alerting the operations crew of a potential problem allows the crew to work at preventive maintenance rather than crisis management. This system should help to make the operation of the plant safer in that maintenance averts emergency situations instead of coping with emergencies after they have arisen.

The desire for more cost-efficient tools has generated much interest in expert system technology. National and international competition is an important factor in most businesses today. Organizations are looking at new technologies that can decrease their cost of operations or increase their efficiency, which is another cost-saving technique. The goal is to stay competitive. Automated Cable Expertise (ACE) is an expert system that was built by American Telephone and Telegraph (ATT) to increase operational efficiency in the area of telephone cable fault analysis.

ATT has automatic test equipment that tests telephone cables. The output of this testing is a database of cable fault information. This information had to be individually analyzed by telephone engineers. This work was labor-intensive, slow, and costly. The ACE system was developed to retrieve the fault information from the data management and reporting system, analyze it, and provide bottom-line recommendations on cable maintenance actions, all automatically. ACE can analyze in one evening what used to take engineers up to a week. Moreover, ACE provides suggestions on the proper procedures that should be followed when performing the maintenance actions. This information allows the organization to detect and fix actual and potential cable problems more quickly and with less engineer involvement. The business consequence is that ATT provides better service to its customers at lower cost because of the introduction of an expert-system-based tool.

The desire to distribute specific knowledge to an organization's operational sites is exemplified by the MUDMAN system development. MUDMAN is an expert system that was developed by the NL Baroid organization with the initial assistance of Carnegie-Mellon University.

NL Baroid is in the business of selling drilling mud and mud engineering consulting services to oil-drilling companies. Drilling mud is a lubricant for the drilling process. It consists of the material naturally found at the drilling site plus additives that are supplied by NL Baroid. NL Baroid has a corporate knowledge-base of over 60 years of drilling mud experience. This experience is contained in technical reports and in the minds of NL Baroid mud experts, many of whom have 30 to 40 years of experience in the business.

NL Baroid wanted to make all of its mud expertise available to mud engineers in the field. NL Baroid engineers would then be able to apply all this expertise to problems in the field. NL Baroid also decided that it would sell the knowledge to other mud engineers. The resulting MUDMAN expert system is thus both a tool to disseminate the organization's knowledge to its operational sites and a product that the organization sells.

Computer-based systems that use the same kinds of rules and reasoning that the organization's experts use should provide many benefits to the organization. Such systems should be easier to develop than conventional systems since the knowledge being transferred to these systems does not have to undergo great transformations. Although the knowledge acquisition and codification processes usually do require knowledge transformation, still a very labor-intensive task, this work should be easier to perform than the specification, design, and transformation tasks that are typical of conventional computer system development.

The resulting systems should be easier for the organization's experts to understand because the system uses the same kinds of rules and reasoning that the experts use. This saves the valuable time of the organization's experts. The experts will also be able to verify that the system is correct since the knowledge codified in the system is in the form they are accustomed to seeing and working with. Acceptance by the experts should be an additional benefit since the experts will understand the system more thoroughly and feel confident that they have been able to audit it properly. The STAR-MD project is developing a medical system based on expert system technology so that it will use rule-based knowledge and reasoning techniques similar to those that medical people use.

Expertise is often needed where it is impossible to have a human expert available at the exact time of the need. The BSM project is developing an expert system with this situation in mind. BSM, in French, stands for *bateau sans médecin* (''boat without a doctor''). The IBM Scientific Center in Paris, in a joint study with the Médecins Sans Frontières organization, is approaching the need for medical decision making and training with an answer that is based on the implementation of an expert system.

The scenario that is being studied in the BSM project is a medical emergency on a boat at sea that does not have a doctor aboard. The second mate would legally be in charge. The second mate would radio for help and would describe the medical problem to a doctor in layman's terms over the radio. The doctor would try to understand the problem without the benefit of seeing the problem firsthand. The doctor would ask the second mate questions in layman's terms and tell him to perform certain examinations, limited by the second mate's capabilities and the resources aboard the boat. The second mate would then provide the doctor with new information. The doctor must then diagnose the problem and provide the second mate with useful recommendations.

The BSM expert system should be able to provide the same kind of assistance to the second mate as the doctor on the other side of the radio link does today.

Expert systems like BSM could be developed to assist with other medical emergencies like the care of victims of natural disaster (such as earthquakes) by civil helpers (such as firemen) who are not doctors.

Expert systems could also be developed to help with other problems that usually require expertise that is not always available when needed.

Many organizations must reach decisions that require the expertise of more than one human expert because no one expert in the organization possesses all the knowledge needed.

The PROSPECTOR expert system includes knowledge from more than one expert in its knowledge-base. The system is designed to assist in determining whether a particular site has a mineral deposit worth mining.

Each major category of mineral deposits is understood by a particular expert geologist. When investigating the potential of a specific site, it is desirable to check for deposits in all or most categories. This implies that an expert geologist for each category will be needed. As data is gathered about the site, each expert geologist will need to study and interpret it with regard to his or her category of expertise.

The PROSPECTOR expert system's knowledge-base includes knowledge from the major categories of mineral deposits, acquired from different expert geologists. The system has the ability to apply this knowledge to make a decision on the mineral value of a site while considering various possibilities.

Experts are often the innovators of organizations. Through their expertise, they develop ideas for products and services. Often these experts lead projects to develop their ideas into commercial products and services or in-house systems. Once the ideas have been fully developed and implemented, the development project should end and routine business activities should take over.

At this point, there is a desire to allow the experts to return to more important tasks, but sometimes their expertise is needed to support what has been developed. Some organizations are looking at expert systems to solve this problem. The idea is to replicate the portion of the experts' knowledge that is needed to support the products, services, or systems by putting this knowledge into the knowledge-bases of expert systems. The support groups should then be able to handle the majority of the problems in supporting the products, services, or systems without the experts. In cases where the expert systems do not provide adequate help, the support groups could get in touch with the experts.

Westinghouse is using Texas Instruments' Personal Consultant expert system shell to develop expert systems that would allow some staff scientists to return to their research while the expert systems take care of much of their routine business. Expert systems are being developed at Westinghouse to support the tasks of training sales representatives on technical products, repairing sophisticated equipment such as X-ray defractometers, and determining replacement material for corroding support plates in steam generators.

Computer-based systems that are in constant evolution have been difficult to develop and maintain using traditional computer systems, products, and technologies. Some organizations are now looking at expert system technology as a possible answer to this problem.

WHAT DO WE WANT EXPERT SYSTEMS TO DO?

New technology discoveries often lead to the hope that problems that were previously difficult or impossible to solve will be solvable with a nominal amount of effort. Human hopes tend to be boundless. Expert system technology provides the computer industry with some new tools and hopes. In essence it is a set of new software techniques being applied to a set of new applications. This technology should not be considered a replacement for other computer technologies. It is better regarded as a new set of tools in the computer professional's tool bag and as an enhancement to existing techniques. The new applications it makes practical are numerous and valuable.

Expert system technology provides system designers with an alternative approach to certain classes of problems. The XCON expert system, built by the Digital Equipment Corporation, is an example where expert system technology provided a solution when other computer technologies failed.

Digital Equipment Corporation sells minicomputers in a manner that allows the buyer great flexibility of configuration. The buyer can purchase a configuration that is specific to his or her needs. This sales approach left DEC with a problem—configuring its products to the specifications of the buyer and, at the same time, making sure that the configurations would function properly. For example, are sufficient numbers of power supplies and cables specified in the purchase request?

The configuration work was being performed by DEC technicians who were trained in minicomputer configuration. The problems with this manual effort were that it was time-intensive and the configurations that resulted included too many errors. This method also required the attention of configuration experts to routine configuration tasks when problems did appear.

During the 1970s, DEC tried many times to automate this configuration task with conventional programming techniques. First a limited-scope order-checking program was attempted. This attempt failed. After studying the configuration problem in more detail and analyzing the required tasks, an automated configuration program was proposed. The next step DEC took was to try to specify the configuration program using conventional computer technology for both the specification work and the resulting computer program. This attempt also failed. At this point, DEC put the project on hold.

Work on the automated configuration program project was again stimulated. This time the interest was developed by people at Carnegie-Mellon University. They proposed a rule-based expert system approach to the configuration problem. After assimilating the basics of the task and choosing an appropriate tool (the OPS language), a prototype system incorporating some 250 rules was developed. This system was tested and demonstrated. It appeared to be on the right track.

Interest in the project grew at DEC. Work began on determining what knowledge the system still lacked. The missing knowledge was identified and applied to the knowledge base. The knowledge base grew to about 750 rules. Somewhere around this time, the experimental system name, R1, was changed to the present name, XCON, which stands for "expert configurator."

The XCON expert system was validated, improved, and introduced into DEC's mainline business operations to perform its intended task of configuring DEC VAX 11/780 minicomputer systems. The system was validated by numerous DEC configuration experts who studied the system's configuration recommendations for representative VAX minicomputer orders. The system went through several improvements, including its recoding into OPS version 5 (from version 4). The recoding effort resulted in a decrease in the knowledge-base size, to 500 rules, because of better knowledge representations. Since its introduction into DEC's operations, the system has experienced significant growth.

The original system to be fielded within DEC could configure the VAX 11/780 using 500 rules. DEC has been constantly expanding the system. The expansions have occurred for two reasons. First, the VAX 11/780 system's options have expanded with time. Second, DEC has extended the capabilities of the system to be able to configure other computer systems that DEC sells. The XCON system today can configure many DEC computer systems including all of the VAX systems, the MICROVAX systems, and many of the PDP-11 and MICRO-PDP-11 systems. The XCON knowledge-base now includes over 10,000 rules. The parts database that the system uses has increased from 400 parts to over 8000 parts.

The XCON expert system is an excellent example of expert system technology providing a solution to a problem that could not otherwise be solved. It has added more than $20 million per year to DEC's profits by eliminating many of the problems with incorrectly configured computers. There are two questions a computer user cannot ask traditional programs. First, why is the program asking for a particular piece of information. The reason the computer requests a particular piece of information might not be obvious to the user. The user might then misunderstand the computer's request and thus furnish the wrong information. Or the user might deduce that the computer is asking for irrelevant information, in which case the computer must have misunderstood the user. The user might lose confidence in the computer and stop using it. Computer programs that are based on expert system technology can be built so that a query of this type can be asked and the program will supply the reason it is asking the question or is asking for a particular piece of information.

Second, a user cannot ask a conventional computer program how the program arrived at a particular solution. Conventional computer programs provide answers to questions, but they cannot explain how they arrived at their solutions. The program's algorithms and the particular data presented to the program for the particular program run would have to be analyzed to determine how the program arrived at a particular result. Programs that are built on expert system technology can provide computer users with explanations of how they arrived at a particular conclusion. These programs will provide this information in various formats. The important information to be provided will include the knowledge used and the inference steps taken to get to the recommended conclusion.

The why and how questions are usually handled by the explanation facility component of an expert system.

Computers can store, manipulate, and retrieve vast amounts of information from their memories. However, the types of information that conventional computer programs can handle effectively have been limited. Conventional computer programs are algorithmic. They handle data in a manner that is set by their algorithms. The algorithms determine the program's operations. The programs operate on the data presented. A large number of applications are properly supported with this type of program. However, some applications are not well supported by this type of program. It is hoped that expert-system-based programs will provide effective support to some of these applications.

Let us look at an example. Since computers can store so much information, why can't organizations use computers to store their important corporate knowledge?

In the past, corporate knowledge was not stored in computers because of two factors. The first was that data storage on automated systems was costly. This situation has now changed. The costs of data storage have decreased dramatically and will continue to drop.

The second factor had to do with how to represent the corporate knowledge in the automated systems. The conventional data representation, storage, and retrieval schemes used on computer systems did not seem to fit the needs of corporate knowledge representation, storage, and retrieval.

Attempts to represent corporate knowledge in an expert-system-based knowledge representation scheme have been successful. Knowledge acquisition is usually supported by a knowledge acquisition component of the expert system, and the knowledge is stored in the expert system knowledge base. Knowledge retrieval occurs during an interactive session between the system and a user. Knowledge retrieval is supported by the user-system interface and the explanation facility.

Expert system technology provides the methods and the tools necessary to represent, store, and retrieve corporate knowledge on a computer system.

In the majority of organizations, most of the key knowledge that the organization depends on in order to function is retained by a small group of people. These people, possibly because of their knowledge, also tend to contribute a majority of the effort. Certain critical knowledge is sometimes held by only one or two people. Often the performance of a person who is not one of these key people is directly affected by the accessability of a key person. Organizational performance most likely would be improved if the key organizational knowledge could be dispersed to a greater number of people in the organization. We would like to be able to acquire key organizational knowledge from these key people, package it, and distribute it to a larger group of people in the organization. The net result of this should be improved performance in many of the organization's people. Present expert system technology will in fact allow us to do this.

Some recent systems have been very large and difficult to understand, manage, and use. It would be helpful to integrate expert systems into these large, complex systems. The expert-system-based subsystems of these large systems could advise users of the options that are available to them and could assist users in the operation of the systems. In the case of large automated process control systems, the expert subsystems could also advise the operators on optimum operating settings and potential problems in the operation of the system. Experiments involving the integration of expert systems with large automated systems have been proposed, and some, for example, for the management of large networks, have been developed.

When a new technology is introduced in the business world, many business people and organizations try to apply it to their products in an attempt to gain a competitive edge. The introduction of expert system technology has created interest in this area. Some businesses would like to integrate an expert system into their products in order to differentiate their products from those of their competitors.

Expert systems could be integrated into test instrumentation equipment. Test equipment that incorporates expert system technology could provide answers rather than just data. The equipment could respond with the observed data and interpretations of it. Instruments providing this additional interpretation service would certainly differentiate themselves from instruments that did not provide this capability.

Helena Laboratories Corporation produces modern clinical laboratory instruments. One instrument is used for a clinical blood test known as the serum protein electrophoresis (SPE) test. Instruments of this type often provide analog and digital data results. The results are then read and interpreted by physicians. Helena Laboratories worked with Sholom Weiss and Casimir Kulikowski of Rutgers University in the development of an expert system that could interpret the SPE test data. After development, this expert interpretative system was packaged into a read-only memory device and was integrated into a microcomputer-equipped SPE instrument product. This product provides analog and digital data information on each test and provides a textual interpretation of the data for each test that is run through the instrument.

Knowledge is an important asset to businesses. Companies with the most accurate and complete knowledge tend to have a competitive edge over other firms in their industry.

Many decisions that must be made involve potentially hundreds and sometimes thousands of chunks of knowledge, information, and data as well as potential choices or courses of action. Human decision makers cannot exhaustively search through and analyze all the knowledge, information, and data. Business decision makers usually do not have the resources required to consider each and every potential choice or course of action. They must rely on some heuristic methods to decrease the amount of knowledge, information, and data to analyze and the number of choices to consider. These nonmechanical reduction methods are likely to remove important knowledge from the analysis or important choices or alternative courses of action from consideration.

If we could capture all the pertinent knowledge, information, and data related to important, recurring decisions of a business as well as the choices or alternative courses of action, could represent and store this business expertise in an expert system knowledge base, and could develop inference mechanisms that could accurately, consistently, and tirelessly judge which knowledge, information, data, and choices to consider and which not to consider for each decision that needs to be made, the resulting expert system could be considered a knowledge power amplifier. This expert system would provide the decision makers of the business with a reduced set of knowledge, information, and data to consider and a reduced number of alternatives from which to choose. The expert system would analyze all the knowledge, information, data, and alternatives with equal consideration. The system would provide the decision makers with reasonable sets of information to analyze and alternatives from which to select. Knowledge, information, and data that are not valuable to the decision at hand would be systematically and rapidly deleted from the field of consideration, and important information would be highlighted to the decision maker. Unimportant alternatives would be deleted by the system. The human decision maker would only have to consider the better alternatives.

When expert systems of this kind are built, the human decision maker, with the assistance of this expert system, is able to make more decisions per

1. Provide computer system designers with a new system design approach.

2. Provide system users with more information (for example, answer how and why questions).

3. Provide the facility to store corporate knowledge.

4. Provide the capability to disburse knowledge to key players in the organization.

5. Assist in the operation of large, complex systems.

6. Produce product differentiation.

7. Amplify knowledge worker (decision maker) capabilities.

8. Use knowledge to provide a competitive edge.

Figure 3.6   What do we want expert systems to do?

unit of time, and the decisions are based on a potentially less hazardous method of initial problem reduction. The decision maker has more time to analyze the relevant information and to consider the important alternatives. In this way, the expert system serves as a tool that amplifies the capabilities of the corporate decision makers.

Expert systems that provide this service are assisting some companies in making decisions on insurance or investments, for example. Companies with such an expert system would not only have this knowledge but would most likely have obtained it by expending the smallest amount of resources. Companies that know which alternatives are best should be in better competitive positions than similar companies that do not have this knowledge.

Expert system technology is a new and exciting technology, and its benefits have only started to become apparent. The potential for beneficial application of expert system technology is very great. Figure 3.6 provides a summary of some of the things we would like to see expert systems do.

REALISTIC EXPERT SYSTEM CAPABILITIES

Whenever a new technology is introduced, it is first applied to a task that is known and understood by the people who developed the new technology. This first application is used to prove the concept and to demonstrate the technology's utility. If interest in the new technology grows, additional attempts are made to apply the technology. If the application of the technology proves useful, the technology gains a certain level of acceptance. Commensurate with the acceptance level, industry will start to use the technology in its products. Expert system technology has experienced these milestones.

Expert system technology, as has already been mentioned, has been applied to numerous tasks in various domains and industries. There are now many examples of what expert systems can do. The technology is becoming popular among computer system designers, who are developing a good feel for when it is appropriate.

As a result of the interest in artificial intelligence and expert systems, many companies are developing products that incorporate expert system technology. Some of these products are already available. The British chemical company ICI and the British software house Isis have marketed the Wheat Counsellor expert system product. ICI sees this system as a marketing tool. Wheat Counsellor helps farmers determine which chemicals are appropriate for the prevention of disease in their crops.

Business people are showing interest in expert system technology, but they are also asking some hard questions:

- What can we do with expert system technology that we could not do without it?
- Can we reduce costs by using expert systems?
- Can expert systems help us create computer systems that are less intimidating to the naive computer user?
- Can we create safer systems and products by integrating expert systems with our present systems and products?
- What returns can be expected on investments in expert system technology?
- Just what should expert systems be capable of doing?

Expert system technology permits us to represent, capture, package, and distribute scarce knowledge and expertise. This knowledge and expertise can include heuristic information and information that is incomplete or inexact. We can develop automated systems that will benefit from this captured knowledge by providing better operations and additional automated assistance to the systems' intended users. These are things that we have not been able to do with other technologies. Automated knowledge banks based on expert system technology can be used to solve many pressing problems that we have not been able to solve with other technologies, including retaining the expertise of a retiring expert, distributing knowledge to areas where it is needed, maintaining corporate expertise level in times of great employee turnover, providing expertise to systems that must operate autonomously (such as interstallar probes), and being able to concentrate on important tasks for indefinite periods of time (as in monitoring essential equipment operations or the military posture of an adversary).

Expert systems can be used by competent workers who are not themselves experts, enabling them to handle problems that normally require the greater knowledge or experience of higher-paid experts. Some applications that require high-resolution, high-cost equipment (for example, robot controllers) can be effectively supported with lower-resolution, lower-cost equipment when provided with expert system support. Cost-effective expert systems can be consulted in lieu of expensive human experts in some cases (such as the Wheat Counsellor expert system). The net result is that expert systems provide opportunities for organizations to reduce costs and save money.

Can expert systems help us create computer systems that are less intimidating to the naive computer user? The answer is yes, in several ways. First, expert system technology can be used to develop an interface capability whereby the user can ask why the computer system is asking for a particular piece of information or how it arrived at a particular solution. Being able to ask these questions should make the user feel more in control of the situation. The computer's responses should provide a greater understanding of what the computer is doing. Usually people are less apprehensive of machines once they understand them better.

A computer system that is based on expert system technology or has incorporated expert system technology in its user-system interface can include knowledge about the user in the knowledge-base. This knowledge could assist the computer system in understanding the user. With this understanding, the computer could provide the user with assistance in using the computer. For example, the computer could fill in information missing from a user request, permitting it to answer the user's question instead of responding to the question with a question. This should make the computer seem more supportive of the user and thus less intimidating.

Expert system technology can help to produce user-system interfaces that are easier for new computer users to work with. User models can be developed with knowledge about the intended users. This user model knowledge can be employed by an expert system or subsystem so that the overall system will be more able to understand the user's requests. Therefore, through expert system technology, we should be able to produce computer-based systems that are less intimidating to the naive computer user.

Many automated systems and products are produced by commercial organizations for themselves or for other organizations that perform some function or control some process. Examples include the monitoring of a chemical plant process, the controlling of a robot, and the controlling of a metal-plating machine. The monitoring and controlling of industrial systems are usually performed by worker-machine teams. Often most of the controlling functions are performed by automated systems with built-in human override capabilities. The automated systems also usually provide important monitoring information for both the automated systems and the human operators to use. The automated systems often use certain monitored data as feedback status information to the automated controllers. The human operators use the monitored information to judge if the system is functioning properly, cost-efficiently, and safely.

The monitoring of certain processes is very important and demands continuous concentration. For some processes, continuous monitoring concentration is demanded of the operators for long periods of time. For other processes, human operators are required continuously to scan large amounts of what is usually routine data, looking for data that might indicate potential or real problems. Human operators are subject to fatigue and boredom. Expert systems could be developed to assist the human operators with their duties. The expert systems could provide continuous monitoring services, handle large data volumes, and respond quickly when the situation requires speed, without making errors or overlooking possible solutions. Although conventional automated systems could provide similar services, they cannot provide the services when given heuristic, incomplete, or inexact information. Human operators are often involved in the monitoring function because of their abilities to work with this kind of information. Expert system technology is the first automated technology that is able to assist in this area.

Safety issues are often involved in the operation of certain systems and processes. If an adverse condition is overlooked or an adverse deviation that is developing incrementally is not noticed, an unsafe situation might develop. Expert systems could be constructed to assist human operators in the monitoring functions so that these adverse situations are detected more often. The detection of unsafe or potentially unsafe conditions would not be dependent on human operators who are subject to fatique and boredom. Thus the integration of expert systems in commercial systems, machinery, equipment, and products should improve safety because important monitoring functions will be assumed by automated systems that will not become tired or bored and therefore will not fail to detect potentially dangerous situations.

The development of useful expert systems requires resources. The investment of these resources to develop expert systems is a concern of business people. Expert system technology is new, so it is difficult to provide a list of guaranteed returns on investments. However, a few examples of what companies have experienced might be helpful in providing some indications.

Digital Equipment Corporation has experienced the following benefits from the XCON expert system:

1. XCON reduced the error rate on the VAX configuration task from approximately 35 percent to 2 percent.

2. XCON reduced customer dissatisfaction because fewer incorrectly configured VAX computer systems were shipped.

3. XCON increased fourfold the number of customer orders DEC could configure without the need for additional configuration experts.

4. XCON decreased the time required to turn around customer orders.

5. XCON improved the customer service level during the ordering phase.

6. XCON reduced costs by over $20 million per year (development costs for XCON were about $10 million).

1. Represent, capture, package, and distribute important knowledge and expertise of an organization.
   - Retain expertise of a retiring expert.
   - Distribute knowledge to areas in the organization where it is needed.
   - Maintain corporate expertise in times of high employee turnover.
   - Provide expertise to systems that must operate autonomously from human operators.
2. Provide another computer science technology that can solve some of the problems that other computer science technologies cannot solve.
   - Work with heuristic information.
   - Work with incomplete or inexact information.
3. Reduce costs.
   - Augment nonexpert workers with expert-level knowledge so that the lower-cost, nonexpert workers can perform tasks that normally require experts.
   - Replace high-cost equipment with lower-cost equipment that is augmented by expert system technology.
4. Create computer systems and computer-based systems that are less intimidating to naive computer users.
   - Provide the users with explanations of why the computer is asking a particular question and how the computer arrived at a particular result.
   - Understand the goals of the user through knowledge about the user in the knowledge-base and thereby assist the user in moving toward these goals.
   - Provide user-system interfaces that are easier for the naive user to work with.
5. Create safer systems and products by augmenting the human operator's monitoring function.
   - Provide continuous monitoring without fatigue or degradation.
   - Provide continuous, error-free data scan services.
6. Provide reasonable returns on the investments incurred in development and operation.
   - Reduce manufacturing errors.
   - Reduce the time required to perform certain tasks.
   - Reduce operational costs.
   - Improve production efficiency.
   - Increase the technical capability of the organization.

Figure 3.7 What expert systems should be capable of doing

The PROSPECTOR expert system developed at SRI International has discovered a molybdenum mineral deposit that has an estimated value of over $100 million. The deposit was located at a site that had already been analyzed by expert geologists, who determined it to have no mineral deposits of commercial quantity and value. Without the aid of this expert system, this deposit might never have been discovered.

Elf Aquitaine is a French oil company. Elf had Teknowledge, Inc., an American knowledge engineering firm, develop the DRILLING ADVISOR expert system. The system is designed to advise operators on a drilling platform on techniques to use to free stuck drill bits. The knowledge applied to the system's knowledge base came from drilling experts.

The expenses related to operating a drilling platform are approximately $100,000 a day, whether the platform is drilling or not. If a drilling rig experiences a difficult stuck-drill problem, the rig might be idle for many weeks until an expert can be flown to the platform. Normally problems experienced on a platform can be handled by the drilling rig supervisor and the crew on the platform. However, when a difficult problem does present itself, it is not uncommon to be forced to wait for an expert.

The DRILLING ADVISOR expert system provides the drilling supervisors with the expertise required to get a stuck drill unstuck and return the rig to normal operation. The system can help rigs get back into operation without potentially waiting weeks for an expert to be flown to the drilling platform. This expert system has the potential to save Elf a lot of money and equipment time.

The STEAMER training system borrows technology from various computer science areas including expert systems and advanced graphics. STEAMER helps to train naval steam propulsion engineers. The system allows the naval engineers to learn how to control the steam turbine systems that are used on large naval ships without the need for an actual ship. STEAMER can provide training on normal operations as well as operations that are associated with problems. Students are provided with real control situations. However, the expense related to having to provide a real ship is saved, and mistakes made by the students do not cause expensive repairs to actual propulsion systems or cause possibly unsafe conditions aboard a naval ship. STEAMER will save the U.S. Navy a lot of money.

In summary, Figure 3.7 provides a list of some of the things that expert systems should be capable of doing.

Expert system technology fits some requirements that other technologies have not been able to fit. An expert system is just another computer science tool that will fit the requirements of some tasks better than other tools and will meet the requirements for some tasks that other technologies have not been able to support.

4 LINKING EXPERT SYSTEMS TO OTHER SOFTWARE

The early expert systems were standalone systems. They did not link to other computer systems. The early toolkits were designed for building standalone systems, often on standalone machines.

Today it is clear that many of the most valuable applications of expert system technology are those in which expert systems access databases used for other purposes or link to other types of software or systems. Many important applications in the future will combine conventional data processing with expert system technology. Knowledge engineering will be combined with information engineering. Much software will have an artificial-intelligence component as a small part of its overall code.

Because of this it has become important that expert systems run on the machines and use the software interfaces that are employed for conventional computing. They must work with the operating systems, database management systems (DBMSs), networks, user interfaces, and programming languages that constitute the world of data processing. Some expert systems tools that were programmed in LISP have been recorded in C and made to run efficiently on data processing machines rather than on specialized LISP machines. It is desirable that these tools link to architectures that are the *de facto* standards of data processing, such as IBM's Systems Application Architecture (SAA). The database management systems of the data processing world will provide expert systems with well-defined, rigorous management mechanisms for knowledge-bases. Expert systems will provide DBMSs with new, innovative techniques and tools for data design and retrieval.

This chapter discusses the linkage of expert systems with:

- Database management systems
- Management information systems

- Decision support systems
- Process control
- Office automation

INTEGRATION OF EXPERT SYSTEMS WITH DBMS

Many, perhaps most, of the valuable applications of expert systems in business and government require data which already exists in large quantities in databases or file systems. This data may be used directly if the expert system software can access the database. Alternatively, the data may be *extracted* from the databases or files and reformatted in the manner needed by the expert system. In other words, the expert system may be *online* to the database, or there may be a bridge between the database system and the expert system. Increasingly in the future the inferencing engines of expert systems will be used in conjunction with database programs and applications.

Expert system technology will benefit DBMS technology in many ways. Expert systems can be developed to assist with logical and physical data designs, for example. An expert logical data designer system could assist the human database designer. An expert physical data designer system could assist the DBMS.

Knowledge about both the domain and logical data design could be incorporated into a single knowledge-base. Operational requirements of the particular organization that relate to the use of the database can also be loaded into the knowledge-base. The resulting expert system could assist the human data designer with the logical database design task. The system could monitor the designer's work and advise the designer of data element omissions in the design and incorrect design specifications. This expert logical data design system could present design suggestions to the human designer. The expert system suggestions would take into account proper logical data design practices, domain-specific data requirements, and organizational requirements. In the future, we should see database design tools that provide expert logical data design and modeling assistance.

An expert physical data designer system could be developed to assist the DBMS with the task of developing a physical data design from the logical design provided to the DBMS. This expert system would not need to operate interactively with a human user; it could work interactively or in a batch mode with the DBMS. The knowledge-base for this physical data designer would include knowledge about the DBMS, knowledge about the logical-to-physical data design tasks, and performance and storage knowledge about the targeted hardware system. The resultant expert physical data designer system could develop physical data design suggestions that meet the logical data requirements and optimize the physical data design for the particular DBMS-hardware system configuration. In the future, we should see expert physical data designer systems integrated in the product lines of the larger DBMS vendors.

Expert systems could also be designed and developed to assist end users in the effective and efficient use of the organization's databases. The knowledge base of a user assistant expert system would include user models and a database model.

The user model knowledge would assist the expert system in knowing what kind of information the user would be interested in getting from the database. For example, the user model could define user contexts. If a user from the payroll department asked for "all Millers" in the database, the expert system would infer "all employees on the payroll with the last name of Miller." If a user from the job assignment section of the personnel department asked for "all Millers" in the database, the expert system might infer "all personnel with a job title of miller." In each case, the expert system could inform the user of a possible conflict in the query request, provide the user with the alternatives and the present system's best estimate of what the user wanted, ask the user if the system's interpretation is correct or if another of the alternatives is what the user meant, and retrieve the information according to the user's responses.

The database model would assist the expert system in the development of efficient interactions with the database and the DBMS. Taking user queries as an example, the expert system would accept the user request and develop an efficient form of the query for presentation to the DBMS. If the user asked for something that was not in the database, the expert system would be able to advise the user of this fact from the knowledge contained in the database model.

An expert system designed to provide advice to database users would assist users in all phases of database use. The expert system could advise the user on how to input data to the database, how to query the database, and how to request reports. If the user asked for something that was beyond the operational boundaries of the database system, the expert system would advise the user of this fact and assist the user in developing an alternative course of action that would satisfy the user's needs or goals.

Other expert systems could be developed to support the DBMS directly. Present DBMSs use many rules; integrity constraints and query optimization are examples. Requests to change a database are screened to assure that certain integrity rules are not violated. Data value and referential integrity are two examples.

Query requests are often optimized prior to data retrieval in order to assure efficient use of the computing resources. The DBMS employs query transformation heuristics. An example is to retrieve the data element associated with the query that has the least number of occurrences first, when the query involves multiple data elements. These rules could be incorporated in an expert system knowledge base.

The expert system could be integrated with the DBMS. The benefits of this architecture would include explicit rule development, storage, and retrieval.

This should result in an improved user interface. For example, the system would be able to provide explanations and justifications for allowing some user requests and disallowing others.

Expert system technology will be able to assist data administrators and database administrators, as well as users, in the effective and efficient use of database management systems and corporate databases. The next logical application of expert systems would be in the area of management information systems.

INTEGRATION OF EXPERT SYSTEMS INTO THE MIS ENVIRONMENT

There are many opportunities to use expert systems in support of the missions and goals of corporate management information systems. Management information systems (MIS) today directly support line managers with operational information about the organization's business. MIS also provide some summary information to managers above the line management level. Today's MISs are often very large systems that are difficult to develop, understand, manage, and maintain. Expert systems could be integrated into present management information systems to make them easier to develop, more understandable, more manageable, and easier to maintain. Expert systems could also be integrated into the MIS to assist directly with certain MIS tasks. In addition, expert systems could be used to provide more support to the strategic, top-level managers of an organization.

Large MIS programs are becoming very complex and are operationally dependent on many MIS components including operating systems, the DBMS, and the communications networks. The development and programming of these systems is becoming difficult. A growing family of tools are becoming available for helping to automate the planning, design, code generation, and maintenance of systems. Some of these, such as the toolset from KnowledgeWare, integrate expert system technology into the tools for CASE (computer-aided software engineering). The repository of CASE tools should be a knowledge-base in which information about the enterprise and its system is steadily accumulated.

MIS users often do not understand the scope and range of MIS services. One of the goals of the information center concept is to provide MIS users with a better understanding of the MIS and help them make better use of its capabilities and services. Expert systems could include the attributes of the MIS. MIS users could present problems to the expert system, and the expert system could advise the user on solving the problem by using the organization's MIS capabilities. This expert system could either be integrated into the MIS or could be a separate advisory system that might be collocated with the organization's information center.

It is becoming more difficult to manage a large corporate MIS effectively. Expert systems could be developed to assist with the management of the MIS.

Prototype expert management systems designed for MIS-type environments are already under development. The IBM Corporation YES system is an example. This expert system was designed with the goal of assisting in the management of the operation of the computer system. Other expert systems could be developed to assist in other MIS management tasks, such as system configuration management, equipment layout planning, and system utilization planning.

The maintenance of large MIS complexes could be assisted by expert system technology. Individual MIS subsystems could have their own expert maintenance systems to look for potential problems, identify causes of present problems, and suggest remedies for system failures. The computer hardware system and the telecommunications system are excellent candidates for expert maintenance systems. Expert maintenance systems could also be designed to suggest or possibly choose alternative operational paths if the MIS resources include such paths. Expert system technology will be used a lot in the future for large-system predictive, preventive, and corrective maintenance.

Expert systems could be integrated into MIS to assist in the performance of mainline MIS tasks. Expert system technology should be considered an additional automated MIS tool, like report generators and graphics packages, that should be used when its capabilities are appropriate. There are fiscal management tasks, for example, that the MIS could perform more efficiently with the aid of expert system technology. An expert system could assist bookkeepers in assigning a particular invoice to a particular account, for example. The expert system would thus help to assure that the invoices are properly classified. This assistance assures that the invoice data is accurately input into the MIS. More accurate data entry should result in more effective support from the MIS.

Most MIS offer minimal support to the day-to-day tasks of strategic, top-level managers. Summary reports of the organization's financial position, inventory levels, and sales statistics are typical of the information the systems provide. This information is very important, but it is historical data. Strategic managers must deal with the future; they must develop future strategies for their organizations.

Future expert systems will support some of the requirements of the strategic, top-level management staff of an organization. Expert systems will incorporate the organization's business model in the knowledge base and will have connectivity to the organization's MIS. Strategic planning expertise and business forecast information should also be incorporated in the expert system's knowledge base.

Many top-level managers today rely on a decision support system (DSS) to assist them with their tasks. Such systems are often extensions of the organization's MIS. There is also an opportunity for DSS to use expert system technology.

INTEGRATION OF EXPERT SYSTEMS WITH DSS

The primary goal of decision support systems (DSSs) is to provide the requisite information and tools needed to support the tasks and activities involved in strategic planning and decision making. The designs of the specific DSS commercial products vary, but they have certain common characteristics. Figure 4.1 shows the components of a generic DSS.

Present DSS products provide strategic planners with the ability to extract and format business data and information on the historical and current status of the organization. Strategic planners can also use the DSS tools to extract and format business data and information from database sources outside the organization. Two notable sources are government and commercial databases. The business data and information obtained from these sources contain historical and present status information of other organizations in the same industry and in different industries. Some databases provide business predictions and trends. This information is helpful to strategic planners, particularly when it can be presented in formats compatible with particular planners' decision-making processes.

Strategic planning and decision making should involve all available appropriate information, analysis methods, and corporate expertise in order to assure the discovery of reasonable alternative courses of action and the ability to choose effectively from the alternatives.

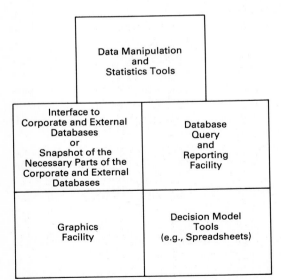

Figure 4.1 Architecture of a generic decision support system

Expert system technology and the decision support concept can be integrated in four ways:

1. By applying expert system technology to some of the current DSS components
2. By developing new DSS components using the expert system technology
3. By developing a new DSS architecture based on expert system technology
4. By developing an automated strategic-planning and decision-making assistant based on expert system technology

Expert system technology can be applied to the data manipulation and statistics tools component, the database query component, and the decision model tools component of the DSS. Manipulating data and choosing the proper statistics to apply to data can be difficult for top-level managers. Through the introduction of expert system technology, these tools can be configured in such a way as to make their use more natural for top-level management. The expert system subcomponent could provide a natural-language interface as well as a flexible interchange between the user and the system while moving toward the user's goals. The knowledge-base would contain knowledge about the organization's data, the proper application of the available statistics tools, and the user's goals. The organization's data and statistics tools use knowledge that can be preloaded. The user's goals might be preloaded, or the system could be designed to query the user for this information at the beginning of a session. With this knowledge, the system should be able to assist the user in manipulating data and selecting the appropriate statistics to apply to the data.

The application of expert system technology to the database query component can provide a natural-language-style interface and can define strategic-planning user models. The resulting query component would provide strategic planners with an intelligent query mechanism that appears to understand their problems and allows the users to converse with the query component in a manner that is natural to their tasks and work styles.

Expert system technology can be applied to the decision model tools component to provide a natural-language interface and to extend the functionality of the component. The resulting component would provide strategic managers with the ability to communicate with the components in a more natural manner. The exchange between user and machine would be based on the user's natural language instead of the machine's language. The exchange could also include jargon and concepts like uncertainty that are germaine to the tasks of strategic planners and decision makers.

The architecture of a decision support system enhanced through the integration of expert system technology in some of the DSS components is presented in Figure 4.2. This enhanced DSS would be easier for the intended users

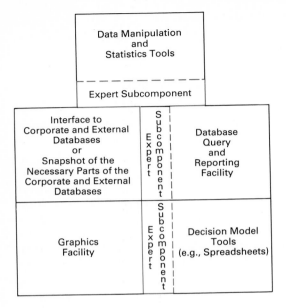

Figure 4.2 An enhanced decision support system architecture

to use, with little need for assistance from technical, computer-system-trained personnel. The opportunity exists, however, to integrate expert system technology into this architecture to produce a DSS that presents a more unified user-system interface.

Expert system technology could be the basis for the development of new DSS components. One new component could be the decision support system interface for the top-level management user. This user-system interface could help the user employ the DSS effectively. The user could start all dialogues with the DSS through this new knowledge-based user-system interface. The user could begin a dialogue by identifying the goal of the particular session. The system could then suggest which knowledge, information, and analysis techniques it has access to and is able to use to move toward the user's goal. The system could ask for agreement. The user would have the choice of agreeing with the system's suggestion or offering alternatives. Through an interchange, an agreement would be developed. The system could then suggest a plan of action and ask for user confirmation. Any time the user suggests something that is in conflict with the system's knowledge, the system would so inform the user. An example might be a user request for the median value of a database field that does not exist in the database. The system would inform the user of this fact and would offer the user an alternative. This would be possible if the user's goal is well related to this request. If it is not, the system could query the user for the subgoal the user is seeking that is to be supported by the answer to the query. With this subgoal information, the system should then be able to suggest alternatives. The system is designed to help the user progress to the user's intended goal, without requiring computer technicians. The system is adaptive; it will not stop supporting the user because the user requested incorrect or unavailable information. Instead, the system provides the user with alternatives that might move the user closer to the intended goal.

The user plus system team would thereby choose strategic-planning and decision-making knowledge, information, and analysis tool resources and formulate a plan of action. At the request of the user, the system would proceed to act on the plan. The user would not necessarily be involved with the work. If the system required assistance at an intermediate step, it could query the user for specific information.

This extended DSS architecture continues to provide the facilities usually identified with DSS. It also provides an interface that is tailored to the intended user and is therefore more understandable and usable. Figure 4.3 portrays a DSS architecture that reflects this enhanced, unified user-system interface.

Another possible approach in integrating expert system technology into the decision support system concept is to develop a new DSS architecture class based on the expert system architecture. This new DSS architecture should not be considered a replacement for the current DSS architectures but rather as an

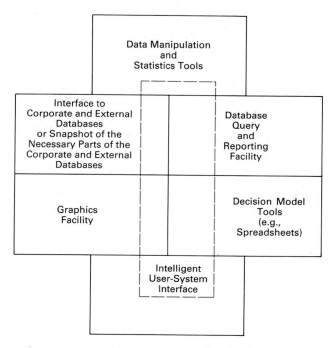

Figure 4.3　An extended decision support system architecture

alternative architecture that might provide more effective support for certain strategic-planning and decision-making tasks. A DSS that is based on an expert system architecture would contain objects in its knowledge-base like these:

- Facts about the organization (for example, "The average general and administrative cost factor assessed on our products by our firm is 14 percent of our production costs for our products.")
- Facts pertinent to the decision-making process from sources external to the organization ("The industry average general and administrative cost factor assessed on products in our industry is 12 percent of the production costs.")
- Rules to help guide strategic planning and decision making ("If any of our cost items is greater than the industry average for that particular cost item, investigate methods to reduce the cost item.")

An expert-system-based DSS could derive its knowledge from the organization's business experts like the chief operational officer and the chief financial officer. The knowledge base could be updated as new business knowledge is gained by the organization from various sources, including business experience and consultants. This DSS form should be helpful in supporting strategic-planning and decision-making tasks where there are business heuristics but no hard data.

The fourth opportunity for expert system technology to enhance the decision support concept is to develop automated strategic-planning and decision-making assistants. These assistants would derive their knowledge from particular business experts in the organization, consisting of the following:

1. Business knowledge and heuristics
2. Organizational knowledge and heuristics
3. Personal knowledge and heuristics

The resulting expert-system-based decision assistants would reflect business norms as represented in the business knowledge and heuristics and would reflect the organizational plans and procedures that are codified in the knowledge-bases derived from organizational knowledge and heuristics. These assistants would also emulate the experts' methods of problem resolution because the experts' personal knowledge and heuristics have been captured in the knowledge-bases of these assistants. These assistants could be used by other employees in the particular business areas. Although these employees do not have the expertise of the experts, the automated assistants could provide the expertise required to perform the necessary tasks. Because the assistants' knowledge-bases include personal knowledge and heuristics of the experts, the decisions made by the human-employee-plus-automated-assistant team could closely approximate the decisions that would have been made by the experts themselves. These systems should be helpful when human experts are unavailable.

There are other areas in a business enterprise where experts might not be always available when they are needed. In some of these areas, expert systems might be appropriate. Process control is a good candidate for expert system support for this reason.

INTEGRATION OF EXPERT SYSTEMS WITH PROCESS CONTROL

Traditional automated process control systems receive real-world status information from sensors integrated into the machinery that is performing the process. These automated systems guide the machinery through its processes through the activation and deactivation of controller devices that are capable of receiving digital control signals. Automated process control systems use the real-time status information and internal algorithms to calculate appropriate control signals that provide feedback to the machinery. Figure 4.4 illustrates a conventional process control system.

The sensor data plus the control algorithms are used by the process control computer to calculate the appropriate feedback data. As the machinery progresses through its process, the process status is constantly being monitored by the process control system. Any time sensor data indicates that something is out of tolerance, the process control computer will send feedback control data to a controller in an attempt to return the process to the desired operating range. This type of operation is often known as event-driven control. Process events

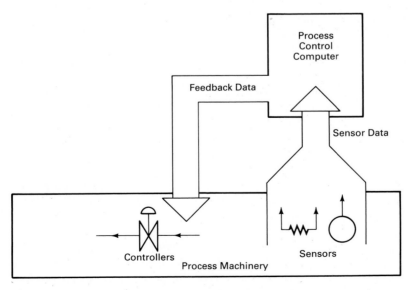

Figure 4.4   A conventional process control system

(for example, if the temperature of the cooling water goes above a predefined limit) stimulate actions (an increase in the cooling water flow rate).

Another type of control operation involves the stimulation of control actions at predefined times or intervals. In this case, the process control computer uses timing data plus its internal process control algorithms to calculate the appropriate feedback control signals.

The integration of expert system technology with automated process control systems can occur at two levels. The first level of integration would involve the use of an expert system to monitor the process and provide advice to the human supervisor. The second level of integration would involve the use of the expert process control system to monitor the process, provide advice, and act on the advice. The human supervisor would be informed of the actions the expert system is taking. The supervisor would have the option to query the system as to why it is doing something and, if necessary, override the expert system's commands. In times of operator fatigue or absence, the expert process control system would be able to keep the process going and provide the required monitoring and control supervision.

The first level of integration of expert system technology with automated process control systems involves the passive monitoring of the sensor and feedback data. The expert assistant system could interpret the data and provide advice to the human supervisor. Figure 4.5 shows how the expert assistant system would be integrated with the process control system.

The expert assistant would be able to provide process status information to

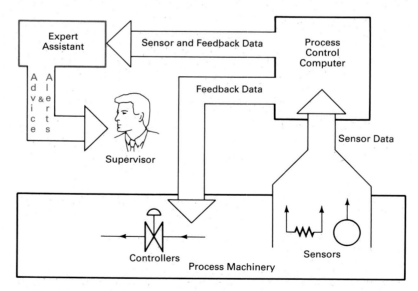

Figure 4.5   A process control system integrated with an expert assistant

the human supervisor upon request. Intermediate process status information can be very helpful. Many traditional process control systems are not capable of providing this intermediate information upon request.

Many process control systems operate around the clock, 365 days a year. Some of these processes must be monitored continuously for safety reasons. The operation of nuclear power plants and chemical processing plants are two examples. This monitoring function can become tiring and monotonous for human process supervisors. It is difficult for human operations supervisors to maintain peak observational alertness. When peak alertness is lost, there is the possibility of a problem situation going unnoticed, risking danger or expense. An expert process control assistant would be of help in such situations. The expert assistant could maintain constant alertness while monitoring the ongoing process. Any problems sensed could be brought to the attention of the human supervisor through an appropriate alert mechanism. Several alert mechanisms could be built into the system. They could alert different people with varying degrees of urgency.

Expert process control assistants could provide two additional services, problem prediction and training. Expert assistants could contain knowledge about the process and machinery design and history, including operational parameter limitations and maintenance history. This knowledge could be used together with the current status information to predict potential problems with the process and equipment. Predicted problems could be brought to the attention of the human supervisor for further consideration.

Expert process control systems could be designed to provide realistic training for new operators and recertification for experienced operators. The training component of the system could be designed to gather live operational data that could be replayed for a trainee on request at some future time. The training component could then use its knowledge and stored operational data to provide trainees with realistic training sessions and helpful responses to questions. The training component could be designed to run concurrently with the operational system or in a stand-alone configuration.

The second level of integration of expert system technology with automated process control systems would involve the passive monitoring of the sensor and feedback data from the machinery and the process control computer and the active development and transmission of feedback control data from the expert process control system. This second category of feedback data would be developed by the expert control system and sent to the process machinery and to the human supervisor. This feedback data would be developed in response to predicted problems or out-of-tolerance situations that are based on heuristics instead of specific data values and algorithms. This level of integration would also be able to provide all the services mentioned for the first level of integration. Figure 4.6 shows an expert process control system integrated within a process control system.

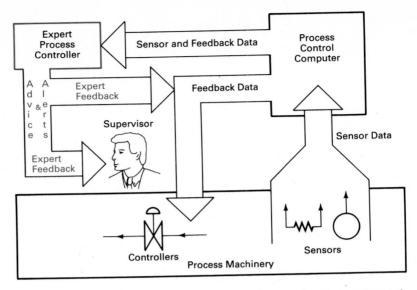

Figure 4.6 An expert process control system integrated with an automated process control system

INTEGRATION OF EXPERT SYSTEMS WITH OFFICE AUTOMATION

Office automation is an attempt to provide automated support tools to the business office environment. Some of the work performed in these office environments tends to be unstructured. It is often difficult to employ strict data formats and computational algorithms in this work. Office workers are often confronted with problems to work on for which there are no predefined solutions. Because of these facts, present office automation (OA) systems have met with only limited success. OA is a prime candidate for expert system technology support.

Among the potential OA application areas that could benefit from expert system technology are two that have already shown promise and could be considered excellent candidates:

1. Mail and message routing
2. Records management and office information retrieval

In many organizations, mail and telex messages are brought to a central location, often the organization's mail room. The mail room personnel are responsible for the proper and timely routing of this material. Often mail and messages arrive at this central location with insufficient address information to make a proper determination of the intended receiver and urgency. The mail room personnel then have to decide who in the organization should see the material for action and for information. The mail room personnel also have to decide how quickly to deliver the material to the chosen receivers. Selecting the correct people to see the material is important to assure that the organization operates properly from the point of view of effective communication. Determining urgency is also important. Delivering the material late could potentially hurt the organization. If the material is a request for a contract with a time limit for response, for example, the organization might lose the opportunity for the contract. By contrast, if nonurgent material is delivered quickly, its transmission cost the organization more than was necessary.

The tendency in many mail rooms is to send the material to all potential addressees and to deliver it all with some sense of urgency. This way the mail room personnel cannot be accused of laxness. The problem with this approach should be obvious: Too much material reaches too many people at too high a cost.

An expert system could be developed for the mail room that could help with making routing decisions. This routing assistant could potentially reduce both the number of people each piece of correspondence is sent to and the urgency of transmission of routine correspondence. This support could translate into lower operating costs. This support could also mean giving important, already overworked personnel less material through which to sort.

Office automation has provided office personnel with the ability to create, access, and store business records. Traditionally, records management, the handling of all the organization's records, was performed by a records management team, and anyone else desiring access to the records had to go through a member of this team, which provided access control, locatability, auditability, and record consistency. However, this system was associated with some operational problems, such as extreme reliance on the record management team and slow response times. OA has rectified some of these operational problems, but it has also introduced some new problems. Auditing and controlling the organization's records can be more difficult with OA facilities.

OA has made it easier to create information packets and records. This ability to create records more easily and more quickly often leads to more records being generated. The greater volume of records then becomes a management and retrieval problem. An expert system could be built to provide support to the records management team as well as to legitimate users of the corporate records and other organizational information repositories. The system could be designed to control the records and information resources and to assist users in the performance of the following tasks:

1. Define users' information needs

2. Where available, select the appropriate information sources, formulate the information search, and locate and access the correct records or files

3. Where unavailable, create, index, and store the necessary information

This expert system could also be used as a training tool. When new employees join the organization, they could use the system to learn what information is relevant to their tasks, what relevant information is available, and how to access it. With this assistance, the new hires could become more effective more quickly and would tend not to redevelop information resources that already exist in the organization.

REFERENCES

1. C. V. Negoita, *Expert Systems and Fuzzy Systems* (Menlo Park, CA: Benjamin/Cummings, 1985).

2. W. Reitman, *Artificial Intelligence Applications for Business* (Norwood, NJ: Ablex, 1984).

PART **II** THE CONSTRUCTION OF EXPERT SYSTEMS

5 VERIFYING SUITABILITY OF TASKS FOR EXPERT SYSTEM SUPPORT

INTRODUCTION It is important to select a domain or problem that is suitable for expert system support. This way, the technology will be properly applied, and the organization developing the system will realize its expected benefits. Figure 5.1 summarizes the task attributes that should be considered.

AN EXPERT MUST BE AVAILABLE To be able to construct an expert system, a human expert must be available. This domain expert should be acknowledged as proficient in the performance of the task that the expert system is to do.

The capability of an expert system built on the expertise of a human expert is limited by the expert's knowledge and expertise and the knowledge engineer's ability to elicit and represent them.

The expert must be able to articulate his or her knowledge and expertise and explain how to apply them to typical problems.

The first step in developing an expert system is to identify the problem to be supported or solved and define its characteristics. A knowledge engineer will work with the domain expert to identify and document the problem.

The knowledge engineer and the expert will look for rules and concepts on which the domain knowledge can be represented. Most of that knowledge will come from the human expert. However, certain fundamental knowledge of the domain may be garnered from books and journals. During this initial work, the knowledge engineer will be looking for a great number of things, these among them:

1. Key concepts about the domain
2. Objects that are important to the domain

3. Rules that seem to govern the domain's objects
4. Relationships among the domain's objects
5. Data and information flow characteristics
6. Processes that are involved with finding solutions
7. Constraints that affect the processes
8. Strategies used by the expert in solving problems

Suitable

- The proposed expert system will save time or money or will enable a task to be performed in a substantially better way; the expert system will truly make a difference to the organization.

- The development costs are such that there will be a substantial return on investment.

- An expert is available.

- Nonexperts require the expertise.

- The task can be fully described with facts, rules, and algorithms.

- The task can be accomplished without the use of common sense, or else the user will easily be able to provide the common sense when working with the computerized knowledge.

- The expertise to be modeled is narrowly focused.

- The time required to perform the task is between a few minutes and a few days.

- The task may have a logical complexity such that no single human expert could perform it without help from computers or manuals.

Not Suitable

- The task is based on hard-to-define knowledge, common sense, or intuition.

- The actions of the expert may require human skills that are difficult to computerize.

- An expert could not describe in detail *over the telephone* how he performs the task (the telephone test).

- The task is performed by most people.

- It is unclear whether the intended users would employ the system.

Figure 5.1   Characteristics of tasks suitable for expert system development

Identification and conceptualization of the domain knowledge are among the tasks performed during the initial stages of expert system development and continue during the knowledge acquisition activities. Without a domain expert, this work would not be possible.

A human expert is a prerequisite resource for the successful development of an expert system. This expert must be available to the knowledge engineer during the majority of the development period.

NONEXPERTS REQUIRE EXPERTISE

One reason organizations are building expert systems is to distribute the knowledge and expertise of their experts to other workers. The organizations' experts are demonstrably more effective in performing their tasks than other individuals. What sets the experts apart is their knowledge and expertise. Many organizations hope that by distributing their experts' knowledge and expertise to the other workers, the others will be more effective in the performance of their work. Expert system technology is the first technology that permits organizations to automate and distribute the expertise and knowledge of their experts.

One trend in our modern society has been the specialization of the work force. Job specialization has occurred in most work areas, including management, research, and production. The result of job specialization is that many organizations have many single-subject experts. Often there is only one person in an organization who can effectively solve a given problem. Developing expert systems to distribute the expertise of the organization's experts allows more of its people to solve more of its problems. This makes the organization less dependent on particular people and makes the overall work force more effective.

The products being developed by many organizations today are complex. This complexity has led to difficulties in operations and maintenance. Experts in organizations design these complex products. These experts, or other experts in organizations, learn how to operate and maintain these products. Once a product becomes popular in the marketplace, more and more people normally become involved in its operation and maintenance. If only a few experts can operate or maintain a product because of its complexity, its sales potential is limited. Through the development and use of expert systems, organizations should be able to distribute the knowledge and expertise required to operate and maintain complex products. Expert systems should be capable of making possible the distribution of important, specific operational and maintenance expertise to nonexpert-level workers so that more workers are capable of operating and maintaining these complex products.

An integral part in the issue of transferring knowledge and expertise is training. Where nonexperts require the knowledge of experts, some training mechanism must be put in place. A task suitable to being supported by an expert system needs to be teachable. Tasks that have been successfully supported with expert systems are often tasks wherein experts routinely teach neophytes the necessary knowledge and expertise for performance at acceptable levels. A notable example of such tasks are found in the manufacturing field. Examples of such expert systems include COOKER ADVISOR, WELD SELECTOR, and DUSTPRO.

Automated machinery and systems are becoming more and more prevalent in modern society. Some of these automated machines, such as automated bank teller machines, are accepted substitutes for human workers. It has become commonplace to trust automatic transaction machines (ATMs), as they are called, to perform such important financial transactions as funds withdrawal and deposit.

Some machines and systems have been developed with the ability to operate autonomously because it was not practical or possible to involve a human operator. An example of this is a probe to be sent into deep space. Machines like space probes require some knowledge of their operations to perform their missions. Expert systems are thus being developed to transfer human expertise not only to other humans but to machines like space probes and automobiles as well.

THE TASK IS COGNITIVE

A task that is cognitive is based on empirical knowledge. Empirical knowledge is a collection of facts that are based on experience. If the knowledge required to perform a task is a collection of facts that are based on experience, most likely the task can be well supported by an expert system. An expert drilling supervisor knows what procedures to follow to release a stuck oil-drilling bit under particular conditions and situations. The supervisor knows these procedures because he or she designed and attempted them successfully in the past under similar conditions. The expert has the ability to correlate the episodes, past and present, and apply the necessary procedures.

If the knowledge required to perform a task is based on natural laws, systems dynamics, mathematical theories, or the like, the task is better supported by more classical computer programming methods. A numeric integration task or a task to calculate the balance of a receivable account would be better supported by classical computer programming. (If the task requires mainly common sense, neither expert system technology nor classical computer programming methods are appropriate. More discussion on this will follow.)

If the full range of information needed to perform a task is primarily based on experience, the task should be supportable with expert system technology.

It is possible to integrate expert system technology with other computer-based technologies. For example, if a task is chiefly cognitive but also requires a few algorithmic calculations, an expert system could be developed to support the task. The expert system would use a programming technique to call up a program to perform the required calculations.

Expert systems manipulate symbolic knowledge. As an example, look at Figure 5.2. The rules in this figure might be part of the knowledge base of an expert system that diagnoses problems with a particular power supply product. These rules are made up of symbols. Some of the symbols, such as IF, have special meaning to expert system control mechanisms. These special symbols delimit other symbols in the rules and provide an indication as to their use. The nonspecial symbols are designed by the knowledge engineer. They are designed to represent some piece of knowledge, for example, "The power supply is plugged into a 110-volt power source." What is between the quotation marks is a symbol, manipulated by the expert system; it is also a readable fact, a piece of knowledge that is represented symbolically.

A diagnostic system like this would start by asking the user what the observed problem is. The system might be designed to have the user select the observed problem from a list of possible problems; an example of such a menu is presented in Figure 5.3.

If the user responded with "2", the system would ask the user if the green input LED is lit. If the user responded with "yes", the system would inform

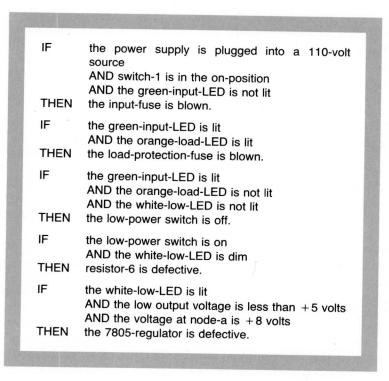

IF   the power supply is plugged into a 110-volt source
          AND switch-1 is in the on-position
          AND the green-input-LED is not lit
THEN   the input-fuse is blown.

IF   the green-input-LED is lit
          AND the orange-load-LED is lit
THEN   the load-protection-fuse is blown.

IF   the green-input-LED is lit
          AND the orange-load-LED is not lit
          AND the white-low-LED is not lit
THEN   the low-power switch is off.

IF   the low-power switch is on
          AND the white-low-LED is dim
THEN   resistor-6 is defective.

IF   the white-low-LED is lit
          AND the low output voltage is less than +5 volts
          AND the voltage at node-a is +8 volts
THEN   the 7805-regulator is defective.

Figure 5.2 Rules from the knowledge base of a power supply diagnostics expert system

What is the observed problem with the N-5557C power supply?

1. Green input LED is not lit.
2. Orange load LED is lit.
3. White low LED is not lit.
4. White low LED is dim.
5. The low output voltage is less than +5 volts.

Figure 5.3   Observed problem selection menu

the user that the load protection fuse is blown. The system was able to develop this response through the use of its inference logic and the manipulation of the symbolically represented knowledge.

For a task to be suitable for expert system support, the task should be cognitive. The knowledge required to perform the work is a collection of facts that are based on experiences. It is also important that it be possible to represent these facts in some symbolic fashion to permit logical manipulation of this symbolic knowledge.

THE TASK MUST NOT REQUIRE COMMON SENSE

Webster's defines *common sense* as sound and prudent but often unsophisticated judgment and the unreflective opinions of ordinary men. Common sense intuitively includes qualities like good judgment and practical understanding. In matters of common sense, it seems that the learned and the unlearned, the philosopher, and the ordinary laborer, the old and the young, and the profoundest thinker and the emptiest talker are on the same level.

Common sense is one quality of human intellect. In the actual perception of a normal, unsophisticated man or woman (as well as of a normal, sophisticated man or woman), the sensations of common sense carry beliefs in corresponding qualities and attach appropriate relationships to worldly objects.

When people are performing a task, they first try to apply their expertise, that is, their skills and know-how. When the task at hand requires knowledge beyond a person's expertise, the person will attempt to draw on generally known factual knowledge, on the discontinuous collection of specific knowledge that the person has collected through the years, and on common sense.

Attempts to codify expertise have been successful. The codification of generally known factual knowledge is also possible, although the magnitude of generally known knowledge data available in the world could easily overwhelm even the largest expert system thus far constructed. The key here is to include only the factual knowledge needed for a particular application. Discontinuous collections of specific knowledge are composed of bits and pieces of expertise from many subjects. This knowledge can also be codified, although its use by a single expert system might not be very effective.

Attempts at codifying common sense using expert system technology techniques have not been successful so far. Common sense seems to be based on the use of a kind of knowledge that requires more concentration and reasoning than collections of knowledge elements. The present state-of-the-art expert system technology techniques rely more on collections of knowledge elements than on reasoning mechanisms. The inference mechanisms of today's expert system are still very elementary.

It might be possible to represent common sense through a collection of knowledge elements, but it would most likely take a very large collection of very dense knowledge. This requirement could not be easily met with today's expert system technology.

It might seem ironic that we can represent and automate human expertise but cannot do the same for common sense. Expert system technology can represent and automate expertise. Common sense is based more on reasoning than on experiential knowledge. It appears, for the time being, that the representation and automation requirements of common sense are beyond the capabilities of present expert system technology.

The good news is that common sense is in abundant supply, and the reasoning required is easy for humans. Neither is true of the knowledge of many important experts. Thus our more urgent need is to capture, retain, and distribute certain specific knowledge of our experts. Expert system technology is supportive of these needs.

THE FOCUS OF THE EXPERTISE IS NARROW

Expert systems derive their power from subject domain knowledge that is specific to the task at hand. The more powerful or capable an expert system must be for a given application, the more domain-specific knowledge must be added to the expert system's knowledge-base. In other words, for all cases to be covered, knowledge about each case must be represented and stored in the knowledge-base. The larger the focus or scope of the task that an expert system must manage, the more knowledge must be present in the knowledge base to support the task.

Present expert system technology limits the amount of knowledge that an expert system can represent, store, and manipulate. Also, the inference mechanisms of today's expert systems are not very powerful; the logic and control mechanisms of expert systems cannot pick up any slack left by the absence of domain knowledge.

To support a task effectively with an expert system that is based on today's technology and capabilities, the expertise to be modeled should be narrowly focused to assure that the system will perform adequately.

It is preferable that the expertise modeled in the knowledge-base of one expert system come from one subject area or one field of expertise. This is not absolutely necessary, however; it just makes system development easier. Expert systems have been developed for the express purpose of integrating related expertise from several subject domains.

If a task can be accomplished effectively by most people or by a large group of people, it is most likely not a good candidate for expert system support.

Tasks that are based on broad, hard-to-define knowledge are not good candidates for expert system support either.

If the task is supported by a human expert, there is a good chance that it is of narrow focus. Important tasks that can be performed well only by experts tend to be well bounded and narrowly focused. Such tasks are well suited to expert system implementation.

THE TIME REQUIRED IS UNDER ONE WEEK

The amount of time it takes the human expert to perform the task that you want an expert system to support should be somewhere between a few minutes and a few days.

If a problem can be resolved in less than a few minutes, the task can most likely be handled more efficiently without using an expert system. Manual methods can handle many different types of very small problems.

A placard could be posted near or on equipment that gives expert advice to equipment operators. Many important placards are posted in airplane cockpits. Although pilots know how to fly airplanes, they can still be assisted by placards that point out important operational characteristics of a particular airplane. These placards often present important expert-level information and knowledge about the operating characteristics of aircraft (see Figure 5.4). Some placards present expert opinions as to how to handle emergency situations in the aircraft. As long as the problems that require placards are few and the amount

When flying in clouds, fog, or haze
or when in close proximity to the ground,
TURN OFF POSITION STROBE LIGHTS.

Figure 5.4 An aircraft placard

of information to be presented for each problem is small, placards effectively handle the need.

Another manual technique for presenting expert advice without an expert system is a checklist. Checklists can be used to assist machine operators in starting, operating, and stopping the machinery and handling problems. As long as the number of alternatives and the amount of information to be presented for each alternative are relatively small, checklists can be effective. With more information, technical manuals, training, or expert systems might be better alternatives. If factors such as fast problem resolution and low training requirements are desired, expert system technology might be the best alternative.

If a task requires an expert's attention for more than a few days, it could be too large for an expert system, given the present state of the art. Research and development continue apace, however; it is quite probable that this limitation will change in the future. If an expert would require more than a few days, the amount of expertise required, and possibly the logic and inferencing required to formulate an answer or solution, is beyond the capabilities of today's expert system technology.

However, there is even hope for the use of expert systems for many of these large tasks by applying the tactics of a famous military strategist: "Divide and conquer!" With some analysis, many of the tasks that take an expert more than a few days to complete can be divided into separate, logical subtasks. Then each difficult task that normally would still require the assistance of an expert would be a candidate for expert system support. The resulting expert systems could then be run individually. There is also supporting research in the area of cooperation among expert systems. This research is showing that it is possible to have several expert systems cooperate toward a common goal. Therefore, it might be possible to take a very large task, divide it up, develop an expert system to perform each specific subtask, and then have these systems cooperate in the fulfillment of the original goal of the original task.

RULE ORIENTATION IS HELPFUL

Present expert systems employ four schemes for representing knowledge: rules, frames, first-order logic, and semantic networks. These are explained in chapter 10. Most expert system shell products on the market employ one of the first three schemes or a combination of them. The semantic network scheme has not been used very much in commercial shell products.

Rule-based systems predominate. Even shells and systems that are based on the frames or logic knowledge representation schemes often employ rule structuring in their knowledge bases. Many frame-based systems, such as CENTAUR, represent important parts of the domain knowledge with rules. The rules are contained in frame slots in the knowledge base. Many logic-based shells, such as ES/P Advisor, use the rule knowledge representation scheme very effectively. Knowledge that is represented with semantic networks can often be translated into a rule representation scheme. This is not to suggest that this should be done; it is only to help to point out that almost any piece of human knowledge that can be effectively represented in an expert system knowledge base by using one of the presently available knowledge representation schemes can also be represented with the rule-based knowledge representation scheme.

If the domain to be supported is based on rules, regulations, instructions, or procedures, expert system technology will most likely be able to provide an effective tool. Examples include the accounting domain (generally accepted accounting practices), standard operating procedures, and government regulations like taxation.

It is helpful when the knowledge to be represented can be represented in the form of rules. With the current state of the technology, rule-based knowledge-bases provide many desirable benefits. For example, when knowledge is represented in the form of rules in the knowledge-base, the knowledge-base data is readable and understandable by people who are familiar with and conversant in the subject. Computer literacy or expert system technology knowledge is not required to be able to read and comprehend the content of the knowledge-base.

Rule-based knowledge-bases tend to be simple, flexible, and composed of discrete elements. The rule knowledge representation scheme provides a powerful yet simple tool for representing human expertise.

If the subject domain is rule-oriented, it should be suitable for expert system support. If the domain is not rule-oriented, it will have to be analyzed further to see if it is suitable for expert system support through the use of one of the other knowledge representation schemes.

RETURN ON INVESTMENT SHOULD BE SIGNIFICANT

The first useful expert systems were very expensive to develop. These systems were built without the aid of the experiential knowledge, shell, and other expert system development tools that are available today. The development of the first expert systems included the design and development of the inference engine, the user-system interface, and the knowledge-base. Knowledge was acquired and manually entered in the knowledge-base without the aid of a knowledge acquisition subsystem. This was a very labor-intensive process and therefore a very expensive one.

The first expert systems were developed on powerful minicomputers and small mainframe computers. These computing resources were expensive. It was assumed at the time that all meaningful expert system implementations required such computing resources, regardless of the application. The only exception was expert system technology instruction.

Early textbooks written about expert systems warned that because the investment in the development of an expert system is very high, only domains and applications that have very high payoffs are suitable for expert system support.

Expert system shells and tools are now available that should aid in the development of expert systems. Some are available on large minicomputers, mainframes, and small, cost-efficient minicomputers as well as some of the larger microcomputers and personal computers. There now exists a body of experiential knowledge in the development of expert systems. A lot of this knowledge is available in textbooks, magazines, and journals. This information should be helpful to people who are building their first expert system. Future expert system developments should be possible at much less cost than the earlier systems.

Expert systems are still new and often must prove their value before organizations are willing to invest in them. It is recommended that a main criterion of the first expert system development for any particular organization be that the resulting expert system will truly make a difference. The organization should be able to see the return on its investment. This advice is not unique to expert system technology; however, it does apply and should be considered. The value of an expert system to an organization might be evidenced in the reduced cost of some operation. The organization might also gain value from an expert system from other business or operational factors. Examples include substituting for an unavailable expert and the ability to let nonexpert-level workers perform tasks that normally require the expertise of experts.

The smallest, simplest expert systems will most likely be rule-based, incorporating perhaps 50 or so rules in the knowledge-base. These systems will be developed with the aid of an expert system shell that runs on a personal computer. The shell will provide knowledge acquisition and explanation facilities. These systems will take approximately two to three months to build. The project will require one knowledge engineer full time plus the time of the domain expert. This time includes all of the development activities from problem identification to testing and delivery.

The largest expert systems will use more than one knowledge representation scheme. The knowledge-base will be large. These systems will be developed with the aid of an expert system shell and additional development tools. The shell and tools will run on mainframes or large AI computers. AI computer architecture will be designed with symbolic processing in mind. The shell will provide knowledge acquisition, explanation, and powerful user-system communication facilities. These large systems will take one to three years to build. The project will make use of numerous knowledge engineers and domain experts during its development.

The value returned to the organization should be proportional to the initial investment. If a small expert system is built, the return can be modest yet still be worthwhile. When large expert systems are built, the return is expected to be large. For large expert system projects, it is proper to make sure that the domain or problem will provide a large payoff.

6 BUILDING EXPERT SYSTEMS

**DIFFERENCES
BETWEEN
BUILDING
CONVENTIONAL
AND EXPERT
SYSTEMS**

The construction of expert systems is similar to the construction of other computer software systems, however, there are some important differences.

The construction techniques for computer applications can be placed on a continuum, as shown in Figure 6.1. On the leftmost end of the continuum is the construction technique that employs procedural languages like FORTRAN and COBOL and basic construction tools such as line editors and compilers. Here the data is explicitly specified and handled by the resultant programs. The programs specify exactly what is to be done to exactly what data in exactly what sequence. *Data and procedures are intertwined* in the program.

Moving to the right, the *procedures and data are separated*. The data is stored in databases. Data management tasks are performed by database management systems. A database management system is a software system that provides all requisite data management services. A DBMS can be home-grown; however, the industry norm is to purchase a DBMS product that appears to have all the functionality required. Database administrators specify data representation, legal data usage, and the like via specialized data management tools. Separate from the data specification, a computer programmer writes a procedural program in a language such as COBOL that explicitly specifies what is to be done in what sequence. However, in this case, the programmer specifies the data by a name that the DBMS understands, and it is the job of the DBMS to provide the correct data to the program for processing. The data and procedures are separated; however, the specification of what data to use and exactly how to manipulate the data is still explicitly the task of the program developer.

Continuing along the continuum to the right, the use of fourth-generation languages with DBMS appears. Fourth-generation languages are partially

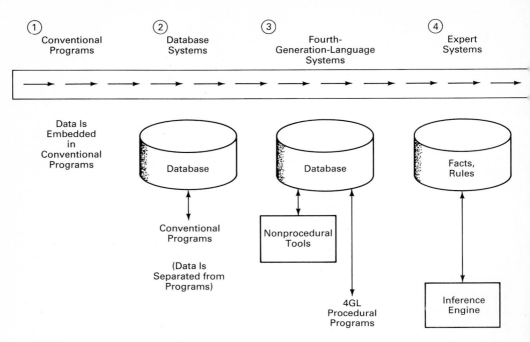

Figure 6.1 A continuum of system construction techniques, with much programming work on the left trending to absence of programming on the right.

nonprocedural, i.e., the developer does not have to specify the sequence in which the data is to be manipulated. Some fourth-generation languages do not require the developer to specify exactly how the data is to be manipulated. They allow the developer to specify the result that is required, and the software creates the code to achieve that result. The task of the application developer still requires some high-level programming.

Moving further to the right, we come to the development of expert systems. In developing an expert system, the specification of what data is to be manipulated and the specification of how the manipulation is to be accomplished are separated. The data is specified in the knowledge-base, and the procedural manipulations of the data are handled by the other system components. In developing expert systems, it is already an industry norm to purchase an expert system shell product and develop the particular expert application using the shell. Most shells provide complete inference and control mechanisms, knowledge-base management systems, user-system interfaces, and explanation facilities. Some shell products also include knowledge acquisition facilities. Therefore, the shell provides all of the manipulation logic. The only task left for the expert system developer is the development of the knowledge-base data. Subject domain expertise is applied to the empty knowledge-base of the expert system shell. The developer acquires the domain expertise data and provides it to the knowledge-base. The developer does not specify how this data is manipulated or what format the data must be in. The developer specifies only what the relevant domain data is.

The fact that the developer is required only to obtain subject domain data points to another difference in the development of an expert system: An expert system developer using an expert system development shell does not have to define any algorithms, procedures, or control structures. There is no need for flowcharts, pseudocode, or any other procedural code design tools. Process specification is one activity an expert system developer using a shell does not perform.

An expert system developer using a shell does not have to get involved in the specification of algorithms. However, an expert system developer must acquire, codify, and transfer subject expertise data. A traditional analyst-programmer would go to a user and ask questions like "What is the format of the input data?" and "What calculations do you want the program to perform?" An expert system builder or a knowledge engineer would go to a domain expert and ask questions like "How can you tell that a problem really exists?" and "What does a solution to the problem look like?" A traditional analyst-programmer uses well-known and established techniques to acquire and document process and data specifications. At the present stage of knowledge engineering, the acquisition and codification of knowledge is very much a trial-and-error affair. It will evolve into a more formal discipline as experience accumulates in constructing expert systems.

The development of expert systems follows the new knowledge engineering discipline. Most other computer software developments follow the software engineering discipline. Although both of these disciplines have as goals the development of computer software, they differ in the use of methodologies, techniques, and tools.

Software engineering uses well-defined methodologies and techniques like structured programming, top-down analysis, enterprise modeling, strategic information planning, data modeling, and action diagramming. These methodologies and techniques are supported by software engineering tools like IEW, IEF, and EXCELERATOR. Software engineering also uses related methodologies and techniques to assure the success of the software development effort. These methodologies include software project management, software metrics, performance measurement, software quality assurance, and software configuration management.

Knowledge engineering is a newer field than software engineering. Knowledge engineering does not yet include well-defined methodologies and techniques, although some have been suggested by people who have been working in this area. Knowledge engineering tools, beyond expert system shells and programming environments, are lacking. Although the shells and programming environments are very powerful, tools that provide better labor efficiencies in areas such as knowledge acquisition and knowledge data consistency are still needed. Tool development will be stimulated through industry acceptance of knowledge engineering methodologies and techniques.

The construction of an expert system is an incremental process. At any time during the construction process, the partially built system will function. The scope and capability of the system will be limited to the depth and breadth of the knowledge that has thus far been applied to the system's knowledge-base. But the system will run and will not come to an abnormal end (abend) when it encounters a case about which it has not yet been given knowledge data. Without any knowledge about the case, the system cannot offer any helpful advice, but it will not abend. This is in contrast with most other computer programs during the development stage. Unless stubs are developed for each unfinished logic area, most partially completed programs will not function, and if they start to function and hit an area where the logic has not yet been coded, they will usually abend without any warning or explanation. Because partially completed expert systems will run, developers can show the intended users the system while it is being developed. This provides the users with the opportunity to offer comments, suggestions, and feedback to the developer during the construction phase.

Most computer programs are designed to provide some specified service. Only the specified service is expected. The industry norm for expert systems has already been elevated to a point where users expect expert systems to provide the specified service (for example, advice) and also provide explanations and justifications to substantiate the proffered advice. Expert system technology lends itself nicely to providing this extra explanation service. However, this is different from most other software developments and must be taken into consideration when developing an expert system.

In a great many cases, completed expert systems are used in highly interactive modes with users. Although other computer programs are being developed with more user interaction, advice-giving expert systems often rely on the user-system interaction to find a solution to a given problem. Therefore, the quantity and quality of information available to the user interactively via the user-system interface is very important. This fact often makes the design and development of an expert system different from the development of other systems like payroll or accounts receivable systems.

Expert systems tend to be more transparent to the end user than most other software systems. By transparent we mean that the system is more understandable as it is in its finished, performing configuration. Expert systems should be designed so that the subject domain knowledge and the problem-solving knowledge are separated. Usually, *the subject domain knowledge is in an expert system's knowledge-base and the problem-solving knowledge is incorporated into the system's inference engine.* An end user will then be able to read through the subject knowledge without having also to view the expert system programming. This makes the system more transparent to the user. The user looks ''through the system'' and can concentrate on only the subject knowledge of interest. The user is not required to be computer-literate, with the possible exception of knowing how to turn the system on and get the expert system running. Computer systems that are custom-designed for end-user expert system work should be designed to enter the expert system of interest automatically when the electrical power is turned on. This way, the user would only have to know where the power switch is.

Expert system development should employ subject domain concepts and ideas directly in the system knowledge-base; this makes the system more understandable to the end user. The problem-solving strategy of the system should cause the system to operate in a manner that is natural to the user. The system's logic flow and the order in which it asks questions should be natural and logical to the end user. If the system's problem-solving strategy is natural to the user, the system will most likely be accepted more readily.

CONCEPTS THAT AFFECT DESIGN AND CONSTRUCTION

The concept of system transparency affects the design and construction of expert systems. If an expert system designer wishes to assure that the completed expert system is truly transparent to the intended user, it is important that the subject domain knowledge and the problem-solving knowledge be separate. For example, if an expert diagnostic system provides a user with the advice that part number 123 needs replacement, the user might want to know the confidence the system has in this advice. The system should be able to provide this information interactively in response to a simple query, and the response should be direct. The user wants to know the confidence factor of the advice; the system should not clutter the response with the calculation procedures used to derive the confidence factor. The confidence the system holds for the advice is information about the subject at hand. How the system calculated the confidence is problem-solving knowledge of less importance to the user.

A key expert system concept is that an expert system provides advice on a specific, well-defined subject. In most cases, for an expert system to support a task effectively, the term *well-defined* usually means ''narrowly defined'' or ''appropriately delimited.'' Contemporary expert systems succeed because they bring large amounts of pertinent knowledge to bear on well-defined problems. In designing an expert system, it is important to limit the subject of the expert system. If the problem is too large, the expert system might not succeed. If a subject domain to be supported by an expert system is large, the expert system designer should look for opportunities to divide and conquer—divide the subject into two or more separate subject areas and design a separate expert system for each. If the separate expert systems could benefit from interaction with other expert systems, there are some architectures that will support such interaction.

(One architectural concept for having expert systems cooperate on a problem is known as the *blackboard*. This concept will be discussed in more detail later.)

It is important to understand that for a subject to be well defined in the context of expert system design does not mean that the subject details are well understood and that the methods of arriving at a solution are well-known procedures. These would be the characteristics of a problem that contemporary data processing could support. Well-defined in this context means that the subject of the expert system being built is defined as narrowly as possible and still provides a valuable service. The subject of the expert system is limited to a specific, well-articulated problem. The method of solution need not be well understood; however, the method of solution must be describable. The domain expert will have to be able to tell the knowledge engineer what the problems are and how solutions are attained. The domain expert does not have to know how the problems developed, why the problems developed, or why the expert's solutions work. The expert needs only to be able to describe the problems as they would be observed by an expert system user and describe the solutions to the problems. No natural laws of physics or matter need be referenced. No algorithms need be used. Only the expert's heuristics, experience, and knowledge data are needed to develop an expert system. It is this data that the expert system designer must take into account.

Another expert system concept that affects design and construction activities is that expert systems attempt to use all relevant knowledge at each problem-solving step. Bringing as much of the domain knowledge to bear at each step as possible is, in part, where expert systems derive their problem-solving power. In order to do this, the design of an expert system must take two technical items into consideration. First, the subject domain knowledge must be represented in such a manner as to make available, at each problem-solving step, all the relevant domain knowledge. Second, the inference mechanism must be designed in such a manner that it can use all of the relevant knowledge.

During the above discussion about the differences between expert systems and most other software systems, the expert system concept of explanation was mentioned. This concept should be kept in mind when designing and building expert systems. A well-designed expert system should be able to explain and justify its line of reasoning and questioning and its advice. Explanations and justifications should be available to the user during and immediately after a consultation. Often the best solution is to include an explanation facility in the design of the system. This facility would communicate to the user through the user-system interface, utilize the knowledge-base for the knowledge it needed to provide the explanations and justifications, and use the inference engine to provide the problem-solving abilities it required to construct its explanations and justifications. In order to provide explanations and justifications, the explanation facility would have to keep track of the consultation session. The explanation facility needs to keep track of how the user and system got to where they are when the user asks for an explanation or justification. User responses and intermediate results must be temporarily saved. The explanation facility could include its own database for this purpose. However, a better design would place this information in a special part of the knowledge-base. This temporary knowledge data store is sometimes called working memory or the dynamic knowledge database.

A human expert is constantly upgrading his or her subject domain expertise through new experiences, the acquisition of new knowledge, and the self-development and self-discovery of new knowledge. For an expert system to continue to reflect abilities similar to those of the expert after whom the system was modeled, the expert system will also require the ability to acquire new knowledge. An effective way to handle this is to include a knowledge acquisition facility in the system's design. This facility would assist with the future transference of expert domain knowledge to the system's knowledge-base.

Some expert systems will operate as part of a totally automatic system. An example of such a system is an expert safety monitoring system for a large chemical processing plant. However, the majority of expert systems built or to be built in the near future will be consultation-type systems that will directly and extensively interface with one or more human users. Expert systems have inherited the concept of user friendliness from their artificial intelligence heritage. This concept conveys design heuristics like these: the system should be easy to use; the user should not be required to have a computer science degree or other formal computer-related training in order to use and benefit from the system; the system should act reasonably to user requests; the system should advise the user of improper requests; the system should work around minor user errors; the system should know something about the user's goals in using the system and assist the user in getting to those goals. This concept leads many expert system developers toward the development of sophisticated user-system interface modules that might include, for example, natural-language capabilities. Because of the intention of the expert system designer and developer to assist a user with a problem, it seems obvious that the expert system itself should not introduce the new problem of how to use and benefit from the expert system. The user-system interface should be an important consideration of expert system designers and developers.

Many expert systems are being developed to work on problems that other computer technologies have not been able to support adequately. Data that is available in some of these problem domains is uncertain, incomplete, or imprecise. For expert systems to be effective in these areas, the system designs must take these data attributes into account. Concepts like certainty factors and fuzzy logic need to be considered. Knowledge representation and inferencing techniques must be designed to handle these data attributes.

The use of certainty factors is one way to handle these knowledge data attributes. Certainty factors provide the expert system developer with a mechanism to represent the confidence the developer has in each piece of evidence the developer wishes to include in the knowledge base. The MYCIN expert system, for example, uses certainty factors from 0 to $+1$ to indicate how strongly facts

in the knowledge-base have been confirmed and uses certainty factors from 0 to
−1 to indicate how strongly facts have not been confirmed. Certainty factors
are not probability functions; they are measures of confidence or certainty.
MYCIN uses a certainty factor model to combine, blend, calculate, and propa-
gate certainty factors and to evaluate advice it offers. Figure 6.2 provides an
example of a MYCIN rule with a certainty factor. In this example, if the antecedents (the IF clauses) of this rule are true, then the evidence gathered provides
a 50 percent (.5) certainty that the consequent (the THEN clause) of this rule is
true for the case at hand.

In conventional data processing, it is expected that all of the requisite data
and information is available prior to running a particular computer program. It
makes no sense to reconcile general ledger accounts with incomplete data. Expert
systems, however, are usually designed with the ability to operate in situations
where some information or data is missing. Knowledge (for instance, rules in a
rule-based expert system) can be included in the knowledge-base to provide
guidance on what to do in cases where information is missing. Better yet, the
expert system's inference engine should be able to handle situations where information it is seeking is not available. For example, in the case of a rule-based
expert system, the inference engine should allow rules to fail where there is
insufficient information or data to evaluate the premises (the IF part) of the rules
without affecting the operation of the rest of the system. Alternatively, the inference engine should allow individual premise clauses to fail where they cannot
be evaluated, without affecting the evaluation of other premise clauses in the
premise (the IF part) of a particular rule. The system is only forced to seek its
knowledge elsewhere; the system's operation is not prematurely terminated. If
a rule or a premise clause of a rule fails for lack of complete information, the
system may or may not be able to reach a conclusion that it can offer a user as
advice. If a rule fails but a different rule applies that is not affected by the lack
of information (because it uses a different set of premises to reach its conclu-

IF
    1. the infection that requires therapy is meningitis, AND
    2. organisms were not seen on the stain of the culture, AND
    3. the type of infection is bacterial, AND
    4. the patient has been seriously burned,

THEN
    there is suggestive evidence (.5) that *Pseudomonas aeruginosa* is one
    of the organisms that might be causing the infection.

Figure 6.2   MYCIN expert system rule example

sion), the missing information does not affect the expert system's ability to offer advice to the user. If a premise clause fails but is logically connected to the other premise clauses by the logical OR and some or all of the other premise clauses can be evaluated, the failed premise clause will not affect the system's ability to reach a conclusion and thus will be able to provide advice to the user. Human experts must often provide advice on the basis of incomplete information; expert systems should be designed to do likewise.

The concept of fuzzy logic will assist expert system builders greatly in the handling of imprecise and inexact data as well as linguistic imprecision. Fuzzy logic quantifies the extent to which inexact concepts are satisfied. The concept of fuzzy logic, for instance, provides a mechanism to represent vagueness. Instead of using classical logic theory that permits a proposition to be either false or true, fuzzy logic allows propositions to be false, true, or true to some degree. The degree of truth would translate to the degree of membership in a particular fuzzy set. The truth values for this logic are the real numbers in the interval 0 through 1. This results in a multivalued logic. Let us look at the concept of being successful in business. When a person says that someone is successful, what does this mean? Many people would consider anyone with a net personal worth of half a million dollars successful. Similarly, many people would consider anyone with a net personal worth of $1000 unsuccessful. But how successful is successful? Figure 6.3 provides one possible answer to this question.

The term *successful* is vague. Figure 6.3 tries to convey a little more information about how to use the term. However, this additional information might still not help an expert system developer or knowledge engineer. Is $800,000 quite successful or successful? Figure 6.4 attempts to represent the concept of being successful through the assignment of real numbers between 0 and 1.

Now the concept "successful" is a little less vague. There is now a correspondence between an amount of net personal worth and a value in the interval between 0 and 1. The fuzzy set provides a subjective evaluation of the concept. If an expert system had to determine, as an intermediate step, if a

Net Personal Worth	Degree of Success
$5,000,000	Very successful
$1,000,000	Quite successful
$500,000	Successful
$100,000	Not so successful
$1,000	Not successful

Figure 6.3   How successful is successful?

Net Personal Worth	Degree of Success
$5,000,000	1.00
$1,000,000	0.75
$500,000	0.50
$100,000	0.25
$1,000	0.00

Figure 6.4   A fuzzy set for the concept "successful"

particular person with a net personal worth of $300,000 is successful, the system could assign a truth value of 0.38. Stated differently, a person with a net personal worth of $300,000 has a degree of membership of 0.38 in the successful fuzzy set.

Real-world properties like tall, short, successful, unsuccessful, warm weather, and cold weather are vague. However, through the use of fuzzy sets and the incorporation of fuzzy logic as an extension to the logic of expert system inference engines, expert systems will be able to represent and work with such vague properties.

ARCHITECTURAL ISSUES

The construction of an expert system includes the designing of the system's architecture. Many issues need to be addressed during this development stage. The goals of the system and the availability and capability of requisite technology need to be matched. An expert system designer must make sure that the system includes all of the required components so that the developed system will fulfill the goals that it is intended to meet. Therefore, system composition is an important issue.

Different expert system technologies seem to support certain classes of problems; therefore, the task the system is to support needs some consideration.

Finally, expert system technology is introducing new techniques, some of which will affect the way organizations do business. Therefore, there will sometimes be the need to consider organizational issues while designing expert systems.

The following are some of the questions that these issues raise. The first six deal with expert system component selection. These are the types of questions an expert system designer must address prior to selecting the components for a system. The seventh question deals with the task dependency issue and how it relates to the expert system architectural design activity. The final question raises the issue of organizational constraints that might affect the development of an expert system that is to support the organization. These, then, are some of the questions that an expert system designer should consider prior to the development of an architecture.

1. What is the system going to be used for?
2. What environment will the system operate in?
3. What computer hardware will the system be developed on?
4. What computer hardware will the system be run on?
5. Who are the ultimate users? What kind of support do they require?
6. Will knowledge acquisition occur during the operational phase? If so, who will enter the knowledge (the user, the expert, or a knowledge engineer)?
7. How are design issues affected by the type of task an expert system is going to do?
8. What organizational constraints might affect the expert system construction tasks?

Let's examine these questions and issues and see how they relate to the building of expert systems.

SELECTING REQUISITE COMPONENTS

If an expert system is being built to monitor and regulate a factory process in real time and the product of the expert system's processes are real-time inputs to the actual process, there is little or no need for a user-system interface or an explanation facility in the expert system's architecture. Instead, there is a requirement for a system-to-system interface between the expert system and the factory system.

If an expert system is being developed to assist a human user with a decision problem where ultimately the user must make the decision, there is a requirement for a well-designed user-system interface and an explanation facility that can provide the user with explanations for the questions the system asks and justifications for the recommendations it provides.

If an expert system is being developed to work on a very well-defined, very narrow subject, like the repair of a very small factory machine, the knowledge base will be small, perhaps only 50 to 100 rules. An expert system with a knowledge base of this size does not need a powerful knowledge database management system. A simple set of file algorithms can handle the knowledge data management requirement. However, if an expert system is being developed that will include a large set of knowledge data, perhaps incorporating a few thousand rules, a more powerful knowledge data management mechanism will be required. It is advisable in this case to use a separate, efficient knowledge data management component.

If an expert system is being developed for a problem where the knowledge of how to solve the problem is still unfolding, a knowledge acquisition facility will be needed. If the user will be adding the new knowledge to the system, possibly the user-system interface will have to service the user interface requirements of the knowledge acquisition facility. If the domain expert or a knowledge engineer will be adding the new knowledge, the knowledge acquisition facility will require its own user interface (the "user" in this case being the domain expert or the knowledge engineer).

Figures 6.5 and 6.6 graphically depict some of the concepts that have been presented in this discussion so far. Figure 6.5 presents a possible expert system architecture for an expert system that will monitor and regulate some factory process. Figure 6.6 depicts a representative expert system architecture for an expert decision assistant system. What is important to see here is that what an expert system is going to be used for can influence the system's architecture.

The environment an expert system is going to be working in is closely tied to the issue of what the system is going to be used for. This environment issue often serves to amplify architectural choices made from the utility issue. For example, look at Figure 6.7. The expert system is monitoring a manufacturing process and is adding additional regulation to the system as necessary. The expert system is monitoring the process and the automated process control system. While performing its monitoring function, it allows the feedback control data to pass through the expert system unchanged. The knowledge in the expert system's knowledge-base allows it to determine when the manufacturing process and the automated process control system together are getting the job done properly. However, if the expert system correlates a given situation with a known dangerous situation (from corporate experience knowledge that is stored in the expert system's knowledge-base), the expert system will modify the feedback data as necessary to assure that the dangerous situation does not develop.

This expert system is being used to monitor a manufacturing process and an automated process control system. If the expert system sees no problems with the process, it will do nothing. When it sees a problem, it will modify the feedback data to the manufacturing process. This system does not interact with a human user; therefore, there is little need for an explanation facility or a user-system interface. However, because the system is to interact with another sys-

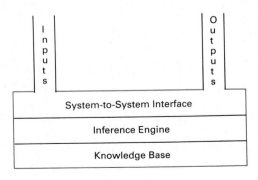

Figure 6.5   An expert factory process monitoring and regulating system

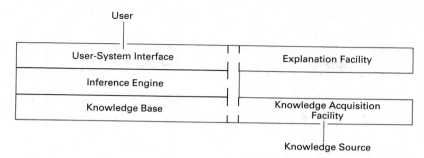

Figure 6.6   An expert decision assistant system

tem, the expert system will require a system-to-system interface. Because the system works with the knowledge it has, there is little need for a knowledge acquisition facility. An offline knowledge acquisition facility could be available to add and modify the knowledge-base when new knowledge is available. The environment in this case might include high data rates for the sensor and feedback data flows. The manufacturing environment might be caustic and corrosive or dirty or very warm. This kind of environment is not conducive to the operation of normal computer hardware. Computer hardware used must either be built into expensive protection shelters or be built to function in this environment, both expensive propositions. It is desirable to keep the size of the computing

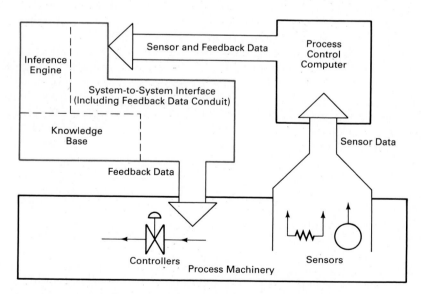

Figure 6.7   An expert monitoring and regulating system in a manufacturing process

machinery to a minimum in order to reduce the costs of introducing the computer hardware into the manufacturing environment. Therefore, the environment requires that the expert system reside in as small a computer system as possible while being able to monitor high data rates. This means that the expert system should have no extra code or components. Components that are not absolutely required must be left out of the architecture of the system that is to run in the actual manufacturing environment. Thus the system will not include a user-system interface, an explanation facility, or a knowledge acquisition facility. A system-to-system interface, however, will be included. This interface will accept sensor data that is passed through the process control computer as well as the feedback data that the process control computer develops. The interface will output unmodified or modified feedback data and provide this feedback control data to the manufacturing process. The resulting architecture will, therefore, include an inference engine, a knowledge-base, and a system-to-system interface. Other components necessary to develop and update the system (such as a knowledge acquisition facility) will be hosted on a different computer system, most likely one that is in a computer system development area.

What computer hardware an expert system is going to be developed on can affect the architecture of an expert system. What computer hardware an expert system is ultimately going to run on can also affect the architecture of the system. The example just given illustrated the second point.

If the development computer system includes a high-resolution, bit-mapped display, it would be nice to use such a tool to its greatest advantage. Both the knowledge acquisition facility and the user-system interface could be designed to take advantage of the display's capabilities. The knowledge acquisition facility, for example, could offer graphical displays of the knowledge in the knowledge-base. Graphical depictions of domain knowledge is often easier to navigate through than knowledge in text form. Graphics can be used either to augment text-based knowledge representation schemes or to replace the text-based approaches with graphics-based approaches like the one used in the IKE® expert system shell product by LMI. Graphics can also be used to augment model representations of the domain problem. LMI's PICON® Process Control Expert System shell product is a good example of this. Figure 6.8 is an example of a PICON display screen during the development of a process control expert system. This figure shows a partially developed rule (in the box in the center of the display) that is being created. Notice that an entity "FR2" is mentioned in the rule and is graphically represented as a component of a real-time process control system to the left of the rule. This upper window is showing part of the complete process; the window at the bottom of the screen is showing the complete process (including the same rule box). The window in the middle of the display is showing a list of words to choose from to continue the development of the rule. For example, it might be appropriate to choose the word *message*. The selected word would be added to the rule and a new list would be displayed. We will return to PICON later.

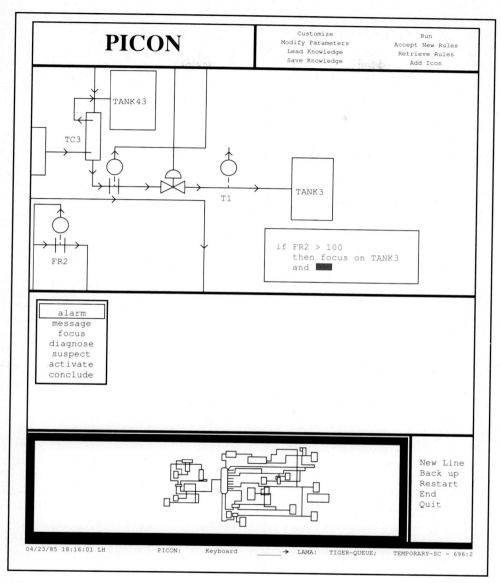

04/23/85 18:16:01 LH   PICON: Keyboard   ⟶ LAMA: TIGER-QUEUE;   TEMPORARY-SC - 696:2

Figure 6.8   Creating a rule using PICON®

Expert system components and shell products are sometimes written in languages that require the use of particular computer hardware. Certain commercial expert system shells require a LISP machine for both development and host computer systems, although this situation is changing. Many of the expert system shell vendors that require a LISP machine for development now support non-LISP-machine host computer systems. In addition, some of the LISP-machine-based expert system shell products are being rehosted onto other computer systems, meaning that the development computer system also need not be a LISP machine. However, if a particular expert system component or shell is available commercially but does not run on the hardware you are using and for some reason you do not wish to use the hardware the component or shell runs on, you will be forced to find another shell and not use that particular component or shell.

If the expert system is going to support a maintenance person in the field, it would be convenient for the expert system to be hosted in a small portable computer or a lap-top computer. If such a computer is used, care must be taken to assure that the expert system will function properly and that the response times are reasonable. The user-system interface should take this kind of hardware into consideration. For example, although many small portable computers do support graphics, the graphics are usually of a low resolution and are monochromatic.

If possible, the best way to start an expert system development project is to develop the system's requirements and goals, then decide which commercially available software tools will best meet the project's overall goals, and finally determine which computer hardware will best support the development and use of the system. This way, the system's architecture is less constrained by hardware limitations.

Hardware issues arise frequently in commercial projects. In real-time applications, the requirements and environment often limit the hardware choices. In the office environment, costs, budgets, and user acceptance are often involved. No matter how the hardware is chosen, the designer should make every possible effort to choose expert system components that use all the capabilities of the hardware efficiently. If, for example, a voice synthesis capability is present or possible, an expert system that is monitoring a real-time process might make use of this voice output capability to communicate warnings to human operators who are controlling the process. This would of course mean that the expert system's user-system interface would have to include or interface to a voice synthesis software component.

The ultimate users should be an important consideration during the design of an expert system. The kinds of support these users require should be studied. How the material is presented to them can make the difference between user acceptance and user rejection. The user-system interface design is crucial here. If an expert system asks questions at too high a comprehension level, the user will not be able to use the tool effectively. The knowledge incorporated in an expert system comes from a subject domain expert, often from within the organization. However, the ultimate users are less expert in the domain, often novices. The goal of the expert system is to help these novices complete some required task without the need of having the human expert present. The language usage in the user-system interface is important. Other communication techniques should be considered as well. Graphics and video media are beginning to provide users with very effective, alternative communication means. Figure 6.9 shows an effective application of graphics support to assist the user in understanding what the expert system wants the user to do, in this case, during the fact-finding phase of a system maintenance task. This figure is one of the screens of a microcomputer-based expert system known as the FMS Communications Diagnostic System developed at Texas Instruments.

Video media like video laser disks and computer controlled laser playback units are being used as audiovisual training aids. Some expert systems (for example, CATS-1 by General Electric) have been developed to assist maintenance teams in the performance of maintaining large, complicated systems (in the case of CATS-1, the systems being maintained are diesel-electric locomotive engines). These expert systems walk through a problem with the maintenance people. When a system determines what the problem is, the system communicates the problem to the user. The system then asks if the user understands the problem. If the user responds in the negative, the system can provide a short tutorial on the subject. The tutorial is on the video disk. After this, the system asks if the user knows how to fix the problem. If the user again responds in the negative, the system is capable of providing tutorials of varying lengths on how to proceed with the repair action. All the time, the video material is automatically selected by the computer. The user is not required to find the correct video-based tutorial material.

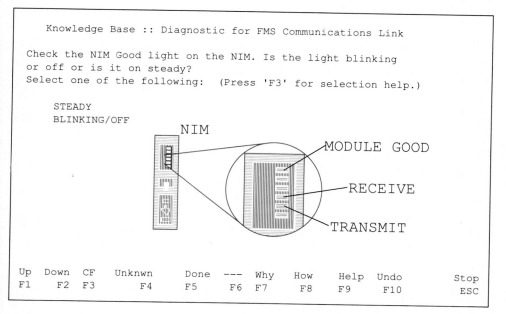

Figure 6.9   A user-system interface with graphics support

Besides graphics presentations on computer displays and video tutorials, expert systems can also assist in referring the user to the proper technical manual, repair manual, or human expert. Some large systems have tens, if not hundreds, of associated manuals. Being able to determine what the problem is and then knowing quickly which manual to refer to for rectifying the problem can often be very helpful. Sometimes the ability to determine what the problem is and knowing where to find the repair information is what distinguishes the expert maintenance foreman from the rest of the maintenance staff.

For many expert system projects, the acquisition of knowledge is a never-ending task. Why is this so? Of the many reasons, six are listed in Figure 6.10.

If knowledge acquisition is going to continue after the system is put into operation, it is important to try to identify who will acquire and input the new knowledge into the expert system. Three candidates are: the knowledge engineer, the domain expert, and the system's user. If the knowledge engineer is going to perform the knowledge acquisition task, all that must be considered is the continued availability of the knowledge acquisition facility software and the ability to connect it to the operational expert system when it is needed. If the domain expert is going to load new knowledge into the knowledge base in the future, a knowledge acquisition facility must be provided that the expert can work with effectively. This facility may or may not be the same knowledge acquisition facility that was used to load the original knowledge base. If the new knowledge is going to be input into the expert system by the system's user, consideration should be given to providing a bridge between the knowledge acquisition facility

1. Experts cannot remember all that is important and relevant to a particular problem until they are put into situations that help remind them of what they have learned or experienced and have since forgotten.

2. Experts do not know everything, and they are always acquiring new knowledge.

3. Knowledge engineers do not always extract all the relevant knowledge from the domain experts; therefore, some expert knowledge may be missing from the expert system's knowledge base.

4. Tasks and conditions change over time; new or different knowledge becomes relevant to the problem and must, therefore, be acquired.

5. Unanticipated situations arise that make additional knowledge necessary.

6. As users understand expert systems and learn how to make these systems work for them, they ask for more.

Figure 6.10   Reasons why knowledge acquisition is often a continuous activity

and the user-system interface. This way, knowledge acquisition would be just another system function available to the user. The knowledge acquisition interface with the user should be formatted in a manner that is similar to the system's operation so that the knowledge acquisition task does not seem totally foreign to the user.

DESIGN ISSUES THAT ARE AFFECTED BY TASK TYPE

Certain expert system design issues are influenced by the type of task a particular expert system is to support. Knowledge engineering is still in its infancy. There is no rigorous body of theory that has survived the test of time. Determining what expert system design features will effectively support a particular task is still a hit-and-miss affair. However, there are experiences of others that have been documented. This information does provide some usable rules of thumb. These heuristics are available for many of the expert systems that have been built to date. However, if an expert system is to be developed to support a task type that has not previously been supported by an expert system, the expert system developer must either interpolate heuristics from other, possibly similar, task types or determine which expert system features best fit the task through trial and error (ideally with the help of an effective rapid-prototyping tool).

Experience has shown, for example, that expert maintenance systems (diagnosis and prescription systems) can be effectively built using a rules knowledge representation and a backward-chaining inferencing mechanism. If the maintenance problem is large, the frames knowledge representation can be used to augment the rules knowledge representation. The maintenance rules would become slot entries in the frames. The frames representation allows the knowledge engineer to divide the domain knowledge into manageable chunks. An inheritance structure can be set up if that will assist the knowledge engineer in loading the knowledge base.

If a knowledge engineer is trying to represent knowledge that has complex interrelationships, the semantic network knowledge representation scheme is most likely the best choice.

Both expert planning systems and expert designing systems have been successfully developed using the production rules knowledge representation and the forward-chaining inference technique.

The logic knowledge representation and the backward-chaining inference technique have been successfully used to "animate" rules, regulations, and laws. Through this "animation," complex and voluminous rules, regulations, and laws that have already been developed into text-based knowledge are loaded into a knowledge-base and then provide users with an interactive consultation tool. This interactive tool will assist in determining which rules, regulations, and laws are applicable to each problem, help develop recommendations, and assist the user in choosing the appropriate recommendation for the problem at hand. An effective expert system shell to do this type of work is called ES/P Advisor from Expert Systems International.

When starting to design an expert system, the task to be supported must be defined and the task type determined. Then a review of the expert system literature should be conducted to determine if it can provide design information and knowledge that is relevant to the particular task type. If design knowledge is available, it will help the designer in the development of the expert system's architecture. If the literature cannot provide help, the designer is breaking new ground and will accordingly have to experiment until he or she has determined an effective architecture.

ORGANIZATIONAL CONSTRAINTS

The introduction of new technology into an organization can be a stressful event. This is especially true if the technology involves changes to organizational policies, procedures, or work structure. Expert system technology will most likely be introduced as a single small project. However, sooner or later in most organizations more expert systems will be added. Some will have little or no impact on organizational policies, procedures, or work structures; others will have some effect. Because the introduction of expert system technology can potentially affect the way an organization performs one or more of its functions, the organization will tend to constrain its introduction until the technology is better understood and, in many cases, has proved itself. There will be a tendency for some people in the organization to support the new technology strongly and want to include it in their operations as soon as possible. Some will be less than supportive and will want to avoid dealing with the new technology. Others will not campaign for the technology's introduction but will agree to use new tools as they prove themselves. There will also be people who will guard the organization's assets against any negative effects. The needs and priorities of many of these people will have to be considered.

Expert system developers will have to take into consideration the constraints an organization might place on expert system projects and how these constraints might affect the design and construction tasks.

The builders of expert decision-making systems will require access to the organization's key decision-making experts and key strategic data and knowledge. These key people and the strategic knowledge are very important assets of the organization. There will most likely be a tendency to protect these organizational assets. The organization might require that some security mechanism be established prior to providing key strategic data, information, and knowledge to a new automated system. After all, the purpose of the expert system is to make certain knowledge and information more accessible to more people, but one goal of an organization that operates in a competitive environment is to limit access to certain key strategic information and knowledge of the organization. The organization might also seek assurances that the expert system builder's motives and objectives are in line with the organization's plans and future objectives. Expert system builders will have to be sensitive to these situations.

An organization might decide to experiment with the new expert system technology through the development of a pilot project. This pilot project will most likely determine the future of expert system technology in the organization. The project will be watched with interest. However, because the pilot project is experimental, the funds released to it will be monitored closely. Actual or potential returns on the investment will be sought. If, on the one hand, the pilot either does not prove useful to the organization or the investment appears to be too great for the returns, in all likelihood, the technology will not be accepted. If, on the other hand, the pilot project proves useful and generates acceptable returns, the technology has a good chance of expansion. The people involved in the pilot system will have to keep this situation in mind during development. The system will have to produce a visible, understandable service, product, or tool that either immediately provides a reasonable return on investment (of funds, personnel, and so on) or provides enough evidence that the potential returns are truly possible. Often this will have to be accomplished in some reasonably short period of time.

If the expert systems to be introduced will affect procedures or propose to replace other entities in the organization (such as technical manuals), often the expert system will be required to prove that it can perform the job accurately and that it does so with some added benefit. Most organizations do not wish to introduce change without some tangible benefit.

Although expert system builders might wish to choose the hardware their systems will be developed on and will run on, many times there will be organizational limitations on these choices. If an organization has approved an expert decision-making system and the decision makers are already using a particular computer for other purposes, the expert system might have to run on that same computer. Cost and user acceptance factors can also motivate such decisions. Expert system builders will have to be sensitive to these situations and be flexible with their design ideas.

The last organizational issue that we will discuss has to do with people and politics. Some people will want to be supported by the new technology. Sometimes their motives will be political. They might believe that by having the new technology supporting them, they will have a competitive advantage over other people in the organization. And this might prove to be true. Others will believe that just by having the technology supporting them, they will look good to the powers that be. Whatever the motive, once the pilot has succeeded, the expert system developer may be swamped with project proposals. The developer must obtain help in ensuring that the projects selected for development will provide bottom-line benefits to the organization.

REFERENCES

1. B. G. Buchanan and E. H. Shortliffe, *Rule-based Expert Systems: The MY-CIN Experiments of the Stanford Heuristic Programming Project* (Reading, MA: Addison-Wesley, 1984).

2. C. V. Negoita, *Expert Systems and Fuzzy Systems* (Menlo Park, CA: Benjamin/Cummings, 1985).

3. R. Turner, *Logics for Artificial Intelligence* (Chichester, England: Ellis Horwood Limited, 1984).

7 THE EXPERT SYSTEM LIFE CYCLE

PROJECT LIFE CYCLE FOR EXPERT SYSTEMS   One of the first steps in a new software development project is to decide on the life cycle steps that will be taken into account for the total project. This framework is needed to be able to plan, budget, monitor, and control the project. The life cycle steps that are often in use today for software system projects are presented in Figure 7.1.

These life cycle steps are usually followed sequentially—a step is not accomplished until the preceding step has been accomplished. However, any step

1. System concept
2. System feasibility study
3. User requirements gathering
4. Requirements analysis
5. Software specification
6. Software design
7. Software coding
8. Software documentation
9. Software unit testing
10. System integration
11. System testing
12. User training
13. User acceptance testing
14. User acceptance
15. Operations/maintenance

Figure 7.1   A conventional software life cycle

might cause the development team to backtrack to redo one or more steps in light of new information obtained during the accomplishment of a step. Backward movements can skip back any number of steps, but forward movements are always accomplished sequentially, without skipping any steps.

In the development of expert systems and other new software systems, a new software life cycle paradigm is suggested. The conventional life cycle form in Figure 7.1 places its emphasis on the construction of the new software system; the end product is the guiding light throughout the process. The new software life cycle paradigm shown in Figure 7.2 segments its emphasis into four areas of interest: system conceptualization and requirements analysis, tool selection, the prototype, and the end product.

The sequence of operations for the life cycle steps in Figure 7.2 follows the same rules that were given for the conventional software life cycle; that is, the steps are followed sequentially, backward movements can occur, and all forward movements are accomplished without skipping steps.

Unless the initial system concept is discarded and the project is restarted,

A. System conceptualization and requirements analysis
1. System concept
2. System feasibility study
3. Preliminary requirements gathering
4. Preliminary requirements analysis

B. Tool Selection
5. Available tools analysis
6. Project tools selection

C. The prototype
7. Prototype development
8. Prototype documentation
9. User training on prototype
10. Prototype use by user
11. User acceptance of prototype

D. The end producer
12. End-product packaging
13. End-product user training
14. User acceptance testing
15. User acceptance
16. Operations/maintenance

Figure 7.2 A software life cycle for expert systems

there should rarely be a need to move backward in the first two segments (A and B). Likewise, if the prototype work (segment C) is performed well, there should be little rework performed in the end-product area (segment D), although newly identified needs would most likely require new prototype work followed by new end-product work. However, it should be emphasized that the prototype work should involve many iterations through the prototype tasks. With each interation the developing expert system will more closely approximate the knowledge of the human expert. Among the inherent benefits of this new software life cycle paradigm are earlier construction of a system, earlier user involvement with the system (the prototype), and shorter backward movements through the life cycle steps.

During step 1, the system concept life cycle, an expert system concept is developed. Often this step will follow a problem-solving exercise in the organization. A problem will be identified and many potential solutions will be presented. Answers are sought to questions like these:

- What is the problem?
- Has the organization solved problems like this one in the past? If so, how was it solved?
- If this is a new type of problem for the organization, what solution options can we identify?

If the organization has on its staff a person who knows about and possibly understands expert system technology, this person might present the technology as a possible solution to the problem at hand, if the person sees a connection between the technology and the problem. If the problem-solving team is convinced about the application of the technology to the problem or if the team has no other potential solution to the problem, an expert system concept might be developed. Questions that need to be answered at this point include these:

- What, more exactly, is the problem?
- How will expert system technology provide a solution to this problem?
- What is the expert system to do? What are the goals of the system?
- How will the expert system accomplish its goals?

Step 2 is the system feasibility study. Here the problem, the system concept, and the supporting technology are studied. Questions to be answered in this step include these:

- What part of the problem are we going to attempt to solve, or are we going to try to solve the entire problem?
- In abstract terms, what is the final system going to be?
- Are other technologies going to be employed as well?

- How is expert system technology going to be applied to the problem?
- Do we have a domain expert available to work on the project?
- Is our system concept viable? Will expert system technology support an effective solution to our problem? Do we have the wherewithal to develop this system?
- Can we develop the system cost-effectively?

If we determine that it is not feasible to develop an expert-system-based product that will solve our problem, we would stop this project development direction and look for other technological alternatives. Otherwise, we would move on to preliminary requirements gathering.

In step 3, we now try to identify as many of the requirements to be levied on the system as is possible at this time. Any and all requirements that can be identified should be identified. (Additional requirements will be developed during the prototype segment, C. Prototypes tend to show the ultimate users graphically what the system can do for them. As users come to understand the system's concepts, they often identify additional requirements.) During the requirements gathering step, we try to answer the following questions:

- What requirements does the system need to fulfill?
- Are any particular approaches required to meet some or all of these requirements?
- How will we know when we have fulfilled the requirements?

The last step in the system conceptualization and requirements analysis area, step 4, is preliminary requirements analysis. The requirements are analyzed and requirements specifications are developed. Requirements specifications cover functional requirements, performance, interface details, and system and software quality and qualification. Questions to be answered during step 4 include these:

- What requirements will the system be able to fulfill?
- What functions will the system provide?
- How will the system perform?
- What are the interface requirements for the system?
- What quality factors are involved in the development of this system?
- How will we qualify the developed system for operational use?
- Does the expert system technology still seem to be appropriate?
- Is the domain knowledge available? Is it sufficient?
- Is the knowledge complete and consistent?
- Is there uncertainty in the subject domain knowledge?

- How is the knowledge acquired?
- What knowledge representation scheme seems to be appropriate?
- What inference technique seems to be appropriate?

Segment C's two steps concern tool selection: available tools analysis, followed by project tools selection.

Expert system shell products should be considered like database management system products. When developing a database, most organizations purchase a DBMS product and populate it with their data. Leaving the development of the DBMS software to the DBMS vendors is usually the most cost-effective approach. The same philosophy should be followed in the development of an expert system. It is recommended that developers purchase an expert system shell and then populate its knowledge base with the organization's knowledge and expertise in a particular subject domain. The first expert systems, just like the first database systems, were developed without the aid of commercial tools. However, there now exist sufficient effective expert system development tools in the marketplace. In most cases, the use of an expert system shell will decrease the time and resources required to develop an expert system.

During step 5, all commercially available tools should be considered. Although many expert system development tools are available, the field can often be quickly narrowed down through certain requirements. For example, if the system is going to be small, say, less than 500 rules, and speed is not an important factor but physical system portability is, the shell must run on a portable personal computer. This immediately eliminates many expert system shell products from further consideration. By contrast, if the system is going to be large, say, over 1000 rules, and speed is a concern, a mainframe or larger machine might be required, and this eliminates expert-system shell products from further consideration. Questions that need to be considered during this step include these:

- What expert system development tools are available in the marketplace?
- What knowledge representation schemes do the expert system shell products support?
- What inference and control mechanisms are supported by the commercially available expert system shells?
- What forms of knowledge acquisition tools come with the shells?
- What are the user-system interfaces like? Are they easy to use?
- What other facilities do these products offer (for example, graphics interfaces or facilities)?
- Will the company offering the product be available to help?
- What hardware do the shells run on? Do any run on hardware that is available in the organization?

- What is the cost of the product versus the functionality it provides?
- What documentation and training are available on the product?
- Are run-time modules and/or licenses available?

The next step, 6, is project tools selection. Matching the project requirements with the available tools, one or more expert system development tools are selected and obtained for the project. This selection process must try to answer questions like these:

- What tools support the required knowledge representation scheme(s)?
- What tools support the required inference technique(s)?
- What tools offer the required facilities like graphics?
- Which tools fulfill all or most of the other project requirements?
- Which tools fit the project budget?

If no tools fulfill the requirements of the project, there are three alternatives:

1. Compromise and use one or more tools that best meet the requirements of the project.
2. Develop your own expert system development tools (a difficult, expensive task that should be avoided in almost all cases).
3. Drop the project and reconsider it in one year (each year, many new expert system development tools will become available, and one of them might fit the requirements).

Once the project tools have been selected, the project team must be trained in their use.

The next major area in the life cycle, segment C, is prototype development. Five life cycle steps are involved: prototype development, prototype documentation, user training on the prototype, prototype use by the user, and user acceptance of the prototype. These steps will probably be repeated in sequence many times.

By the time we get to steps 7 through 11, we have selected and studied a problem and have determined that expert system technology is appropriate for the development of a cost-effective solution. We have done some initial knowledge acquisition; that is, during our problem definition and specification work, we have studied the subject domain and have learned a lot about our problem and its related subject area. We have selected a set of computer-based development tools that will assist in the efficient development of a stand-alone expert system or an expert system component of a larger computer-based system. We have identified our system's user or user group and are now ready to develop our prototype. We now move into the knowledge engineering tasks.

Knowledge engineering is a relatively new discipline involved with the development of specific software systems, known as knowledge-based systems, which include expert systems. Many ideas and concepts used in knowledge engineering are borrowed from other disciplines including software engineering, cognitive psychology, and artificial intelligence. Knowledge engineering is concerned with three aspects of knowledge:

1. Knowledge acquisition (what to say about the subject)
2. Knowledge representation (how to say it)
3. Knowledge use (what to do with it)

During the development of an expert system prototype, the following knowledge engineering and software engineering tasks are performed:

- Knowledge acquisition
- Knowledge representation
- Expert system design
- Expert system shell programming
- User-system interface programming
- Subfunction programming

The development of an expert system is often performed in an iterative manner. The six tasks are usually performed in sequence, albeit many times. First (step 7), the knowledge acquired prior to prototype development is studied, and an attempt is made to represent it. A preliminary expert system design is developed, and the expert system is programmed using the selected expert system shell. This programming includes knowledge representation coding (such as rules), user-system interface coding (such as display formats), and subfunction coding (such as data conversion routines). The first-out "rough draft" version is experimented with. If this rough draft system seems to be headed correctly toward the desired solution, its development continues. If not, its development stops and a new attempt is started.

Once a rough draft version is determined to be acceptable, this version is documented (step 8). Fortunately, many knowledge-bases are readable and understandable; therefore, the knowledge-base documentation effort should be minimal. Also, many commercial shells offer automated documentation tools that include source code reformatters and logic tree graphics. Often, however, the user-system interface and the subprograms require traditional software documentation activities. Also, a user manual will have to be developed. However, many expert systems require minimal operational documentation for users. The amount of documentation required is a function of the design and quality of the user-system interface.

The user is told the status of this rough draft prototype version and is provided with requisite training so as to try it out and comment on it (step 9).

If a user is new to systems developed with expert system technology, the technology and its goals should be explained. Hyped up descriptions should be avoided, as they tend either to raise user expectations to levels difficult to fulfill or to intimidate the user, possibly to the point of unwillingness to participate. The explanation should mention that expert system technology is but one more computer software development technology. This new technology brings with it new development techniques and tools. The resulting system is a computer software system that often can run on regular business computer systems. To the user, what is different with the resulting system is the classes of problems for which expert systems attempt to provide solutions. If the user is given an effective introduction to the technology and agrees, first, that the problem to be supported is a real problem and, second, that an automated solution might be successful, the user should be a capable and willing project participant.

After training to the user's satisfaction, the user is given the opportunity to try out the system (step 10). A development person should be available to answer the user's questions and record user comments and suggestions.

These prototype development steps will most likely be performed many times. Each time, the system should improve in its performance. Each time, the user should be more knowledgeable about and comfortable with the system. The user should start to develop ideas and new requirements, which should be fed into the development.

The user, along with the development team, which usually includes a domain expert and a knowledge engineer, will decide when the prototype is ready for user acceptance (step 11). At this time, the user will notify the organization that the prototype is ready to be packaged into a functional system. The user should write a short acceptance report. In it, the user should articulate what work, if any, still remains to be done.

The final life cycle steps, 12 through 16, move the development prototype, version "X," to an operational product for the organization. The end-product area includes packaging, user training, user acceptance testing, user acceptance, and operations/maintenance life cycle steps.

During end-product packaging (step 12) any remaining work should be completed. System documentation should also be completed, especially the user manual. If the system is to interface to other systems used in the organization, the interfaces must be readied for use. If the system is going to fit into an existing operational area in an organization, the requisite procedural changes will have to be identified so that the expert system can be properly integrated into the work flow.

The end-product user training (step 13) should include introduction of the final product to the user or user group, articulation of how all outstanding work items were completed, publication of the user manual, explanation of the requisite organizational procedures, and full training in the product, either in actual operation connected to the organization's work flow or as close to this situation as is feasible. Any and all user questions must be addressed at this time.

After reaching a state of readiness, the user should run tests (step 14) to see if the system and its interfaces are ready for implementation. These tests should evaluate the performance and the utility of the system. They need to answer questions like these:

- Does the system ask questions in a consistent and natural manner?
- Does the system depict the expert's heuristics properly and completely?
- Does the system provide advice that the expert agrees with?
- Does the system reach its conclusions in a reasonable amount of time?
- Can the user understand and use the advice the system provides?
- Does the system provide solutions that help the user complete the tasks at hand?
- Are the system's explanations and justifications sufficient and understandable?

Any potential problems the user identifies during testing must be resolved prior to user acceptance. If the potential problems are not in fact real problems, the situation needs to be resolved to the user's satisfaction. If the problems are real but minor, resolution might be handled at this step. If not, the project needs to regress to the point in the life cycle where the problem can be rectified.

When the user has completed training and testing and is convinced that the product is ready for operational use, the user should notify the organization of acceptance (step 15).

The organization then must take the required actions to move the accepted expert system into the mainstream operation of the organization. Full operability should be achieved at this time, and preplanned operations and maintenance procedures for the system should be put in place (step 16). The introduction of the system should solve the problem it was designed to solve. As more experience and knowledge are gained about the problem, the maintenance activities should include the addition of new knowledge into the system's knowledge-base. The system should continue to support the organization, solve its subject problem, and have its knowledge-base expanded as the organization learns more about the problem. The system will help solve the problem. It will also be a repository of all corporate knowledge relating to the subject problem area.

KNOWLEDGE ACQUISITION TASKS

Knowledge is the key to a useful expert system. The acquisition and representation of knowledge are among the most important of expert system development tasks. For this reason, we will devote some time here to the subject of knowledge acquisition.

Knowledge acquisition, simply put, is the acquisition of knowledge, experience, and rules of thumb from a human expert. Knowledge representation is the codification of this subject domain knowledge so that the knowledge can be used by a computer-based expert system.

If knowledge acquisition is to occur, a human subject domain expert must be selected. A logical question to ask is, "How is an expert identified?" Two common techniques for identifying domain experts are (1) by reputation, someone who seems to get results, and (2) by management recommendation.

Knowledge acquisition is the acquisition of expertise from one or more domain experts. It is usually accomplished by a knowledge engineer. Subject domain knowledge and experience information is transferred from the domain expert to the knowledge-base of an expert system (Figure 7.3). The data placed into the knowledge-base includes modular collections of codified subject domain knowledge and advice. The more complete and accurate this transfer is, the more capable the resulting expert system will be.

For a knowledge engineer to transfer knowledge from an expert to an expert system, the engineer must interview and interact with the expert. Since the expert will most likely not understand expert system technology, the expert will not know where to begin. The knowledge engineer will have to plan for the interviews. The knowledge engineer will also have to study prior to the interviews. The reason for this planning and studying is to assure that the interviews are purposeful and that the knowledge engineer can understand what the expert is saying during the interviews. During an interview, the knowledge engineer must help and guide the domain expert. An effective technique of guiding the expert involves asking the expert some important but general questions. These questions help elicit subject domain knowledge and information and guide the expert by providing a framework for the information sought by the knowledge engineer. These questions should be general so that the knowledge engineer

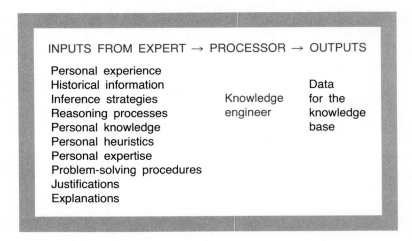

INPUTS FROM EXPERT → PROCESSOR → OUTPUTS

Personal experience
Historical information   Data
Inference strategies   Knowledge   for the
Reasoning processes   engineer   knowledge
Personal knowledge   base
Personal heuristics
Personal expertise
Problem-solving procedures
Justifications
Explanations

Figure 7.3   Knowledge acquisition from a domain expert

does not bias the expert's information. Figure 7.4 gives examples of questions that a knowledge engineer might ask a domain expert.

After these general questions have been asked and the responses have been recorded, the knowledge engineer should analyze the knowledge data acquired, validate the acquired knowledge data, and elicit some more specific information.

The knowledge engineer should develop an overview or summary of the material acquired from the expert. This overview can be used to see where each detail fits into the larger picture. As the knowledge engineer analyzes each knowledge detail and sees how it fits into the scheme of the problem or the solution, he or she should be able to see where needed knowledge data is missing. This missing data serves as the basis for questions to be asked of the domain expert at the next interview.

The knowledge engineer can validate the acquired knowledge data by presenting the expert with new problems that require the use of the acquired knowledge data and observe the expert's use of this knowledge in the context of the new but related problem. Through this knowledge-use demonstration, the knowledge engineer should be able to assess the legitimacy of the acquired knowledge data. If more than one expert is available, the knowledge engineer can also present similar problems to other experts and observe their use of the acquired knowledge.

Two more specific information categories deal with case analysis and historical analysis. The knowledge engineer can elicit more specific subject domain knowledge data and information through the use of these subject analysis techniques.

- What do you, the expert, know that the nonexpert or novice needs to know?
- What questions *can* we (or maybe more appropriately, the expert system) ask the user?
- What questions *should* we ask the user?
- What should the presentation (of questions, answers, and user-system information interchanges) be like?
- Are any computations involved with our problem?
- What are the facts (that relate to our problem)?
- What are the rules (that operate in our problem space)?
- What other knowledge information (experience data) can you provide?

Figure 7.4   What does a knowledge engineer ask an expert?

For case analysis, the knowledge engineer could introduce an analysis session with the following opening guidance:

> Please choose an important case. Tell me about the problem's subproblems and their solutions as they relate to the specific case.

This case information can be used to help acquire new knowledge information and to help the knowledge engineer understand and validate contextual references and knowledge placement. The context of the case will help the knowledge engineer understand the subject problem. The context will also help the knowledge engineer validate knowledge pieces and place them relative to other knowledge pieces in the subject knowledge collection.

The other more specific line the knowledge engineer can take deals with the history of the problem. The knowledge engineer could move the discussion into this area with the following opening:

> Please tell me the history of the subject problem. Please include any historical facts that would make this problem more understandable. For example, what events led to this being a problem that needed the help of an expert like yourself?

These discussions should provide the knowledge engineer with new problem domain information and insight.

Thus we can see that by interviewing the domain expert, the knowledge engineer can acquire a lot of information about the problem that is to be supported by an expert system. A natural question here might be, Is this the only way a knowledge engineer acquires knowledge for an expert system's knowledge-base, or are there other ways to acquire subject domain knowledge?

Interviewing the domain expert is the most important means of acquiring subject domain knowledge. However, there are other sources of domain knowledge that the knowledge engineer can often use in the acquisition of knowledge on a particular subject. The left column in Figure 7.5 lists knowledge domain data sources that might be available to the knowledge engineer for a particular subject.

Figure 7.6 provides a list of knowledge acquisition techniques that a knowledge engineer might use to acquire knowledge from the sources listed in Figure 7.5. For example, studying a new subject domain might include reading documents and research reports on the subject. These knowledge sources are sometimes the most current literature sources on a subject. If the subject is well documented, books might have been published on the subject. Where a subject has a large amount of data, often databases will exist. If the particular industry or discipline tends toward automation, these databases might be computer-based, making data retrieval quicker. Using the knowledge acquisition techniques listed in Figure 7.6 with the knowledge sources listed in Figure 7.5, the

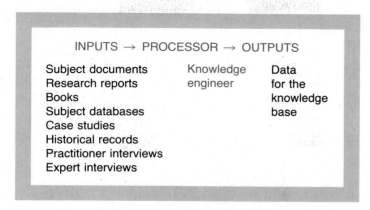

INPUTS → PROCESSOR → OUTPUTS

Subject documents	Knowledge	Data
Research reports	engineer	for the
Books		knowledge
Subject databases		base
Case studies		
Historical records		
Practitioner interviews		
Expert interviews		

Figure 7.5   Knowledge acquisition

knowledge engineer should be able to compile an initial, workable expert system knowledge-base.

After all the knowledge acquisition questions have been answered by the expert and all the other knowledge acquisition techniques have been attempted, there might be the feeling that all accessible knowledge has been acquired. However, this is often not the case. Let us explore why this is so. Why is there possibly more knowledge to access, and how does the knowledge engineer go about acquiring it?

Figure 7.7 shows the knowledge acquisition process. It demonstrates that the knowledge acquisition process is iterative. The amount of effort expended and the number of times the project must iterate through the process loop is

- Study the subject.
- Observe the subject problem to study the surface behavior of the problem.
- Observe domain experts and practitioners performing tasks.
- Discuss the problem area with experts and practitioners.
- Study the behavior of the experts and the practitioners to attempt to uncover their underlying knowledge and thought processes.
- Query the domain experts and get descriptions of typical problems or situations that they have to contend with.
- Develop and evaluate cases; present experts with problems and ask them to solve the cases while "thinking aloud."

Figure 7.6   What does a knowledge engineer do for knowledge acquisition?

- Acquire initial subject domain knowledge.
- Prototype the knowledge data and place it in an expert system development shell for knowledge data test purposes.
- Give the prototype system a sample task.
- Let the expert comment on the system.
- If the knowledge base is reasonably complete, exit this bracket.
- Let the expert infer what is missing in the knowledge base.
- Acquire the missing knowledge.
- Add the missing knowledge to the knowledge base.
- Reiterate these steps.
- • Continue to the next expert system development step.

Figure 7.7   The knowledge acquisition process

usually dependent on the size of the system to be built, the depth and breadth of the tasks to be supported, and the quality of the knowledge as it is acquired. Expert system knowledge bases are often built as the knowledge data is obtained. A prototype shell is selected, and the knowledge data is applied to the knowledge base of the shell as it is acquired. If at any point in the development of this prototype knowledge base it is observed that the chosen expert system shell and its attendant knowledge representation scheme or schemes do not effectively represent the domain knowledge, a new expert system shell with a different knowledge representation scheme would be chosen, the acquired knowledge data would be recodified, and the project would continue. Therefore, it can be seen that although we are discussing the knowledge acquisition steps at the moment, we often move back and forth through other life cycle development steps, as was mentioned earlier in this chapter.

The next three figures offer some reasons as to why the knowledge acquisition process is an iterative process. Figure 7.8 explores a few reasons, centering on the domain experts and the domain knowledge data.

Figure 7.9 presents some of the reasons why knowledge acquisition tends to be a continuing activity. As organizations move with development and our changing society, the tasks that people perform in these organizations change. Tasks that the expert systems perform and support will potentially change also.

In any given domain that is supported by expert system technology, there is always the possibility that new situations will arise. In an expert system that helps locate natural resources, for example, a new natural resource might be discovered or a new method might be invented for finding a known natural

- Experts cannot remember all that is important until they are put into situations that remind them of what they forgot.

- Experts do not know everything during the initial knowledge acquisition activity; experts are constantly learning more about their subject domains through new experiences and study.

- Knowledge data is often imperfect, and there is often a constant tendency to improve it.

Figure 7.8   Why is knowledge acquisition incremental?

resource. Knowledge about the new natural resource or the new technique for finding a natural resource would then be added to the expert system's knowledge-base.

Expert systems tend to train users while supporting them. Because of the explanation and justification capabilities of these systems, the users tend to become more and more knowledgeable in the subject domain material. At the same time, users become more accustomed to the expert systems and come to understand these systems and how they can help. If the users perceive expert systems as beneficial to them, they will tend to ask that additional knowledge be put into the knowledge-base. They themselves will present new situations that they believe should be supported by expert systems. As the users become more knowledgeable, these requests will most likely be well founded and should therefore be considered seriously.

Figure 7.10 lists some of the reasons why knowledge is added to the knowledge-bases of functioning, already helpful expert systems. Whenever new knowledge is acquired and is deemed important, that knowledge must be added to the expert system knowledge-base in order for the system's users to be able to take advantage of it. Because the knowledge-base is the repository of the system's knowledge and because the knowledge is the power of the system,

- Tasks that expert systems support change over time.
- New or additional situations arise.
- As users understand their systems, they ask for more.

Figure 7.9   Why does knowledge acquisition continue even after the system is completed?

- To add newly acquired knowledge
- To make minor refinements to the knowledge-base
- To make major refinements to the knowledge-base
- To expand system functionality for current tasks; to provide more complete knowledge services for the current tasks
- To expand system functionality for new tasks; to provide the users with support in other important task areas

Figure 7.10   Why knowledge is added to the expert system after the system is operational

whenever users want the system to behave in a more refined manner, the system's developers wish the system to operate more distinctly on the subject material, or the users and the developers wish to have the system's functionality extended, new knowledge data must be added to the knowledge-base of the expert system.

Knowledge acquisition should continue as long as new solutions to the problem the expert system is going to support are still being sought and discovered. Knowledge acquisition should occur in parallel with human expert discovery. When an organization obtains new data, information, or knowledge on the subject that an expert system supports, that data, information, or knowledge should be applied to that expert system's knowledge-base.

To develop an operational expert system, the knowledge representation, expert system design, expert system shell programming, user-system interface programming, and subfunction programming tasks must also be performed. These tasks will be accomplished in an iterative manner that includes knowledge acquisition. However, some of the tasks will not be performed as often after the system is operational. The knowledge acquisition, knowledge representation, and shell programming activities will continue as long as new knowledge is being obtained; the other activities will be conducted to a lesser degree as needed.

Let us now move on to discuss these other expert system construction tasks.

EXPERT SYSTEM CONSTRUCTION TASKS

The goal of the expert system construction tasks is to transform the acquired subject domain knowledge into an operational computer-based expert system. These tasks will include activities related to expert system technology (such as knowledge representation coding) and activities related to other computer system and software development technologies (such as user-system interface coding).

Another way to look at this goal is to start with an expert system shell and populate the shell with the subject domain knowledge, thereby transforming the shell into an operational expert system. This perspective is illustrated in Figure 7.11. The use of a commercial expert-system shell makes the expert system construction job both easier and faster. Taking the expert system shell, the expert system developer has three tasks: developing the knowledge-base, developing the user-system interface if the shell software does not provide this, and programming any required subfunctions.

Developing the knowledge-base is somewhat like system design on the one hand and like writing a manual on the other hand. The knowledge engineer must represent the logic of a human expert in the knowledge-base.

The coded knowledge looks a little different from what a programmer is accustomed to seeing. Learning the new form is easy, and some front-end software packages allow the knowledge engineer to code predicate logic in a form that resembles the rule knowledge representation form.

The frame and semantic network knowledge representations require similar logic organization; however, their representation forms look less like conventional software logic.

In developing a knowledge-base, software tools that are very similar to other software development tools are used. Knowledge-base editors and debugging tools are good examples.

Knowledge-base editors are similar to text or source code editors. Knowledge-base editors are used to develop and change knowledge-base text, check for correct syntax, and manage changes to the knowledge-base. These editors often use word-processing-like entry paradigms that are easy to use for knowledge data entry. Syntax checking is often provided so that errors like improper keyword use are caught early, during the knowledge data entry task, rather than later when the knowledge-base is compiled or run. Since expert systems are often built in an incremental manner, changes to the knowledge-base are more the norm than the exception. Because of this, change management of the knowledge-base entities is important. Some knowledge-base editors mark knowledge-base changes with who performed the change and the time and date of the change action.

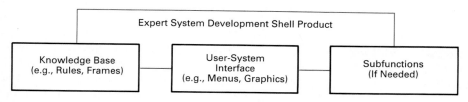

Figure 7.11 Expert system construction

The knowledge engineer uses debugging tools to discover faults in the knowledge-base in the same way that a computer programmer would use a debugging aid to find a logic error in a computer program. Debugging tools provide various services to the knowledge engineer, including tracing and breakpointing and the management of user input and test set databases.

Tracing provides navigation information for a particular session. As an expert system user or a knowledge engineer runs through a session with the expert system, the trace facility captures information on how the session navigated through the knowledge base. After the session, the knowledge engineer can analyze the trace information.

Breakpointing provides the knowledge engineer with the capability to stop the expert system when a particular point in the knowledge-base is reached. This provides the knowledge engineer with the ability to look at the knowledge-base in a particular state that was arrived at during its operation. This facility could be used by a knowledge engineer to debug some piece of knowledge that seems to be causing an error or abnormal termination of the expert system.

User input databases are used to store all of the user responses, choices, and user-provided knowledge of particular sessions. These databases can then be used by knowledge engineers during debugging activities. They can also be used to help knowledge engineers design appropriate test cases for future use.

Test set databases are used to store sets of expert system test cases. These test cases are known to provide a particular set of results. Whenever a knowledge engineer modifies the knowledge-base, he or she can run these test cases against the revised expert system knowledge-base to see if the desired results occur. With test set databases, the knowledge engineer can see if desired changes were in fact made and all other information remained unchanged.

Programming the knowledge-base is often like a documentation project. As a matter of fact, some expert systems are computer-based, dynamic models of existing documentation. One example is an expert system that an insurance company developed to help computer operators with job control problems. This particular expert system provided knowledge and information from the job control language manual as well as from other expert sources. A business school developed an expert system that performs comparative analyses of different treatments on various accountancy problems. This expert system used accountancy standards documents as one of its knowledge sources.

Programming a knowledge-base is sometimes similar to developing documentation entities like logic flow diagrams and logic trees. The knowledge data represents the components of the logic flow diagrams or the logic trees and their relationships. The actual construction of the logic flow diagrams or the logic trees occurs dynamically; that is, the expert system develops the logic flow or the tree during run sessions with users. The knowledge engineer can build large flow diagrams or trees incrementally as the knowledge is acquired. The expert system will construct the logic flow diagrams or the logic trees each time it runs. Each run might involve new knowledge and new responses from the users;

therefore, the actual logic flow diagrams or logic trees constructed, and thereby traversed, might be different. The expert system will construct an appropriate logic representation given the knowledge it has acquired and the responses the users have provided.

The human race has long documented its expertise in the form of writings, books, manuals, logbooks, and the like. Expert system technology gives us another way of documenting expertise which is superior in many ways.

Developing a knowledge-base is different from programming a COBOL or FORTRAN program. A programmer using FORTRAN or COBOL would be concerned with what happens in the program or software system. Typically, procedures would be defined in relationship to the way they interact with each other and the way data moves and changes in the software system. A knowledge engineer using a commercial shell like ART or Personal Consultant would be concerned with some of the procedures just like the programmer but would be more concerned with what the data (the expertise) is, how choices of which data to use are made, and why those choices are made. The knowledge engineer is more concerned with the how and the why than the what. The knowledge engineer analyzes the flow of knowledge (its paths) during an expert's consultation and then tries to build an expert system that reflects that knowledge flow and, thereby, provide a similar, valuable consultation to the expert system user. The knowledge-base content will be largely determined from this analysis performed by the knowledge engineer.

Knowledge-base programming must be in accordance with the specifications and constraints of the expert system development shell chosen by the knowledge engineer. The shell chosen will greatly influence the form the expert system will take. The knowledge engineer must choose a shell that reflects the complexion of the problem, the knowledge data, and the solutions. Once the shell has been selected, if selected properly, the knowledge engineer will be able to represent the expert's knowledge and other subject domain knowledge that has to do with the problem the expert system is to support. Equally important, the expert will be able to understand the codified knowledge. In this way, the expert can verify the validity of the knowledge-base content.

The actual tasks that are performed for knowledge-base programming are shaped and formed by the expert system shell chosen. For example, the use of the Insight 2 + expert system shell means that the knowledge engineer will use the Production Rule Language (PRL) for knowledge representation and the inference strategy will either be forward or backward chaining. The coding can only be described in terms of a particular expert system shell. (Information on some commercially available expert system shells is provided later in this book.)

Coding a knowledge-base is somewhat like programming a database system. The goals of the two systems are different; therefore, the data and specification information presented to them are different. However, the tasks are similar. Parallels can therefore be drawn.

If you were to develop a small, personal computer database for a mailing list application, you might use a DBMS product like dBase III, Rbase 5000, or the microcomputer version of Oracle. You would study the problem over a short period of time, study the DBMS product that you are going to use, and then program the application. Because these products are easy to use, you might code the application up the way you thought it should be, populate the database with a few pieces of information, and let the user test it out and make comments. The entire effort would be accomplished in a few days, possibly a week if you were not familiar with the DBMS product. (We are assuming that you are computer-literate and have done some programming.)

If you were to develop a small, personal-computer-based expert system for repair consultant application, you might use an expert system shell like Personal Consultant. Insight 2 + , or EXSYS. You would study the problem over a short period of time, study the expert system product that you selected, and then program the application. Again, because these products are easy to use, you might code the application or a part of it and let a domain expert test it out and send comments back to you. The entire effort would be accomplished in a short amount of time, possibly as little as three or four days if the application was very small and you were computer-literate and were familiar with expert system concepts.

The development of large database and expert system applications are also similar. Programming a large database would use a large computer system and a DBMS product like ADABAS, IDMS, or IMS. Programming a large expert system application would require a large computer system and an expert system shell product like ART, KEE, or KnowledgeCraft. The amount of time to develop a large database or expert system application could take from six months to a few years.

An expert system shell product includes a defined but empty knowledge-base. Subject domain expertise must be represented in a manner consistent with the knowledge representation techniques of the chosen shell. The domain knowledge is codified and placed in the shell's knowledge-base. When the expert believes that the expert system properly handles the problem class it is designed to support, the knowledge-base programming can be considered complete. However, as the expert learns and gains new knowledge, this new subject domain knowledge should also be provided to the expert system via knowledge-base enhancement programming activities.

Programming the user-system interface is an important task. Often user acceptance will be affected either positively or negatively by the interface provided. The user's first impressions of the system are greatly influenced by the user-system interface.

In programming the user-system interface, the modality of the system must be taken into consideration. There are two common operational modes for expert systems today:

- Acting as a consultant to a user who is performing a task
- Acting as a teacher to a user who needs to perform a task

A third operational mode that should become popular in the future for certain applications (such as factory automation applications) is the actor mode, where the expert system actually performs the task. Most likely these systems will include monitoring, feedback, and override devices so that users can monitor and, when necessary, override the expert system's task performance.

What is important here is that the intended system modality needs to be supported by the user-system interface.

If the system is to provide consultation support to a user, the user should be able to interact with the system in a forthright, time-sensitive manner. If the user has a problem that requires action within two minutes, the expert system cannot require three minutes of dialogue with the user prior to providing assistance. An expert consultation system should communicate in the language the user is accustomed to using when working on the task that the expert system is supporting.

If the system is providing instruction to a user, it is less constrained to a definite time schedule; however, the system should be designed so that the student does not get bored because the system is too slow. An expert instructional system should provide the user with the proper terminology and jargon but should not assume the student's knowledge of the terminology. The system should also be able to present its knowledge to the student in several ways. If the student does not understand a concept, the system must provide a different view of the concept to help the student learn the concept.

Expert control systems require user-system interfaces that permit a human operator to take on a monitoring function. Since the human operator will not be controlling the process, he or she may become bored; the user-system interface must therefore take this into consideration. For example, one expert control system uses a combination of a red flashing light and a large screen display. If the expert control system believes something important is occurring that the operator should be aware of, the red flashing light rotates until the operator pushes an acknowledgment button. The information is presented on the large screen display. The large screen display is easy to read and is always available for the operator to view. This screen can be used by the operator to monitor all ongoing processes. The user-system interface also includes controls that the operator can use either to cooperate with the expert control system or to override it when the operator believes it is necessary to do so. Human-operated control systems have been in use for a long time. The human operators have developed standard operating procedures for these systems. It is important for expert control system designers to take these standard operating procedures into account when building their systems. Expert control systems must perform effectively; they must correctly control the processes they have been developed to control. Expert control systems, for the most part, will also have to cooperate with human operators; therefore, they also must perform in a manner that is not perceived by the operators as antagonistic.

Another user-system interface consideration is presentation. Like all computer-based systems, expert systems can be designed and constructed with a variety of presentation formats. Figure 7.12 lists some of the presentation formats an expert system builder might consider.

Presentation format is important. A case history should bring the point home. One expert maintenance consultation system was developed to assist factory workers in fault isolation and repair of some of their equipment. The system was developed using an expert system shell product that included an excellent user-system interface. The resulting expert system looked professional, was easy to use, and included an excellent explanation facility. However, the system was not well accepted. Research determined that the user-system interface was poorly designed for the intended user, factory workers. Many factory workers are good at motor coordination and graphical analysis but are less effective at using and analyzing textual information. The expert system provided only a text-based user-system interface. To solve the problem, the user-system interface was enhanced with graphics designed to support understanding of the textual material. This interface enhancement helped achieve greater user acceptance.

Programming any required subfunctions is generally one of the last steps in constructing an expert system. The work done in this step is to provide the system with data and information that may be coming from some external source, is in a different format, or requires some calculation that the expert system logic is not capable of performing. Subfunction programs would be written to convert the data and information to the desired format or units of measure or to provide the requisite computational support. For example, an expert control system might be provided with temperature data from a process sensor using the Celsius scale, and the operator is more used to Fahrenheit temperature readings. A numerically oriented subprogram could be written to convert the Celsius readings to Fahrenheit and provide this new data to the symbolically oriented expert system.

- Full, conversational text
  - scrolling
  - full screen
- Abbreviated text
  - menus
  - keywords
- Graphics
  - monochromatic
  - multicolor
- Combinations of the above

Figure 7.12   User-system interface presentation formats

Expert system shell products are being provided with more and more computational support. Basic arithmetic functions are almost always provided now, and many shells provide other computational capabilities, such as trigonometric functions. With these capabilities, more of the required computations can be performed within the shell, reducing the need for subprograms.

Some subfunctions have been developed to interface expert systems with other computer-based processing in an organization, for example, corporate databases. Some expert systems are now providing capabilities to interface with databases without the need for subfunctions. An example of this is the interface that the Insight 2+ expert system shell provides to use dBase II or dBase III databases. As new capabilities are needed that combine expert system technology with some other technology, subfunctions will be developed to interface the technologies. As particular interfaces become more popular, the expert system shell development companies will include such interface capabilities in their shell products.

From all of these discussions on the construction of expert systems, it should be apparent that the development of an expert system is in some ways very similar to the development of other computer-based systems; yet there are requirements for building expert systems that are unique to this technology. The next chapter will discuss requirements related to the development of expert systems.

8 EXPERT SYSTEM CONSTRUCTION REQUIREMENTS

Three resources are required to build expert systems: software, hardware, and personnel. Human experts and knowledge engineers are required in the development of expert systems. The domain knowledge is elicited from the domain expert by the knowledge engineer. The third person involved with expert systems is the ultimate user. The user makes use of the expert system while performing work tasks. The expert system has been developed with the goal of assisting its user in the performance of work tasks by providing requisite, valuable problem domain knowledge.

SOFTWARE

From the software point of view, there are basically two approaches to building expert systems. The first approach is based on programming languages and programming tools. The second approach is based on the use of expert system shells.

Building expert systems with a programming language and its associated tools often means developing all of the requisite expert system functional components (such as an inference engine) as well as developing the problem domain knowledge-base. The development of the functional components might take even longer than the development of the problem domain knowledge-base.

The purpose of expert system shells is to provide an expert system developer with most, if not all, of the requisite expert system functional components. Figure 8.1 presents a list of the components that an expert system shell might provide. These components will be described in more detail later. Suffice it to say that the use of an expert system shell that provides the components listed in Figure 8.1 saves the trouble and expense of developing these components. The development of these components using a programming language might require years of effort.

- User-system interface
- Explanation facility
- Inference engine
- Knowledge database management system
- Knowledge acquisition facility

Figure 8.1   Expert system components often provided in expert system shells

The distinction between the programming languages (and tools) and the expert system shells is important. However, the issue really is more properly represented as a continuum rather than two poles. For example, OPS5 is a programming language. However, OPS5 provides an inference engine and a rudimentary knowledge-base management system. The idea behind using an expert system shell is that the requisite expert system components are provided so that the expert system developer does not need to perform many of the programming tasks. Task-specific shells go even further by providing a task outline, thereby eliminating the need to develop the outline in the knowledge-base. The developer's tasks are related to knowledge acquisition and codification. However, to provide the developer with functionality as well as flexibility in the design of an expert system, some expert system shells, such as ART and KEE, include programming language constructs.

There is a great difference between programming an expert system in a language like LISP or C and developing an expert system with the aid of an expert system shell like ART, KEE, Insight 2 +, or Personal Consultant Plus.

Sometimes there are debates over the development of expert systems in symbolic languages like LISP and PROLOG versus programming languages like C and Pascal. As long as the user-system interface is appropriately developed for the user's needs, the resulting expert system will often be as effective in one language as it would be if it were coded in another language. So if the end product is affected little by the choice of the language the delivery system is coded in, one might then ask, What factors should be considered when choosing a language?

Factors to consider in the selection of a programming language, if one is to be used, include the development environment, the appropriateness of tool capabilities versus problem domain requirements, the ability of the development environment to allow a developer to experiment with solution paradigms, and maintainability. The development environment of a programming language is often very important. For example, some of the programming environments built around the LISP programming language and some of its dialects, like InterLISP-D, are impressive. LISP environments often include requisite programming tools like source code editors as well as knowledge engineering tools like object-oriented constructs. However, very effective and complete development environments are also available for some programming languages like C and Pascal.

The ability to experiment with many solution paradigms quickly and effectively is often important in the development of new expert systems. Expert system technology is still new enough that sufficient guidance and expertise of the form "If the problem to be solved is of type X, then use the Y solution method and tool Z" does not exist. Rather, expert system developers have two options. The first is to look for a problem that has been effectively supported by an expert system and closely approximates the problem at hand. The developer could then use the same tools and techniques used by the developer of the existing expert system. The second option is to analyze the problem, infer which techniques and tools might work, create one or more expert system prototypes, and see what works. If this second option is chosen, the ability to experiment with numerous solution paradigms is important.

Languages that have been used to develop expert systems provide the greatest potential for being able to offer expert system developers the ability to experiment with solution paradigms. Languages that have been used for expert system development will offer the best chances for finding generalized code and subprograms that support specific expert system requirements like inference engine implementations. LISP and PROLOG have certainly been used for expert system developments, and a large number of expert system component implementations exist in these languages.

Maintainability is a concern to all software system developers, and the developers of expert systems are no exception. Developed expert systems that are going to be used operationally in an organization must be maintainable. If the user organization is able to maintain expert system software, in the implemented language, there should be no problem. However, if the user organization is not capable of maintaining the delivered system, capable personnel will have to be hired, consultants will have to be called in, or the developing organization will have to support the delivered system.

Two factors affect maintainability from the programming language perspective: the maintainability of code generated in the language of choice and the availability of competent maintenance personnel trained in the language of choice. There are many theories about the maintainability of programming languages. Whether a program written in Pascal is more maintainable than a program written in LISP is a point of debate in the computer science field. There are a lot of variables involved in this debate. The structure of a language, the tools available for a particular language for the maintenance activities, the extensibility of a language, and the ability to understand a program written by someone else as that ability is enhanced by the structure of the particular programming language are all examples of maintainability issues among programming languages. It is difficult to assess which programs are more maintainable strictly from a language standpoint. From the expert system perspective, the issue might naturally jump from looking at programming languages only to looking at programming languages versus expert system shells. The expert system shells might prove to be more maintainable.

The second maintainability issue, that of the availability of competent maintenance personnel trained in the language of choice, is an easier point for an organization to investigate. The organization can survey the capabilities of the software maintenance staff within the organization and of those outside the organization that either traditionally have supported the organization or would be available to support the organization. This survey will give the organization an idea of what languages the organization can presently support. If an organization chooses, it could also train its software maintenance staff in a new language. Here, again, the choice should include expert system shells as well as programming languages.

The argument then returns to developing expert systems in languages like LISP versus using expert system shells. In many, if not most, commercial implementations of expert systems, the use of shells makes a lot of sense from a business standpoint. The expert system development project will most likely use fewer human resources, take less time to develop, and cost less money if an expert system shell is used and if the particular shell used provides the appropriate knowledge representation and inferencing capabilities needed for the task at hand.

If convinced, a developer might accept the premise that an expert system shell might save the project time and money, and then the developer might start asking questions like these:

- How do I pick a shell?
- Does it matter which language the shell is written in?
- Does it matter which hardware the shell runs on?

Some of the answers to these questions will be provided in forthcoming chapters. However, let us at least partially address these issues here.

Each commercial shell provides one or more knowledge representation schemes and one or more inference mechanisms. Each shell provides its own set of tools (for example, knowledge editors) and capabilities (for example, rule development through data induction). The selection of a shell should take these technical issues into consideration. The problem to be solved must be analyzed. The knowledge representation and inference schemes required to solve the problem must be determined. And the tools needed to develop the expert system efficiently must be considered.

Besides the obvious technical issues related to the selection of an expert system shell, a company should also consider some of the important related business decisions. An organization will not only purchase a shell but will also invest its own resources in training on and initial use of the shell. By the time a company has developed a system around an expert system shell, the company will have invested a significant amount of money beyond the cost of the shell.

Since the company is going to invest its precious resources in the training and use of the expert system shell, it should be sure that the supplier of the expert system shell is going to stay in business and be available to the company, as needed, for maintenance. It is also important for the company to ascertain the vendor's ability to develop and deliver enhancements as new capabilities become available.

From strictly a technical capabilities standpoint, an expert system shell should be able to be developed in almost any programming language and should be able to provide the end user with effective expert system support. The language an expert system shell is written in is not as important as the form and function of the expert system shell. Often the language used for the initial development of an expert system shell is dependent on the capabilities of the development environment of the particular language. From that standpoint, often programming environments developed around languages like LISP are selected. However, once an expert system shell is developed and its concepts and design are well understood, it has been determined to be a reasonable task to recode the shell product in languages like C and Pascal. Often the reason for porting a shell product from a LISP environment to an environment developed in a language like C or Pascal is tied to a choice or desire to use a particular piece of hardware.

The choice of the hardware used with expert system shells to develop expert systems is often tied to two important factors. The first factor is the ability of the hardware to support an effective user-system interface, and the second factor is tied to online memory and data storage capabilities. The hardware should be able to support the large online memory requirements and data storage requirements that expert systems often require. As long as a piece of hardware effectively supports these two factors, it is proper to use an expert system shell on this hardware for a particular problem. This means that some computing hardware that used to be considered inappropriate for expert systems is now being reconsidered and in some cases has already been successfully used for them. One popular expert system shell that used to be available only on LISP machines is now available on the IBM PC/RT product. The IBM PC/RT is considered by some to be a powerful personal computer and by others to be an entry-level workstation. In fact, products like the IBM PC/RT blur the distinction between high-end personal computers and low-end workstations. In the future, more and more expert system shells and the expert systems developed with them will be showing up on all forms of computing machinery, including mainframe computers, minicomputers, workstations, and personal computers, as well as on LISP machines.

HARDWARE   The first expert systems and expert system shells were developed on either specialized machinery like LISP machines or on more conventional machines like the DEC-10 system using specialized software tools.

As LISP machines became more readily available, more and more of the development of expert system shells and expert systems was accomplished on these machines. As these shells and systems came to the marketplace, they were available only on LISP machines. These facts led to the belief that LISP machines were a prerequisite for the development and use of expert systems.

LISP machines were developed with the goal of making the development of a certain class of systems more effective. This class of systems includes expert systems. Often it is more effective to use a LISP machine in the development of expert system shells and expert systems. However, if an effective and comprehensive expert system shell product is available on a computer system that is not a LISP machine but does provide an effective user-system interface and the requisite memory and data storage requirements, there is no reason not to consider that particular expert system shell–computer system combination for the development of an expert system.

Given a particular problem and the selection of an appropriate expert system shell, any computer hardware suite that effectively supports the expert system shell should be seriously considered. For example, if it has been determined that the KEE expert system shell will provide the requisite components and functionality, any computer hardware suite that KEE runs on can be considered. Expert system shells like KEE, originally available only on LISP machines, are now or will soon be available on minicomputers like the DEC VAX, workstations like the Sun-3, and personal computers like the IBM PS.2 linked to mainframes.

Shell products like these are also available on mainframe computers as well as LISP machines. Figure 8.2 provides a cross-reference of a sample of what programming languages and expert system shells run on what hardware. This figure shows that many software resources exist and are available on all computer hardware forms for the development of expert systems. Developers of expert systems can choose appropriate hardware-software combinations for each problem on which they choose to work.

Expert system technology will become more and more an adjunct software engineering paradigm that software system developers will have available to them when developing new automated systems.

Although expert system shells will be available on many forms of computers in the future, the use of LISP machines is still an important asset in expert system development. For this reason, and for the reason that there is

	Programming Languages					Expert System Shells				
	LISP	PROLOG	OPS5	C	Pascal	ART	KEE	Insight 2+	EXSYS	PC Plus
LISP Machines										
LMI (GigaMos)	•	•			•	•	•			
Symbolics	•	•		•	•	•	•			
Texas Instruments	•	•		•		•	•			
Xerox	•	•	•				•			
Mainframes										
DEC	•	•	•	•	•	•	•	•	•	
IBM	•	•	•	•	•					
Minicomputers										
DEC	•	•	•	•	•	•	•	•	•	
Hewlett-Packard	•	•	•	•	•					
Workstations										
Apollo	•	•	•	•	•					
IBM	•	•	•	•	•		•			
Sun	•	•	•	•	•	•	•			
Personal Computers										
Apple	•		•	•	•			•		
Compaq	•	•	•	•	•	•	•	•	•	•
IBM	•	•	•	•	•		•	•	•	•
Texas Instruments	•	•	•	•	•					•

Figure 8.2 Computer hardware–expert system tools matrix

little written about LISP machines in other books, we will provide a chapter on the LISP machines that are commercially available.

There are two important reasons to understand what LISP machines are. The first has to do with the fact that to understand how expert system shells were originally developed, it is good to have a basic understanding of the machines that were used to develop many of the initial shell products. The second reason has to do with being able to compare other computer hardware to hardware that is known to be effective for the development and use of expert systems.

If there is any question as to whether an expert system will run efficiently on a particular piece of computer hardware, the developer has basically three choices. The first choice is to implement the expert system on available hardware and see if it supports the requirements properly. The second choice would be to consider hardware alternatives and select the one that best fits the system requirements. The third alternative is to use a LISP machine similar to one that has been used for a similar expert system. More is known about expert systems running successfully on LISP machines than on other computer hardware; however, this will change in the future.

STAFF

To develop an expert system, three personnel resources are required. Domain experts have traditionally been the source of the problem domain expertise. Knowledge engineers are needed to transfer the experts' domain knowledge to expert system knowledge bases and to develop the expert systems. Nonexperts have traditionally been the users of the expert systems. Expert systems have often been developed to assist a group of users who would otherwise have to go directly to the domain expert each time they had a problem. With expert systems, these users can consult with the system first. If it provides the information they need, they will not have to bother the domain expert. If the expert system is not able to help them, they could consult with the expert.

The success of an expert system implementation hinges on an effective integration of the human expert's knowledge, the knowledge engineer's expert system and knowledge-base development, and the needs and capabilities of the system's intended users.

The expertise, experience base, training, and domain knowledge of experts all help experts assist the nonexperts in an organization. When a member of an organization has a problem, this person usually has several sources of information available. The person's own knowledge and experiential information base is one possible source. When the problem extends beyond the person's knowledge, this person can either research the problem in the organization's technical library or seek out an expert in the subject area within the organization. Often the problem is researched and questions still exist, and these questions need answers. At this point, the human expert of an organization is the only choice left to the nonexpert for solving the problem. The ability of the organization to solve the problem now depends entirely on the organization's expert. The only other choice would be to obtain the information outside the organization, and for competitive or other financial reasons this option is not always available.

If a particular expert is always being sought out, this expert's knowledge might be a good candidate for an expert system implementation.

The knowledge engineer has many responsibilities in the development of an expert system:

1. Deciding the applicability of the expert system technology with respect to problems requiring support
2. Having knowledge of applicable expert system technology
3. Having knowledge of available expert system development tools
4. Choosing the correct technology for a particular problem
5. Choosing the correct tool that supports the requisite technology
6. Acquiring and codifying the expert's knowledge
7. Coding and developing the expert system
8. Refining the expert system's knowledge-base
9. Introducing the intended users of the expert system to the developed system
10. Training the users in the operation and effective use of the system.

Knowledge engineers will often have to rely on a multiplicity of skills from a variety of academic areas including computer science and cognitive psychology. They must be able to interview experts, acquire knowledge from the interviews, detect patterns of knowledge from disjointed information provided by the expert, and codify acquired knowledge in the language of the chosen expert system building tool (this task is analagous to computer programming).

The knowledge engineer transfers the expert's knowledge from the expert to the surrogate expert, the expert system. The purpose in performing this act is to provide the expert's knowledge to others in the organization who need the knowledge to perform their tasks. These individuals are to be the users of the developed expert system.

For an expert system to return the investment an organization puts into its development, the system must be used, and it must make the work of its users more effective. The system must provide difficult-to-obtain information to its users, or it must help its users solve a problem that without the expert system would either go unsolved or force the organization to bring in an expert. The former is often unsatisfactory; the latter might not be possible, if the expert has retired or moved geographically out of reach.

Use is an absolute requirement for an organization to realize a return on its investment in an expert system. Therefore, except for expert systems that operate in a totally automated environment, the user is an absolute human resource requirement.

Expert systems must be designed and developed with their intended users in mind. The user-system interface must fit into the user's environment. The text provided to the expert system user must be understandable and reasonable to that user. If the user is accustomed to certain forms of presentation (graphs, gauges, lights, signs), the expert system designer should take these forms into consideration.

The user should also help in the development of the system. The user will be able to provide guidance on what he or she needs and in what order and form information should be asked for or presented. The user will be able to tell the knowledge engineer when the system is understandable. Sometimes the ex-

The Problem Domain Expert

- Provides expertise and empirical knowledge
- Critiques the expert system as it evolves

The Knowledge Engineer

- Has knowledge of current expert system technology
- Has knowledge of available expert system development tools
- Selects the appropriate expert system technology and tool for the problem at hand
- Acquires and codifies the expert's knowledge into the expert system knowledge base
- Refines the knowledge in the expert system
- Introduces and trains the intended users in the use of the system
- Observes the system in operation and refines it so that it performs as valuable a job as possible

The Intended User

- Verifies that the system is understandable and usable
- Critiques the system as it evolves
- Uses the system in the performance of job tasks

Figure 8.3 Expert system personnel responsibilities and duties

pert will provide the knowledge engineer with key problem-solving knowledge but will leave out some intermediate knowledge pieces. The user will be able to assist the knowledge engineer in identifying these oversights.

The user knows the tasks required and can provide this information to the knowledge engineer, who will need this information to identify the structure of the work that the expert system is to support. With work breakdown information, the knowledge engineer will be able to structure the expert system in the most effective manner.

In the end, the user will use the developed expert system, which should assist the user in the performance of tasks, ideally to the point that the assistance saves the organization personnel resources or decreases worker error.

Figure 8.3 provides a summary of the personnel responsibilities and duties related to the development and use of an expert system.

SUMMARY

In this chapter, the three resources required for the construction of expert systems (software, hardware, and personnel) were identified and discussed.

For the personnel resource requirements, three people were identified as being necessary for the development of expert systems: the domain expert, the knowledge engineer, and the user.

The software and hardware resource requirements identified in this chapter are the subjects of the chapters in the next part of this book, Part III.

PART **III** TOOLS FOR BUILDING
EXPERT SYSTEMS

9 LANGUAGES

The first expert systems, including DENDRAL, MACSYMA, and MYCIN, were written in the LISP programming language. Many of the first significant expert system shells were developed on LISP machines in this language. Examples of these shells include ART and KEE. Early personal-computer-based expert system shells were also written in LISP (for example, Personal Consultant by Texas Instruments) or PROLOG (such as M.1 by Teknowledge). The OPS5 programming language was originally written in LISP. OPS5 has been used to develop a few significant expert systems, including XCON and XSEL.

Expert system and tool developers chose languages like LISP, PROLOG, and OPS5 for various reasons. The developers wanted specific features made available by the language they were using, including the ability to handle symbolic manipulation efficiently and support for incremental program development.

The artificial intelligence community invested heavily in developing programming environments for AI languages, most notably the environments that have been developed for the LISP programming language.

Computer hardware systems known as LISP machines will be discussed in detail later in this book. These machines have been specifically designed to provide effective LISP development workstations. They were developed in the United States. Japan is presently working on AI workstations that are based on the PROLOG programming language. The goal of these PROLOG machines will also be to provide effective development workstations, in this case to support the development of AI software like expert systems in PROLOG.

Expert systems and tools have also been built in other programming languages. Some have been designed, prototyped, and in some cases developed in languages like LISP and later ported to other languages like C and Pascal.

Languages like LISP and PROLOG tend to perform less efficiently on traditional computer hardware like DEC VAX and IBM mainframe systems than languages like C and Pascal. Programs written in languages like C and Pascal also tend to run more efficiently than the AI languages on personal computers.

Although special-purpose expert systems will continue to be built on LISP machines, in the future many more expert systems will be built for the more traditional computer hardware.

As expert system technology becomes better understood, its utility will become more obvious to the more traditional management information system (MIS) divisions and shops of the corporate world. Expert systems will become identified as ''just another data processing tool.'' The corporate MIS shops have, in the past, shown only limited interest in special-purpose hardware. Today there is even greater reason for employing environments that facilitate portability of code, connectivity, standards, access to existing dababases, and ease of use by existing staff. There should always be a market for LISP machines, but it will be limited to research and development operations and specialized applications such as weapons systems and intelligent machines, rather than to the more traditional business operations that are usually identified with the MIS shops.

If LISP machines are not accepted by groups like corporate MIS shops and if programs written in languages like LISP do not run efficiently on the computer systems that corporate MIS shops use, what is the future for the AI languages?

The future of AI languages like LISP and PROLOG will be determined mostly by the research and development (R&D) community. The R&D community will most likely continue to use AI languages for the development of new expert system tools and ideas. Expert system developers will also continue to use AI languages for expert system prototype development for domains that are not supported by commercially available shells. AI students will still be taught AI principles with the AI languages. Expert system researchers and some developers, as well as AI students, need the AI languages.

We will examine three popular AI languages: LISP, PROLOG, and OPS5. The discussions will include descriptions of the languages, analyses of their strengths, and examples of the code for each language.

We will not present sufficient tutorial material to enable programming in these languages; for this, see the references at the end of this chapter.

LISP

LISP is a widely used artificial intelligence language whose name is derived from *LISt Processor*. An overview of LISP will be presented, followed by a discussion of LISP features and structures and a tutorial that will help explain how LISP works.

LISP was the first symbolic processing language. It was developed in 1958 at the Massachusetts Institute of Technology by John McCarthy, initially as a programming language in which researchers could efficiently implement computer programs capable of reasoning. LISP became popular because of its symbol manipulation capability. It became the language chosen by many for AI applications development.

Today LISP is also being used in various domains including compiler writing, VLSI design systems, mechanical computer-aided design systems, animation graphics, and expert systems. Special-purpose LISP machines have been developed and are being used by many LISP programmers. LISP machines are minicomputers that have been architected to run programs written in the LISP programming language.

LISP Key Features

LISP became a popular AI programming language because it offered a wide range of features, one of which was the capability of symbol manipulation in the form of list structures.

The use of lists, collections of items contained within parentheses, to represent associations between symbols has been key to efficient symbolic processing. Due to this fact, the word *list* has been included in the description of many symbolic processing tools and features. Symbolic processing is sometimes referred to as list processing. The following are examples of LISP lists:

```
(+  54 267)
(STEVE COTY JUDI)
(VEHICLES (PLANE (DC9 DC10) AUTOMOBILE (FORD RENAULT)))
```

In the last list, (DC9 DC10) and (FORD RENAULT) are themselves lists contained in a larger list:

```
(PLANE (DC9 DC10) AUTOMOBILE (FORD RENAULT))
```

This list, in turn, is contained in a larger list that also includes the element VEHICLES.

The representation of a list in computer memory is a series of cells containing two parts or fields (see Figure 9.1). In any given cell, one of two situations is possible: One field may contain a symbol while the other contains a pointer to the next cell in the list, or each cell may contain a pointer to a symbol or to another cell.

By using lists, a programmer does not need to know the size or structure of the data at the time the program is being written. In many programming languages, the exact size and structure of the data that is to be processed must be determined in order for the computer to allocate enough memory space. In LISP, the size and shape of any given list can change continually without having any effect on the execution of the program.

Other LISP features include recursion, interactive interpreters, treating LISP programs as data, and LISP programming environments.

Recursion is a technique that has proved important in intelligent problem

The list (STEVE COTY JUDI) will be used for this illustration.

1. A cell

2. In the simple list representation, a symbol is contained in the first field in each cell, and the second field, except for the last field, contains a pointer to the next cell.

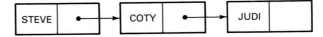

3. In the more complex list representation, each cell contains a pointer to a symbol in its first field, and except for the last cell, each also contains a pointer to the next cell in its second field.

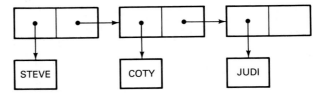

Figure 9.1   List representation in memory

solving. Recursion is a program structure that allows LISP to solve such problems as finding the factorial of a number. By definition, the factorial of a positive integer is defined as follows:

- The factorial of 1 is 1.
- The factorial of an integer greater than 1 is that integer multiplied by the factorial of the next lower integer.

To calculate the factorial of a number, one must first calculate the factorial of the next lower number; and to calculate the factorial of that lower number, one must first calculate the factorial of the next lower number; and so on. The recursive factorial procedure is stopped when the factorial of 1 is reached (the factorial of 1 is 1 by definition); then all of the other factorials can be calculated as can the desired result (see Figure 9.2).

The technique used in Figure 9.2 to calculate the factorial of a number cannot be represented in all programming languages, because some languages do not support recursion; LISP does.

With LISP, time is not wasted waiting for an entire program to be interpreted each time a change is made in that program. This is because LISP incor-

The exclamation point stands for *factorial;* calculating the factorial of the integer 4 is performed as follows:

$$4! = 4 \times 3!$$

$$3! = 3 \times 2!$$

$$2! = 2 \times 1!$$

$$1! = 1 \text{ by definition}$$

Now that we know that $1! = 1$, and we have equations for $2!$, $3!$, and $4!$, we can go ahead and calculate $4!$:

$$1! = 1$$

$$2! = 2 \times 1! = 2 \times 1 = 2$$

$$3! = 3 \times 2! = 3 \times 2 = 6$$

$$4! = 4 \times 3! = 4 \times 6 = 24$$

Therefore, the factorial of 4 is 24.

Figure 9.2 Recursive calculation of the factorial of 4

porates an interactive interpreter that translates each instruction during the execution of the program. This interpreter feature is important. Without it, a great deal of time might be wasted while waiting to compile LISP programs before being able to execute them. AI programs are known for many trial-and-error processes typically required during development, and this feature helps developers by allowing them to work in this trial-and-error mode. LISP compilers also exist for the rapid execution of completed programs.

LISP is an interactive language. LISP programs allow programmers to interact with their programs during all the phases of development. Programmers can experiment with various programming techniques during program development and can also provide information to the program during program execution.

LISP offers a rich programming environment. Its environment is composed of groups of programs designed to expedite program development and execution thanks to features such as a text editor, a debugger, and a windowing system. These and other LISP tools exist to help programmers in the development of their applications.

LISP programs can be used as data by other LISP programs. LISP programs can modify or add instructions to themselves (this feature is known as extensibility) and create new LISP programs. Declarative and procedural knowledge are easily integrated because LISP data and programs are in exactly the same format. The monitoring of the execution of instructions is available; it is possible to know which LISP instructions have been executed, in what order the executions of each instruction took place, and with what frequency each instruction was executed. These are benefits of the unique LISP language design.

LISP Structure

Although LISP is a powerful programming language, its basic structure is simple and straightforward. It is composed of combinations of the following language elements: atoms, lists, and procedures.

The atom, the smallest unit in LISP, may be a number or a symbol. The following are examples of atoms:

7	PAUL	A
33.6	R2B2	+
.3354	IS-BIGGER-THAN	ADD1

The first column contains numbers; the other two columns are symbolic atoms or symbols. Symbols can be used to represent almost anything, including numbers, words, people's names, and LISP function names. Symbols can be combinations of letters, numbers, and a few special characters such as hyphens. LISP also incorporates the following special symbols:

T	truth, yes
NIL	falsehood, emptiness, no

LISP procedures are included in lists to specify what to do with different atoms. In lists where procedures are present, the first element in each list will always be the procedure. The remaining elements are the arguments for the procedure. There are two types of procedures in LISP:

1. Primitives are built into LISP. Examples of such procedures are: +, *, QUOTIENT, EQUAL. In the list (+ 5 6), the primitive + specifies that arguments 5 and 6 should be added together.

2. Procedures are defined by programmers through the LISP function DEFUN *(DEfine FUNction)*. As an example, we could define a function called HALF that would compute the value that is half of any given number:

(DEFUN HALF (N) (QUOTIENT N 2))

Once a function has been defined, LISP can directly evaluate expressions that use the specified procedure.

LISP Dialects

Since its creation in 1958, many versions of LISP have been created to satisfy numerous user groups. In an effort to standardize LISP, CommonLISP was created. All existing versions of LISP (known as LISP dialects) fall into two main categories: the versions derived from Bolt, Beranek, and Newman (BBN) LISP and the versions derived from MacLISP.

BBN LISP originated in the Bolt, Beranek, and Newman firm in the Boston area and was transported to the Xerox Palo Alto Research Center (PARC) in California. It was at PARC that such LISP dialects as INTERLISP *(INTERactive LISP)*, INTERLISP-D, and VAX LISP were derived from BBN LISP. INTERLISP-D was designed for the Xerox 1100 series of workstations. VAX LISP was designed for the Digital Equipment Corporation VAX computer system.

MacLISP was created at M.I.T. Franz LISP, ZETALISP, and GC-LISP *(Golden Common LISP)* were derived from MacLISP. Franz LISP was created at the University of California at Berkeley and runs on the UNIX operating system. ZETALISP was created for LISP machines such as the Symbolics 3600. GC-LISP was developed for personal computers, including the IBM PC.

LISP Tutorial

This section is designed to introduce basic LISP primitive, function, and symbol manipulation concepts. The LISP concepts to be introduced are (1) the notion of predicate, (2) the use of QUOTE, (3) the use of the CAR, CDR, SET, and CONS primitives, (4) the defining of functions, and (5) the making of conditional statements.

A predicate is a LISP function that provides yes (T) or no (NIL) answers to any question. For example, if we want to find out whether we are dealing with a number or a symbol, we can define the following predicates (→ means "evaluates to"):

NUMBERP (as in "number predicate") will test if the input is a number or not:

(NUMBERP 7) → T
(NUMBERP Z) → NIL

SYMBOLP will test whether or not the input is a symbol:

(SYMBOLP X) → T
(SYMBOLP 5) → NIL

QUOTE or ′ is a special LISP form that returns exactly what is input, for example:

```
'(HELLO STEVE) → (HELLO STEVE)
'HORSE         → HORSE
```

The CAR primitive is used to retrieve the first element of a list:

```
(CAR '(X Y Z))    → X
(CAR '((X Y) Z))  → (X Y)
```

The CDR primitive is the complement of the CAR primitive and is used to retrieve all but the first element of a list:

```
(CDR '(X Y Z))    → (Y Z)
(CDR '((X Y) Z))  → (Z)
```

SET assigns a value to a symbol:

Expression	Symbol	Value
(SET X '2)	X	2
(SET SWITCH '(POWER ON))	SWITCH	(POWER ON)

The CONS *(CONStruct)* primitive is used to insert a new element at the beginning of a list:

```
(CONS 'X '(Y Z))            → (X Y Z)
(CONS 'ATTENTION SWITCH)    → (ATTENTION POWER ON)
```

Notice that in the last example we have assumed that the symbol SWITCH has a value that was previously assigned to it; in this case the value was previously assigned by the SET primitive.

LISP functions are defined through a special form called DEFUN, DE, DEF, or DEFINE, depending on the LISP dialect used. For example, if we want to define a function called HALF that will return a number that is half of a given number, we will use the following:

```
(DEFUN HALF (N) (QUOTIENT N 2))
```

Here, N is the name given to the function HALF argument.

```
(HALF 16) → 8
```

(HALF PAUL) will generate an error message because PAUL is a symbol, not a number.

Identically, we can define the following:

```
(DEFUN SQUARE (N) (TIMES N N))
(SQUARE 4) → 16
(DEFUN CALL-UP (A B) (LIST 'HELLO A 'THIS 'IS B 'CALLING))
(CALL-UP (STEVE JAMES)) → (HELLO STEVE THIS IS JAMES CALLING)
```

Notice that in the last example we have used LIST, which is a function used to create a list, for example:

```
(LIST 'A '(B C) 'D) → (A (B C) D)
```

To create conditional statements in LISP, the special form IF is used. This form has three arguments: a condition, a true part, and a false part. If the condition is true, only the true part is evaluated by the IF form. If the condition is false, the true part is skipped, and only the false part is evaluated. Here are some illustrative examples:

```
(IF (ODDP 4) 'ODD 'EVEN) → EVEN
(IF (ODDP 5) 'ODD 'EVEN) → ODD
(IF (SYMBOLP 7) (PLUS 4 5) (TIMES 6 7)) → 42
```

LISP Summary

LISP is a list-oriented computer programming language. It is an artificial intelligence programming language that is capable of effective symbol manipulation. LISP is used today to develop expert systems and various other computer software systems that require extensive symbolic processing.

PROLOG

PROLOG (*PROgramming in LOGic*) is a widely used AI programming language. We shall examine a historical overview of PROLOG, a description of some of its features and structures, and a presentation of its different dialects.

PROLOG was developed in France in 1973 by Alain Colmerauer and his research team at the University of Marseilles. It was first used for natural-language processing. It became a popular programming language among AI developers for symbolic manipulation applications. Using the results obtained by the French research group, Robert Kowalski of the University of Edinburgh in Scotland developed a theory of logic programming. PROLOG experienced a boom in popularity in 1981 when the Japanese decided to base the research for their fifth-generation computer systems on PROLOG. PROLOG has been used to develop expert system shells, including the original version of M.1, and expert systems.

As indicated by its name, PROLOG supports logic-based knowledge representation and programming methods; it uses logic to solve problems. Using PROLOG, programmers describe their problems in terms of facts and rules. PROLOG searches for possible solutions to the problems presented to it.

PROLOG Program Structure

PROLOG programs consist of facts, rules, and questions. The facts are used to represent the existence of relationships between objects. For example, the sentence "Peter owns a car" is a fact that contains two objects, "Peter" and "car," and a relationship between them called "owns." The PROLOG form of this sentence is

owns (peter, car).

Here are some PROLOG notation and syntax rules:

- Names of objects and relationships begin with a lower-case letter.
- Relationships are written first, followed by objects enclosed in parentheses; objects are separated from each other by commas within the parentheses. In PROLOG, relationships are called predicates and objects are called arguments (of the predicates).
- The end of each fact must be marked by a period.

The order in which the objects are presented in the facts is important. For example, the fact "owns (car, peter)." is totally different from "owns (peter, car)." The former would normally be translated into English as "Car owns Peter," which is not what is wanted. Figure 9.3 provides more examples of PROLOG facts.

The number of arguments in a given fact is not limited. In PROLOG, a collection of facts is called a database.

A question in PROLOG resembles a fact that is preceded by ?- (a question mark immediately followed by a hyphen). For example, the fact

owns (peter, car).

can be transformed into the question

?- owns (peter, car).

This question can be translated to "Does Peter own a car?" or "Is it a fact that Peter owns a car?"

For a given question, PROLOG will search the database for facts that match the fact contained in that question. Facts match when they have identical predicates and identical arguments arranged in the same order. When a match

rich (neal).   "Neal is rich."
female (judi).   "Judi is female."
mother-of (mary, betty).   "Mary is the mother of Betty."
play (paul, bill, soccer). "Paul and Bill play soccer."

Figure 9.3   Examples of facts in PROLOG and their English translations

to a question is found, PROLOG answers "yes" to that question. In the case when no match is found, the response "no" is given. Figure 9.4 provides an example.

As illustrated in Figure 9.4, the response to each question is given by PROLOG in the line following the question.

In PROLOG, any object beginning with an upper-case character is a variable. If we want to determine who the mother of Betty is, we ask the question

$$?- \text{mother (X, betty)}.$$

PROLOG will respond with

$$X = \text{mary}$$

In the question, X is a variable. PROLOG gets its value by matching the question with the facts contained in the current PROLOG database.

Conjunctions of facts are formed by placing commas between the facts to

PROLOG Database	Questions and PROLOG Answers
rich (neal).	?- rich (neal).
female (judi).	yes
mother (mary, betty).	?- male (judi).
	no
	?- mother (mary, sue).
	no
	?- mother (mary, betty).
	yes

Figure 9.4   A PROLOG database and accompanying questions

be conjoined. For example, if we want to say "James is wealthy and owns a car," we can write

wealthy (james), owns (james, car).

Rules in PROLOG have the form F1 :- F2. The symbol :- is read "if," and F1 and F2 are facts. F1 is called the head of the rule and describes the fact the rule is trying to establish. F2 is called the body of the rule and represents the goal that must be satisfied for the head to be true. If we want to establish the fact that Marilyn is the sister of Steve, we write the following rule:

```
sister (marilyn, steve) :-
    female (marilyn),
    parents (marilyn, P),
    parents (steve, P).
```

The English translation of this rule is:

Marilyn is the sister of Steve if
Marilyn is a female and
Marilyn's parents are P and
Steve's parents are P.

PROLOG supports various data structures, including constants, structures, and lists. There are two types of constants: atoms and integers. Examples of atoms that are words are

mindy   steve   owns   likes

Examples of symbols that are atoms are

?-   :−   =

Integers are whole numbers ranging from 0 to 16383. These numbers do not contain a decimal point. Standard PROLOG implementations do not support negative integers.

Structures are objects consisting of collections of other objects called components. Examples of structures are:

owns (james, car)
owns (james, car (cimarron, cadillac))

The English translation of the second example is "James owns a car called a Cimarron by Cadillac."

A list is a collection of elements, such as atoms and structures, that are put in a certain order inside a pair of square brackets. The first element of a list is called the head of the list. The remaining elements constitute the tail of the list. Lists can contain other lists and variables. Figure 9.5 provides some PROLOG list examples as well as the head and tail components.

PROLOG Features

PROLOG incorporates a wide range of features, including a control mechanism, built-in predicates, and effective debugging facilities.

Backtracking and cut constitute the basic control mechanisms. Backtracking is the process PROLOG goes through when handling multiple requests. PROLOG takes each part of each request in sequential order and tries to match the parts with something in memory. If PROLOG cannot succeed in matching any given part, it will not be able to continue to the next part; instead, PROLOG backtracks and looks for other ways of matching the earlier parts, in order to locate a match for the item causing the stop. To illustrate backtracking, we will use the following database:

```
student (robert, 18).
student (mark, 20).
student (judi, 18).
student (john, 18).
```

From this database containing facts about the names and ages of some students, we will try to find all possible pairs of students who are 18 years old. The translation of this goal into PROLOG would be

```
?- student (Person1,18),
   student (Person2,18),
   Person1 <> Person2.
```

This query asks PROLOG to find all pairs of Person1 and Person2 where Person1 is aged 18, Person2 is aged 18, and Person1 and Person2 are different. What will happen? At first PROLOG will try to find a solution to the first

List	Head	Tail
[x, y, z, w]	x	[y, z, w]
[x]	x	[ ]
[[our, car], maroon]	[our, car]	[maroon]
[[x + y], [z − w]]	[x + y]	[z − w]

Figure 9.5   PROLOG list examples

subgoal, student (Person1,18). It will continue to the next subgoal only when the first subgoal is satisfied. The first subgoal is satisfied with "Person1 = robert." Now PROLOG can satisfy student (Person2,18) by also taking "Person2 = robert." Now PROLOG tries to verify the last subgoal, Person1 <> Person2. Since Person1 and Person2 are both "robert," this subgoal fails. PROLOG backtracks to the previous subgoal, which is student (Person2,18) and searches for another solution. By taking "Person2 = judi," the second subgoal is reached, and the third subgoal, Person1 <> Person2, is also satisfied, since "robert" and "judi" are different. At this point, the entire goal is satisfied. PROLOG then backtracks in an attempt to find another possible solution. Since the second subgoal, student (Person2,18), can be satisfied by taking Person2 as "john," PROLOG tries the third subgoal once again. It succeeds since "robert" and "john" are different. At this point, another solution to the goal is found.

In another attempt to find other solutions, PROLOG will once again backtrack to the second subgoal, but it finds that all the possibilities have been considered for this subgoal. So it backtracks to the first subgoal. It finds that the first subgoal can be satisfied by taking Person1 to be "judi." The second subgoal now succeeds by taking Person2 to be "john." Here again, the entire goal is satisfied since "judi" is different from "john."

The final solution is with Person1 and Person2 as "john." For this case, the third subgoal fails, and PROLOG must backtrack to the second subgoal, but there are no new possibilities. PROLOG backtracks to the first subgoal and finds that all the possibilities have been exhausted. At this point, the execution terminates.

Here is the list of all the pairs of students that were obtained:

Person1 = robert	Person2 = judi
Person1 = robert	Person2 = john
Person1 = judi	Person2 = robert
Person1 = judi	Person2 = john
Person1 = john	Person2 = robert
Person1 = john	Person2 = judi

We have a total of six solutions. Notice that Person1 = robert and Person2 = judi is one valid solution and Person1 = judi and Person2 = robert is another valid solution. If this duplication of pairs is not wanted, an additional subgoal must be specified to exclude them.

The cut control mechanism is used to prevent backtracking under certain circumstances. PROLOG cannot backtrack past a cut. The symbol used to represent a cut is the exclamation mark (!). The cut is used for two reasons: to avoid wasting memory space and to avoid wasting time. For instance, when it is evident to a programmer that a particular possibility will never result in a satisfactory solution, the programmer can use a cut to prevent PROLOG from backtracking to it. This permits the program to operate faster and to use less memory space since the number of backtracking points to be considered is reduced. To illustrate the use of the cut, we will use our database containing facts about the names and ages of the students, together with the following goal:

```
?- student (Person1,18), !,
   student (Person2,18),
   Person1 <> Person2.
```

With the cut symbol following the first subgoal, only the first solution of that subgoal will be considered; there will be no backtracking to this subgoal for other solutions. The solution for the whole goal will then be

```
Person1 = robert   Person2 = judi
Person1 = robert   Person2 = john
```

For the goal

```
?- student (Person1,18),
   student (Person2,18),!,
   Person1 <> Person2.
```

The solution is one pair, "Person1 = robert" and "Person2 = judi." In this goal, the position of the cut tells PROLOG that we are satisfied with the first valid solution of subgoal 1 and subgoal 2.

PROLOG has built-in predicates that can be used directly to perform actions, including entering new clauses in a program, classifying terms, affecting backtracking, creating complex goals, handling files, evaluating arithmetic expressions, reading and writing characters, and observing PROLOG program executions.

PROLOG contains debugging features that allow programmers to watch programs, pinpoint bugs, and make corrections by using its tracing facility.

PROLOG Dialects

Since its creation in 1972, PROLOG has had such success that different dialects have been created to satisfy a wide range of users. Some of the well known PROLOG dialects are PROLOG I, PROLOG II, and Micro-PROLOG.

PROLOG I is the first version of PROLOG that was created in 1973 by Alain Colmerauer at the University of Marseilles. PROLOG I is also referred to as Marseilles PROLOG.

After the release of PROLOG I, Colmerauer and his team spent a few years trying to improve this version. In 1982 they announced that they had come out with "the ultimate PROLOG." This new version of PROLOG was named

PROLOG II by its authors. The innovation in PROLOG II is the ability to handle infinite terms or cyclic structures.

In a successful attempt to install PROLOG on an 8-bit microcomputer, McCabe created Micro-PROLOG in 1981. This version of PROLOG is the language selected by Kowalski, the founder of predicate calculus, and his team at Imperial College in London, for their research. The basic differences between Micro-PROLOG and the other versions are essentially in the syntax of programs and in the way querying is done.

PROLOG Summary

PROLOG is a symbolic programming language that was developed in France. Because of the wide variety of features it incorporates, PROLOG has become popular. It is a language chosen by many for the development of their artificial intelligence systems, including expert system shells, like the original version of M.1, and expert systems. PROLOG has various dialects that support its use on mainframe computers, minicomputers, LISP machines, and microcomputers.

OPS5

OPS5 (Official Production System 5) is a knowledge engineering language that supports the rule-based representation method. It incorporates a pattern matcher, an interpreter that includes a forward-chaining mechanism, and various programming tools such as editing and debugging tools. OPS5 is a member of the OPS family of programming languages developed at Carnegie-Mellon University. Implementations of this language exist in BLISS, MacLISP, and Franz LISP. Commercial implementations of OPS5 have been developed by companies including the Digital Equipment Corporation and Verac Corporation. OPS5 implementations are available for a variety of computer hardware systems, including LISP machines (such as Xerox 1108), minicomputers (DEC VAX), and microcomputers (IBM PC).

OPS5 Programming Structure and Features

An OPS5 program is composed of two sections: a declaration section and a production section. The declaration section includes the definitions and descriptions of all the data object types and all the user-defined functions contained in the program. The production section contains all the production rules. During the execution of an OPS5 program, the manipulated data is found in working memory, and the rules are in production memory.

OPS5 supports the use of various data types that can be grouped in two main categories: primitive data types and compound data types. The primitive data types, also known as scalar types, include numbers (integers and floating-

point numbers) and symbolic atoms. A symbolic atom is a sequence of characters. Examples of symbolic atoms are

> private
> 385 __Westbury __Drive
> name

In OPS5, the compound data structure is an element class, and each component of an element class is called an attribute. The class name and the attribute names should be symbolic atoms. Any given element class in an OPS5
program should be declared as follows:

> (literalize Classname
>   attribute1
>   attribute2
>   •
>   •
>   attributeN)

where Classname is the class name, attribute1. . .attributeN are the attribute
names, and literalize is an OPS5 command (see Figure 9.6 for an illustration of
the literalize command).

```
(literalize Vehicle ;  Element class representing mode of
                    ;  transportation
    type           ;  name attribute of a vehicle, or nil
    make           ;  name attribute of a vehicle, or nil
    model__year    ;  year the vehicle was made, or nil
    odometer       ;  positive integer, or nil
)

(literalize Person ;  Element class representing people
    first__name    ;  first name of person
    last__name     ;  last name of person
    area__code     ;  positive integer, or nil
    phone__no      ;  telephone number, or nil
    sex            ;  indicates whether person is male or
                   ;  female
    birth__date    ;  person's birth date
)

(literalize Start)  ;  Element class for initialization
```

Figure 9.6   Compound data examples in OPS5

In Figure 9.6 we have three class names: Vehicle, Person, and Start. The Vehicle element class has four attributes: type, make, model__year, and odometer. The Person element class has six attributes: first__name, last__name, area__ code, phone__no, sex, and birth__date. The Start element class has no attributes and is used to initialize the program. The symbolic atom ''nil'' is used as the value to which all the attributes are initialized. The semicolon is used to mark the start of a comment.

In OPS5, there is a special type of attribute, called the vector attribute, that, in contrast with the other attributes, can have more than one scalar value. Each element class can have only one vector attribute, and each vector attribute must be declared. In Figure 9.6, the birth__date attribute for the Person class may have three values: the day, the month, and the year of birth. The general form of a vector attribute is the following:

$$(\text{vector-attribute} \quad \text{attribute1}$$
$$\text{attribute2}$$
$$\bullet$$
$$\bullet$$
$$\text{attributeN})$$

There are various ways of declaring vector attributes. Two commonly used forms of declaration are presented in Figure 9.7.

In OPS5, data manipulated during the execution of a program is kept in working memory and constitutes the elements of the working memory. Each data element in working memory is made up of an attribute value element. If no specific value is attached to a given attribute, the ''nil'' default value is

```
(literalize Person first__name last__name area__code phone__no
        sex birth__date)
(vector-attribute birth__date)
(literalize Vehicle type make model__year odometer
        brand__of__tire)
(vector-attribute brand__of__tire)

AND

(vector-attribute birth__date brand__of__tire)
(literalize Person first__name last__name area__code phone__no
        sex birth__date)
(literalize Vehicle type make model__year odometer
        brand__of__tire)
```

Figure 9.7   Declaration of vector attributes

assigned to that attribute. Attributes are distinguished from their values by the prefix operator ↑ attached to them. Each working memory element is created by a make command. In Figure 9.8, the use of the make command will create two working memory elements.

An integer value called the time tag will be attached to each working memory element created. This integer value is used to determine when a specific working memory element was first entered or last modified. The larger the time tag, the more recent the element it refers to was entered or modified. So if the make commands in Figure 9.8 were executed, a printing of the working memory would look like:

```
1:  (Vehicle    ↑type car    ↑make Cadillac    ↑model__year  1985
    ↑odometer 21,000)
2:  (Person    ↑first__name Steven    ↑last__name Marks
    ↑area__code 301    ↑phone__no 956-6756    ↑sex male)
```

Production rules in OPS5 have the form ''antecedent → consequent.'' The antecedent is made up of one or more condition elements that are to be matched against some working memory elements. The consequent specifies the actions to be taken in case of a match between the antecedent and working memory elements. The antecedent is also referred to as the left-hand side (LHS) of the rule, and the consequent is referred to as the right-hand side (RHS) of the rule. Each side of an OPS5 production rule is composed of one or more lists.

In OPS5, there are two ways of entering production rules in the system:

- By using the top-level command ''p'' (for production), rules are entered before the execution begins.

- By calling the action ''build'' on the right-hand side of a rule, rules can be added during execution.

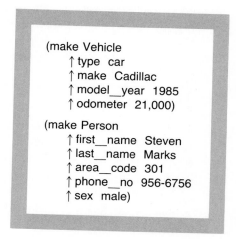

```
(make Vehicle
    ↑type  car
    ↑make  Cadillac
    ↑model__year 1985
    ↑odometer  21,000)

(make Person
    ↑first__name  Steven
    ↑last__name  Marks
    ↑area__code  301
    ↑phone__no  956-6756
    ↑sex  male)
```

Figure 9.8 Using the make command

To illustrate the use of rules in OPS5, consider an example in which we want to write a program to maintain a database of people's names. Whenever a new name is encountered, we would like to add a new object to represent that name. We would like an OPS5 implementation of this:

> IF   there is a Person with the name <nameA>
>   AND the name <nameA> doesn't exist in the database,
> THEN   create a database entry for a Person named <nameA>.

The OPS5 translation of this could be:

```
(p  make-new-name
    (Person    ↑ last-name  <nameA>)
  - (Person    ↑ name  <nameA>)
    →
    (make Person    ↑ name  <nameA>))
```

In this production rule, make-new-name is the name of the rule. The two clauses (Person   ↑ last-name <nameA>) and -(Person   ↑ name <nameA>) constitute the LHS of the rule. The clause (make Person   ↑ name <nameA>) constitutes the RHS of the rule. The use of angle brackets (as in ``<nameA>'') indicates that the expression in brackets is a variable. The nameA variable will match any last-name that does not exist in the database. If we want to express the fact that there is no working memory element that will match a given condition, we use the minus sign at the beginning of that particular condition. In our example, the condition element ``- (Person   ↑ name <nameA>)'' will match if there is no element in the working memory of class Person with a value for the name attribute equal to nameA.

The RHS of an OPS5 production rule is composed of one or more list structures. Each list contains an action to be performed as the first element of the list, followed by the arguments of that action. Various predefined commands exist that can be used in the RHS of rules to specify the actions to be taken. Here are some of the actions that can be taken:

- The "make" action is used to create new working memory elements.
- The "remove" action is used to remove elements from working memory.
- The "modify" action is used to modify one or more attributes of a particular element of working memory.
- The "write" action is used to write messages to a terminal or to a file.
- The "build" action is used to create new rules for production memory during program execution.
- File actions such as "openfile," "closefile," and "default" are used to manage files.

The RHS can also contain functions such as these:

- "compute" to do arithmetic operations
- "accept" and "acceptline" to read inputs directly from files or a terminal

The OPS5 Control Mechanism

The basic control mechanism in OPS5 consists of matching, selecting, and executing production rules. In the matching process, the OPS5 inference engine attempts to match the LHS of rules against working memory elements. The LHS of a rule is said to match with working memory if the following conditions are met:

- There is a match between each nonnegated condition element and a working memory element.
- None of the working memory elements match with negated condition elements.
- Each element variable is bound to the working memory element matched.
- Only a single value is bound to any given variable appearing more than once in the LHS of a rule.

In the case where more than one rule is produced in the matching process, the OPS5 inference engine will go through a conflict resolution process to determine which rule to use first. An OPS5 programmer has the choice between two conflict resolution strategies, called LEX (lexigraphic ordering) and MEA (means-ends analysis). In the LEX conflict resolution strategy, the following is performed on the conflicting set of rules:

1. Refraction is performed to ensure that the conflict set is free of instantiations previously used or fired.
2. Recency orders of instantiations are formulated according to the recency of the time tags attached to the working memory elements matching condition elements.
3. Specificity selects the more specific rules when no instantiation dominates.
4. If no dominant instantiation is found in steps 1 to 3, the inference engine makes an arbitrary choice between the competing rules.

The MEA contains the same conflict resolution steps as LEX, except it adds a step that places emphasis on the recency of the working memory element that matches the first condition element of the rules. This conflict resolution strategy is often used when backward chaining is needed. The MEA conflict resolution steps are as follows:

1. Refraction
2. Recency of first condition elements

3. Recency of other condition elements

4. Specificity

5. Arbitrary choice

OPS5 Summary

OPS5 is a knowledge engineering language that supports the rule-based knowledge representation scheme. It offers effective control strategies that principally support forward-chaining inferencing, but it is also possible to support backward-chaining tasks with OPS5. OPS5 has been used to develop expert systems, notably XCON and XSEL at Digital Equipment Corporation. OPS5 is a very effective tool for producing expert systems whose tasks naturally fit into the forward-chaining paradigm, such as planning and configuring.

REFERENCES

1. R. A. Brooks, *Programming in Common LISP* (New York: Wiley, 1985).

2. L. Brownston, R. Farrell, E. Kant, and N. Martin, *Programming Expert Systems in OPS5* (Reading, MA: Addison-Wesley, 1985).

3. W. F. Clocksin and C. S. Mellish, *Programming in PROLOG* (Berlin: Springer-Verlag, 1981).

4. G. L. Steele, Jr., *Common LISP: The Language* (Burlington, MA: Digital Press, 1984).

10 EXPERT SYSTEM SHELLS

The key to the efficient building of expert systems today is to use expert system shells with components that support all the requirements of the systems to be built. The basic components of expert systems were presented earlier (see Fig. 1.6):

- Inference engine
- Knowledge-base
- User-system interface
- Explanation facility
- Knowledge acquisition facility

When an expert system construction project is completed, these five components must be in place and must work together to obtain the desired results. Whatever construction tools are used should assist the expert system builder with the efficient development of these components and with the entities going into the knowledge-base.

SHELL COMPONENTS

Most commercial shells available today provide most of the construction capabilities required to build productive expert systems. These capabilities are usually grouped logically into functional components. The actual shell components provided by the various shell vendors vary. Also, similar shell components in various expert system shell products may differ in functionality. These variations exist for many reasons, including these:

- Vendors' intended market
- Vendors' views of what is needed

- Vendors' background and capabilities
- Product age
- Third-party add-on market
- Knowledge engineer experience level being targeted

Even though expert system shell components vary, most fall into one of seven categories:

1. Knowledge engineers' development aids
2. Knowledge acquisition aids
3. Knowledge data management tools
4. Inference engines
5. User-system interfaces
6. Explanation facilities
7. Language interfaces

Knowledge engineers' development aids assist knowledge engineers with the development of expert systems. These aids provide capabilities necessary to build effective systems that are otherwise not provided by the other six component categories. These aids include screen formatting, graphics development aids, and multipurpose editors.

Screen formatters assist knowledge engineers in the development of customized terminal screen presentations. These formatters assist with specification requirements for such screen attributes as color, video presentation, and location.

Graphics development aids assist with the creation of graphics-based presentations. These aids often provide for the development of graphics entities known as icons as well as complete graphical presentations. Icons are portions of larger graphics pictures that represent some specific physical entity (such as a machine) or a specific conceptual entity (such as an alphabetic letter shown in a particular font).

Multipurpose editors provide expert system builders with various capabilities like text editing. These editors assist with creation, modification, and deletion capabilities. These functions might be used, for example, to develop the text portion of a consultation recommendation.

Knowledge acquisition is often considered the bottleneck or critical item in the critical path in the development of expert systems. Therefore, knowledge acquisition aids are crucial to cost-effective expert system development. Knowledge editors and induction tools are examples of knowledge acquisition aids.

Knowledge editors are special-purpose editors. These editors assist expert system builders in the population of the knowledge-base with knowledge data. These editors often are specifically configured to accept the knowledge data in exactly the form that is determined by the specific knowledge representation form. Sometimes these editors include certain basic knowledge data integrity-checking capabilities. For example, a knowledge editor for a rule-based knowledge-base could check that all rules have at least one IF condition clause and one THEN action clause. This kind of checking could be performed while the knowledge data is being loaded into the knowledge-base of the expert system. Any errors the editor detects could be brought to the attention of the knowledge engineer loading the data. The capability to check for knowledge data integrity will be improved on in the future.

Induction tools have the potential of developing knowledge data directly from the information sources that typically exist in many organizations today. Examples of these information sources include databases on computers, spreadsheets on personal computers, and manual records (such as bill of material records). If an organization wanted to develop a rule-based expert configuration system and had many years of records in a database on what parts went into what products for specific customer specifications, an induction tool like First Class (from Programs in Motion, Inc.) could be used to develop rules from the database records. These rules could then be augmented with manually developed rules that would correlate this knowledge with an expert's knowledge on how to use the induced knowledge when developing a new proposal configuration for a new client or where the proposal configuration is similar but not identical to past proposal configurations. Through the use of the induction tool, more than half of the rules for this expert system could be developed automatically, thus reducing the knowledge acquisition time and resource requirements of the knowledge engineer.

Knowledge data management tools provide very much the same services to expert systems that database management systems provide to management information systems. Knowledge-base management systems (KBMS) accept knowledge data from the expert system builder, store it, manage it, and provide it to the inference engine or explanation facility upon request.

The inference engine component of the expert system shell is the foundation of the inference engine of the expert system under development. The control logic for the expert system is based on this inference engine component. In many cases, this component should be all the control logic the expert system requires. In some cases, a minor portion of the required logic will be coded by the knowledge engineer and loaded in the knowledge-base.

The user-system interface (USI) component is the most important component when it comes to user acceptance of the system. It is important to ensure that the expert system shell provide all or most of the USI functionality for two reasons. First, without a comprehensive USI, the developed system will be more difficult for a user to learn and use. Second, the knowledge engineer will have to develop the requisite USI functionality, and this development can require a great deal of time and effort.

USI functionality can include menu generators, natural-language modules, and graphics presentation modules. The menu generation capability allows the knowledge engineer quickly to develop pick-what-you-want menus from which users can select pertinent options. Menu selection is a very intuitive USI paradigm. Natural-language capabilities assist users in the use of the developed systems. Natural-language modules assist knowledge engineers in the development of user-system interfaces that employ language and terminology that are natural and understandable to the intended users. Graphics presentations are often valuable aids in helping users understand questions and recommendations presented by expert systems. Graphics presentation modules help knowledge engineers incorporate graphics into the USI. Graphics presentation modules retrieve graphics files developed with graphics editors and present them in a manner that is specified by the expert system builder. Graphics will often be used when an expert system is trying to show spatial relationships between objects that are easier to represent with pictures than to describe with words.

Explanation facilities assist the expert system builder with the development of the expert system explanation facility. Often the expert system shell products provide the full facility. Only the actual explanations are missing since they are peculiar to the specific application. Most expert system shells derive the actual explanations from the knowledge data provided by the expert system builder, the knowledge engineer. Therefore, the knowledge engineer must keep the explanation function and use of the knowledge data in mind when formatting and inputting the knowledge data into the expert system knowledge-base. With this in mind, the knowledge engineer will be developing both the knowledge-base and the explanation capability at the same time. Therefore, in many cases, no explicit, separate work is needed to provide an explanation facility.

Language interfaces are important where the expert system design calls for the system to perform data manipulation that is not germane to expert system technology. An example of such manipulation is numeric analysis. Computer programming languages like Pascal and FORTRAN and program packages like Lotus 1-2-3 and Borland's Eureka: The Solver can handle a numeric task more efficiently than the expert system.

The language interface functions provided with most expert system shells allow the expert system builder to interface programs external to the expert system with the system. These interfaces provide a conduit whereby data can be passed between the expert system and other programs. The programming languages chosen by the expert system builder will be selected on the basis of language applicability to the requirements and the builder's familiarity with computer languages and general-purpose computer programs like Lotus 1-2-3.

For the expert system to use a program written in a computer language external to the expert system shell, two items are needed. First, the external program must be developed or purchased. Second, there must be a means by which to exchange the data. The first item must be taken care of by the expert system builder without any benefit from the expert system shell. The second item is often provided to some degree by the expert system shell. A data exchange function is very helpful to the expert system builder. Many expert system shells provide mechanisms for importing external data into the system and exporting data out of the system.

Some expert system shell components and tools are developed for the purpose of supporting the development of expert systems. Others are developed to assist users in running the developed expert systems. Still others are developed to support both the development and the run-time environments. Figure 10.1 provides a Venn diagram of development and run-time environment sets of components and tools.

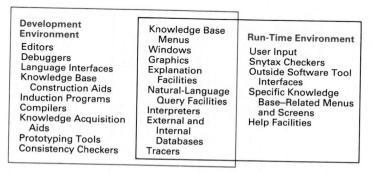

Development Environment

Editors
Debuggers
Language Interfaces
Knowledge Base
   Construction Aids
Induction Programs
Compilers
Knowledge Acquisition
   Aids
Prototyping Tools
Consistency Checkers

Knowledge Base
   Menus
Windows
Graphics
Explanation
   Facilities
Natural-Language
   Query Facilities
Interpreters
External and
   Internal
   Databases
Tracers

Run-Time Environment

User Input
Snytax Checkers
Outside Software Tool
   Interfaces
Specific Knowledge
   Base—Related Menus
   and Screens
Help Facilities

Figure 10.1   Development and run-time components and tools

KNOWLEDGE-BUILDING SUPPORT COMPONENTS

Induction tools, debugging tools, knowledge-base editors, interpreters, and consistency checkers are examples of the many tools that might be included in expert system shells to aid in the development of expert system knowledge-bases. Figure 10.2 shows many of the knowledge-base building tools that are often made available by expert system shell vendors.

Debugging aids, such as tracers, consistency checkers, and editing aids, are typical components of knowledge-base building tool sets provided in commercial expert system shells. The particular facilities provided depend on the design structure of the shell and what the vendor feels is important. For example, some shells integrate debuggers and editors, while others provide separate components.

Editors are often associated with changes and modifications of knowledge data entities in the knowledge base. Other editors are associated with the design facilities of menus, mathematical expressions, English text, and data formulation. Some editors are compatible with those found in programming languages like the dBase II and III–compatible Insight 2+ database editor.

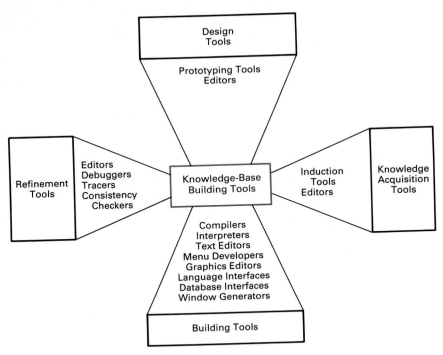

Figure 10.2   Knowledge-base building tools

Editor syntax checkers acknowledge grammatical and structural errors in the knowledge-base. Some editors reiterate the error and give the user an explanation of why it is incorrect; others only state that an error exists. Consistency checkers denote conflict in knowledge-base logic.

Debuggers are generic; they have a broad range of capabilities. Debuggers are incorporated in knowledge acquisition tools. These are some of their more common features:

- *Trace facilities* are used when analysis and evaluation of a system's reasoning process is required.

- *Verification facilities* are comparison devices used for evaluations of consultations; consultations are compared with stored information that relate to or appear similar to the consultation.

- *Break packages* are used when knowledge developers desire to discontinue a program prior to completion in order to examine, update, correct, or delete knowledge information from a run.

- *Debuggers* permit developers to run structured problems as a means of detecting system bugs, failures, and inconsistencies in the knowledge-base.

Some debuggers are specific programs built into knowledge-building tools. These programs operate like subroutines, each checking for specific information. They are programs to check for consistency, completeness, or general programmatic issues.

Programs designed to check for completeness work on the same premise as an editor. These programs check for missing data entities in knowledge data. Programs that check for consistency look for redundancy in data (for example, two rules fired simultaneously, both having the same conclusion). Other programs search for conflict in information (two rules fired for the same condition, yet conflict in their conclusion) and for subsumption suspected (two rules possessing identical outcomes, but one contains limitations that restrict the proposed outcome). Programmatic issues usually fall in line with syntactic and systematic analysis of the developing system. These issues are knowledge-base-dependent.

Some systems have menus or windows built into their structural design. These facilities aid in the friendliness of the overall system. Menus and windows are user interface facilities. In some expert system shells, development menus are designed to assist novice developers in building knowledge-bases. These systems are equipped with explanation facilities that are linked to components of the editor.

Rule development by example or rule induction is a facility for knowledge acquisition when the developer is a novice knowledge engineer or there is a desire to develop rules quickly from some preformatted information. Systems constructed in this fashion require the developer to input examples of specific problems and the required course of action in order to obtain a solution. The developer need not understand procedural rule formulation or other knowledge representation forms. The information provided by the developer is compiled in a knowledge-base that is then displayed to the developer in the form of a matrix or spreadsheet. Any displaced or missing information in the matrix can be filled in by the developer by implementing another example and its solution.

Another component found in many knowledge-base construction tools is a graphics interface. Several tools have graphics interfaces for development. This interface is in the form of a lattice (a visual representation of the system's logic flow). The ART and KEE expert system development tools provide this mechanism. As the developer structures the various attributes, he or she can also use the attributes to build a lattice. With some of these tools, a browser is used to build the lattice. A window display of each section of the lattice is displayed as it grows. The final product is a graphical display of the system's reasoning patterns. Figure 10.3 presents a lattice and some of the associated top-level rules. The knowledge-base can be run by the inferencing process during a consultation while providing the user with visuals of the reasoning process.

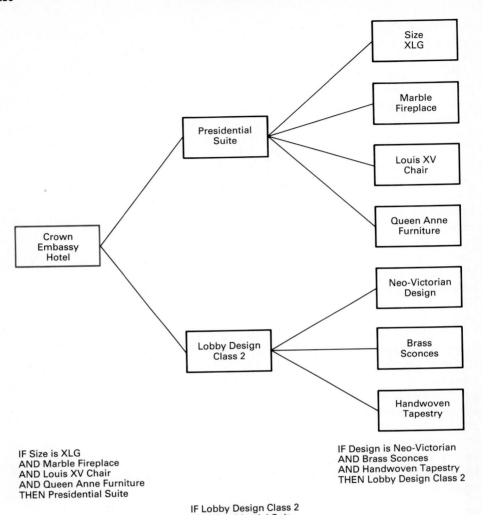

IF Size is XLG
AND Marble Fireplace
AND Louis XV Chair
AND Queen Anne Furniture
THEN Presidential Suite

IF Design is Neo-Victorian
AND Brass Sconces
AND Handwoven Tapestry
THEN Lobby Design Class 2

IF Lobby Design Class 2
AND Presidential Suite
THEN Crown Embassy Hotel

Figure 10.3   Example of a knowledge-base lattice

USER-SYSTEM INTERFACE TOOLS

Many components incorporated in expert system shells are designed to make the user-system interaction more flexible and friendly. Common features include graphics interfaces, menus, windows, explanation features, and natural-language dialogue. Figure 10.4 is a chart of some of the commercial expert systems shells and the user interface and developer interface components they provide.

KNOWLEDGE-BASES, BLACKBOARDS, AND DATABASE INTERFACES

Blackboard architecture is a unique feature not common to many expert systems and shell products. In a blackboard, various knowledge-bases are used in a manner similar to databases. The knowledge-bases communicate through a central source, the blackboard. The knowledge-bases can vary in their information type. The user may store or retrieve information from any of the knowledge-bases while still using any combination of information to solve problems.

Insight 2+	Personal Consultant	M.1	KEE	S.1
User Interface				
Natural-language capability Explanation facilities Screens Function key interaction Help and explain features	Screens Windows Natural-language interface Function key interaction Help and explain features	Natural-language interface Windows Explanation facilities	Screens Windows Graphical represen-tation Natural-language interface	Screens Windows Explanation facilities
Developer Interface				
Database-compatible editor Compiler Graphics interface Language interface Debugger Function keys Editor Help facility	Graphics interface English text Menus Windows Function keys Editor	English text Display and explain features Graphics interface	Explanation features Inference trees Natural-language interface	Screens Windows Editor Debugger

Figure 10.4   Commercial shells and their components

This architecture employs a central inference engine and a central working memory. The knowledge entities are independent of one another, yet there remains a central controlling mechanism at all times. A blackboard provides a way of recording and tabulating intermediate decisions about a particular problem. Some blackboards categorize the decision process into three parts: plan of action, agenda of actions not yet taken, and final decision. The blackboard architecture was used to structure HEARSAY III, an expert system that deals with speech understanding. HEARSAY III uses multiple knowledge-bases that interact through the blackboard.

Expert system–database marriages have become quite popular. Through this type of combination, many commercial users of expert systems can use data from mainframe computers, minicomputers, and personal computers.

EXPLANATION FACILITIES

The process of decision making performed by the inference engine during a consultation session reflects the reasoning process of an expert. During the knowledge elicitation period, this information is transformed into the knowledge-base of the expert system. However, the end user is often not an expert in the particular domain of a consultation. Therefore, some form of explanation utility is required to inform the user of the reasoning path the system is taking to solve the specific problem. The explanation utilities express the reasoning process of the system in various forms, including explanations after a given question, explanations of why a particular question is asked, and help via more detailed information.

When designing an explanation facility, the developer should use the language of the user's domain. The explanation utility should be capable of handling a variety of queries about the knowledge-base. A common feature used by most developers is retrospect reasoning—how the inference engine addresses a particular question. This is requested via a why feature. Figure 10.5 provides an explanation example.

This concludes our discussion of expert system shell components. We will now provide further details on the knowledge representation schemes and reasoning schemes used in expert system shells and systems today.

TECHNICAL DETAILS OF SHELLS

Shells typically provide a limited set of knowledge representation and inference engine control logic paradigms. We will look at the various knowledge representation methods that can be used in knowledge-bases and the various control mechanisms that can be used in expert system inference engine components.

The formal lobby furniture is: Neo-Victorian
                                 Modern

Why?

Because:

First-level   IF design is neo-Victorian
reasoning   AND brass sconces
                     AND handwoven tapestry
                     THEN lobby design Class 2

Why?

Because:

Second-level   IF formal lobby
reasoning   THEN design is neo-Victorian

An explanation for the same question, requested by an EXPLAIN command, might read as follows:

It is important that the present designers know the history of the Crown Embassy Hotel if they are to re-create the decor of the original designers. Neo-Victorian furniture was in the formal lobby of the first model of the Crown Embassy Hotel, not modern or early American.

Figure 10.5   Explanation example

KNOWLEDGE REPRESENTATION SCHEMES

The knowledge-base is the part of an expert system that contains the knowledge about a specific domain. Domain knowledge can be organized in many ways. We will discuss five knowledge representation methods: rules, frames, semantic networks, first-order logic, and hybrids. Each of the first four methods can be used alone or in conjunction with others, to form a hybrid (the fifth method) in a given knowledge-base.

Rules

The rule knowledge representation scheme is the most popular. Systems using the rule knowledge representation scheme are sometimes called production systems. The rules or productions are used to represent relationships in terms of condition-action pairs:

IF   (condition)
THEN (action)

The condition part of a rule is also referred to as the premise, antecedent, or left-hand side (LHS). The action part is also referred to as the conclusion, consequent, or right-hand side (RHS).

To illustrate the use of rules, consider the following example in which rules are used to give recommendations on the mode of transportation to use depending on distance and weather conditions.

Rule 1: IF distance is 1 mile
AND weather is sunny
THEN transportation is bicycle.

Rule 2: IF distance is 3 miles
AND weather is sunny
THEN transportation is bicycle.

Rule 3: IF distance is 20 miles
AND weather is sunny
OR weather is rainy
THEN transportation is automobile.

Uncertainties can be expressed in rules by attaching certainty factors to the premises or conditions of rules. For example, if we want the mode of transportation to be automobile in the case that there is an 85 percent chance of rain and the distance to travel is 5 miles, we can use the following rule:

Rule 4: IF distance is 5 miles
AND weather is rainy CONFIDENCE 85
THEN transportation is automobile

Several facts can often be assimilated into a more general form through the use of variables. For example, rules 1 and 2 can be put together through the assimilation of the first IF conditions:

IF distance in miles $<=$ 3
AND weather is sunny
THEN transportation is bicycle.

Frames

Another method of representing facts and relationships in a knowledge base is the use of frames. A frame is a group of attributes that describes a given object. Each attribute is stored in a slot, which may contain default values, rules, or procedures for changing the values attached to the attributes. The procedures in a given slot are executed when the information contained in that slot is changed.

As illustrated in Figure 10.6, information contained in a frame can be represented using both declarative and procedural information. A declarative

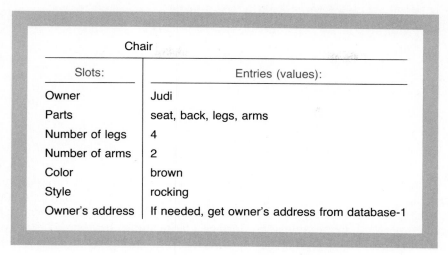

Chair	
Slots:	Entries (values):
Owner	Judi
Parts	seat, back, legs, arms
Number of legs	4
Number of arms	2
Color	brown
Style	rocking
Owner's address	If needed, get owner's address from database-1

Figure 10.6   Frame for Judi's chair

statement is an assertion that a given piece of information is true. For example, from Figure 10.6, we can say that the number of legs of Judi's chair is four. This is a declarative statement about the number of legs of Judi's chair. A procedural statement contains instructions to be executed in a given slot. An example of procedural statement is "If needed, get owner's address from database-1."

The use of frames assumes that the knowledge to be represented can be represented in "chunks" or blocks of data. Each block of data in a frame is presented as a slot. Each slot has the capability of housing specific values about the data or information contained in it. Slots might also contain pointers to other frames or other displays of knowledge. Frames can be linked together. This linkage gives rise to inheritance. If frame 1, containing information about the use of training tools, and frame 2, containing types of training tools, are linked together, knowledge from frame 1 would be inherited by frame 2. An advantage in using frames is that related information can be used repeatedly without the development of repetitive blocks of knowledge data. For example, all training tools are the same type, and frames associated with training tools are linked together. Procedural information in frame 1 can be transferred to frame 2. No repetitiveness is required in usage instructions since the procedures are inherited from frame 1.

A structure that is frame-like but differs in its handling of inheritance is known as an object-attribute-value (O-A-V) triplet. Factual knowledge can be represented using O-A-V triplets. In this association, attributes are characteristics of objects. Each attribute may take on a specific value. With O-A-V triplets, attributes work similarly to slots. Knowledge can be arranged to represent various associations with O-A-V triplets. Objects sharing relationships can be represented in a tree:

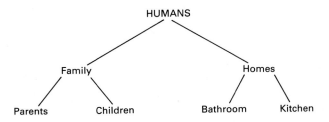

The top object, humans, is the apogee of the reasoning pattern concerning knowledge about humans. In some cases, objects below the top object can have more than one association. Take "Children." The object "Children" represents nonadult persons and requires no further clarification. If desired, however, "Children" could be subgrouped into "Male" and "Female," as shown in the following illustration.

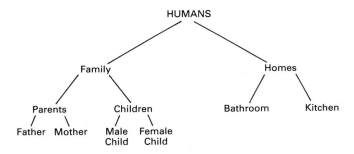

Objects can also represent uncertainty. In our example, it is possible that the parents may be someone other than the mother and father. We can add certainty factors to "Mother" and "Father." This provides a level of certainty or confidence that the mother and father are the parents.

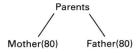

O-A-V triplets may also be used to represent *static* and *dynamic* aspects of knowledge. In some knowledge-base structures, certain facts are unchanged in each new condition, whereas other things change from one situation to the next. The change in situations is known as the dynamic aspect of knowledge, and the lack of change is known as a *static* condition. In viewing the training knowledge-base, it is a given that learning tools are present in every aspect of training. However, the application methods vary from one training phase to the next.

The type of knowledge data organization selected when utilizing O-A-V triplets is contingent on the desired knowledge representation. A combination of O-A-V structures is also possible. An example that is often used is a tree structure showing all the objects and the certainty factors associated with each object. This representation can be linked with production rules.

Semantic Networks

The semantic network is a graphical knowledge representation method composed of nodes linked to each other. The nodes are used to represent objects, concepts, or events. The links between the nodes are called arcs and represent relationships between objects. Commonly used links include "is-a" and "is-part-of." The relationships between objects create inheritance hierarchies in the network. This means that in a given network, objects can inherit properties from other objects in the network. Figure 10.7 provides an illustration of a simple semantic network.

In Figure 10.7, dog has the property of being a mammal, and since Lassie is a dog, she inherits that property. A semantic network is an effective knowledge representation method to use when the relationships between objects are complex.

Semantic networks present an alternative to structural representation for the knowledge-base developer. New nodes and arcs can be added at any point in the development. Like frames, semantic networks provide inheritance relationships. Viewing our sample tree, a semantic network would be depicted as follows:

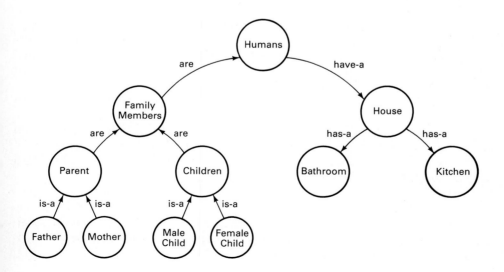

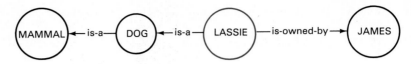

Figure 10.7   A simple semantic network

First-order Logic

Declarative knowledge can be represented through the use of different logic systems: propositional calculus, predicate calculus, first-order predicate calculus, and Horn clause logic. Propositional calculus is a logic system used to verify whether a given proposition is true or false (Figure 10.8).

Considering that the following two statements are true:

● Lassie is a dog.
● If Lassie is a dog, then she is a mammal.

a propositional calculus logic system will tell us that the following statement is also true:

● Lassie is a mammal.

Figure 10.8   Illustration of the use of propositional calculus

Predicate calculus is an extension of propositional calculus that also determines whether a proposition is true or false. Predicate calculus also allows the use of relationships and generalization statements (Figure 10.9).

First-order predicate calculus is a logic system that is commonly used in AI. It is a variation of predicate calculus in that it allows the use of functions and other analytic features. For example, if we apply an "is-owned-by" function to Lassie, the value "James" will be returned.

Horn clause logic is a subset of first-order predicate logic. Negation and disjunction are not supported in Horn clause logic. PROLOG, a computer programming language sometimes used to develop expert systems, supports Horn clause logic.

INFERENCE SCHEMES

In expert systems, the inference engines are responsible for deciding how and in what order the knowledge data in the knowledge-bases should be used. It

Considering that the following two statements are true:

- Lassie is a dog.
- All dogs are bigger than all cats.

predicate calculus permits us to conclude that:

- Lassie is bigger than all cats.

Figure 10.9   Illustration of the use of predicate calculus

is responsible for the control and execution of the reasoning strategies used by expert systems. Reasoning strategies used in expert systems include backward chaining, forward chaining, various search strategies, problem reduction, pattern-matching procedures, unification, event-driven methods, and hybrids.

   Backward chaining and *forward chaining* are strategies used to specify how rules contained in a rule-based knowledge-base are to be executed. To illustrate how these two reasoning mechanisms are used, consider the following set of rules:

> 1:   IF weather is sunny
>   AND distance $<=$ 20 miles
>   THEN transportation is bicycle.
>
> 2:   IF transportation is bicycle
>   THEN no passenger insurance is considered.
>
> 3:   IF no passenger insurance is considered
>   THEN transportation insurance cost = 0.

Backward Chaining

Suppose that we want to establish the fact that "transportation insurance cost = 0" assuming that we only know that the weather is sunny and the distance is 15 miles. The backward-chaining method works backward from the conclusion.

> Is this fact known?   → NO.
> Can it be obtained from a rule?   → YES, by rule 3.
> Which fact(s) needs to be known?   → "no passenger insurance
>   should be considered."

Is this fact known?	→ NO.
Can it be obtained from a rule?	→ YES, by rule 2.
Which fact(s) needs to be known?	→ "transportation is bicycle."

Is this fact known?	→ NO.
Can it be obtained from a rule?	→ YES, by rule 1.
Which fact(s) needs to be known?	→ "weather is sunny" and "distance <=20 miles."

| Are these facts known? | → YES, "weather is sunny" and "distance = 15 miles." |

Therefore, it is true that: "transportation is bicycle."
Therefore, it is true that: "no passenger insurance is considered."
Therefore, it is true that: "transportation insurance cost = 0."

We started with the fact that we wanted to prove (our goal), and we tried to establish all the facts needed to reach that goal. This reasoning method is called backward chaining. In general, backward chaining is applied when a goal or a hypothesis is chosen as the starting point for problem solving. Backward chaining is sometimes called *goal-directed*, *top-down*, or *consequent-driven* reasoning.

Forward Chaining

The forward-chaining reasoning mechanism goes forward from antecedents to the conclusions they generate. Suppose that we want to prove "transportation insurance cost = 0," assuming we know that "weather is sunny" and "distance = 15 miles."

Is this fact known?	→ NO.
Which facts do we know?	→ "weather is sunny" and "distance <= 20 miles."
What facts follow from it?	→ "transportation is bicycle" by rule 1.
Is this what we want to prove?	→ NO.
What facts follow from this?	→ "no passenger insurance is considered," by rule 2.
Is this what we want to prove?	→ NO.
What facts follow from this?	→ "transportation insurance cost = 0," by rule 3.
Is this what we want to prove?	→ YES.

Thus we have established from "weather is sunny" and "distance <=20 miles" that "transportation is bicycle." From "transportation is bicycle" we have established that "no passenger insurance is considered." Finally, from that we have established that "transportation insurance cost = 0," which was our goal.

The reasoning mechanism used here is called forward chaining; it is also known as *data-driven*, *bottom-up*, and *antecedent-driven* inferencing. It is best used to solve problems in which data is to be used as the starting point for problem solving.

A combination of forward chaining and backward chaining can be used to get to problem solutions quickly when dealing with large search spaces. The combination of bottom-up and top-down searches produces quicker results. This search strategy can be applied when solving complex problems.

Depth-first and Breadth-first Schemes

Inference engines also use various search strategies to locate pertinent knowledge data in knowledge bases, including depth-first or breadth-first searches. To illustrate these search techniques, let us consider the following rules:

1:   IF weather is sunny
    AND distance < = 20 miles
    THEN transportation is bicycle.

2:   IF transportation is bicycle
    THEN no passenger insurance is considered.

3:   IF no passenger insurance is considered
    THEN transportation insurance cost = 0.

4:   IF no insurance company exists
    THEN it is impossible to get insurance.

5:   IF it is impossible to get insurance
    THEN transportation insurance cost = 0.

We will apply both depth-first and breadth-first search strategies on these rules, together with the backward-chaining paradigm (Figures 10.10 and 10.11).

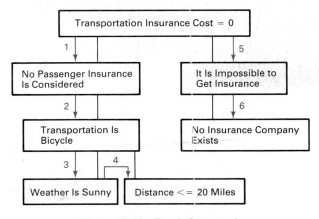

Figure 10.10   Depth-first search

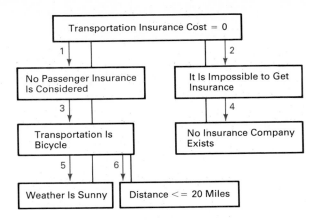

Figure 10.11   Breadth-first search

In a depth-first search, the order in which the goals are considered is illustrated in Figure 10.10. If the only provable fact is "no insurance company exists," the inference engine would go through six steps before proving that "transportation insurance cost = 0."

In a breadth-first search, all the steps at any given level are examined before going to the next lower level. Figure 10.11 illustrates this.

In a depth-first search, the focus is on the specific details of a problem, whereas in a breadth-first search, the problem is worked in a more general fashion.

Heuristic search techniques employ rule-of-thumb strategies to help solve problems. These techniques use some intelligent scheme to reduce the search space, that is, to prune the logic tree. With these techniques, there is no guarantee that the best solution for a given problem will be reached, only that a satisfactorily correct solution will be found and identified. Heuristic search techniques include *means-end analysis* and *hill climbing*.

Means-end Analysis

The *means-end analysis* technique, also referred to as the difference reduction technique, combines forward- and backward-chaining mechanisms in a way that permits moves toward the solution of a problem by first obtaining the solutions to the major parts of the problem and then obtaining the solutions to the smaller subproblems. This process tries to diminish the distance between a current state and the goal state by setting up subgoals. When all the subgoals have been reached, the main problem is solved. For example, if we know a heuristic that can be used to get to a goal state and it happens that we are able to use it from our current node, we might try to get to a nearby node from which the heuristic can be applied. We can repeat this process until we get to the desired goal.

Hill Climbing

Hill climbing is a search technique derived from the search strategy called generate and test. The generate-and-test strategy consists of the following steps:

1. Generate a possible solution.
2. Test the solution.
3. If the solution is acceptable, stop; otherwise, go back to step 1.

Hill climbing contains the basic search procedures used in generate and test and the capability of getting and using feedback from the test procedure that is used to decide in which direction to move in the search space. In hill climbing, whenever the goal state is not reached, the difference between that goal state and the current node is calculated. By comparing the calculated differences between states, we can determine whether or not we are getting closer to the goal state. In the case where we are moving away from the goal state, we can backtrack and select a different path. In the case where we are moving toward our goal state, we continue the present solution path. Through the use of these heuristics, we can get to the goal state more quickly than through the use of the basic generate-and-test scheme.

Problem Reduction

Problem reduction is a technique used to represent problems in a structure that makes problem solving easier. It consists of decomposing a given problem into sets of smaller problems—a divide-and-conquer strategy. The decomposition is stopped when all the generated subproblems have solutions. The subproblems' solutions are consolidated to get the solution to the bigger problem. The transformations used in problem decomposition are defined as operators. Each operator is capable of transforming a problem into subproblems that are to be solved.

Problem reduction can be represented using AND/OR graphs (Figure 10.12). AND/OR graphs are constructed using five rules:

1. Each node represents a single problem or a set of problems that need solution.
2. A primitive problem is defined by a terminal node.
3. Each possible application of an operator to a problem must be assigned a directed arc from the problem node to the node that defines the subproblem set created by itself.
4. Directed arcs must be formed between member problems and the subproblem set node to which they belong.
5. In the case that only one application of an operator is possible, even though this operator produces more than one subproblem, the resulting OR node that represents the subproblem set may be eliminated.

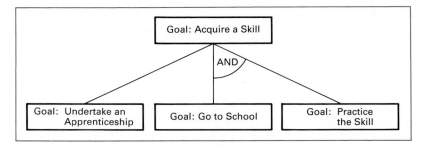

Figure 10.12 A simple AND/OR graph

Pattern Matching

Pattern matching is a technique used to describe objects, events, or processes in terms of their respective features and the relationships between them. A pattern can be viewed as a kind of sketch of an element contained in a database. Each pattern is a structure made up of different variables. A pattern is considered to match another structure if it can be made identical to that structure by replacing its variables with specific values. Pattern matching is used in conjunction with other reasoning strategies. For example, in backward chaining, the selection of another rule in a chain occurs when the THEN action clause of the rule to be selected matches the IF condition clause of interest.

Hierarchical Generate and Test

Hierarchical generate and test is a search technique used for searching large search spaces. It is a variation of the generate-and-test strategy in which possible solutions of a given problem are first generated and then the solutions that do not meet appropriate criteria are eliminated. Hierarchical generate and test is often used in large data interpretation and diagnosis problems where obtaining all possible solutions is necessary. Hierarchical generate and test is based on the concept of putting as much heuristic knowledge as possible into the generate portion of this strategy. This translates into a smaller search space for the tester to have to evaluate, thereby reducing the time it takes to find a valid solution.

Unification

Unification is a strategy used to compare different lists of items (often referred to as atoms) and determine how they can be made identical. The following is an example of two lists on which unification can be attempted:

(father-of robert steven)
(father-of robert X)

In general, if we want to unify two lists, we first verify whether their first elements are the same or not. If they are the same, we start comparing the remaining elements of the lists. If the first elements of both lists are different, we can conclude that unification is impossible for these two lists regardless of their arguments. For example, the two lists

(father-of robert steven)

(mother-of natalie marilyn mindy)

cannot be unified. If there is a match between the first elements of the lists, the remaining elements can be checked, one pair at a time, according to these rules:

1. Identical constants, functions, or predicates match.
2. Different constants, functions, or predicates do not match.
3. A variable can match another variable, any constant, or a function expression (not containing any instances of the variable being matched).

During unification, substitutions that are used to generate identical lists are to be made in a consistent manner. Consider the following expressions:

(A a a)

(A b h)

The A's in each list match. Then we compare a and b and see that they can match if we substitute b for a. The substitution can be represented as b/a. For the last pair, a can match h if we substitute h for a using the substitution h/a. But it is not possible to substitute b and h for a. So, to have consistent substitutions throughout the whole set of pairs, we apply the b/a substitution to all the remaining elements and get

(A a b)

(A a h)

Now it is possible to unify these expressions by using the substitution h/b. At this point, the unification is complete. We have used a combination of two substitutions to succeed. This combination of two substitutions is written as

(h/b) (b/a)

When confronted with a combination of substitutions, such as $(X1/X2, X3/X4, X5/X6, \ldots)$ $(Y1/Y2, Y3/Y4, Y5/Y6, \ldots) \ldots$, all the substitutions of the rightmost list are first applied, and the result is used to apply all the substitutions of the next list until all the substitutions have been applied.

Event-driven Control

An *event-driven control* scheme is based on the fact that data or information is considered to be time-dependent. In this technique, one can get to the next step only if new information allows it or if the prior step has created conditions that make it necessary to go to the next step. Except for the time factor consideration, this technique resembles forward chaining. The event-driven technique is appropriate to real-time operations such as process control.

Uncertainties

When dealing with *uncertainties* in knowledge-base data, numeric techniques can be used. Each uncertain event or fact has a numeric value called a certainty factor or confidence factor attached to it. For example, in the rule

> IF weather is raining
> THEN Paul takes his automobile CF 70.

CF 70 is the certainty factor attached to the rule. The meaning of the whole rule is that there is a 70 percent chance that Paul takes his automobile when it is raining.

There are situations where, if a given rule is applied more than once, the same conclusion can be reached each time but with different degrees of confidence. For example, let us suppose that the following rule has been called twice in a consultation:

> IF distance = 10 miles
> THEN transportation is bicycle.

If "transportation is bicycle" was concluded at first with a confidence factor of 60 and later with confidence of 70, these two confidence values are combined. This is because when the first conclusion is made, "transportation is bicycle" was entered into the context of the session along with the confidence factor of 60. This confidence factor value is not forgotten. When the second conclusion is made with a confidence factor of 70, the two are combined as shown in Figure 10.13.

As illustrated in Figure 10.13, one way to combine the two confidence factors is as follows:

1. Take the difference between the first confidence factor value (60) and 100 percent certainty (100), which is 40.

2. The difference (40) is multiplied by the confidence factor of the second conclusion (70) to give an increment of 28 percent.

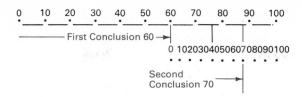

Figure 10.13 Graphical representation of the combination of two confidence factors

3. The increment (28) is added to the original confidence factor value to arrive at the combined value of 88.

Using this technique, the final confidence value resulting from the combination of the two confidence factors (60 and 70) is 88.

    In general, a confidence factor is an integer between -100 and $+100$ (or a real number between -1.0 and $+1.0$). If a conclusion or a fact has no certainty factor attached to it and it is selected, it is assumed to have a value of 100. A confidence value of 100 means that the conclusion or the fact is absolutely true. A confidence factor value of 0 means that the fact is unknown, and a negative confidence factor value indicates that there is evidence against the conclusion or fact. A confidence factor value of -100 indicates that the conclusion or fact is absolutely false.

    Confidence factors can be applied in a conjunctive proposition, a disjunctive proposition, or a negative proposition (Figure 10.14).

1. With a conjunction:
   IF weather is sunny CF 60
   AND distance $<=$ 20 miles CF 50
   THEN transportation is bicycle.

2. With a disjunction:
   IF weather is rainy CF 60
   OR bicycle is broken CF 50
   THEN transportation is automobile.

3. With a negation:
   IF weather is rainy CF 90
   AND NOT there is automobile CF 10
   THEN transportation is bicycle.

Figure 10.14 Illustration of the use of confidence factors

Hybrid Schemes

Some expert system shells allow different knowledge representation methods to be used simultaneously; in this case, the knowledge representation method is referred to as a *hybrid knowledge representation scheme*. An example of an expert system shell supporting hybrid knowledge representation is the Knowledge Engineering Environment (KEE). KEE allows the use of frame-based and rule-based knowledge representation methods. Different reasoning strategies can be used simultaneously in a single system. Such a combination is referred to as a hybrid reasoning strategy. KEE is an example of an expert system shell incorporating multiple reasoning strategies including forward chaining and backward chaining.

11 COMMERCIAL EXPERT SYSTEM SHELLS

The term *expert system shell* has been used to mean different things to different people. The term *shell* has its history in the evolution of general expert system building tools.

The first expert systems, including MYCIN and DENDRAL, were constructed using the LISP programming language, with no help from any generalized expert system building tools. These systems proved the concept of expert systems as a viable and useful automated paradigm.

With the acceptance of expert system technology, more researchers and developers wanted to build more expert systems. However, they also desired to develop expert systems in less time than it took to build the first ones. Believing that the unique attribute of any one expert system implementation was based on its knowledge-base entities, different groups proceeded to extract the knowledge-base entities from different developed expert systems. The team that worked on MYCIN succeeded in developing an expert system building tool that consisted of the MYCIN expert system minus the knowledge-base entities for MYCIN's specific problem domain, blood diseases. The team named this tool EMYCIN. EMYCIN is known by both the names Empty MYCIN and Essential MYCIN. The idea here is that you have a complete ready-to-run system except for the actual problem domain knowledge entities. All that an expert system developer has to do is to acquire and codify problem domain knowledge in EMYCIN knowledge representation form, compile the system, and be ready to use it. This saves the developer the time it would take to build the other essential elements of an expert system.

Because tools like EMYCIN are total expert system structures and provide the form of an expert system, people started calling these kinds of tools shells or expert system shells. Therefore, the term *shell* for many people means an expert system building tool that is rigid in form and limited to the problem domains it can support. Historically, the term *shell* is limited to this particular category of expert system building tool. Expert system shells became associated with tools that are expert systems with unpopulated knowledge bases.

Some of the expert system building tools on the market exemplify this historic perspective; others do not.

Some expert system building tools offer choices of knowledge representation schemes and inference and control schemes. Expert system builders can pick and choose when developing large and complex expert systems. These new tools are considered by many not expert system shells but expert system programming environments.

Any set of software tools that is expressly designed to assist in the development of expert systems beyond programming languages like LISP, PROLOG, OPS, KNOWLEDGE TOOL, and SMALLTALK can be considered expert system shells. In particular, any expert system building tool that is designed to be used by non-AI scientists and researchers should be considered an expert system shell.

In this book we use the term *expert system shell* to mean any comprehensive set of tools that assist a knowledge engineer or an expert system builder in building expert systems. In this chapter we will look at a representation of expert system building products that are commercially available today. Some of these products are targeted for LISP machines, some for personal computers, and some for general-purpose computers. As has already been seen, there will be a tendency for these tools to support more than one class of computer machinery in the future. What is important to look at when reading about these tools is what the tools will provide over having to develop the basic expert system software.

Expert system shells can be compared to DBMS products. When developing a large database, most firms today buy a commercial off-the-shelf DBMS product like IMS or Oracle and populate it with their own unique data. Although a DBMS product can easily cost as much as $250,000, most firms have found that it is more cost-effective to purchase one than to develop a similar capability in-house.

Expert system shell products can be considered as cost effective to purchase as DBMS products. As Figure 11.1 shows, an expert system shell encompasses all of the generic expert system logic required in building an expert sys-

Figure 11.1   Why use an expert system shell?

tem. A simple 300-rule expert system that would take less than three months to develop with a shell would take over a year to develop from scratch. Another benefit in using an expert system shell product is that the vendors of these products are for the most part more knowledgeable about the basic technology than are the companies that might want to use these products to develop end-user expert systems. Another advantage is that the user of the shell benefits from the construction experiences of the shell vendor and its clients.

Choosing an expert system shell product is very much like choosing a DBMS product. Lessons learned and procedures used in selecting a DBMS product can be used in the development of an expert system shell selection process. Figure 11.2 provides a list of some of the issues that relate to the selection of an expert system building tool product.

The following sections are provided to give an idea of what is available in the marketplace. However, because these tools are new and because research and development efforts are producing new features almost every month, actual current product information should be sought from the vendors at the time an organization is about to select an expert system shell. The following sections provide a good cross section of what is available in the marketplace.

AUTOMATED REASONING TOOL (ART)

The development of the Automated Reasoning Tool (ART) was started in 1979 in InterLISP (a dialect of LISP, widely used and popularized by Xerox) and was subsequently ported to ZetaLISP when Inference Corporation targeted the Symbolics and LMI LISP machine markets as the initial marketing foci for ART. The current release of ART is implemented in Common LISP.

Research has developed a number of knowledge-based problem-solving

1. The product supports the knowledge representation scheme needed.
2. The product supports the inference techniques needed.
3. The product provides good development tools.
4. The product provides a good user interface.
5. The vendor will be around to help.
6. The product runs on hardware that is available.
7. Cost is in line with functionality.

Figure 11.2　Choosing a shell

paradigms and methodologies. The differences between these paradigms are characterized by variations in knowledge representation (such as rules and frames) and inference control mechanisms (such as forward chaining and backward chaining). ART is one of the few, and one of the first, commercial general-purpose expert system development tools that has integrated different problem-solving paradigms and combined them with a powerful application development tool kit. ART's integrated development and run-time support environments provide a versatile tool for the efficient construction of a variety of expert systems.

As is often the case with high-end software products, customer assistance and support add to the utility and efficiency of the product. As shown in Figure 11.3, ART has a good support structure for the customer. This support includes hands-on training, a hotline service, a user group and user newsletter, tutorials, and reference manuals. A knowledge engineering center exists in Houston, Texas, where the customers' knowledge engineers can obtain assistance from a senior knowledge engineer from Inference Corporation while developing expert systems.

ART is intended to be used primarily for large-scale expert system applications. It is a powerful and somewhat complex tool that entails a large initial investment for the product and training. However, the popularity of ART suggests that its customers believe that they can realize enough savings from ART-based applications to justify the initial investment. The true benefits and cost effectiveness of ART can be realized in the context of applications development that is sufficiently complex and large of scale to warrant the use of a powerful tool like ART.

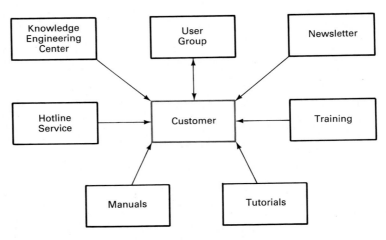

Figure 11.3 ART customer support

The Structure of ART

ART can be decomposed into five major components: a knowledge representation language, a knowledge base compiler, an inference engine, the ART interface synthesis tool (ARTIST), and the ART Studio. These components represent an integration of rule-based programming, symbolic knowledge representation, logic programming, object-oriented programming, nonmonotonic reasoning, and user interface features in a single architecture. The integration of these techniques yields one of the most broadly applicable tools currently available.

ART provides a diverse and robust mechanism for representing and modeling a variety of knowledge structures. The representation of such knowledge is accomplished by using the representation types provided by the ART knowledge representation language. As we shall see, some of the representation types and their attendant terminology are unique to ART. They are not supported by other commercial tools.

Knowledge Representation

The basic mechanism for representing objects and classes in ART is a frame-like structure called the schema. A schema is a collection of facts about objects that are stored in slots associated with a schema. ART provides a number of system-defined slots as part of the basic schema structure. The user can add more slots to any schema. Schemas can be related to each other via parent-and-child relationships using system-provided slots such as HAS-INSTANCES and SUBSET-OF.

Schemas are used to represent objects in a way similar to other object-oriented systems. Schemas possess an inheritance capability. In the case of multiple parents, ART allows for multiple inheritance. The inheritance mechanism is mutable in that properties (such as slots) expressed in parent objects are generally inherited by all child objects unless the system is told not to carry the properties along to a child. This is an important and useful characteristic of the inheritance mechanism that supports the expression of exceptions in conceptual taxonomies represented by schemas.

ART has a unique way of handling the message-passing aspect of object-oriented programming. It uses its rule language for this purpose. Messages that get data from objects are implemented by a pattern in a rule. Messages that send data to an object are implemented by the action part in a rule. Instead of providing an explicit message-passing protocol, ART has an enhanced rule language that provides an equivalent capability with some interesting advantages.

Rule-based message passing relaxes the strict association of a message-passing procedure with only a single object or class. The same rule can retrieve or modify attributes (slots) in more than one object (schema). This approach represents the middle ground between strict object-oriented programming and the relaxed data encapsulation of traditional procedural languages. By not providing procedural message passing, the ART approach avoids the problems of incremental development and modifiability faced in procedural programming. Another advantage of rule-based implementation of object-oriented programming is that messages can be interpreted in a more holistic context. Temporal and structural constraints can become factors in message interpretation, which would be tedious to achieve in more traditional object-oriented programming.

Using rule-based programming for message passing is ART's approach to carry over the benefits of the knowledge-based approach to object-oriented programming. This tailors object-oriented programming closer to the knowledge-based approach.

The most unusual feature of ART is the viewpoint structure, which provides ART with the capability to support a variety of problem-solving strategies such as hypothetical reasoning, logical dependencies, temporal scoping of knowledge, and blackboard modeling. Viewpoint is used to record changes in the knowledge-base at a given instant or at a given stage in a process. From a functional point of view, a viewpoint is an explicitly recorded collection of elements extracted from the application knowledge-base along with their values at a given time during the processing that is intended to represent some intermediate state of the knowledge-base.

This capability is useful in a number of ways. It can be used to record interesting states during a process that represents the changes entailed by certain significant events. It can be used to record the order in which events occur. It can also be used to record the path taken by the system from the problem definition to the solution state. Viewpoints can be used to store alternative or competing possibilities as ART tries to find a solution.

Viewpoints are used to implement the concept of hypothetical worlds, which is used to organize, compare, and contrast alternative possible actions and conclusions in the problem-solving process. Such hypothetical reasoning is represented as a tree-like structure of related viewpoints. The process of sprouting new viewpoint nodes in the hypothetical reasoning tree is rule-driven and can happen whenever ART finds that an additional hypothetical possibility exists.

ART creates viewpoints using its schema feature. Therefore, inheritance also works within viewpoint structures. That is, newly created viewpoints inherit the history of choices made in their ancestral viewpoints.

In traversing viewpoint hierarchies, ART explores both depth and breadth within guidelines that can be set by the knowledge engineer. ART can be advised to remove unproductive branches of a viewpoint structure. Efficient encoding of an application in ART can produce an effective expert system.

Another concept in ART is facts. The term *fact* is used somewhat differently in ART as compared to other systems. In ART, a fact is a fundamental unit of knowledge that has two components: a proposition and a viewpoint. A proposition in ART is a statement that is considered a fact in other systems and is intuitively recognized by most people as a fact. For example, "This office is open'' is a proposition. ART, however, considers a fact also to include a scope or a perspective from which a proposition is viewed. This aspect of a fact is made explicit in ART by associating a fact's viewpoint with its proposition. Therefore, in terms of the above example, a complete fact in ART could be "This office is open on Wednesday,'' where "on Wednesday'' represents the scope within which the proposition "This office is open'' is valid. This approach to representing facts is used in ART to support logical dependencies. This allows facts to be retracted if, at a later point in a process, certain supporting information becomes known to be false.

As we have seen, some of the ART representation structures are used to implement more than one concept in ART. Viewpoints, for example, are used as a scoping mechanism for facts as well as to support hypothetical and temporal reasoning. Facts represent individual units of knowledge, whereas schemas are used to represent taxonomies. Inference Corporation also suggests that schemas can be viewed as a mechanism to describe a collection of facts that represent an object or class of objects that share certain properties. This set of knowledge structures can model a variety of application domains.

We shall now discuss the rule language and inferencing aspects of ART. This discussion will illustrate how ART combines its knowledge structures and rules to implement different problem-solving techniques.

A versatile feature of ART is its rule system. The way ART provides support for organizing and exploiting a rule base is sophisticated and effective. The rule system includes several types of rules, each with a specific role in ART's inferencing process. ART's categorization of rules helps organize problem-solving expertise in a natural and efficient manner.

ART allows forward and backward chaining to be integrated at the rule level. Because of ART's ability to reason with backtracking, it allows asynchronously arriving data to be used during backward chaining. Computations invalidated or enabled are immediately recognized, and any decisions that become inconsistent are eliminated by the inferencing mechanism. The knowledge engineer does not need to invoke the backward-chaining mechanism procedurally because ART is able to generate goals automatically when they are needed.

In ART, patterns are used to specify a collection of possible data objects by describing their common structure. Patterns contain variables in places where data objects are allowed to differ. Thus patterns describe a general condition that many different sets of facts might satisfy. Another way of understanding patterns is to view them as propositions with variables. Patterns can include logical operators, logical quantification, and arbitrary predicates and procedural restrictions encoded in LISP.

A rule in ART is implemented as a combination of a pattern and an action. The pattern represents some set of conditions that must exist in the knowledge base before ART can propose to take the action specified in the rule. ART uses the concept of goals to provide the underlying mechanism for associating rule antecedents (patterns) with their associated consequences (actions). Goals are explicitly represented data objects that can be processed by rules in the same manner as facts. ART also uses goals to drive its backward-chaining process.

ART categorizes rules as general-purpose, hypothetical, constraint, and belief rules. The categorization is based on the nature of the action specified in the rule. Different actions invoke different aspects of ART's inferencing and control mechanism. General-purpose rules are the most common and are similar to how rules are represented in other rule-based expert system building tools. They perform specific, deterministic operations on a knowledge-base. Here is an example of a general-purpose rule:

```
RULE:   Calculate Area
   IF   (Length-of Rectangle Known)
  AND   (Breadth-of Rectangle Known)
  AND   (Area-of Rectangle Unknown)
  ———→
  THEN  (Calculate Area-of Rectangle)
          (Area-of = Length-of * Breadth-of)
```

Hypothetical rules drive ART's hypothetical reasoning capability. Hypothetical rules use a function called SPROUT to generate competing viewpoints or possibilities. ART is able to explore the implications of the competing alternatives as part of its inferencing mechanism. Hypothetical rules in ART are intended to represent the kind of decision making reflected in the following example:

```
RULE:   Fire Source Undiscovered
   IF   (Schema Nursery-School-Fire-1 (Source Unknown))
  ———→
  THEN  (Inform Investigator Fire-Dept)
          (hypothesize
          (Schema Nursery-School-Fire-1 (Source Accident))
          (Schema Nursery-School-Fire-1 (Source Arson))
          and explore possible implications)
```

In the example, ART would consider (or assume) the source of the fire to be either an accident or arson and proceed to discover the implications of both assumptions. If at a later state in the process the source of the fire became known, ART would discard the wrong assumption and all conclusions that were based on it.

ART also uses rules to place constraints on hypothetical plans or viewpoints. A constraint represents a situation that is not allowed to occur in valid viewpoints. If a constraint is violated, the hypothetical world in which this violation occurs is said to be poisoned. *Poison* is ART's term for discarding a viewpoint. Thus poisoned hypothetical worlds are eliminated from future consideration. A constraint rule might be expressed as follows:

RULE: Cost/Benefit Constraint
 IF   (Cost > Income)
──────→
THEN   (Poison this Plan)

In this case, any hypothetical plan in which costs were found to exceed income would be poisoned and pursued no further. Poisoning is handled by ART as a fact associated with a viewpoint. It is therefore inherited like a property by descendant viewpoints.

A disadvantage of using too many constraint rules is that they will consume resources in generating situations that are only going to be eliminated. The combination of hypothetical and constraint rules creates a problem-solving process that is termed generate and test. Generate-and-test solutions tend to be easy to implement but are inefficient to run. They are, however, a good starting point for testing the logic of a solution and can be refined and made more efficient later in the development of an expert system by adding more explicit testing.

Constraints in ART can also be expressed using the DefContradiction construct, which establishes incompatible facts associated with one or more viewpoints. A rule that expresses constraints has to be declared as having a high priority or salience (ART does this automatically for DefContradiction) so that testing for undesirable situations is always at the top of the agenda. ART also provides functions to build constraint rules that test for circular paths in problem-solving logic.

At some point, an ART-based application must stop its consideration of the various hypothetical alternatives and make a decision. The final type of rule, a belief rule, is used for this purpose. A belief rule expresses a desired solution as a pattern. It is used to recognize desirable viewpoints, either to end processing or to streamline it. If ART determines that a viewpoint exactly matches some desired solution, it considers that viewpoint believed. The action of believing can be initiated by a rule or a process. ART also manages the interaction between poison and belief. For example, if two alternatives are contradictory and if one becomes poisoned (false), the other automatically becomes believed (true). Establishing belief in a viewpoint initiates a restructuring of the hypothetical viewpoint tree. The believed viewpoint is combined with all of its ancestral viewpoints and becomes the new root viewpoint of the tree. If during the restructuring certain viewpoints become orphaned, ART determines whether they are compatible with the new root, and if so, they are connected as its descendants in the tree.

The various types of rules give the knowledge engineer a versatile mechanism for shaping and influencing the inferencing and control associated with the problem-solving process. ART supports both monotonic and nonmonotonic reasoning. ART's ability to reason with backtracking is intended to support the notion of logical dependencies. That is, ART records evidence that suggests a particular solution and is able to withdraw conclusions or discard evidence that is later established to be false. This also provides ART with the capability to reason with uncertainty.

The successful integration of all of ART's features makes ART a sophisticated and diverse tool. In addition to its problem-solving capabilities, ART also has a well-integrated interactive development environment that includes tools for designing and debugging knowledge-based applications and for developing custom graphics end-user interfaces.

Interactive Development Environment

A sophisticated tool like ART that supports the construction of complex expert systems and a wide range of applications must provide an equally sophisticated set of tools to facilitate the product's usability. ART's multiwindow user interface has a rich set of features and tools, including a comprehensive help system, a knowledge-base browser, an execution monitor, a keyboard-based command entry system that supports command abbreviation and spelling correction, a mouse-accessible menu system, and a graphics package for the creation of end-user interfaces. Two utilities that support these features are ART Studio and ARTIST (ART Image Synthesis Tool).

ART Studio provides the framework for two tools: the knowledge-base browser and the execution monitor. When ART is activated, the execution display windows of the Studio are displayed. The layout of the window is shown in Figure 11.4. There are eight windows in all, and each is devoted to a different task.

The global command window at the lower right corner of the screen displays a static, mouse-sensitive menu of ten basic commands like EXIT and HELP, as well as commands to browse through schemas and viewpoint structures. The global commands can be executed at any time during a user session.

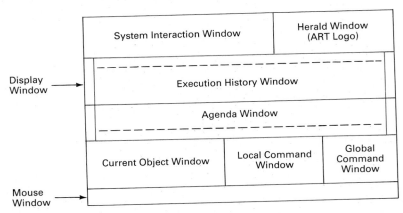

Figure 11.4   ART Studio execution display windows

The local command window displays mouse-sensitive menus of commands relevant to the task at hand.

The current object window at the lower left corner of the screen displays textual descriptions of schemas, rules, and viewpoints and is used during browsing or debugging.

The display window shares screen space with the execution history and agenda windows. The global command RECONFIGURE is used to toggle the assignment of screen space set up among these windows. The display window is used for displaying graphs of schemas and viewpoint structures and can also be activated by certain debug options.

The agenda window is used to display the activation agenda. The activation agenda is the list of rules that ART is considering executing during the execution of an expert system. ART will only execute the top rule in the agenda before reevaluating the state of the knowledge-base and revising the agenda.

The execution history window is used to display the trace or record of the execution steps of an expert system.

The system interaction window is used as a textual interface to ART. It is used for commands typed in by the user and for status messages and questions displayed by ART.

The herald window is used for displaying the Inference Corporation logo and copyright notice.

The mouse documentation window is a reverse-video one-line window at the bottom of the screen that displays the current interpretation of the mouse buttons.

The design of the Studio interface is intended to facilitate the use of the browser and monitor utilities. The browser allows the user to examine, modify, or create items in the knowledge-base such as schemas, facts, rules, and viewpoints. It uses context-dependent, mouse-sensitive menus for the user to select various kinds of options. If the user wants to examine the schemas or viewpoint structures, the browser creates a graphical display of the inheritance structure. The user can then use commands in either the global command window or the local command window to move between nodes (schemas or viewpoints) in the graphics display and examine them at different levels of detail. ART provides a full-screen editor that can be used in the browser context. Changes made to schemas can be tested for correct syntax with the help of the ART parser.

The execution monitor has two functions: It helps the knowledge engineer debug the expert system, and it serves as the run-time interface between the expert system and the user. Support for debugging includes provisions to set step-by-step traces that can be associated with one or more rules or with facts, viewpoints, agenda, or goals. Context-sensitive menus (menus that display different sets of options depending on the current context) are used to help the user select various debugging options. One such option, the break option, applies to rules and is used to halt the execution of the expert system temporarily whenever it tries to execute a rule to which a breakpoint has been assigned. The debugging facility also allows the specification of a precise number of rules to be executed before interrupting program execution. The execution monitor provides statistics of the internal state and the execution behavior of the system. When the debugging features are on, diagnostic messages are displayed dynamically.

The Studio facility supports both mouse- and keyboard-based interaction. Its capabilities include spelling correction, command abbreviation, and hierarchical menu presentation. Studio also supports incremental refinement of an expert system with integrated text editors. It allows for incremental compilation of refinements to a knowledge base. This makes it possible to determine quickly the impact of such refinements on the system. In addition, the display in each window is optimized to maximize the information content. Scrolling and zooming capabilities allow the developer to explore large networks of schemas and viewpoints. Studio's capabilities to support the end-user interface are enhanced by ARTIST.

ARTIST is an interactive tool for building end-user interfaces for ART-based applications. The graphics editor of ARTIST allows for the design of window layouts, construction and animation of graphic icons, and creation of icon libraries. ARTIST also includes utilities to build hierarchically organized menus and command line interpreters. These features make it possible rapidly to prototype and test a variety of interaction styles and user interfaces tailored to different levels of end-user expertise and different aesthetic preferences.

ARTIST is integrated within the overall ART structure. All graphic objects are represented as ART schemas, and all animation is done by rules. This declarative interface representation allows displays presented to the user to be modeled as schemas. This ensures consistency between the application's internal model and the view it provides to the user. Other advantages are derived from this approach. The symbolic representation of the user interface allows applications to reason about the user view, which makes certain run-time adaptations possible. Internal changes automatically invoke rules that update the user view to reflect the changes. Changes to the user view are accomplished by changes to the schemas and not by executing procedure calls. Similarly, inputs by the user are stored in schemas that trigger rules to update the internal model. Thus interface consistency is assured in ART. The data-directed nature of forward-chained rule-based programming makes it simpler to build a mixed-initiative user interface in which either the application or the user can initiate the interaction.

The current Common LISP–based version of ART is available on the TI Explorer LISP workstation, the Symbolics LISP machines, the LMI Lambda LISP machines, and the DEC AI VAX computer. Future versions will run on the IBM PC RT, Sun workstations, and certain UNIX machines.

In summary, ART is a powerful and effective expert system building tool. ART includes a rich interactive development environment. Many of the features in ART are unique to ART.

The Inference Corporation

ART is a product of the Inference Corporation, a commercial software company that was founded in 1979 and is based in Los Angeles, California. Inference is a high-tech company that specializes in the development and marketing of artificial-intelligence-based software products. ART is Inference's popular high-end expert-system-building product.

EXSYS

EXSYS is a knowledge engineering tool for developing expert systems. It is composed of three main programs written in the C programming language: EXSYS, EDITXS, and SHRINK. EXSYS is the main program. It runs operational knowledge bases. EDITXS is an editor that can be used to generate knowledge-bases. SHRINK is a utility program that can be used to rearrange a knowledge-base in order to make the running of the whole system as efficient as possible. EXSYS is designed to work on personal computers and can accommodate up to about 5000 rules, depending on the amount of available memory. It supports the rule-based representation method. EXSYS provides backward- and forward-chaining reasoning mechanisms. It allows knowledge-bases to be interfaced with external systems and programs such as database management systems and spreadsheet programs.

EXSYS is easy to use. It does not require an understanding of any special knowledge engineering language such as LISP or PROLOG. It was developed by Exsys, Inc., in an effort to make the development and use of expert systems possible by most commercial organizations.

Key Features

The EXSYS expert system shell product includes a tool called FASTER. FASTER will reorganize a knowledge base in an effort to decrease its run time. Large knowledge-bases require much longer run times and thereby more computing resources than small ones. FASTER has been created to reduce the run time of large knowledge-bases. With FASTER, the order in which the rules were initially entered in the knowledge base might be changed in a manner that permits control algorithms to run more efficiently. The result of consultations will remain the same whether or not FASTER has been used; FASTER will only speed up the consultation.

A user can query EXSYS as to why a particular piece of information is required and how information is used to reach a conclusion. This feature is important during both the expert system development period and consultation. In the first case, this facility assists the developer in determining whether the system's line of reasoning makes sense or not. In the second case, this facility becomes the means by which the user can query the system as to why it is asked for a particular piece of information or how it developed a particular conclusion.

During a consultation with an expert system, the user answers questions asked by the system. Using these answers and the knowledge data in the knowledge-base, the system develops conclusions. With EXSYS, the user has the capability of determining how a conclusion or recommendation is affected if a change is made in one of the user's answers. EXSYS provides this through its *sensitivity analysis* capability. During sensitivity analysis, one answer is changed while the others are maintained constant. The system provides the user with a conclusion for each case. The user can perform as many of these what-if tests as are needed.

EXSYS contains a rule editor called EDITXS. EDITXS permits rules to be directly written in the EXSYS environment. This allows for direct testing of rules being entered and facilitates rule correction.

Compared to knowledge engineering languages like LISP and PROLOG, C is a programming language that allows programs to run faster and use less memory in traditional computer systems. For this reason, C was used instead of a knowledge engineering language to develop EXSYS.

A user does not need to know any special programming language to be able to use EXSYS for developing an expert system or to consult with an expert system built with EXSYS. This is because English phrases are used to create knowledge-bases. The developer and user need only understand the subject domain.

EXSYS has the capability of interfacing with external systems and programs like database management systems and spreadsheet programs. EXSYS can also be interfaced with automatic test equipment. This means that EXSYS can be used in many application areas. If a particular problem cannot be totally solved by the expert system, EXSYS can call an external program capable of solving that problem. The solution is then captured by EXSYS for further analysis. EXSYS can provide data to external programs for analysis and receive data back from external programs.

EXSYS allows the user to show a degree of belief on a given fact or event through the use of *certainty factors*. Certainty factors can be used in rules and can be attached to conclusions provided to a user. If there is more than one answer to a given problem, EXSYS can attach a certainty factor to each answer and rearrange the answers in order of likelihood.

In EXSYS, certainty can be assigned by using one of the following scales: 0 or 1, 0 to 10, and 0 to 100. When the 0 or 1 scale is used, the 0 corresponds to the absolute meaning that the solution should be rejected and the 1 corresponds to an absolute meaning that the solution should be accepted as true. For the 0 to 10 scale, 0 represents absolutely false and 10 absolutely true; the numbers between are used to represent degrees of certainty. The 0 to 100 scale is similar to the 0 to 10 scale, except that the range is 0 through 100. This scale provides more granularity in certainty specification.

The size of a knowledge-base is limited by the amount of memory available in the computer being used. EXSYS makes efficient use of memory; therefore, relatively large knowledge-bases can be developed with it. A small EXSYS program can accommodate approximately 700 rules in a 192K memory space. Approximately 5600 rules can be handled in a 640K memory space.

Knowledge Representation

The knowledge representation scheme in EXSYS is rule-based. The rules have the following general structure:

IF   (condition)

THEN   (action)

Here is an example of a simple EXSYS rule:

IF   your car is broken
         and
         the amount of money needed to fix it $>$ its value
THEN   buy a new car.

Control System

Backward- and forward-chaining inferencing mechanisms are used by EXSYS. For example, backward chaining is the means by which EXSYS is capable of solving problems according to the following scheme: Use the solutions obtained from small subproblems to generate information needed to solve larger problems (see Figure 11.5). Another view of backward chaining is to look at the top-level problem, if it is immediately solvable, and solve it. If it is not immediately solvable, back up to the next subproblem level and see if this level is solvable.

Rule 1:
     IF   it is hot
     THEN put the air conditioner on.

Rule 2:
     IF   the temperature is $>$ 80 deg. F
     THEN it is hot.

Notice that rule 1 is solved when the expert system has the information it needs to find true the condition specified in rule 1 or rule 2.

Figure 11.5 Backward chaining in EXSYS.

If it is, solve it, and then try to solve the top-level problem. If the subproblem is not solvable, back up to the next level subproblem. If it is solvable and the problem is still not solvable, search out another subproblem to solve that will help in solving the top-level problem.

EXSYS does not require its developers or its users to have any knowledge of a programming language to be able to use it effectively. All the inputs to and outputs from the system are expressed in English phrases. EXSYS has its own rule editor in which rules can be entered and automatically tested. This helps to save time during the expert system development process. EXSYS can be used in a wide variety of application areas because it is a general-purpose expert system shell and because it is capable of exchanging information with external systems and programs. EXSYS makes efficient use of computing resources.

Exsys, Inc.

Exsys, Inc., is a knowledge engineering company with headquarters in Albuquerque, New Mexico. The company's basic objective is to offer products and services related to expert systems development at a relatively low price. The personal computer version of EXSYS is the company's most popular product.

INSIGHT 2+

Insight 2+ is an expert system shell product designed for developing personal-computer-based expert systems. It is a software package that has its own knowledge engineering language called Production Rule Language (PRL), its own editing facility, and its own programming and data manipulation language called DBPAS. DBPAS is derived from the Pascal and dBase programming languages. PRL is used for knowledge-base creation. DBPAS is used for generating dBASE II and dBASE III databases and for developing small Pascal programs. The editing facility is used to enter knowledge-bases and programs into the Insight 2+ environment.

Insight 2+ supports a rule-based representation paradigm and is capable of both forward (limited) and backward chaining. It is designed to run on personal computers having at least 256K of memory space available.

Insight 2+ was developed by Level Five Research, Inc., and constitutes an improved version of an initially developed product called Insight 2 that was capable only of backward chaining.

Key Features

Insight 2+ has its own knowledge-base development language called PRL. PRL is easy to learn and use. Previous programming experience is not required to be able to master it. PRL requires the knowledge-base elements to be arranged in a particular sequence. The following is the order in which the elements of a PRL knowledge-base should be:

1. Knowledge-base title
2. Declaration of facts shared by chained knowledge-bases
3. Fact type declarations
4. Parameter initialization statements
5. Control element selectors
6. Goals of the knowledge-base
7. Rules that support the goals
8. Textual information
9. Knowledge-base termination declaration

The knowledge engineer is not obliged to use all nine elements in an Insight 2+ knowledge-base to make it functional; however, a title, one or more goal statements and accompanying sets of rules to support them, some control elements to guide Insight 2+ in the handling of certain knowledge-base information, and the word END on the last line of the knowledge-base should be provided. It is also advisable to include some explanatory texts and commentaries.

Figure 11.6 provides an illustration of a PRL knowledge-base. It contains the following PRL elements:

- A title
- One control element called THRESHOLD, which represents the minimum certainty value with which each premise of a given rule should be verified before Insight 2+ will consider the conclusion of that particular rule. The threshold value can be any integer in the interval 0 to 100. If there is no threshold value in a given knowledge-base, Insight 2+ will use a default threshold of 50 in its evaluation of the rules
- Three goal statements and their supporting rules
- Some commentary statements preceded by an exclamation mark
- The word END to mark the end of the knowledge-base

Insight 2+ has its own programming language called DBPAS. DBPAS was derived from the Pascal and dBase programming languages. DBPAS is the means by which the user can create databases and allow knowledge-bases to interact with external dBase II and dBase III databases. Programs created using DBPAS have the same structure as standard Pascal. Figure 11.7 provides an example of the basic structure of a DBPAS program.

There is a slight difference between the structure of a DBPAS program as

```
TITLE The Transportation Adviser
!
! The confidence factor level
! at which a conclusion needs
! to reach
!
THRESHOLD = 65
!
! Define the goals of the knowledge-base
!
1.  The mode of transportation is a car
2.  The mode of transportation is an airplane
3.  The mode of transportation is a ship
!
! Rules that support the goals
!
RULE for car
IF The traveling distance is within city limits
AND It is raining
THEN The mode of transportation is a car CF 80
!
RULE for airplane
IF The traveling distance is beyond city limits
THEN The mode of transportation is an airplane CF 70
!
RULE for boat
IF The traveling distance is beyond continent limits
AND There is no airplane available
THEN The mode of transportation is a ship CF 95
!
END
```

Figure 11.6   Illustration of an Insight 2 + knowledge-base

shown in Figure 11.7 and that of a standard Pascal program. In the DBPAS program, the word *end* marking the completion of the program is followed by a semicolon. Insight 2 + allows the created DBPAS programs to be tested and debugged before they are used with Insight 2 + knowledge-bases.

Both the knowledge-bases created using PRL and the DBPAS-generated programs need to be compiled before they can be run. The compiled PRL knowledge-bases will have the extension .KNB attached to their names and the compiled DBPAS programs will have the extension .PCO attached to their file

```
Program name (input, output);
Const
   identifier = identifier;
Var
   identifier: type identifier;
Procedure name (parameter list);
begin
   statement;
   statement;
end;
begin
   statement;
   statement;
end;
```

Figure 11.7 Basic structure of a DBPAS program

names. The noncompiled PRL knowledge-bases and DBPAS programs have the extensions .PRL and .PAS, respectively.

Insight 2+ has two editors: one text editor and one database editor. The text editor can be used to generate and edit PRL and DBPAS programs as well as some other programs. This editor is similar to both WordStar and the TURBO Pascal editor. It also supports the use of graphics characters. The database editor is used to generate and edit databases. It is also a means to view dBase II and dBase III database files.

In Insight 2+, access to all of the major functions is through the use of the main menu. This menu can be used to accomplish the following functions:

- Run a knowledge-base
- Edit a knowledge-base
- Compile a knowledge-base
- Run a DBPAS program
- Edit a DBPAS program
- Compile a DBPAS program
- Edit a database

Most of these functions can also be performed by directly issuing commands from the keyboard.

This expert system shell has an explanation facility from which the user is able to visualize the system line of reasoning and the system's responses to queries. This facility is important during expert system development and during a consultation. In the expert system development stage, the system developer is capable of testing and debugging a system through this facility. During a consultation, this facility is the means by which the user is able to examine and evaluate the facts and responses provided by the system.

Insight 2+ is an expert system shell that has its own knowledge engineering language, PRL, and two editors (one used for creating and editing knowledge-bases and the other for creating and editing databases). Insight 2+ supports forward- (limited) and backward-chaining inference mechanisms and is designed to run on microcomputers.

Level Five Research, Inc.

Level Five Research, Inc., is a knowledge engineering company with headquarters in Indialantic, Florida. The company's basic objective is to offer products related to the development of expert systems. Insight 1 and Insight 2+ were the company's most popular products. The new version of Insight 2+ is called Level 5 and is marketed by Level Five's new parent company, Information Builders, Inc.

KNOWLEDGE ENGINEERING ENVIRONMENT (KEE)

KEE is an integrated knowledge engineering tool for developing expert systems. It includes a general-purpose knowledge engineering language that is used primarily for frame-based and object-oriented knowledge representations. It also supports rule-based and procedure-oriented representations. It is implemented in Interlisp and runs on the Xerox 1100, the Symbolics 3600 series, and the Texas Instruments Explorer computers.

KEE can accommodate multiple knowledge-bases and has an interpreter that can handle both forward- and backward-chaining mechanisms. It contains a graphics utility used in debugging and interfacing with the user. It also contains an explanation facility through which the user can visualize KEE's line of reasoning and the meaning of the commands incorporated into KEE. KEE was developed by IntelliCorp in the early 1980s to be used specifically in genetic engineering. Later IntelliCorp promoted KEE as a general-purpose expert system development tool.

Knowledge System Development Support

KEE can accommodate four different knowledge representation schemes (frame-based, object-oriented, rule-based, and procedure-oriented) and both forward and backward chaining. This makes KEE one of the most efficient and flexible knowledge engineering tools, one that can satisfy all kinds of users and handle a wide variety of problems.

A method used to represent objects and their attributes is the network structure. The objects are organized in a hierarchy wherein the lower-level objects inherit attributes from the higher-level objects.

In KEE, objects are represented by frames called units. Each unit has attributes represented by slots. This frame-based representation makes KEE a time-saving tool because, through the inheritance property among objects, the time needed for data entry is reduced. Attributes common to several objects need not be specified for each of them, but rather need only be specified for the higher-level objects; the lower-level objects will inherit the attributes. The fact that attributes need only be entered at one level and are then inherited by the lower-level objects assures consistency in the information entered. Knowledge-base maintenance is also enhanced.

Frame-based representation language attributes (slots) can be either descriptive or procedural, as shown in Figure 11.8.

This figure represents another important feature of KEE. Although it resembles frame-based representation in many aspects, this knowledge representation method is unique because it permits all of the objects to communicate

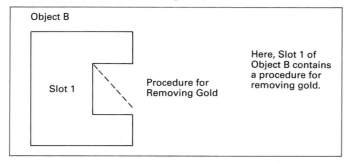

Figure 11.8   Object-oriented representation

with one another by sending and receiving messages. In KEE, this object orientation permits unification of knowledge representation, access to LISP, and the use of graphics and active values.

In KEE, as in any other rule-based representation language, both the heuristic knowledge obtained from the human expert and the logic procedures required to perform a given activity are translated into rules; for example:

> If a fire breaks out in the house,
> Then call the fire department.

Rules are easy to use, and they can be used to explain reasoning paths. Variables can be used in rules to accommodate any object in a given class.

In KEE, the use of procedures (also referred to as subroutines) increases the efficiency in the coding. This code efficiency is realized through a reduction in code duplication.

The KEE Inference System

The inference system is called Rule System 2 (it is an updated version of an earlier inference system called Rule System 1). This inference system allows a lot of flexibility in the design and writing of rules and makes debugging easy. Rule System 2 supports the following functions:

- Forward and backward chaining; these two chaining mechanisms can be represented graphically for viewing or debugging
- The use of variables in rules
- The use of LISP; this is done through LISP functions called ''methods.'' They are located in the knowledge-base as slot values.

Rule System 2 allows debugging to be done through the use of graphics. It makes use of rules with active values (a special kind of method used to respond to or execute specific changes in the knowledge-base) possible. This permits the monitoring of the value of attributes through the use of monitors or demons.

Creating a Knowledge-Base in KEE

Knowledge-bases can be created in KEE in two ways:

1. Through the use of a menu-driven system (See Figure 11.9) from which the selection of commands is done using a mouse
2. Through the use of a special KEE language called TellAndAsk.

These two knowledge-base creation options are very easy to use and are available to the user for adding and retrieving information from the knowledge-

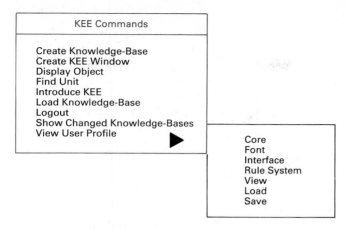

Figure 11.9   Top-level menu in KEE

base. A KEE knowledge-base can have five basic structural elements (see Figure 11.10):

1. Units (which are objects)

2. Slots (which are attributes of units)

3. Slot values (which describe the units to which they are attached)

4. Facets (which describe slots)

5. Facet values (which articulate the values of the facets)

       For example, a knowledge-base called ANIMALS might have elephants and dogs as objects. A unit to represent an elephant, ELEPHANT, has a slot called WEIGHT, with the value of 1000. The WEIGHT slot can have a facet called DIMENSIONAL.UNIT, with the value of POUNDS.

       The selection of a command from a menu can generate a submenu of specific options. Besides this top-level command menu, there are also menus at

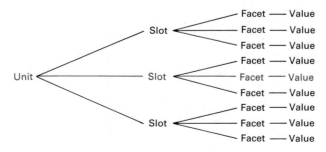

Figure 11.10   Schematic view of the structure of a unit

the knowledge-base level, the unit level, and the slot level. The meaning of all the commands can be seen through an explanation window.

Use of Active Images in KEE

The KEE system has a powerful graphics package called ActiveImages. Through the use of this package, active images are used to represent units and slots, monitor or set slot values, and invoke methods. All the images created for a given unit or knowledge-base can be put together into what is called an Image Panel. Figure 11.11 illustrates the use of an Image Panel for a knowledge-base called TRANSPORTATION.KB. In this Image Panel, the object MY.CAR is represented by an icon. This panel also provides a means to monitor and control MY.CAR's ODOMETER and MY.FUEL SYSTEM's PUMP.

In summary, KEE is a powerful and versatile knowledge engineering tool that supports frame-based, object-oriented, rule-based, and procedure-oriented representation paradigms. It supports both forward and backward chaining. It incorporates effective user interface tools that provide friendly expert systems to end users.

IntelliCorp

IntelliCorp is a knowledge engineering company with headquarters in Menlo Park, California. It was founded in 1980. Since its creation, IntelliCorp has developed software in the field of genetic engineering and has also developed tools for building expert systems. The company provides services related to

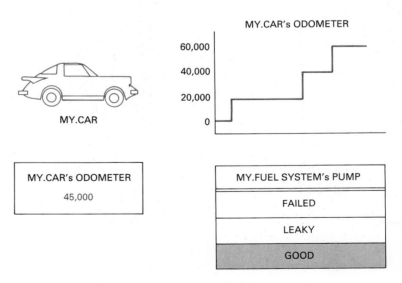

Figure 11.11   Image Panel for TRANSPORTATION.KB

building expert systems on a contract basis. IntelliCorp also provides clients with extensive training and apprenticeship program options.

KNOWLEDGECRAFT KnowledgeCraft is a powerful knowledge engineering tool for building expert systems. It is a general-purpose software package that includes a knowledge representation language called Carnegie Representation Language (CRL) and a knowledge-base editor. KnowledgeCraft supports frame-based, logic-based, rule-based, and object-oriented knowledge representation methods for expert system development. It also supports database system development.

   KnowledgeCraft contains utilities that assist with the creation of graphics and menu systems and allows for the use of natural language. It incorporates numerous control mechanisms, including an OPS5 forward-chaining system and a PROLOG-like inferencing system. KnowledgeCraft is implemented in Common LISP and can run on many workstations, including some LISP machines.

   KnowledgeCraft was developed by Carnegie Group, Inc., based on concepts and methods that originated at Carnegie-Mellon University.

Key Features

One of the most important features of KnowledgeCraft is CRL. CRL is the language used for knowledge representation in KnowledgeCraft. It permits the use of frame-based representation methods in which the basic representational unit is called a schema (see Figure 11.12). Each schema is composed of slots. Slot values are used to represent information about an entity. With CRL, information can be inherited from one schema to another, and linkage is possible among schemas.

   CRL allows the user to define relations between schemas and inheritance semantics. Relations such as SUB-ACTIVITY-OF and HAS-SUB-ACTIVITY are user-defined relations, and each has its own inheritance characteristics indicating how information is passed between schemas.

   Figure 11.12 illustrates the use of schemas for representing activities. Schema 1 and schema 2 are subactivities in the process of developing computer circuit boards. Schema 1 is concerned with the development of specifications for the central processing unit 1 (CPU1). Schema 2 is the CPU1 development activity. Schema 1 is a subactivity of schema 2; this implies that schema 1 will inherit some schema 2 characteristics. For example, the project leader, Jim Smith, specified in schema 2 will be inherited by schema 1.

   CRL provides the capability of metaknowledge representation to describe the knowledge-base further. For example, in schema 2, a metaknowledge can be used to give more information about the person who chose Jim Smith to be the project leader. In schema 1, a metaknowledge can be used to show that the value of project leader is inherited from schema 2.

Schema 1: make-CPU1-board-spec Schema

```
{{make-CPU1-board-spec
   IS-A: engineering-activity specification-development
   SUB-ACTIVITY-OF: develop-board CPU1
   INITIAL-ACTIVITY-OF: develop-board-CPU1
   EXPECTED-COMPLETION-DATE: "August 7, 1986"
   INITIATED: t
   COMPLETED: nil
   DESCRIPTION: "Develop specifications for the CPU board"}}
```

Schema 2: develop-board-CPU1 Schema

```
{{develop-board-CPU1
   IS-A: engineering-activity board-development
   SUB-ACTIVITY-OF: develop-computer
   HAS-SUB-ACTIVITY: make-CPU1-board-spec
   PROJECT-LEADER: Jim-Smith
   DURATION: (6 mo)
   DESCRIPTION: "Develop CPU board CPU1"}}.
```

Figure 11.12   Illustration of the use of schemas

CRL permits the use of procedures or subroutines with slots. Those procedures are executed when slot values are changed. There are different kinds of procedures that can be attached to slots; one commonly used procedure is one that fires when the value of a slot is about to be modified or when information is about to be added to a slot or removed from it. In Figure 11.12, a procedure can be attached to the duration slot so that the project manager gets an alarm message whenever he or she is getting close to the expected project completion date. Another procedure can be used to determine completion dates of each activity whenever a change is made to the project completion date.

With CRL, the user can define a control scheme that will guide the system in searching for inheritable information. This avoids wasting time in the searching procedures and also makes efficient use of memory space because of a reduction in information duplication. In Figure 11.12, the system could be directed where specifically to look for certain information. For example, the system could be directed to look for information concerning the project leader in the HAS-SUB-ACTIVITY relation.

The user can also use CRL to define some guiding procedures the system would follow in the case of an error. For example, in a project management system, if a manager tries to set a task budget at a higher level than the project's budget, an error will occur. The user can be provided with specific steps to follow in order to correct the error. CRL can be used as a monitoring device for a KnowledgeCraft database system. It can monitor the schema traffic.

KnowledgeCraft incorporates engineering aids that provide knowledge engineers with flexibility in knowledge-base development and the creation of effective user interfaces. Some of these aids are a window manager, a graphics package, a task manager, knowledge-base editors, and debugging facilities.

The window manager is the device that permits the creation and manipulation of multiwindow displays. The graphics package gives the user the ability to create two-dimensional graphics displays. It includes basic graphics elements like string, line, circle, rectangle, box, polygon, and spline. The task manager allows the manipulation of several tasks simultaneously. KnowledgeCraft schemas can be accessed by the user to make changes. Schemas are presented graphically in tree form. KnowledgeCraft incorporates debugging facilities that can be easily accessed. Debugging aids include trace windows that permit viewing of the system's line of reasoning so that errors can be detected and corrected.

Inference Mechanisms

The KnowledgeCraft inference mechanisms include both OPS5 and PROLOG control schemes in combination with CRL. The CRL-OPS combination provides KnowledgeCraft with a forward-chaining rule-based system, while the CRL-PROLOG combination provides a backward-chaining capability. Both CRL-OPS and CRL-PROLOG can be used simultaneously in a single application.

In summary, KnowledgeCraft is a knowledge engineering tool that supports several knowledge representation methods. It has its own knowledge representation language called CRL and its own knowledge-base editor. It incorporates a graphics package and supports icons. KnowledgeCraft is implemented in Common LISP and can be run on many workstations, including LISP machines.

Carnegie Group, Inc.

The Carnegie Group is an artificial intelligence research organization whose specialty is knowledge engineering software development. It was founded in 1983 by a group of computer scientists from Carnegie-Mellon University. The company headquarters is in Pittsburgh, Pennsylvania.

Since its creation, the Carnegie Group has developed software tools for knowledge engineering and has provided educational and consulting services to both the public and private sectors. Some of the company's most successful products are KnowledgeCraft and LanguageCraft. LanguageCraft is an environment that permits the creation of natural-language interfaces to software systems, including knowledge engineering software.

M.1

M.1 is an expert system shell that can be used for developing small, personal computer–based expert systems. It was first implemented in the PROLOG programming language. Later, M.1 was rewritten in the C programming language to gain portability and speed. M.1 will run on the IBM PC, PC/XT, or PC/AT microcomputers. It is one of a few personal computer–based knowledge engineering tools that gives the knowledge engineer the capability of preparing a finished end-user expert system. M.1 is regarded as a knowledge engineering language in the family of rule-based languages. It was developed in the early 1980s by Teknowledge, an international knowledge engineering company.

Key Features

Unlike some of the other knowledge engineering tools, M.1 is easy to learn and can be successfully used in a short period of time without the need of long-term artificial intelligence training.

The fact that M.1 uses English-like language syntax makes it easy for knowledge engineers to develop their knowledge-bases quickly. Little time is spent trying to understand some language codes, as is the case when using knowledge engineering languages, such as LISP and PROLOG. With M.1, inputs and outputs can be read easily without translation.

The M.1 knowledge-base is modular. Knowledge elements (rules and facts) in M.1 are independent of each other, since each can be entered, altered, or removed without affecting any other.

M.1 has debugging features that are easy to use; among them are these:

- An inference tracing mechanism that allows the knowledge engineer to follow the system activities
- A knowledge-base patch facility for making temporary changes to the knowledge-base
- A knowledge-base auditor that keeps track of inferences and conclusions for later examination
- A knowledge-base browser capable of listing all the rules and facts that contain particular expressions

The use of variables is a powerful feature because it allows a knowledge-base to contain all relevant facts with fewer entries. The following example contains a set of rules for giving recommendations on the mode of transportation depending on the distance and weather conditions.

```
Rule 1:   If distance = 1 mile and
             weather = sunny
          then transportation = bike or walk
```

Rule 2:   If distance = 2 miles and
               weather = sunny
           then transportation = bike or walk

Rule 3:   If distance = 3 miles and
               weather = sunny
           then transportation = bike or walk

Rules 1, 2, and 3 can be replaced by the following single rule thanks to the use of a variable. The replacement rule would be as follows:

Rule 4:   If distance = x and
               x $<=$ 3 miles and
               weather = sunny
           then transportation = bike or walk

This is a simple illustration of the use of variables in M.1. In more complex situations, variables can be used to decrease the number of rules in a knowledge-base.

Text file format for the knowledge-base allows the accomplishment of knowledge-base entry using a standard text editor such as WordStar. The knowledge engineer creates a file that will contain the knowledge-base and loads it into M.1. Once the knowledge-base has been loaded, a consultation is possible.

M.1 has a window-style interface that permits real-time viewing of the internal reasoning process of the system.

End-User Features

It is easy for a user to go through a consultation with an expert system created with M.1 for the following reasons:

- A consultation is accomplished through questions and answers in English.
- At any point during or after a consultation, the user can query the system as to why a question is asked, what the current conclusions of the system are, or how conclusions were reached.
- M.1 contains a help facility to assist the user when needed.
- M.1 has the ability to handle intuitive and uncertain knowledge; this allows the user to attach a degree of belief to the value of an expression. This is done through the use of certainty factors. These certainty factors are integers between 0 and 100 where 100 represents complete certainty and 0 represents no belief at all—the value is felt to be false.
- M.1 runs on IBM personal computers.

Knowledge-Base Representation

M.1 is a member of the family of rule-based languages. Its knowledge-bases are composed of rules and accompanying sets of facts and metafacts. The rules are representations of the heuristics obtained from human experts in the form of if-then statements:

> If PREMISE
> Then CONCLUSION

Facts are knowledge-base entities showing expressions that have values (expression = value), such as

> Distance = 10 miles
> Hair color = black

Metafacts are mostly question statements in the form "question (expression) = text," for example:

> Question (Distance) = "How far are you going?"
> Question (Hair color) = "What is the color of your hair?"

The M.1 Inference Engine

The inference engine is a general problem-solving mechanism; it is responsible for reasoning and solving problems through a backward-chaining mechanism. The M.1 inference engine is activated when a consultation begins. It first searches for knowledge-base goal expressions. Once a goal expression has been identified, it then searches the cache that stores the conclusions of the consultations for the desired goal result. If this search in the cache is unsuccessful due to the nonexistence of the desired result, the inference engine will then search the knowledge-base for entries that can facilitate obtaining the desired goal. Once a goal is satisfied, the system outputs the result to the user, along with its corresponding confidence factor.

It should be noted that the M.1 inference engine can search for numerous goal expressions in one consultation. However, each goal expression will be sought in the order in which it appears in the goal statement in the knowledge-base. As an example, for the M.1 goal statement

> Goal = X, Y, Z

the inference engine will first search the knowledge-base for X, then for Y, and then finally for Z.

Teknowledge

Teknowledge is an international knowledge engineering company with headquarters in Palo Alto, California. It was founded in 1981 by a group of artificial intelligence researchers from Stanford University and the Rand Corporation. The company's basic objective is to offer products and services related to building expert systems.

Since its creation, Teknowledge has developed several software tools for knowledge engineering. These products are targeted to personal computers, minicomputers like the DEC VAX system, and LISP machines. Teknowledge has also developed prototype expert systems for a variety of industrial applications, including drilling (for Elf Aquitaine) and computer order-entry and system configuration (for NCR).

PERSONAL CONSULTANT AND PERSONAL CONSULTANT PLUS

Personal Consultant and Personal Consultant Plus are expert system shells that facilitate the creation of expert systems that run on personal computers. These two products represent Texas Instruments' continuing investment in artificial intelligence and knowledge engineering products, which also includes the Personal Consultant Easy expert system shell.

Personal Consultant

Like many other knowledge engineering tools, Personal Consultant traces its roots to a research system in artificial intelligence. It is based on the EMYCIN program, a system developed by W. van Melle in 1979 as part of his doctoral dissertation at Stanford University. The EMYCIN project has its underpinnings in the MYCIN system developed by E. H. Shortliffe and his team in the mid-1970s, also at Stanford. MYCIN represents one of the earliest successful expert systems. Representing 50 person-years of development effort, MYCIN was the first large expert system to perform at the level of the human expert in a domain of practical significance, the diagnosis and treatment of infectious blood diseases. It also vindicated the school of thought in artificial intelligence that has maintained that simple control and inference techniques combined with sufficient domain knowledge can exhibit sophistication and expertise comparable to human expert performance.

Recognizing the extensive effort that went into developing MYCIN, the purpose of the EMYCIN project was to make the domain-independent parts of MYCIN reusable for solving other diagnosis-type problems. This would make it easier to try the MYCIN approach on other classes of problems (such as repair and debugging). EMYCIN became a pioneering effort in the reuse of software tools for building and executing expert systems. It embodied the control and inference structure and the support utilities (explanation capabilities and debugging aids) of MYCIN. To this MYCIN shell, utilities were added to expedite encoding domain-specific expertise.

The first successful application of EMYCIN was the PUFF expert system developed at Stanford University in 1979. It demonstrated EMYCIN's ability to prototype expert systems rapidly. From then on, it was just a matter of time before systems like EMYCIN were enhanced and refined into commercial expert system shells. Texas Instruments' Personal Consultant is one such product. Personal Consultant represents the first wave of expert systems shells for the PC market. These products are characterized by their close functional resemblance to their academic precursors.

From the perspective of the users of Personal Consultant, to maximize its utility and apply it most effectively, users must be familiar with its capabilities and understand the nature of applications for which it was designed. In this context, it is worthwhile noting that MYCIN-like control, inference, and knowledge representation structures were developed for, and have been most successful in, building diagnostic and interpretation systems of limited complexity.

Such problems are characterized by small search spaces, reliable data, and reliable knowledge. These characteristics permit correspondingly simple system architectures. Thus MYCIN/EMYCIN-like systems such as Personal Consultant employ exhaustive backward-chaining search, and their reasoning is monotonic, so they avoid the need for retraction of intermediate decisions. Control is primarily determined by the order of antecedents in the rules. Personal Consultant also employs a MYCIN-like algorithm for determining certainty factors that provides a heuristic technique for combining uncertain and incomplete data with experts' rules of inference.

In spite of this somewhat simple underlying architecture, Personal Consultant embodies considerable accumulated knowledge engineering expertise and powerful knowledge engineering tools that have been tested for many years in the research laboratories and have been used successfully in solving knowledge engineering problems. Therefore, using a product like Personal Consultant is desirable for the expert systems developer, especially for the developer with a weak artificial intelligence background. Personal Consultant provides a number of interactive utilities that enable the expert system developer to interact with the product conveniently to accomplish the various tasks involved in building an expert system. With the inference engine and control structures already provided, the developer can immediately focus on the knowledge acquisition and knowledge-base development process.

Personal Consultant has a window-oriented user interface and an interactive environment to generate and test expert systems. Personal Consultant provides a structure editor and a simplified rule entry language to support knowledge-base construction. In addition, there are several aids, such as trace and explanation facilities, for debugging and validating the expert systems. Personal

Consultant also provides access to the underlying language, LISP. This allows experienced knowledge engineers to tailor Personal Consultant.

The capability to access the underlying language to tailor or enhance the expert system shell is more important than it may seem at first. Expert system shells are designed to be both developmental tools and the run-time execution environment for the expert system. Knowledge engineers employ these user interface features to design the user interfaces for expert systems that they develop. However, each expert system has a unique set of users whose specific needs and characteristics may necessitate customization. Having access to the underlying language makes it possible not only to add special functionality to expert systems but also to develop custom user interfaces. Personal Consultant's user interface utilities are straightforward and easy to use and are quite efficient for building good user interfaces for small or prototype expert systems. Users interact with Personal Consultant by typing answers to questions posed by the system or by selecting appropriate responses from menus. The SnapShot utility facilitates the use of graphics in the expert system's user interface. Screens for interaction are well designed. Capabilities to use function keys, expand abbreviated answers, and provide English-like explanations to questions like HOW and WHY all add up to considerable convenience and ease for both the knowledge engineer and the end user.

Personal Consultant requires a PC, MS-DOS, two diskette drives or one diskette drive and one hard disk, and at least 512K bytes of RAM. Overall, users of the Personal Consultant are reported to be satisfied with its performance and ease of use.

Personal Consultant Plus

Even though commercial expert system shells have been around for only a relatively short time, a new generation of refined and enhanced expert system shells is already entering the market. Personal Consultant Plus, an enhanced version of Personal Consultant, is an example of this new generation of knowledge engineering tools. Personal Consultant Plus offers faster execution, enhanced knowledge base capacity of up to 2000 knowledge base elements (twice that of Personal Consultant), extended knowledge representation features (such as frames and metarules), and an enhanced graphics program interface that allows graphics and other programs to be used in Personal Consultant Plus applications. In addition, the original rule entry language, the Abbreviated Rule Language (ARL), has been extended to all system functions, which makes the rule input process faster and easier.

As knowledge engineering continues to mature, there is a trend to integrate various knowledge representation techniques, inference mechanisms, and control structures into hybrid knowledge engineering tools. The new generation of knowledge engineering tools like Personal Consultant Plus increasingly reflect this integrated approach. Such tools are also more efficiently implemented as a result of experience with the older generations of knowledge engineering tools. The user interface utilities of these new knowledge engineering tools have improved considerably. It is easier and more efficient to use these products to develop user-friendly systems. The accompanying documentation, which was in many instances rather opaque in older products, has also improved. This has also contributed to improved usability.

The meteoric rise in the popularity of expert systems has sent many organizations scrambling to develop products to capitalize on this new demand. This race gave little time for some companies to think out their initial products. These products approximated the functionality of academic systems, and the quality of documentation was not as good as it might have been.

The new generation of expert system building tools reflects a level of maturity the knowledge engineering market has attained over the years. Companies like Texas Instruments who have made a serious commitment to the knowledge engineering market have consolidated high-caliber in-house knowledge engineering teams. Experience with narrow single-paradigm and integrated multiparadigm systems has also influenced the functionality and capabilities of the new generation of tools. Personal Consultant Plus is one of the first integrated expert system shells for the PC market.

With Personal Consultant Plus, TI has enhanced the capabilities of Personal Consultant. We will discuss the enhancements of Personal Consultant Plus. This discussion will highlight developments in knowledge engineering and issues worth considering in selecting an expert system shell.

Personal Consultant Plus is characterized as a frame-based system by TI because it uses rule sets labeled as frames as a knowledge representation structure. A frame is a collection of parameters that together describe a stereotyped object. Frames were first proposed as a knowledge representation structure by Marvin Minsky in 1975, and they were subsequently popularized with the introduction of a number of frame-oriented representation languages, such as FRL and KRL. The notion of inheritance associated with frames is particularly useful from the developer's perspective because it allows parameters and features of parent frames automatically to become part of child frames, thus obviating the need to respecify redundant information.

Personal Consultant Plus uses three principal knowledge structures to represent knowledge-bases: frames, parameters, and rules. Each of these structures is designed for a specific role. Frames are used to model and organize the domain entities and concepts, the world of an expert system. Associated with a frame are rules and parameters. Personal Consultant Plus can work with only one knowledge-base at a time. Each knowledge-base has a root frame that is the starting point of the domain representation and is intended to capture the most general concepts and descriptions, which should be common and applicable to all subframes (representing subconcepts and subentities of the domain). A hierarchical structure comprised of the root frame and one or more subframes is called a frame tree.

Personal Consultant Plus uses special pieces of information, called properties, that control various aspects of a consultation. Properties are associated with frames, parameters, and rules. Frames, for instance, have properties like GOALS, OCCURRENCES, and INITIALDATA. GOALS are lists of parameters that constitute the objectives of frames. Consultations with Personal Consultant Plus involve instantiating frames and determining their GOALS. OCCURRENCES designate the number of times that frames can be instantiated during a consultation. For example, if a frame represents cars in a parking lot, then by using the OCCURRENCES property, the expert system can enforce a maximum number of cars that may be parked in that parking lot. The INITIALDATA property represents information that is required from the user of the expert system before the system tries to determine any parameter values within a frame. For example, if a parameter in a frame represents cities to be visited, the expert system may use the INITIALDATA property to determine the month or season, which may influence the value of that parameter. Properties therefore play important roles in building knowledge-bases. Personal Consultant Plus provides defaults for many of the properties that describe frames. These default values can be modified after initial knowledge-base construction.

Entities, concepts, or situations (associated with the domain) are represented in frames through the use of parameters. Parameters can be organized in groups to keep logically associated parameters together. The system automatically creates a parameter group for each frame. Parameter groups can be associated with more than one frame. Parameters also have properties like type, the type of value that can be assigned to it; transition, a textual description of the parameters; and prompt, used to prompt the user if a value is needed for the parameter and legal values. Also, each parameter has a numeric value, called the certainty factor. The certainty factor is a measure of belief that the parameter value is correct.

The third major element of a Personal Consultant Plus knowledge-base is the rule. The primary purpose of rules is to infer the value of parameters and to communicate information to the user. Rules are intended to represent the heuristics and expertise of the expert system. The system organizes rules in rule groups. Like parameter groups, rule groups keep rules that relate to a specific tool together. The system will automatically create a rule group for each frame. A rule group can be associated with more than one frame. It is important to remember that when frames share a rule group, they must have access to the same parameters. For this reason, frames that share rule groups must also share the parameter groups that correspond to the rule groups.

A rule is comprised of an IF and a THEN statement. These are both made up of one or more clauses, which contain system functions (provided by Personal Consultant Plus) and/or user-defined functions. Personal Consultant Plus has a special notation called ARL. ARL provides an abbreviated format for entering system functions required in rules. Both ARL statements and LISP statements can be used in rules.

There are a number of properties associated with rules. The basic properties of a rule (IF, THEN, SUBJECT) describe the function of the rule and the rule group to which the rule belongs. Another property, ANTECEDENT, is used to create a forward-chaining capability in an expert system. If a rule's ANTECEDENT property has no value, the rule is tested only when the values in its THEN part are needed (this is the normal backward-chaining procedure). However, if the ANTECEDENT property is YES, the rule is tested when the values of the parameters in the IF statement of the rule are known. Applying rules in this way constitutes forward chaining. Providing forward chaining in this way has one disadvantage: Rules whose ANTECEDENT property is not YES can only be used in the backward-chaining mode, whereas at times it would be useful to be able to use the same rule for both forward and backward chaining. Rules also have an EXPLANATION property that can be used to control the way a rule is explained during a consultation.

Five groups of system functions are provided by the system to build rules. Predicate functions are used in the IF statement of a rule and always return a value of TRUE or FALSE. Conclusion functions and text functions are used in the THEN statement. Arithmetic and auxiliary functions can be used in either the IF or the THEN statements. User-defined functions can also be used in rules.

The inheritance mechanism applies to parameters but not to rules. That is, parameter groups associated with frames are inherited by subframes. However, rule groups are not inherited and have to be explicitly associated with each frame, as needed.

Personal Consultant Plus allows user-defined properties to be associated with rules and parameters. These properties can be used, for example, to document rules in the knowledge base. In addition, these properties can be used in conjunction with user-defined functions to add more functionality to the system.

Personal Consultant Plus has a feature called the self-referencing rule. A self-referencing rule is a rule that references a parameter in the IF statement and then concludes a value for the same parameter in the THEN statement. Self-referencing rules are used if no other rule is available to provide a parameter's value.

The metarule is an important feature of Personal Consultant Plus. Metarules are used to determine the usefulness of object rules and to reorder the object rules. This way, the system applies the most relevant rule first. Metarules can be used by the knowledge engineer to influence the flow and efficiency of a consultation.

Personal Consultant Plus uses the VARIABLES construct to store globally accessible information that is outside the structured knowledge base. This construct is like a variable in a conventional programming language. It can be used to set global flags, influence the inferencing process, and provide values for various properties.

Access methods are another kind of parameter property that are used to trigger actions based on parameter access. Access methods are useful in performing actions such as reading an instrument and performing calculations. The concept of access methods is similar to the notion of active values and demons in object-oriented languages.

A deliverable expert system built with Personal Consultant Plus does not need the complete Personal Consultant Plus product for run-time support. Personal Consultant Plus consists of two kinds of utilities: the development tools and the consultation support utilities. A deliverable expert system needs only the consultation support utilities, along with the knowledge base and any related LISP files (if the knowledge engineer created any LISP routines).

Personal Consultant Plus is a state-of-the-art PC-based expert system shell. Though speed and memory space continue to be obstacles in building large expert systems on PCs, the increased capabilities offered by Personal Consultant Plus make the task easier and more practicable.

TI recommends the Personal Consultant Easy system as a learning tool for developers who are interested in learning more about expert system technology. Personal Consultant Easy is also recommended for quick prototyping of initial concepts and for developing small- to medium-scale commercial rule-based expert systems. Personal Consultant Plus, with its enhanced capabilities (enhanced speed, diverse knowledge representation techniques, and so on), is recommended for more sophisticated commercial systems.

Texas Instruments

Texas Instruments is an international high-technology company. Its headquarters is located in Dallas, Texas. Artificial intelligence is one of many high-technology domains that Texas Instruments has invested in heavily. TI develops and markets LISP machines, expert systems shells, and natural-language tools. TI also develops and sells textbooks and lecture materials in these subject areas.

PICON

PICON is one of a new breed of expert system shells designed to integrate expert system technology with other automated systems technologies.

PICON (Process Intelligent CONtrol) is a knowledge engineering tool for developing real-time expert systems in the domain of process control. It allows knowledge representation through the use of rules and schematic representations of a process. PICON operates on the LISP Machine Inc. (LMI) LISP machine called the Lambda/PLUS. The LMI machine is connected to a distributed process control system. PICON supports both forward- and backward-inferencing mechanisms.

PICON was developed by the Process Division of LMI, initially to assist a process operator in diagnosing the causes of a given process alarm. It now has the capability of controlling and monitoring intelligently a process operating in real time.

The Structure of PICON

PICON is composed of the following four elements: an inference engine, a knowledge-base, a user interface program called AI-BASE, and a C-coded software package called RTIME (Real-Time Intelligent Machine Environment) that gives PICON the capability of monitoring real-time processes.

The PICON Inference Engine

The PICON inference engine is responsible for PICON reasoning and problem-solving capabilities. It is able to use forward and backward chaining to search through the rules, reach conclusions, and direct the LISP processor and RTIME in accomplishing a particular task.

When a significant event is about to happen and RTIME notifies the LISP processor, it will wait for the inference engine to indicate the parts of the process on which special attention should be focused.

The inference engine can generate advice and alarm messages for the operator.

Because of the quick response needed to handle real-time processes, PICON's inference chaining is not done through the commonly used pattern-matching mechanism. Instead, it is done through use of methods that provide quick retrieval and application of rules and procedures needed in a particular situation. One of the methods that enables the inference engine to act quickly is to state explicitly in the inference rules which rules to apply next. The following is an example of such a rule structure:

IF T25 > 250 deg-f
THEN apply rules for "too hot."

Here, T25 refers to the temperature of sensor T25. This rule will invoke a set of rules dealing with high temperature at sensor T25.

AI-BASE

AI-BASE is a program that enables an engineer to develop and edit a knowledge-base. It is composed of three parts:

- AI-PARSE, which permits the analysis of the syntactic relationship of each part of the rules entered using a structured natural language provided with AI-BASE
- TRANSLATE-PARSE, which translates the parses into LISP
- AI-DBMS, through which rules and data are stored in and retrieved from the knowledge-base

The Knowledge-Base

The PICON knowledge-base contains two parts: a schematic representation of the process and a rule-based representation of the process operator heuristics. The schematic knowledge is created through the use of a menu-driven system and a graphics package. A mouse is used to select icons representing the plant components and to make the needed drawings (see Figure 11.13). The rules are entered into the knowledge-base through the use of a menu with the mouse or

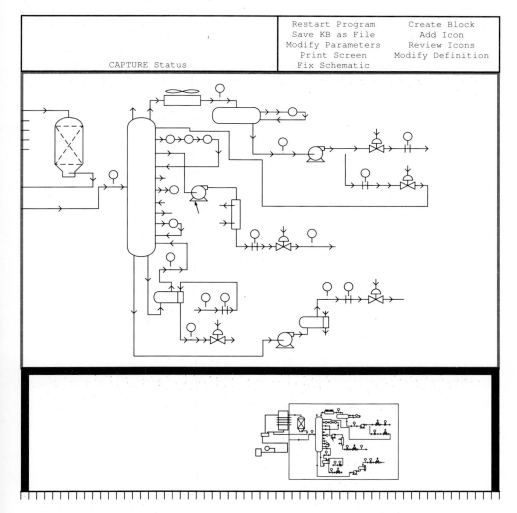

Figure 11.13   Schematic capture of process knowledge

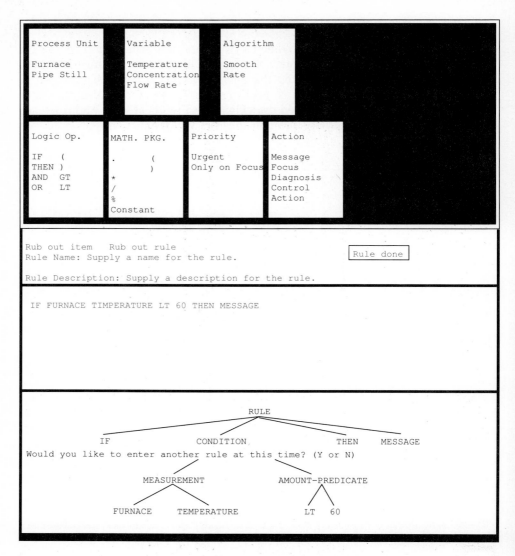

Figure 11.14   Heuristic knowledge capture

through AI-BASE by typing them (see Figure 11.14). Rules in PICON have a frame-like structure and can have the following slots:

- Antecedents
- Actions (with priorities)
- Conclusions (with certainty factors)

- Name of rule
- Description
- Overall worth
- Type of rule
- Other information

Rules in PICON are organized in a hierarchy composed of primary and secondary rules. The primary rules are used for periodic checks on the process conditions, whereas secondary rules are used for specific purposes. The secondary rules always have to be activated by primary ones. Rules have an IF or WHENEVER part and a THEN part. Figure 11.15 provides a few examples.

PICON also contains activation rules. These rules begin with one of the following keywords:

activate

focus

diagnose

suspect

Figure 11.16 illustrates the use of some of these words in rules.

PICON is an expert system shell that permits real-time monitoring and controlling of a process control system. It supports the use of two knowledge representation methods: graphics to represent the process and rules to represent the process operator heuristics. PICON is capable of both forward and backward chaining. PICON can be considered a parallel processing process in that the LISP-based expert system runs on the LISP machine, while, in parallel, RTIME (PICON's real-time component) runs on a UNIX processor. PICON can be considered a solution for optimizing the quality of control needed in a process control system. PICON can decrease process control costs because the process

```
Rule-1:   If t5 > 250
          Then message "Temperature in furnace 7 is high."
Rule-2:   Whenever p6 varies by 15 psi:
          If increase then message
            "The pressure at p6 has risen 15 psi!";
          If decrease then message
            "The pressure at p6 has decreased 15 psi!"
```

Figure 11.15   Examples of PICON rules

Rule-3:   If t5 > 212 deg-f
           Then activate rules for scan interval = 60.

Rule-4:   If t5 > 270
           Then focus on furnace-7.

Figure 11.16   PICON activation rules

can be run with fewer operators, more knowledgeable control can lower operating costs, or dangerous conditions might be able to be predicted by the system, giving the operators more time to check and thereby reducing costs related to these conditions.

Real-Time Interface

PICON can access real-time process data through RTIME. This software operates on a MC68010 processor in the LMI Lambda/PLUS machine and permits LISP-based programs running on the Lambda LISP processor to communicate with real-time processes. RTIME performs the following activities:

- Acquires and transmits data periodically at a specified frequency. The critical measurement points of the process are checked more frequently than the less critical (up to 20,000 measurement points can be monitored by RTIME).
- Parallel processes data through the use of algorithms and inferential functions specified by the LISP processor (the inferencing mechanism used here is forward chaining and is referred to as low-level inferencing).
- Notifies the LISP processor when a significant event in the external system is about to happen and then waits for recommendations from the LISP processor.
- Maintains data and results obtained in shared memory accessed by both RTIME and the LISP processor.

The LISP processor is responsible for the higher-level inferencing (such as backward chaining), directing RTIME in its data collection activities, and scheduling the monitoring of the process.

LISP Machine Inc.

LISP Machine Inc. (LMI) was a knowledge engineering company located in Massachusetts. The company's objective was to offer products and services related to building expert systems using LISP machines and LISP/UNIX machines. The Process System Division of LISP Machine Inc. was seeking ways to apply expert system technology to process control. It was this division that created PICON. LMI has been acquired by GigaMos Systems, which is carrying the LMI objectives forward.

RULEMASTER

RuleMaster is a knowledge engineering tool for developing expert systems. It is a general-purpose software package capable of generating rules from examples. Its two major parts are RuleMaker and Radial. RuleMaker induces rules from examples. Radial is a language system for interpreting these rules.

The creation of RuleMaster is based on concepts and methods developed by Professor Donald Michie of Edinburgh University in Scotland. RuleMaster was developed by experts from both Professor Michie's organization (the Turing Institute) and Radian Corporation (Austin, Texas); it is marketed by Radian Corporation.

RuleMaster offers forward- and backward-chaining mechanisms. It is written in the C programming language and runs on UNIX operating systems. Versions of RuleMaster exist that work on DEC VAX computers, Sun Microsystems workstations, and AT&T and IBM personal computers.

Key Features

Rule induction is the use of examples to generate rules. This is an interesting feature. With it, a human expert does not have to create rules; the expert has only to provide RuleMaster with examples, and RuleMaster will develop rules from the expert's examples.

RuleMaster uses a Pascal-like language called Radial to develop knowledge bases with a structure that will facilitate their manipulation and provide a better understanding of their knowledge data. A Radial program is a body of executable procedures and data elements organized in modules capable of communicating with each other. The modules are in a hierarchical tree structure. The communication between them is governed by a rule of "visibility" defined as follows:

Module X is visible to module Y if and only if X is a child of Y or X is visible to the parent of Y.

Figure 11.17 illustrates a tree representation of Radial modules. The circled modules are the only modules visible to module m. The module at the top of the tree cannot be referenced by any other module.

RuleMaster has an explanation facility that is useful for expert system development and consultation. In the first case, knowledge engineers building an expert system make use of this facility to check if the system's reasoning pattern is correct. In the second case, a user consulting with the system can request an explanation whenever needed.

RuleMaster accepts facts and rules with a degree-of-belief factor attached to them. This provides the knowledge engineer with the ability to represent the expert's certainty in the heuristics.

RuleMaster can interface with external systems, programs, data files, and sensors. This allows expert systems created with RuleMaster to be integrated with other systems an organization uses or is developing.

Control System

RuleMaster handles both declarative and procedural knowledge representation when the set of examples provided to it is transformed into rules using Radial. The set of examples represents the declarative knowledge. Radial generates the procedural knowledge.

The forward-chaining capability provides RuleMaster with the ability to build expert systems capable of planning and monitoring. This forward-chaining mechanism is also used by RuleMaster to present explanations about its line of reasoning. The backward-chaining mechanism gives RuleMaster the capability of developing expert systems for diagnosis. This capability is used by Rule-Master's reasoning facility.

Two search methods used by expert systems are depth-first search and breadth-first search. Depth-first search refers to the ability of an expert system to work effectively on narrow but difficult problem domains. Breadth-first search refers to the ability to go through a wider but less difficult or complex

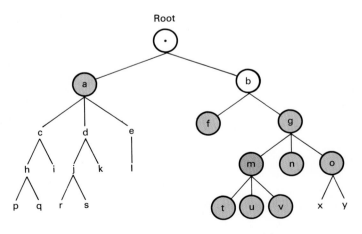

Figure 11.17   Modules visible to module *m*

problem domain. In RuleMaster, Radial can be used to generate rules that will help in determining the better method.

Rule checking is done at two stages: when a set of examples is provided to RuleMaster and after it has generated corresponding rules. In the first case, checking is done to assure compatibility among the examples. Also, some error checking is performed. In the second case, checking is done to assure correct linkage between rules.

Control can be exercised in RuleMaster through the use of a sophisticated approach called the blackboard. The blackboard construct allows independent groups of rules to communicate among themselves through a central database.

Example of a RuleMaster Application

RuleMaster can be used in various domains. Two major categories are diagnosis and control. Diagnosis refers to the ability of an expert system to use the knowledge provided to it to detect causes of problems in a system. RuleMaster has been used in fault isolation, monitoring, forecasting, and data evaluation. Control refers to the ability of an expert system to modulate the behavior of a given system. For example, RuleMaster has been used in the chemical industry to control chemical processes. An example RuleMaster application is the transformer fault diagnosis expert system developed for the Hartford Steam Boiler Inspection and Insurance Company to decrease the costs associated with sudden breakdowns of power distribution transformers. This expert system gives recommendations based on transformer oil analysis. Figure 11.18 illustrates some

H2	thermal	H2/C2H2	temperature		action	next state
high	—	high	low	→	(likely,	GOAL)
med	absent	high	low	→	(likely,	GOAL)
high	—	high	moderate	→	(possible,	GOAL)
med	absent	high	moderate	→	(possible,	GOAL)
high	—	high	high	→	(unlikely,	GOAL)
med	absent	high	high	→	(unlikely,	GOAL)
med	present	—	moderate	→	(unlikely,	GOAL)
med	slight	—	moderate	→	(unlikely,	GOAL)
low	—	—	—	→	(unlikely,	GOAL)
—	—	low	—	→	(unlikely,	GOAL)

Figure 11.18   Example set for a corona rule

examples used to check whether or not the condition known as a corona is present in a transformer. From those examples, RuleMaster will automatically generate rules using Radial (see Figure 11.19).

RuleMaster is an expert system development tool that is capable of generating rules from examples. It has its own interpretative language called Radial and has the capability of explaining its line of reasoning, interfacing with external systems, and handling uncertain facts and rules. RuleMaster can be used for building expert systems for diagnosis, monitoring, training, and control.

Radian Corporation

Radian Corporation is a knowledge engineering company with headquarters in Austin, Texas. Since its creation in 1969, Radian has been providing services and software and hardware products to both the government and the private sector. Radian is responsible for the continued development and marketing of RuleMaster. Radian offers knowledge engineering and expert system consulting services as well as its expert system shell product, RuleMaster.

```
IF (temp IS
    "low" : IF (H2/C2H2) IS
        "high" : IF (H2) IS
            "low" : ( "unlikely" → result, GOAL )
            "med" : ( "likely" → result, GOAL )
            ELSE ( "unlikely" → result, GOAL )
        ELSE ( "unlikely" → result, GOAL )
    "moderate" : IF (H2/C2H2) IS
        "high" : IF (H2) IS
            "low" : ( "unlikely" → result, GOAL )
            "med" : IF (thermal) IS
                "absent": ( "possible" → result, GOAL )
                "slight" : ( "unlikely" → result, GOAL )
                ELSE ( "unlikely" → result, GOAL )
            ELSE ( "possible" → result, GOAL )
        ELSE ( "unlikely" → result, GOAL )
    ELSE ( "unlikely" → result, GOAL )

GOAL OF corona
```

Figure 11.19 Corona determination rule induced from Figure 11.18 examples as expressed in automatically generated Radial code

TIMM   TIMM (The Intelligent Machine Model) is a general-
                                        purpose tool for building expert systems. This soft-
ware package supports a frame-like knowledge representation method and has
an inference engine that uses analogical reasoning to generate rules and to reach
conclusions. TIMM can also be used to interconnect several expert systems.

 TIMM is written in FORTRAN-77 and exists in two versions, a personal
computer (PC) version and a mainframe version. The PC version can accommodate up to 500 rules, whereas the mainframe version can accommodate up to
5000 rules. Both versions are easy to learn and use; a developer does not need
to be a knowledge engineer or a computer programmer to be able to use TIMM.
TIMM was developed in the early 1980s by General Research Corporation
(GRC), a California-based company specialized in high-technology research.

Key Features

TIMM is a knowledge engineering tool that guides developers through step-by-
step procedures needed to accomplish a given task. TIMM creates knowledge-
bases by asking questions in English and from the answers provided generates
the rules and facts needed in the knowledge-base.

 TIMM can be used in a variety of computer systems, ranging from microcomputers to mainframe computers. As a result, TIMM is available to many
users.

 An expert system built with TIMM can be used to communicate with other
expert systems or to access database files.

 In its knowledge representation structure, TIMM allows the use of symbolic and numeric data, discrete and continuous variables, and certainty factors.
Inheritance of values and decisions is possible between linked systems.

 One important feature of TIMM is its ability to perform analogical reasoning to generate rules and to reach conclusions. When beginning to use TIMM
for building an expert system, a developer has to provide the following information:

- The name of the new expert system
- A list of possible decisions that can be reached
- A list of factors that can influence the decision reached
- Some illustrative examples in which the human expert specifies the correct de-
  cisions to make for some given combination of factors

 The various examples are provided in a frame-like structure and constitute
the analogs from which TIMM derives the decision rules to apply for any given
situation.

 In Figure 11.20, we confine ourselves to the use of only 4 of TIMM's 12

Figure 11.20   Sample session with TIMM

In this example, there are only two possible decisions—take a car or take a plane—and two factors—distance and road condition. The possible values for the factor "Distance" range from 200 miles to 1000 miles, where as the possible values of the factor "Road Condition" are "Bad" and "Good."

The following matrix gives a summary of the decision to be made for each combination of factors (the decision "take a car" = C, and the decision "take a plane" = P).

Distance ====== Road Condition	200	300	400	500	600	700	800	900	1000
Good	C	C	C	C	P	P	P	P	P
Bad	P	P	P	P	P	P	P	P	P

What Happens in Each Mode of Operation:

The Build mode of operation (B):

The following is a summary of some of the information generated in B mode:

- The new expert system name = Transportation Adviser
- The choice of decisions to be made = Take a Plane
                                          Take a Car
- Factors that influence the decision = Distance
                                          Road Condition
- Possible values for the factor "Distance":
              minimum value = 200
              maximum value = 1000
- Possible values for the factor "Road Condition" = Good
                                                      Bad

The Train mode of operation (T):

The following are some examples of combination of factors and decisions that we provide to TIMM as its training cases for making decisions:

*Distance	= 200	*Distance	= 200
Road Condition	= Good	Road Condition	= Bad
Decision	= Take a Car	Decision	= Take a Plane

Figure 11.20 *(Continued)*

*Distance   = 500
  Road Condition = Good
  Decision   = Take a Car

*Distance   = 500
  Road Condition = Bad
  Decision   = Take a Plane

*Distance   = 600
  Road Condition = Good
  Decision   = Take a Car

*Distance   = 1000
  Road Condition = Bad
  Decision   = Take a Plane

*Distance   = 1000
  Road Condition = Good
  Decision   = Take a Car

The Exercise mode of operation (E):

At this stage, TIMM is able to make decisions by itself and explain how it arrived at them. TIMM also attaches a reliability factor to its conclusions.

When provided with the following information:

Distance = 200
Road Condition = Good

TIMM will conclude:

Decision = Take a Car (100)
(Reliability = 100)

TIMM will then ask the user whether or not its decision is correct or whether there is a need to explain how the decision was reached. If there is a need to explain how the decision was reached, TIMM will start by explaining that the combination of factors presented here is similar to the following training case:

Rule 1:

If: Distance   = 200
         Road Condition = Good

Then:
       Decision   = Take a Car (100).

TIMM will try to match any new set of factors to its existing set of examples generated by the expert during the training session. By doing that, TIMM is said to be reasoning by analogy. The examples are referred to as analogs.

The Generalize mode of operation (G):

In this mode, TIMM will give the following general rules, which will encompass all possible cases:

If:
     Distance   = <500
     Road Condition = Good

(Continued)

Figure 11.20   (Continued)

Then:

  Decision   = Take a Car

If:

  Distance   = >500
  Road Condition = Good

Then:

  Decision   = Take a Plane

If:

  Distance   = <1000
  Road Condition = Bad

Then:

  Decision   = Take a Plane.

major functions (see Figure 11.21): Build (B), Train (T), Generalize (G), and Exercise (E). The Build function is used to define the type of problem that would be solved by the system, list all the different decisions that could be reached, and identify all the factors that can affect the decision. The Train function is used to generate rules and the needed knowledge base from all the facts and examples provided by an expert. The Generalize function is used to generate general rules from sets of specific rules. The Exercise function is used to consult with TIMM and obtain a conclusion to a particular problem.

In summary, TIMM is a versatile knowledge engineering tool that builds knowledge bases. It uses analogical reasoning to reach its conclusions. This tool provides in its knowledge representation repertoire the use of symbolic and numeric values and discrete and continuous variables. TIMM can be used on a variety of computer systems including personal computers and mainframes.

General Research Corporation

GRC is a high-tech development company with headquarters in Santa Barbara, California. It was founded in 1961 under the name Defense Research Corporation. In 1977, GRC became a subsidiary of a major corporation called Flow General, Inc.

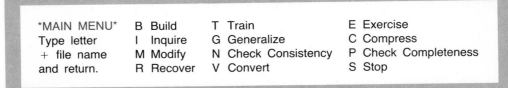

MAIN MENU	B Build	T Train	E Exercise
Type letter	I Inquire	G Generalize	C Compress
+ file name	M Modify	N Check Consistency	P Check Completeness
and return.	R Recover	V Convert	S Stop

Figure 11.21   TIMM's main menu

The company decided to emphasize research in the area of artificial intelligence in 1977. The objective was to make AI techniques readily accessible to the business community.

Since its creation, GRC has provided high-tech-related services and products to both the public and private sectors. One of its products is the TIMM expert system building tool.

12 HARDWARE FOR EXPERT SYSTEMS

Expert systems are computer software systems. Computer hardware is a prerequisite for expert system development and use. Expert system technology is a product of artificial intelligence research that has occurred and is still occurring at university research laboratories and FORTUNE 500 company research facilities. These research establishments have traditionally used specialized computer systems known as LISP machines or LISP workstations to host their artificial intelligence research.

LISP machines are computer systems of varying sizes, both from a physical standpoint and from a computing standpoint. LISP machines are often deskside units ranging in height from 2 to 6 feet. They usually measure between 6 inches by 2 feet and 2 feet by 4 feet. Most LISP machines are single-processor, single-user systems. LISP machines usually comprise the LISP machine system unit and a user-system interface component. The LISP machine system unit usually contains the LISP processor, memory, disk drives, and requisite support hardware such as communications ports and power supplies. Processor memory and virtual memory are usually relatively large for a single-user system. Up to 30 megabytes of processor memory and up to 1024 megabytes of virtual memory are typical. The user-system interface component usually includes a large (up to 19-inch) high-resolution display screen, often employing a bit map of up to 1024 by 1024 bits. The user-system interface component also includes keyboard and mouse input devices.

Since LISP machines are usually single-user systems, most are equipped with communications ports so that these machines can interoperate with other computing facilities in an organization or at other organizations.

These machines are called LISP machines because they are architected to optimize the development and running of software systems written in the LISP programming language.

Other powerful single-user workstations support the development and use

301

of artificial intelligence software like expert systems but have not been architected to optimize LISP operations. These AI machines do not include specialized LISP processors but do offer other computing attributes of LISP machines including large, high-resolution screen displays; keyboard and mouse input devices; and large memories.

The software offered by the LISP machine and AI workstation vendors includes software engineering environments for the LISP programming language as well as other languages like PROLOG and SMALLTALK. Some of the vendors also offer non-AI languages, including C, Pascal, and Ada. These hardware vendors and third-party software vendors also offer a variety of knowledge engineering tools that assist knowledge engineers in the development of expert systems.

Other features that set LISP machines apart from other computer systems include tagged architecture for run-time data-type checking, wide internal data paths, microcoded LISP instructions, hardware to perform memory management activities like garbage collection (retrieval of memory space), large high-speed stack buffers, and parallelism between specific processes within the machine.

Today, although most computer systems are rated as to their potential computing power on one of two scales, *mips* (millions of instructions per second) or *flops* (floating-point operations per second), LISP machines are commonly rated on a different scale, *lips* (logical inferences per second). The first LISP machines had the capability of handling 1000 logical inferences per second. Present LISP machines can handle on the order of 10,000 to 50,000 lips. American and Japanese researchers hope to be able to create LISP machines that can handle in excess of 100 million lips soon.

LISP machines are specialized computer systems. They are used for special purposes and needs. Although LISP machines provide effective workstations, other workstation configurations that are more general-purpose are competing well with LISP machines and workstations for artificial intelligence and, in particular, expert system development and delivery machine business. General-purpose high-power workstations have been taking over much AI processing from LISP machines.

LISP machine vendors are responding to the competition by providing machines with more general-purpose computing capabilities in addition to the specialized LISP capabilities. They are also including more connectivity options by providing organizations with the requisite hardware and software to connect their LISP machines to their management information systems and their process control systems.

One important trend to watch is that of the leading expert system development tool vendors porting their tools over to more traditional computer systems like the Digital Equipment Corporation VAX computer line and to general-purpose workstations like the IBM PC/RT and the Apollo and Sun workstation products and the IBM PS and its clones. These computers are less expensive and are already in place in many organizations.

LISP machine vendors will be attempting to compete with these developments by the software vendors by producing more powerful versions of their products for lower investment costs. This trend has already started and should be evident in the LISP machine and workstation information provided in the remainder of this chapter.

LISP MACHINE INC.

In this section, we will describe the LISP Machine Inc. (LMI) family of LISP machines called Lambda and some of the software packages that are available to run on this computer hardware. LMI was acquired by GigaMos Systems.

The first computers developed by LMI were the Series III CADR family of computers in 1980. The development of the CADR, the first stand-alone LISP language processor, was initiated at M.I.T. LMI was founded in 1980 by Richard Greenblatt and Stephen Wyle in an effort to enhance the problem-solving capability of LISP machines.

The first Lambda computers were developed in 1981 by combining existing LISP technology and a newly developed computer architecture called the NuBus. With the NuBus came a new generation of LISP machines found to be more flexible and more expandable than existing LISP machines. LMI took advantage of this technology and sought to make LISP and LISP machines into tools that could be used to solve a variety of problems.

Lambda System Components and Key Features

The LMI Lambda was the first LISP machine with a multiprocessor capability that allowed LISP to run simultaneously with other software. Its basic components include the NuBus, a system diagnostic unit, a LISP processor, and a high-resolution graphics display. The LMI Lambda also incorporates interesting features like Multibus compatibility, multiprocessing, and networking capabilities. In addition to the LISP processor, a UNIX processor is available for the Lambda system. With a multiprocessor LMI Lambda machine, different processes can run in parallel, communicate with each other, and cooperate in problem-solving activities.

The NuBus is a bus architecture design capable of handling both general-purpose and special-purpose processors. It provides for the effective exchange of information among processors. The NuBus supports 32-bit microprocessor systems. It provides the LMI Lambda with its multiprocessor capability. A LISP processor and a UNIX processor are two processors that can be used in Lambda systems. Figure 12.1 illustrates the LMI NuBus architecture.

The System Diagnosis Unit monitors bus and board functions and performs system configuration tasks. Most Lambda system failures can be detected by this unit.

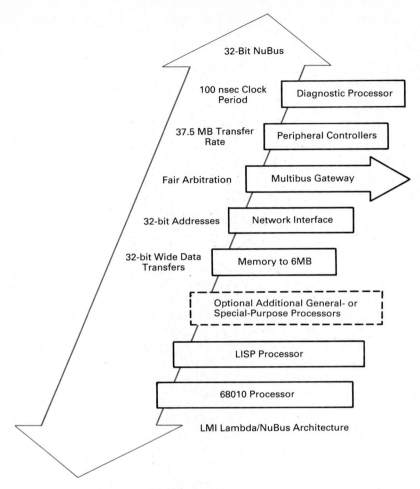

Figure 12.1   LMI Lambda/NuBus architecture

The LISP processor constitutes the fundamental component of a Lambda system. Along with the LMI LISP microcompiler, the LISP processor provides the environment necessary to create sophisticated LISP application programs. This LISP processor is a 32-bit microprogrammable processor designed to handle complex software architecture.

Lambda systems include Multibus. Lambda users have the capability of employing Multibus-compatible board-level products from more than 100 manufacturers.

Although the LISP and UNIX processors are independent of each other, a communication link exists so that programs that reside on one processor can interoperate and exchange data with the other processor.

Lambda systems can be formed into networks to allow for the possibility of information sharing between systems and users.

Lambda Machine Descriptions

The LMI Lambda family contains a variety of machines designed to satisfy most LISP machine user needs. This family of computers includes the following machines: the Lambda, the Lambda/PLUS, the Lambda 2*2, the Lambda 2*2/PLUS, the Lambda 3*3, the Lambda 4*4, and the Lambda/E.

The Lambda constitutes the foundation of the Lambda family. It can be upgraded to the Lambda 2*2/PLUS by adding processors. Its multiprocessor architecture and Multibus make it a powerful and expandable machine.

The Lambda/PLUS is a Lambda machine that has a 68010/UNIX coprocessor in addition to the LISP processor. In this machine, the two processors can communicate with each other. The UNIX processor can be used for many purposes including the running of non-LISP process control programs.

The Lambda 2*2 contains two Lambda LISP processors that share common memory and disk storage. This Lambda system comes with two high-resolution 19-inch displays, two keyboards, and two mice. The two processors have equal accessibility to the ZetaLISP-PLUS and the LM-PROLOG environments.

The Lambda 2*2/PLUS contains two LMI LISP processors and a UNIX processor. It is a powerful and versatile system that can simultaneously provide LISP, PROLOG, and UNIX programming environments.

The Lambda 3*3 offers three Lambda LISP processors that run independently of one another. This system allows three users to use the ZetaLISP-PLUS and LM-PROLOG programming environments simultaneously.

The LMI Lambda 4*4 simultaneously supports four LISP/PROLOG users.

The LMI Lambda/E is the most compact of all the LMI LISP machines. This system is manufactured by Texas Instruments. It includes a 32-bit LISP processor, 2 megabytes of physical memory, 140 megabytes of Winchester disk storage, and a ZetaLISP-PLUS programming environment.

Lambda Software

The LISP software used in Lambda systems is called ZetaLISP-PLUS. ZetaLISP-PLUS offers developers a LISP programming environment that also includes a wide variety of software development tools. This creates an environment in which programs can be written efficiently. Here are some of the programming tools used in ZetaLISP-PLUS and their functions:

- The LMI Window System permits the creation of customized windows. Each window can have its own process.
- ZMACS is a real-time editor that is integrated into the LISP environment. The existence of the mouse and the LMI Window System in the Lambda machines makes this an effective editor.

- The Inspector is used to examine and modify LISP structures.
- The Window Error Handler is a graphics-oriented debugging tool.
- Common LISP is integrated with ZetaLISP-PLUS to facilitate the interchange of software between the LMI systems and other Common LISP systems.
- InterLISP-D is an optional tool that can be added to the Lambda system to support InterLISP-D programs.
- FLAVORS is an object-oriented programming paradigm.

ZetaLISP-PLUS provides the Lambda machines with an environment in which the power of LISP can be simultaneously used with LM-PROLOG, Common LISP, System V UNIX, Extended-STREAMS interface, and the hardware support of the Lambda LISP processor. It constitutes a LISP environment where approximately 10,000 compiled functions and 30,000 symbols reside. The LMI machines were the first to offer Common LISP.

LM-PROLOG is derived from the PROLOG language; it is available to support logic programming. LM-PROLOG operates within ZetaLISP-PLUS and allows PROLOG programs to be called from LISP functions.

The System V UNIX augments the Lambda systems so that the LISP environment can be interfaced with other programming languages like C, FORTRAN 77, and Pascal.

The Extended-STREAMS interface provides the interface between the LISP and the UNIX environments. It enables parallel processing between both the LISP and PROLOG programming environments and the UNIX programming environment.

The Lambda LISP machines also have the following software available: RTIME, AI-BASE, IKE, AND PICON. PICON is a software package for developing real-time expert systems for process control. IKE is an expert system building tool. RTIME is the software used by PICON to process real-time data. AI-BASE is a LISP package that assists developers in the construction of knowledge bases; it supports rules, models, flowchart procedures, and decision tree knowledge representations.

In summary, the LMI Lambda systems are powerful LISP machines with multiprocessor capabilities. Some of the systems contain more than one LISP processor, and some contain a UNIX coprocessor and allow processing of LISP and PROLOG in parallel with UNIX. Every Lambda system has an integral Multibus that allows interfacing with a wide variety of peripherals. ZetaLISP-PLUS is the basic LISP environment that comes with the Lambda machines.

LISP Machine Inc.

LISP Machine Inc. (LMI) was engaged in AI research and in the development of LISP machines using LISP and UNIX processors. LMI developed significantly important software packages, such as the PICON expert process control system shell. GigaMos Systems, LMI's new owner, has its headquarters in Lowell, Massachusetts.

SYMBOLICS

The 3600 series of Symbolics machines will be presented in this section. The discussion will include hardware and software descriptions as well as the application domains in which Symbolics machines are being used.

The Symbolics 3600 series of LISP machines is made up of the most powerful symbolic processing systems currently available. They can be used for the development of any LISP-based application program. This family of LISP machines offers sophisticated end-user systems into which application programs can be integrated for delivery to end users. A wide range of software is available for these machines.

The Symbolics 3600 series machines were developed by Symbolics, Inc. This company was founded in 1980 and has its headquarters in Cambridge, Massachusetts.

Symbolics Machines

The Symbolics 3600 series includes the following hardware systems: Symbolics 3640, 3670, 3645, 3675, 3610AE, 3620, and 3650. The Symbolics 3645 and 3675 systems are enhanced versions of the 3640 and 3670, respectively; they offer as much as a 50 percent performance improvement over their predecessors thanks to an added feature called the Enhanced Performance Option (EPO). It is possible to upgrade the 3640 and 3670 systems to their enhanced versions by adding an EPO to each of them.

The EPO consists of two components: the Instruction Fetch Unit (IFU) and the Extended Control Store Option (ECS). The IFU is responsible for decoding instructions obtained from the main memory while the processor is performing other operations; this reduces the processor's wait time for instructions to come from main memory. The ECS permits the accommodation of Symbolics products such as Symbolics PROLOG, for which additional microcode is needed. With the ECS, extra central storage is available.

The Symbolics 3600 family is based on a 36-bit architecture that supports the creation of AI applications. It incorporates tools that provide rich development environments in which productivity is improved. The time and cost involved in the development of application systems are both decreased. These machines are being used to solve a wide range of problems in software engineering, VLSI design, CAE/CAD/CAM, expert system development, signal interpretation, natural-language understanding and translation, vision, robotics, training, and simulation.

The Symbolics 3600 family of computers offers an environment in which the ZetaLISP language and a wide variety of software can be accommodated.

ZetaLISP is a programming language that offers a support environment that incorporates all of the standard LISP features as well as a wide variety of extensions such as FLAVORS.

The Symbolics 3640 and 3670 support environments have the following features:

- A high-resolution bit-mapped graphics display
- A window system
- An Inspector utility to examine data structures
- A Peek utility to examine the state of the system's resources
- A display-oriented debugger
- A font editor
- A file system editor
- An electronic mail capability
- A networking facility

Additional software options exist for use with the Symbolics 3640 and 3670. This optional software includes FORTRAN-77, Pascal, PROLOG, an InterLISP Compatibility Package, and MACSYMA. Each of these software packages will be discussed shortly.

To complement their programming environments, the Symbolics 3640 and 3670 systems provide powerful hardware for symbolic processing. Their hardware features include the following:

- A proprietary tagged memory architecture for run-time data-type checking and generic operations
- A stack-oriented architecture with large stack buffers
- A front-end microprocessor
- A hardware-assisted garbage collection facility for memory efficiency with low software overhead
- A floating-point accelerator (FPA) option

In addition, a standard 3640 system configuration provides the following:

- A 30-inch system cabinet containing the processor, I/O controllers, memory, disk, and options
- Physical memory up to 28 megabytes
- Virtual memory up to 261 megabytes

- Four backplane expansion slots (one dedicated to the FPA)
- Disk capacities from 140 to 380 megabytes

In addition to the standard list, the 3670 system configuration provides the following:

- A 55-inch system cabinet containing the processor, I/O controllers, memory, disk, and options
- Physical memory up to 28 megabytes
- Virtual memory up to 1 gigabyte
- Fifteen backplane expansion slots (one dedicated to the FPA)
- Disk capacities from 167 megabytes to over 3 gigabytes

The 3640 is a single-user workstation ideal for the development of small to medium-sized applications. It can be put in a network where it can be linked with other 3640s, 3670s, and file server and host computer systems.

In parallel with application development systems such as the Symbolics 3640 and 3670, Symbolics offers machines for delivering applications to end users. These delivery systems allow large applications to be delivered at an affordable price without compromising on functionality or performance. Applications delivered on these systems can take advantage of the following features:

- Symbolics Common LISP environment
- Networking software
- Operating system functions
- Symbolics LISP environment window system and editor
- FORTRAN, PROLOG, Pascal, and Ada
- Error-checking devices
- High-resolution color graphics
- Tools to support application products throughout their life cycles

The Symbolics 3610AE system is a delivery system used to run symbolic processing applications that were previously developed on the larger 3600 systems. It is compatible with the Symbolics development processors. It incorporates a processor, a high-resolution monochrome display, a keyboard, a mouse, and integrated Symbolics LISP software. The 3610AE system can accommodate a wide variety of features including multitasking in a single address space, an advanced window system, and the FLAVORS object-oriented programming language. This system will run any of these functions when they are contained in a developed application.

The Symbolics 3620 machine is appropriate for smaller development projects. It provides a general programming environment in which program developers can use features such as Symbolics Common LISP, FLAVORS object-oriented programming, window management, networking software, graphics, multitasking in a single address space, multilanguage programming, editors, debuggers, and electronic mail. The 3620 system contains five expansion slots for additional memory, a floating-point accelerator for numerically intensive applications, mass storage, printers, or additional I/O ports. Like the 3610AE, the 3620 can be used as a delivery system; it too is compatible with the other Symbolics 3600 computers. Compared to the 3610AE, the 3620 can accommodate larger application systems. The general environment provides an operating system written in LISP, a flexible user interface, Symbolics documentation, multiple language support, and various program utilities.

The Symbolics 3650 is designed to accommodate the development of mid-range projects. It can also be used as an applications delivery system or as a file server for small networks. This machine provides multiple expansion possibilities. The 3650 system provides a general programming environment that allows both the development of mid-size applications and an effective utilization of applications by end users. The 3650 includes a processor, an I/O controller, an Ethernet interface, a 368-megabyte disk, and 15 expansion slots for additional options.

The Symbolics 3675 and 3645 are the Symbolics machines that incorporate the enhanced performance processor that allows them to provide up to a 50 percent increase in performance when compared with their predecessors, the 3670 and the 3640. The 3675 includes a 4-megabyte standard main memory, a 474-megabyte disk or a 300-megabyte removable disk, the EPO with the IFU, and the ECS. The 3645 configuration includes a 4-megabyte standard main memory, one or two 190-megabyte disks, and the EPO.

Software Options

The 3600 application software development environment is very sophisticated. It includes software tools, development utilities, and a wide range of programming languages including FORTRAN 77, Pascal, PROLOG, Ada, and Inter-LISP.

The FORTRAN 77 Tool Kit permits FORTRAN 77 programs to be developed, debugged, and run on the Symbolics 3600. It allows routines to be incrementally compiled and executed without having to be linked and loaded; this accelerates program development. This tool kit contains the following items:

- A FORTRAN 77 compiler
- Extensions to ZMACS, the standard 3600 text editor, to permit the editing of FORTRAN programs

- A run-time library
- A debugger

The Pascal Tool Kit supports ISO Standard Pascal. This tool kit converts the Symbolics machines into ideal workstations for Pascal programmers because rapid prototyping and development of Pascal-based application programs are allowed. With this tool kit, routines can be incrementally compiled and executed independently of the program to which they belong.

Symbolics PROLOG allows the use of standard PROLOG features in the Symbolics LISP environment. PROLOG programs written according to the DECsystem-10 PROLOG standard can be run without modification on Symbolics machines.

The Symbolics Ada programming environment permits Ada programmers to have access to Symbolics LISP, Common LISP, FORTRAN, Pascal, and PROLOG while developing Ada applications. Ada programmers are provided with all of the Symbolics software development tools including a window-oriented symbolic software debugger, online documentation, and a window system.

MACSYMA is a software package designed to help solve mathematical problems analytically. It is designed to support scientists, engineers, and mathematicians in solving mathematical problems. In an interactive mode, users converse with MACSYMA through a mathematical language while the system automatically maintains a complete record of all interactions. A user who has no prior computing experience can interact with the system and solve complex problems. MACSYMA is currently being used in application areas such as acoustics, algebraic geometry, computer-aided design, economics, structural mechanics, solid-state physics, fluid mechanics, and numeric analysis.

The InterLISP Compatibility Package is a tool that permits InterLISP to be used in the ZetaLISP environment where InterLISP can be intermixed with or converted to ZetaLISP code. This package allows InterLISP programs to be maintained and extended.

In summary, the Symbolics 3600 family of LISP machines represents the state of the art for LISP machine technology. It offers environments in which a wide variety of programming languages such as Common LISP, ZetaLISP, PROLOG, FORTRAN 77, Pascal, and Ada can be used. The family includes machines designed to meet the needs of both application system developers and end users. This family of LISP machines provides a solid foundation for the solving of complex artificial intelligence problems in a variety of application domains.

Symbolics, Inc.

Symbolics, Inc. was founded in 1980 by a group of researchers from the M.I.T. Artificial Intelligence Laboratory. It is a leading company in the development of LISP machines. It has more than 1500 systems installed in the United States and throughout the world. Headquartered in Cambridge, Massachusetts, Symbolics has regional sales offices in many major cities in the United States.

TEKTRONIX   The Tektronix family of artificial intelligence computer systems will be presented in this section. We will describe some of the computer hardware included in this family and some of the programming languages and software packages that are available for use on them. Notice that we will not refer to the TEK 4400 computer systems series as LISP machines or LISP workstations, since they are not. Rather, the TEK 4400 series is a series of large microprocessor-based systems that have been designed to help develop systems like expert systems but are not architected in a manner to optimize the LISP programming language.

Tektronix Workstations

The Tektronix family of AI computer systems is known as the Tektronix 4400 series. It includes the following workstations: the TEK 4404, the TEK 4405, and the TEK 4406. The TEK 4404 is the oldest of this series; it was introduced in August 1984. The TEK 4404 will not be presented here; instead we will describe the more recent Tektronix AI workstations, the TEK 4405 and the TEK 4406.

The TEK 4405 is a single-user system designed to be used for the development of AI applications including expert systems. The TEK 4405 incorporates a high-performance microprocessor, the Motorola 68020. A 68881 floating-point coprocessor and a 1-megabyte high-speed dynamic RAM memory are also included in this machine. Information can be stored on a 45-megabyte hard disk or on a 320-kilobyte floppy. There is an option of adding 2 or 4 megabytes of additional RAM and an additional 90-megabyte hard disk. The TEK 4405 incorporates a UNIX-like virtual memory operating system that allows multitasking. The TEK 4405 facilities that support the user interface include a 13-inch monochrome bit-mapped graphics display, a mouse, and a keyboard.

The TEK 4406 is the most powerful of the TEK 4400 series. It is a single-user system that incorporates a Motorola 68020 microprocessor, a high-speed 68881 floating-point coprocessor, 2 megabytes of dynamic RAM (expandable to 6 megabytes), a 90-megabyte hard disk, and a 320-kilobyte floppy. An additional 90-megabyte hard disk can be added to the system. The TEK 4406 display is a 19-inch CRT that is bit-mapped and provides text, graphics, and icons. The user can interact with the screen through a three-button mouse or a keyboard joystick. The TEK 4406 also incorporates a UNIX-like virtual memory operating system. The TEK 4406 can access host computing systems through a standard terminal evaluation protocol.

TEK Software and Programming Environment

The predominant programming language used on the TEK 4400 series computer systems is TEK SMALLTALK-80, a Tektronix version of the object-oriented SMALLTALK language. TEK SMALLTALK-80 provides an environment that supports quick program prototyping. It also provides for the development of graphics-oriented applications. The SMALLTALK-80 system comes with a text and graphics editor, a compiler, a debugger, and a windowing system.

Other programming systems that can be used on the TEK 4400 series include TEK Common LISP, the Franz dialect of LISP, and MPROLOG. TEK Common LISP is an implementation of Common LISP, an AI programming environment considered standard by many. TEK Common LISP integrates several features obtained from various LISP implementations. This programming system supports the development of sophisticated applications. TEK Common LISP provides the Common LISP programming environment to TEK 4400 series applications developers. It incorporates features such as a compiler with built-in debugging tools, a lexical scoped interpreter, a package system for symbol name differentiation, and an interactive user interface system. Franz LISP is a popular dialect of LISP that is a product of Franz, Inc. MPROLOG is a programming language derived from PROLOG. It is designed to accommodate logic programming.

Tektronix, Inc.

Tektronix, Inc. is a high-technology company that develops information systems hardware and software as well as other high-technology tools. Tektronix has a division called the Computer Research Laboratory, Knowledge-based Systems Group, that has developed a variety of tools and application systems for AI applications like expert systems. Some of the products developed by Tektronix include GLIB, a knowledge engineering language for rule-based representation, and FG502-TASP, a system designed to assist technicians in the diagnosis of malfunctioning Tektronix FG502 function generators.

TEXAS INSTRUMENTS

The Explorer system is a sophisticated LISP workstation that allows for the development of complex applications. This system was designed for symbolic processing and the creation of high-quality graphics. It contains numerous features, one of which is the NLMenu system, a feature that permits the user to develop application systems through a natural-language interface. Explorer is well suited to be used as an end-user system.

The Explorer programming environment offers powerful tools designed to facilitate the development of complex application systems. This programming environment can also accommodate a wide variety of software packages, including communication software that permits Explorer to be linked to other computer systems including IBM mainframes.

Explorer was built by Texas Instruments in an effort to provide the AI community with a system that can be used for the development of sophisticated computer-based systems.

Explorer Hardware

The Explorer workstation offers a variety of features designed to give application systems developers flexibility in the accomplishment of their tasks. These features offer an ideal environment for the development of high-performance LISP programs and high-quality graphics.

Explorer hardware is composed of the following elements: the NuBus, the local bus, a processor, memory boards, a system interface board, a mass storage subsystem, and a bit-mapped display for the user interface (see Figure 12.2).

The NuBus system allows for high-speed exchange of data among processors, memory, mass storage, special devices, and other computer systems. It incorporates the following features:

- Processor-independent architecture with multiprocessor support that allows processors or other devices meeting the user's needs to be added
- 32-bit addressing and the capability of supporting 8-bit, 16-bit, and 32-bit data transfers
- Block transfers of multiple words
- 37.5-megabyte-per-second data transfer rate
- 10-megahertz bus clock
- Synchronous operation
- Simple bus protocols

The local bus is used by the processor to access main memory and the graphics bit map directly.

Explorer incorporates a processor specifically designed for the efficient execution of LISP data structure manipulation. This microcoded processor is an enhanced version of a processor that was originally created at M.I.T. The processor offers a full 32-bit data path and a 16,000- by 56-bit writable control store for microcode. The processor also incorporates features needed for demand paging, garbage collection, and tagged data support. The newer Explorer II includes T.I.'s LISP chip processor.

The Explorer system contains two memory boards capable of handling up to a total of 4 megabytes of memory. The system interface board provides the following features:

- A fiber-optic link to various devices including the display unit and the serial and parallel ports
- A graphics controller responsible for storing the high-resolution display image and acceleration of the window operations
- Parallel and serial ports for printers and other devices
- Miscellaneous hardware including clocks, timers, nonvolatile memory, and power failure event logic

The mass storage subsystem contains a mass storage controller. This device is responsible for handling the requests issued from the processor and the

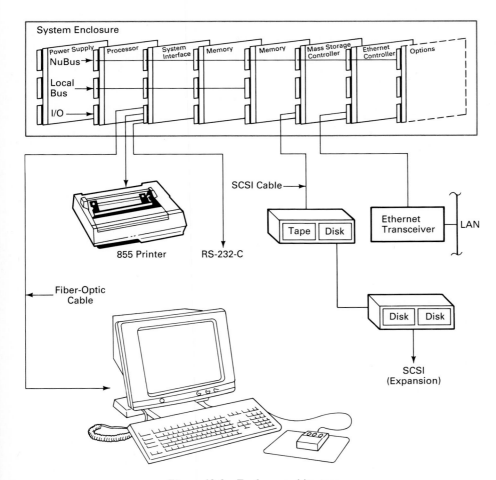

Figure 12.2   Explorer architecture

transfer of commands, data, and status between memory and mass storage. The controller also provides the interface needed to the industry standard small computer systems interface (SCSI). The mass storage subsystem is contained in one or more mass storage enclosures. Each mass storage enclosure contains a combination of two storage devices. These storage devices can be 112-megabyte disks or 60-megabyte magnetic tape units. Up to four enclosures can be chained together in a single Explorer system.

Explorer Software and Programming Environment

The Explorer software and programming environment offers advanced features that enable application systems developers to develop systems easily and rapidly. This environment consists of a user interface, the LISP language, and a variety of tools and facilities.

The user interface consists of hardware and software that allows the users to gain access to all the system facilities. Its hardware component is composed of the following:

- A display unit that provides a high-resolution bit-mapped display from which all system activities can be watched. This display can accommodate the use of multiple fonts and the development of high-quality graphics. It also incorporates microphone and headset connectors that can be used when speech options are added to the system

- A keyboard

- An optical mouse that permits a direct manipulation of items on the display screen

The user interface software includes a window system that provides for the management of the display information. This interface software also provides users with guidance on how to use the system efficiently.

The Explorer software system is written in LISP and supports Common LISP and ZetaLISP. It is the LISP programming environment that provides Explorer with features like these:

- Symbolic processing capability allowing for the use of symbols and symbolic structures to represent real-world objects or concepts

- Flexibility in the design and development of application systems

- The ability to customize LISP to fit developers' needs

- A variety of programming tools

In addition to the LISP, Common LISP, and ZetaLISP programming environments, Explorer offers high-level extensions such as a FLAVORS system. The FLAVORS system permits the use of object-oriented programming in which each flavor is an object representing a family of other similar objects. Methods, which are functions containing the operations to perform on a given object, can be attached to each flavor.

The Explorer system offers a variety of program development tools that permit rapid application system development. With these tools, a developer is able to develop programs piece by piece and execute them incrementally. Thus partially developed programs can be executed. These tools make the program development activity easier because associated tasks are simplified.

Program development tools used in Explorer include these:

- ZMACS Editor is a real-time display editor that offers a wide range of features, including commands, that permit the manipulation of texts as units; each unit can be moved, copied, deleted, transposed, have its fonts changed, or be changed to upper case or lower case.

- LISP Listener provides the user with a direct link to the LISP interpreter.

- LISP Compiler converts LISP functions into machine code and checks for errors.

- Debugging tools assist in locating and correcting bugs in LISP programs and include a window-based debugger, a break facility that stops the execution of a program, a trace facility that can be used when there is a need to trace a particular function, a step facility that permits the monitoring in the evaluation procedure of a LISP form, an advice facility, and an error condition handler through which the user is able to specify the way the user wants the program to handle any given error condition.

- Inspector is a window-oriented program that allows data structures to be monitored so that corrective actions can be taken when needed.

- Command Interface Toolkit (CIT) permits the creation of user interfaces for Explorer-based applications.

The Explorer system provides a variety of software options that can be incorporated into application programs. These software options allow developers to integrate sophisticated features such as natural-language interfaces, graphics tools, database management system capabilities, publication development tools, and knowledge engineering tools with their applications. The currently available software options include the Graphics Toolkit, the Natural Language Menu System, the Relational Table Management System, Formatter, and Personal Consultant.

The Graphics Toolkit is a software library that permits the manipulation of graphics objects and displaying of the results on Explorer's bit-mapped display screen. It contains the following set of tools:

- The Graphics Window System (GWIN), the component that contains the procedures allowing graphics objects to be manipulated and combined with each other and supports the drawing of shapes in windows

- The Graphics Editor, a program that permits the creation of pictures directly on the screen without having to use any LISP code; it is handy for making charts and diagrams.

- The Tree Editor, which graphically displays in a tree structure any data organized in a hierarchical form; it is a collection of procedures that can be used to build application programs (see Figure 12.3).

The Natural Language Menu (NLMenu) system is a software package that supports the creation of natural-language interfaces to applications developed on Explorer. The NLMenu provides users with windows containing words and phrases that they can select for building their own sentences (see Figure 12.4). With this natural-language interface, non–computer specialists are able to use many Explorer-based applications.

The Relational Table Management System (RTMS) is a database management system designed for the LISP environment. It is a collection of procedures that allows relational tables such as the one shown in Figure 12.5 to be created

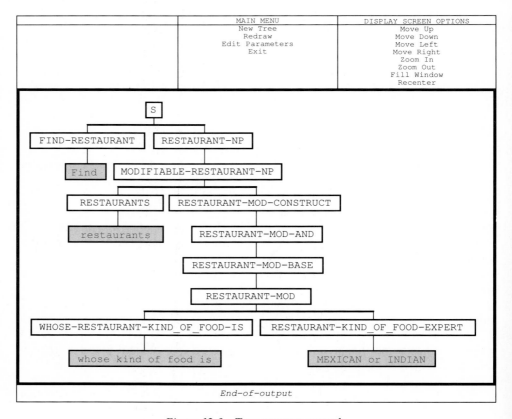

Figure 12.3   Tree structure example

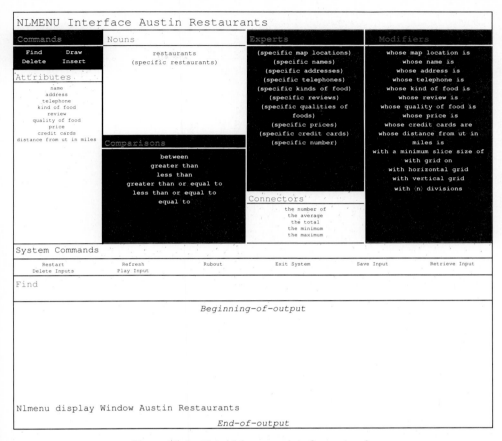

Figure 12.4 Natural-language interface example

and manipulated in the LISP environment. RTMS supports user-defined relations.

The Explorer system offers knowledge engineering tools that allow users to build expert systems. These knowledge engineering tools include the following:

- A PROLOG tool kit that contains a PROLOG interpreter and a sample expert system tool. The PROLOG interpreter incorporates both LISP and PROLOG codes. It can be called from the LISP environment. The sample expert system tool can be used to build small rule-based expert systems that reason through the PROLOG inference engine.

- A graph representation language called Grasper. Grasper is a software tool that permits knowledge to be represented as a network of objects. It includes functions to create, delete, bind, evaluate, and show the existence of elements in a network.

PARTS					SUPPLIERS			
NUMBER	PNAME	COLOR	WEIGHT	SUPNO	SUPNO	SNAME	CITY	STATUS
32	BOLT	GREEN	14	88	21	A&T	PARIS	30
45	CAM	BLUE	12	21	34	CF	NICE	50
65	COG	TEAL	14	43	76	PC&H	ATHENS	20
79	NUT	RED	12	76	88	UNITED	AUSTIN	50
83	SCREW	GREEN	15	19	89	TRANS	BOSTON	10

Figure 12.5   Example of relational database tables

The Formatter is a tool that can be used to create high-quality publication documents such as reports and manuals. It is responsible for the details of formatting, page layout, and typography.

Personal Consultant is an expert system building tool. Personal Consultant represents knowledge in a rule format and develops inferences via the backward-chaining control paradigm.

Explorer is capable of exchanging data with IBM mainframe hosts through a communications link provided by the Explorer System Network Architecture (SNA) Communications package. With this package, files can be transferred directly between Explorer systems and IBM hosts using file transfer programs. This communications package consists of an Explorer software package and a hardware protocol converter. Up to nine Explorers can be connected to an IBM host through a single converter.

The Explorer system can be connected to other LISP machines or to conventional computers in local area networks using the Ethernet interface.

In summary, Explorer is a LISP workstation built by Texas Instruments. It incorporates powerful program development tools such as a graphics package, a natural-language interface, a LISP editor, a compiler and an interpreter, debugging and performance monitoring facilities, and a tool kit for database management. This sophisticated development system also contains a PROLOG interpreter and inference engine. An Explorer workstation can be connected to other Explorers or computer systems through the use of a local area network or a SNA communications link. The Explorer machine is designed to satisfy the needs of applications developers and end users.

Texas Instruments

Texas Instruments is an international high-technology company with headquarters in Dallas, Texas. Artificial intelligence is one of many high-technology domains in which Texas Instruments has invested heavily. TI develops and markets LISP machines, expert systems shells, and natural-language tools. TI also develops and sells textbooks and lecture materials for these subject areas.

XEROX

Xerox decided in the early 1970s to invest a large amount of its resources in AI technology development. Today, Xerox is among the leading companies capable of offering a reliable line of AI hardware and software. This company offers its users training in how to use its products as well as service and technical support by well-trained engineers and technicians.

Xerox AI Workstations

Xerox offers AI workstations that support the development of sophisticated expert systems. The AI language used in these machines is called InterLISP-D and is derived from LISP. The InterLISP-D environment also supports other programming tools and languages like LOOPS and Quintus PROLOG. LOOPS provides developers with procedure-oriented, object-oriented, data-oriented, and rule-oriented knowledge representation methods. Quintus PROLOG provides Xerox AI workstation users with the PROLOG logic programming language.

The Xerox family of LISP machines contains the following workstations: the Xerox 1108 series, the Xerox 1132 series, and the Xerox 1185 and 1186 workstations.

The 1108 series, the oldest of these workstations, offers a variety of options in system configuration. These options include a main memory capacity between 1.0 and 3.5 megabytes and a disk drive capacity from 10 to 300 megabytes. With the 1108, there is also the possibility of enhancing the efficiency and productivity of AI application development through the use of two options, the Extended Processor option and the Extended Memory option. The Extended Processor option extends the capabilities of a standard 1108 processor by providing the following:

- An expanded control store and an IEEE standard floating-point processor, both of which are designed to increase the 1108 numeric and graphic capabilities
- A parallel I/O port that permits the 1108 to be connected to various I/O devices

The Extended Memory option increases the 1108 main memory capacity from 1.5 megabytes to 3.5 megabytes. This enables system developers to design and develop larger applications.

A Xerox 1108 workstation is delivered with the following components: a processor, a display, a keyboard, a mouse, a floppy disk drive, and a hard disk drive. The hard disk has a capacity of 10, 29, or 42 megabytes. The display has a 17-inch screen with a high-resolution bit map. The mouse is either a three-button optical mouse or a two-button mechanical mouse. Both the floppy disk drive and the rigid disk are contained in the processor enclosure, which also houses six printed circuit boards: the I/O processor, the central processor, the high-speed I/O processor, memory storage, memory control, and the options board. There is an RS-232 serial port next to the processor. The 1108 includes the InterLISP-D programming environment. The 1108 also has a Busmaster option that provides the 1108 with the capability to support diverse peripherals like color monitors, printers, and speech and music devices. This augmentation of the 1108 capability, based on the Busmaster, allows the connection of IBM PC Bus– and Multibus–based peripheral devices.

The Xerox 1132 LISP workstation can be used for developing medium-scale applications. It is more powerful than the 1108. A standard 1132 includes 2 megabytes of main memory that can be upgraded to 8 megabytes and 80 megabytes of disk memory that is upgradable to 315 megabytes. The system comes with a 17-inch CRT display, a high-resolution bit map, and an optional color display interface. The 1132 includes the InterLISP-D programming environment.

The Xerox 1185 and 1186 LISP workstations are the newest of the Xerox product line. They can be used for system development and as end-user devices. Their key features include these:

- High-performance processors allowing for the efficient execution of AI programming languages
- An optional coprocessor able to run software written for personal computers, such as the IBM PC, with the simultaneous execution and windowing of both the 118X and PC environments on the display
- 32-megabyte virtual memory
- Xerox Ethernet local area network connection capability
- 15-inch or 19-inch high-resolution monochrome display
- Mouse
- 1.1 megabytes of memory, expandable to 3.7 megabytes by increments of 500 kilobytes
- 10-, 20-, 40-, and 80-megabyte hard disk drives
- An optional 360-kilobyte formatted floppy disk drive
- Expansion slots for future growth
- Communication serial ports

Software and Programming Environment

The programming environment provided by Xerox is based on the InterLISP-D programming language and its derivatives such as LOOPS. InterLISP-D is an improved version of AltoLISP, an implementation that ran on a personal computer called the Alto. InterLISP-D is a dialect of the LISP programming language. The InterLISP environment provides the following user facilities: syntax extension, uniform error handling, automatic error correction, an integrated structure-based editor, a compiler, a debugger, and a filing system.

InterLISP-D, combined with the Xerox LISP workstation's high-resolution graphics, provides the user with an effective display facility. It incorporates tools designed to facilitate the development of applications. Some of these tools are the Display Editor, the Inspector, the Programmer's Assistant, the Debugging Tools, and the Program Analyst. The Display Editor and the Inspector allow interactive, structure-based editing of programs and data and access to all objects in the system. The Programmer's Assistant is an aid designed to provide developers with an error analysis capability, an input-monitoring function, a spelling corrector, and a file management capability. The Debugging Tools permit brake, trace, and machine status interrogation functions. The Program Analyst is capable of displaying the structure of programs for inspection and assisting the user in program modification.

The Xerox LISP workstations also support other programming paradigms and languages like LOOPS and Quintus PROLOG. LOOPS is designed to extend the InterLISP-D programming environment. It supports the use of procedure-oriented, object-oriented, data-oriented, and rule-oriented knowledge representation methods. LOOPS was developed in the early 1980s by the Knowledge System Group at the Xerox Palo Alto Research Center. It includes tools such as break packages and editors. The Quintus PROLOG programming language allows the use of English-like, logic-based programming. It was jointly developed by Xerox and Quintus Computer Systems, Inc., a company specializing in the development of PROLOG. Quintus PROLOG can accommodate sophisticated applications. It provides developers with a PROLOG interpreter and compiler that support development, editing, interpretation, and compilation of whole or portions of PROLOG programs.

In summary, Xerox offers a family of LISP workstations that can be used either as application systems development tools or as end-user workstations. They provide users with a wide range of features designed to facilitate development activities and operational use. The programming environment includes the InterLISP-D programming system. This environment permits the use of various programming tools, including LOOPS and Quintus PROLOG.

Xerox Corporation

Xerox Corporation is a high-technology company that has produced many effective tools for industry, including computer hardware and software. Xerox is committed to the promotion of information system and artificial intelligence technologies. Xerox formed the Xerox Palo Alto Research Center (PARC) in 1970. PARC is a research laboratory with a mission to explore all of the potentials of information system use and develop related product ideas. PARC is known for its research in the areas of integrated circuit electronics, materials science, and cognitive science. Major PARC accomplishments in the area of expert systems include the development of languages and tools such as Inter-LISP-D, LOOPS, KRL, and SMALLTALK.

13 DEVELOPMENT OF A LARGE EXPERT SYSTEM

XSEL
There are no set standards for what differentiates a large expert system from a small expert system. However, for rule-based expert systems, a generally accepted heuristic is that rule-based expert systems with over 1000 rules in their knowledge bases are considered large expert systems. Only a small proportion of rule-based expert systems at present exceed that size.

The XSEL expert system is an important example to consider for several reasons. First, it is a large system. Second, it is in productive, daily use. Third, it ties into other data processing systems, such as corporate databases. Fourth, and perhaps most important, XSEL is used in the mainstream of operations for its corporate host.

BACKGROUND
XSEL is a product of the Digital Equipment Corporation's Intelligent Systems Technologies Group. This group is responsible for both the XCON and XSEL expert systems.

Digital Equipment Corporation is a leading manufacturer of computer systems. Originally known for manufacturing small minicomputers that could be custom-configured to meet a client's requirements exactly, DEC today provides a complete computer hardware line from microcomputers to large computer systems and still provides its customers with the ability to specify custom configurations. DEC also sells computer software that runs on its machines.

DEC's hardware product line is very large. At the low end, DEC sells microcomputers like the DEC MATE and the VAX MATE. Moving up, DEC sells a line of micro PDP-11 and PDP-11 minicomputers. Going higher up the line, DEC sells microVAX, VAX station, and VAX computer systems. Each of these product areas includes standard systems, packaged systems, and system building-block systems.

Beyond the computers themselves, computer systems include many computer peripheral devices such as disk drives, tape drives, and communications devices. DEC computer systems can be configured with many DEC peripheral computer devices.

When a DEC sales representative visits a potential customer, the DEC representative has potentially thousands of possible products to consider when trying to meet the customer's needs. Adding to the complexity is the frequent introduction of new products to the market that is typical of the computer industry. To be and to remain a leader in this industry, DEC is constantly introducing new computer systems and components. Often the new introductions provide greater capabilities for lower cost. Therefore, customers are often eager to have the salesperson describe the newest products.

The computer sales market has become very competitive. Therefore, computer salespeople must be able to meet with a potential customer, learn what the customer needs and wants, and quickly and efficiently propose a computer system to that potential client.

DEC's à la carte selling style has pluses and minuses. On the plus side is the design flexibility DEC offers its customers. Often a customer can obtain a computer from DEC that exactly fits the particular requirements. This makes the client happy. It also helps DEC in the competitive marketplace since the client is not required to purchase packaged systems that often include costly components that the client does not need and will not use. Therefore, DEC can offer systems that wholly meet the bid requirements at very competitive prices. On the minus side is the extra burden this selling technique places on the DEC sales force. The DEC sales force must convert a potential client's requirements list into a DEC computer system. This process entails designing a computer system from DEC components that meets two sets of constraining factors, the client's requirements and the components' requirements. The salesperson's task is to develop a DEC computer hardware product that satisfies all of the client's requirements and constraints.

The XSEL expert system was developed to assist the DEC sales force with the complex, often time-pressured task of developing and delivering DEC computer system proposals to potential customers.

XSEL is one of a family of expert systems that DEC has developed. Many of these systems were developed with the help of Carnegie-Mellon University, located in Pittsburgh, Pennsylvania.

Among the other family members are XCON, which produces more detailed computer system configurations using XSEL inputs; XSITE (Expert Site Preparation Tool), which helps with the design and layout of a computer room that uses DEC hardware; and IDT (Intelligent Diagnostic Tool), which assists technicians in diagnosing computer systems that fail strict DEC manufacturing verification tests.

DEC has over two dozen major expert system projects going on as internal operations. Interestingly, DEC appears to be more committed to expert system technology than might be deduced from its product offerings.

XSEL was originally developed through a collaborative effort between Carnegie-Mellon University and DEC researchers. Other DEC expert systems like XCON were also initially produced through similar collaboration. Through these projects and additional internal experience, DEC has perfected a program management plan for the elaboration of expert systems.

DEC's expert system program management plan has ten stages, listed in Figure 13.1. Initial program definition involves the identification of requirements and potential solutions, risk and cost assessments, and concept plan development.

Project feasibility and organizational support are researched in the second stage. A prototype development team is assembled to include knowledge engineering, domain expertise, and management capabilities. At this time, a design document, a business plan, and an initial prototype are developed and presented.

If support for the project emerges, a program plan is developed. During this third stage, development team members are selected and their training needs are identified, the program direction is articulated better, and a preliminary program schedule is drawn up.

The next step is to provide the requisite training to the team and to determine an appropriate means to communicate with and involve the users in the project. Some program assessment might also be performed at this time.

In the fifth stage, a more detailed design document is created and project

1. Initial program definition
2. Building of initial prototype
3. Program plan
4. Education and user involvement plan
5. Design document
6. Basic shell
7. Adaptive development
8. Field test
9. Product release to production
10. Production

Figure 13.1   Expert system management plan

plans are written. Change management procedures and hardware requirements are also developed at this time.

The basic expert system shell is built next. At this time, users and experts get to run this preliminary system and make comments and suggestions. It is at this point that DEC starts to consider how to integrate the system with the rest of the organization. The basic shell goes through iterations of changes until there is agreement on the system's content and a commitment to continue and host the system is obtained.

Expert system development is an iterative process. The population of domain knowledge into an expert system's knowledge-base usually takes several development steps. DEC bundles these development iterations into the adaptive development stage. Here, more and more domain expertise is added to the developing system. DEC also designs its interfaces to other systems and writes the requisite documentation at this point in the project.

The host organization evaluates the developed system in the user's work environment during the field-testing stage. System integration into the organization and system implementation activities occur at this time.

The system is now released for productive use. Final installation and user training are accomplished, and a problem reporting and resolution mechanism is established.

The system is now in full productive use. The host organization is using the system and updating its knowledge-base as the problem domain and business requirements dictate.

DEC has developed this thorough management guide through experience. The company's Intelligent Systems Technologies Group in Hudson, Massachusetts, has taken this concept much further than is discussed here. Contact a DEC representative for more detailed information.

The creation of XSEL began in 1980. Actual code development started at Carnegie-Mellon during fall 1980. Initial DEC support of the system began two years later. DEC support and use of the system has continued since then. XSEL has received good support from its intended user community, the DEC sales force.

XSEL, like most DEC expert systems, was built using DEC domain experts and DEC and Carnegie-Mellon knowledge engineers. Also like most other DEC expert systems, XSEL is used and supported internally. Some DEC expert systems might be sold to DEC hardware customers in the future.

SYSTEM GOALS   DEC's goals with XSEL include supporting the DEC salespeople in the field and assuring accuracy in the computer system configurations that DEC salespeople provide to their clients. Further, DEC wanted this system to support the whole organization. To this end, XSEL has been integrated into the mainstream operations of the organization. DEC systems like XSEL and XCON are excellent examples of integrating expert systems with other systems in the organization and with the organization itself.

This integration has required both technical and organizational activities. The technical activities included training people in the organization, supplying the requisite computer hardware at the intended user locations, connecting the user hardware to a DEC network, and putting together a team to ensure that the expert system's knowledge has and continues to have enough breadth and depth to keep the system effective. Organizational activities included obtaining host organization commitment for the system, defining host organization requirements, ensuring that the host organization's requirements are met, and ensuring that the systems integrate well into the organization's work stream and with the in-place systems.

The XSEL development team knew that they could not force XSEL on the sales force. Therefore, another goal of the XSEL development team was to create a tool that assisted the intended users, the DEC salespeople, so well that they themselves would seek the system out. In other words, give the user something that makes the user's job easier, more effective, or more rewarding, and the user will want to use the system. Positive experiences and word of mouth are very effective in large organizations like DEC.

In the computer sales market, many potential clients request many proposals. It is difficult to weed out the serious requests from the others. Therefore, computer salespeople must develop many product proposals, many of which result in new questions and modifications that can take up a lot of time, often as much as the original proposals. DEC wanted XSEL to decrease the time salespeople spent on these proposals and changes.

System design goals included the ability of the salespeople to obtain assistance while working with potential customers on proposals, starting with initial, presales meetings with the customers.

From initial customer contact through to system installation, computer system configuration has been and continues to be a concern at DEC. A business-directed goal of XSEL, as well as some of the other DEC expert systems like XCON, is to provide accurate, consistent, properly designed configurations. This goal was cosponsored by manufacturing, engineering, and field service as well as by sales and marketing.

XSEL SYSTEM DESCRIPTION

XSEL is a large expert system. It uses the rule knowledge representation scheme and the forward-chaining inferencing technique. XSEL was originally developed using the OPS4 (Official Production System, Version 4) programming language and later was ported over to an improved OPS language, OPS5.

OPS5 is a general-purpose, production rule language. It provides rule memory and working memory support. It also provides an interpreter to test, select, and execute rules appropriate to each session. An OPS5 rule is of the form

IF condition
THEN action

OPS5 condition patterns or clauses are often referred to as the left-hand side (LHS) of the rules. OPS5 action specifications are often referred to as the right-hand side (RHS) of the rules.

XSEL provides the user with an interactive, line-oriented, terminal screen user-system interface. As a session progresses, the system's questions, provided information, and the user's responses scroll up from the bottom of the terminal screen. Figure 13.2 provides a listing of an XSEL session (all user responses are in red).

The session documented in Figure 13.2 starts after the user has already logged on to the computer and has requested XSEL. Notice that the system provides a main menu from which the user may make a selection. The system then requests the user to make a main menu selection. The user can respond with a choice (abbreviated responses are allowable) or press the RETURN key and the default specified inside the square brackets will be used as the user's selection (in this case, EXIT).

In this session, the user responded with "con," the system understood the selection to be CONFIGURE, and it presented the user with the Configure Menu. The user then responded with "cr," which the system understood to be CREATE (a new configuration). The system then asked for a configuration identification, and the user responded with the name of the client's firm.

With this initial dialogue completed, the system asked the user to wait while the main XSEL program was loaded into the computer for use.

XSEL then asks the DEC salesperson a set of questions and the salesperson responds. Notice that user response 11 is "help." The system reacts to this response by providing the user with a list of valid user responses.

The next interesting response to note is user response 15: "show 861Xa." Here the user asked the system to provide more information pertaining to the default selection, and the system so responded.

As the session continues, XSEL develops the computer system configuration that satisfies the user's choices and its rules on this subject. Sometimes the system will add components to complete user requirements or system configuration requirements. For example, the twentieth system communication stated that it was adding system components to fulfill an earlier user memory request (user response 10).

The system has the capability to filter out superfluous user dialogue as exemplified in the user response 18 and XSEL's ability to understand "terminals" and continue, ignoring "gorilla-proof."

Figure 13.2 A session with XSEL

```
XCON/XSEL VERSION 4.7-1
MAIN MENU

     RELEASE        —READ RELEASE NOTES
     CONFIGURE      —PREPARE A SYSTEM CONFIGURATION
     LAYOUT         —PREPARE A SITE LAYOUT
     RERUN          —SUBMIT CONFIGURATION FOR VERIFICATION
     COMMENT        —GENERATE PROBLEM REPORT
     PROFILE        —SEE OR CHANGE USER PROFILE
     QUEUE          —SEE THE VERIFICATION QUEUE
     EXIT           —EXIT MAIN MENU

   MAIN MENU SELECTION [EXIT]
1  ? con
   CONFIGURE MENU

     CREATE         —CREATE A NEW CONFIGURATION
     CHANGE         —CHANGE AN EXISTING CONFIGURATION
     MODEL          —MODEL AN EXISTING CONFIGURATION
     LIST           —LIST YOUR CURRENT CONFIGURATIONS
     SHOW           —SHOW CONFIGURATION CONTENT
     TYPE           —SEE A CONFIGURATION PICTURE
     DELETE         —DELETE EXISTING CONFIGURATION
     EXIT           —EXIT CONFIGURE MENU

   CONFIGURE MENU SELECTION [EXIT]
2  ? cr
   CONFIGURATION ID [DONE]
3  ? OXKO CORPORATION
   PLEASE WAIT WHILE EXPERT SALES ASSISTANT IS INVOKED

   XSEL V4.7-1

   ENTER CUSTOMER NAME
4  ? Steve Oxman

   BRIEF DESCRIPTION OF THIS CONFIGURATION [NONE]
5  ? Example

   SYSTEM FAMILY CHOICE
            VAX     THE VAX FAMILY OF COMPUTERS
            PDP     THE PDP-11 FAMILY OF COMPUTERS
   SYSTEM FAMILY CHOICE [VAX] ←   The user presses the ENTER key,
6  ?                              thereby selecting the default choice
                                  "VAX."
```

(Continued)

Figure 13.2 (*Continued*)

```
VAX SYSTEM SELECTION MENU
        8700      VAX8700 OR VAX8800 SYSTEM
        8600      VAX8600 OR VAX8650 SYSTEM
        8500      VAX8500 OR VAX8550 SYSTEM
        8200      VAX8200 OR VAX8300 SYSTEM
        11785     VAX-11/785 SYSTEM
        11780     VAX-11/780 OR VAX-11/782 SYSTEM
        11750     VAX-11/750 SYSTEM
        11730     VAX-11/730 SYSTEM
        11725     VAX-11/725 SYSTEM
        MVAX1     MICROVAXI SYSTEM
        MVAX2     MICROVAXII SYSTEM

    VAX SYSTEM CHOICE [8200]
 7  ? 8600

    OPERATING SYSTEM CHOICE [VMS]
 8  ? _____ ◄──── The user presses the ENTER key,
                                    selecting the default choice.
    POWER [120 VOLTS 60 HERTZ]
 9  ? _____ ◄

    ENTER LINE ITEMS ONE AT A TIME. PLEASE ENTER A SYSTEM AS
    LINE-ITEM  1. ENTER 'STANDARD' TO USE STANDARD SYSTEMS
    FLEXIBLE MENUS.
    LINE-ITEM 1 [SYSTEM]
10  ? system with 16 megs

        SYSTEM HAS MANY VARIANTS.

    CPU-FAMILY [8600]
11  ? help

        FOR THIS QUESTION, I WILL ACCEPT VALID COMMANDS OR
        ONE OF THE FOLLOWING:
            8600            8650

    CPU-FAMILY [8600]              The user presses the ENTER key,
12  ? _____ ◄──  selecting the default choice.

        THERE ARE A NUMBER OF SYSTEM TYPES AVAILABLE. THEY
        ARE:
            SBB-KERNEL          SBB      SBB-UPGRADE
    TYPE [SBB-KERNEL]
13  ? _____ ◄

    SUBTYPE [861XA]
14  ? help

        FOR THIS QUESTION, I WILL ACCEPT VALID COMMANDS OR
        ONE OF THE FOLLOWING:
            861XA           861CC
```

Figure 13.2 (Continued)

```
     SUBTYPE [861XA]              The user asks for more information
15   ? show 861xa            ←  about the default selection.


     861XA-AE       8600 QK001-UZ 4MB 120/60              350000 MLP
     861XA-UA       861XA IDTC UPGRADE VMS 120/60         350000 MLP

     SUBTYPE [861XA]
16   ? _____

     THE FOLLOWING SATISFY THE FUNCTIONALITY YOU SPECIFIED.
              861XA-UA      861XA-AE
     PLEASE SELECT ONE [861XA-UA]
17   ? _____
          IN ADDITION TO THE MEMORY INCLUDED WITH THE
          861XA-UA:

          ADDING 3 MS86-BA (12 MEGABYTE) TO THE
          CONFIGURATION TO FILL YOUR MEMORY
          REQUIREMENTS, PENDING REVIEW.

     LINE-ITEM 3 [DONE]           The system understands "2 terminals"
18   ? gorilla-proof terminals ← and ignores "gorilla-proof."
          TERMINAL HAS MANY VARIANTS.
     ADVANCED-VIDEO [YES]
19   ? _____
     GRAPHICS-CAPABILITY [YES]
20   ? _____
     SCREEN-DISPLAY [AMBER]
21   ? _____
     LINE-TYPE [20MA]
22   ? _____
     PRINTER-PORT [YES]
23   ? _____
     THE TERMINAL WITH THESE CHARACTERISTICS IS THE
     RT240-EE. HOW MANY OF THE 2 TERMINALS SHOULD BE
     RT240-EE [2]
24   ? _____
          (NOTE: YOU MUST ADD KEYBOARDS FOR RT240'S IF
          THEY ARE TO BE USED AS TERMINALS.)
                                   "Ghost" means that the 2 vt220
                                   devices are already owned by the
     LINE-ITEM 4 [DONE]            customer and should be configured
25   ? ghost 2 vt220         ↙  but not priced.
          VT220 HAS MANY VARIANTS.
     SCREEN-DISPLAY [AMBER]
26   ? _____                      (Continued)
```

335

Figure 13.2 *(Continued)*

THE FOLLOWING SATISFY THE FUNCTIONALITY YOU SPECIFIED.

      VT220-C   VT220-F2

PLEASE SELECT ONE [VT220-F2]

27 ? _____

HOW MANY OF THE 2 VT220 SHOULD BE VT220-F2 [2]

28 ? _____

LINE-ITEM 5 [DONE]

29 ? ra81-aa

LINE-ITEM 6 [DONE]

30 ? uda50

      THE ONLY UDA50 AVAILABLE IS THE UDA50-A*.

LINE-ITEM 7 [DONE]

31 ? tu80

THE TU80 IS BOTH A PARTIAL AND A FULL COMPONENT NAME. DO YOU WANT THE COMPONENT WHOSE PARTIAL NAME IS TU80 [YES]

32 ? _____

THE ONLY TU80S AVAILABLE ARE:

      TU80-AA*   TU80-CA

PLEASE SELECT ONE [TU80-AA*]

33 ? _____

LINE-ITEM 8 [DONE]

34 ? floating-point

      I DO NOT KNOW WHAT YOU MEAN BY 'FLOATING-POINT'.

LINE-ITEM 8 [DONE]

35 ? show key-words

      I DO NOT KNOW WHAT YOU MEAN BY 'KEY-WORDS'.

LINE-ITEMS 8 [DONE]

36 ? fp861

      I DO NOT KNOW WHAT YOU MEAN BY 'FP861'.

LINE-ITEM 8 [DONE]

37 ? la38-ha

      THE LA38-HA IS NOT CURRENTLY MARKETED BY DIGITAL.

      THE SUBSTITUTE HAS CHARACTERS-PER-SECOND 180 INSTEAD OF 30.

      THE SUBSTITUTE HAS SUBTYPE LA120 INSTEAD OF LA38.

Figure 13.2   (Continued)

PLEASE SELECT ANOTHER COMPONENT.
LINE-ITEM [1 LA120-DA]
38 ? _____

LINE-ITEM 9 [DONE]
39 ? tsv05-bb

THE TSV05-BB CANNOT BE ORDERED FOR A VAX8600 RUNNING
UNDER VMS.

I CANNOT FIND ONE JUST LIKE THE TSV05-BB THAT WILL WORK
HERE SO I NEED TO ASK YOU QUESTIONS ABOUT ITS
SUBSTITUTE.

FORWARD-SPEED [NEVER MIND]
40 ? help

FOR THESE QUESTIONS, I WILL ACCEPT VALID
COMMANDS OR ONE OF THE FOLLOWING:
100 IPS   45 IPS   125 IPS
NEVER MIND

FORWARD-SPEED [NEVER MIND]
41 ? 125 ips

IF YOU CHOOSE TO PLACE THE TSV05-BB ON YOUR
CONFIGURATION AS A SPARE, REENTER IT NOW.
OTHERWISE SELECT ANOTHER COMPONENT.
LINE-ITEM [1 TU77-AF*]
42 ? _____

LINE-ITEM 10 [DONE]
43 ? _____

MODIFY MENU:

ADD   —ADD LINE-ITEMS TO THIS   ← XSEL allows the
                 CONFIGURATION   user to modify the
INSERT   —INSERT A LINE-ITEM BETWEEN   configuration.
                 TWO OTHERS
DELETE   —REMOVE LINE-ITEMS FROM THIS
                 CONFIGURATION
REPLACE   —REPLACE A LINE-ITEM WITH
                 SOMETHING ELSE
OVERRIDE   —RETURN WITHOUT CHECKING
EXIT   —RETURN TO CHANGE MENU

MODIFY MENU SELECTION [EXIT]
44 ? _____

PLEASE WAIT WHILE I CHECK YOUR CONFIGURATION
FOR COMPLETENESS.

(Continued)

Figure 13.2   (Continued)

IN ORDER TO HAVE A COMPLETE SYSTEM-BUILDING-BLOCK
CONFIGURATION, YOU MUST CHOOSE A LOAD-DEVICE FROM ONE
OF THE FOLLOWING:

TU81E-AA*   TU81-AA*

LOAD-DEVICE [TU81E-AA*]

XSEL finds some requisite items missing
and notifies the user.

45 ? _____

IN ORDER TO HAVE A COMPLETE SYSTEM-BUILDING-BLOCK
CONFIGURATION, YOU MUST ALSO CHOOSE A COMM-DEVICE
FROM ONE OF THE FOLLOWING:

DELUA-M   DMF32-M   DMZ32-M*   DHU11-M   DSRVA-AA

COMM-DEVICE [DELUA-M]

46 ? _____

    I AM SWAPPING YOUR 1 RA81-AA WITH AN EQUIVALENT
    NUMBER OF RA81-AA* FOR THE MOMENT.

DO YOU WANT AN OPTIMUM SERVICE PACKAGE [NO]

47 ? _____

DO YOU WANT A SOFTWARE SERVICES STARTUP PACKAGE [NO]

48 ? _____

THIS CONFIGURATION IS NOT COMPLETE WITHOUT AN OPERATING
SYSTEM MEDIUM. IF YOU HAVE ANOTHER VAX8600 WITH VMS IN
THE CORRECT MEDIUM AND WITH LICENSES, YOU DO NOT NEED
TO ADD VMS HERE. DO YOU HAVE ANOTHER SYSTEM WITH VMS
[NO]

49 ? _____   XSEL helps the user to avoid omissions.

    ADDING 1 QK001-HM TO YOUR CONFIGURATION FOR
    SYSTEM-BUILDING-BLOCK COMPLETENESS.

YOUR CONFIGURATION REQUIRES A SPECIAL POWER
RECEPTACLE (60 AMP) THAT MAY BE DIFFICULT TO OBTAIN
IN THE FIELD.

PLEASE SELECT RECEPTACLE. [12-19321-02]

50 ? _____

    ADDING 1 12-19321-02 TO YOUR CONFIGURATION
    NECESSARY FOR SYSTEM INSTALLATION.

    YOU NEED 2 VT22K COUNTRY-KIT(S) TO MATCH YOUR 2
    VT220(S).

    VT22K HAS MANY VARIANTS.

COUNTRY [USA/CANADA]

51 ? _____

KEYBOARD [WORD-PROCESSING]

52 ? help _____

338

Figure 13.2 (Continued)

FOR THIS QUESTION, I WILL ACCEPT VALID COMMANDS
OR ONE OF THE FOLLOWING:
WORD-PROCESSING   STANDARD

KEYBOARD [WORD-PROCESSING]
53 ? standard

THE VT22K WITH THESE CHARACTERISTICS IS THE VT22K-AA.
HOW MANY OF THE 2 VT22K SHOULD BE VT22K-AA [2]
54 ?

HOW MANY OF YOUR 4 TERMINALS WILL BE HARD-WIRED OR ON
A TERMINAL SERVER [4]
55 ? 0

HOW MANY OF THE 4 DIAL-UP TERMINALS WILL BE USED
SIMULTANEOUSLY [4]
56 ?

HOW MANY MODEMS DO YOU WANT [1]
57 ?

MODEM HAS MANY VARIANTS.

LINES-SUPPORTED [1]
58 ? help

FOR THIS QUESTION, I WILL ACCEPT VALID COMMANDS
OR ONE OF THE FOLLOWING:
1   16   12
8   4

LINES-SUPPORTED [1]
59 ? 4

BAUD-RATE [9600 BAUD]
60 ?

THE FOLLOWING SATISFY THE FUNCTIONALITY YOU SPECIFIED.

DFMO4-AC   DFMO4-SC

PLEASE SELECT ONE [DFMO4-AC]
61 ? show dfm04-ac
DFMO4-AC   4LINE STAT MUX W/9600BPS MODM   5525 MLP

THE FOLLOWING SATISFY THE FUNCTIONALITY YOU SPECIFIED.
DFMO4-AC   DFMO4-SC

PLEASE SELECT ONE [DFMO4-AC]
62 ?

THERE IS NOT ENOUGH HARDWARE TO SUPPORT YOUR VT220-F2.

(Continued)

Figure 13.2   (Continued)

ENTER PARTS TO SUPPORT THE CONFIGURATION OF YOUR
VT220-F2 [1 DECSA-DA],

63 ? _____

THE VT220-F2 FOR WHICH I AM ADDING THE DECSA-DA IS
GHOSTED. SHALL I GHOST THE DECSA-DA ALSO [YES]

64 ? _____

ADDING 1 GHOST DECSA-DA TO YOUR CONFIGURATION
FOR SUPPORT.
ADDING 1 TU81 TO YOUR CONFIGURATION TO SUPPORT
YOUR TU81E-AA*.
ADDING 1 TMO3-FN TO YOUR CONFIGURATION TO SUPPORT
YOUR TU77-AF*.
ADDING 1 RH780* TO YOUR CONFIGURATION TO SUPPORT
YOUR TMO3-FN.
ADDING 1 TU80 TO YOUR CONFIGURATION TO SUPPORT
YOUR TU80-AA*.
ADDING 1 DZ11-N TO YOUR CONFIGURATION TO SUPPORT
BOTH OF YOUR RT240-EE.
ADDING 1 TEU77-FB TO THE CONFIGURATION WHICH INCLUDES
YOUR RH780*
YOUR TMO3-FN AND
YOUR TU77-AF*.
ADDING 1 TU81E-AA TO THE CONFIGURATION WHICH INCLUDES
YOUR TU81 AND
YOUR TU81E-AA*.
ADDING 1 TU80-AA TO THE CONFIGURATION WHICH INCLUDES
YOUR TU80 AND
YOUR TU80-AA*.
ADDING A RA81-AA TO REPLACE
YOUR RA81-AA*.
ADDING A MS86-BB TO REPLACE
ALL 3 OF YOUR MS86-BA.
ADDING 1 UDA50-A TO THE CONFIGURATION WHICH INCLUDES
YOUR UDA50-A*.

YOU NEED 1 DECSK COUNTRY-KIT(S) TO MATCH YOUR
1 DECSA(S).

DECSK HAS MANY VARIANTS.   XSEL adds items when it finds them
                                  to be a requisite.
COUNTRY [USA/CANADA]

65 ? _____

THE DECSK YOU WANT IS THE DECSK-AA.

ADDING 1 QK726-UZ TO YOUR CONFIGURATION SINCE
QK726-UZ IS A PREREQUISITE FOR DECSA-DA.

Figure 13.2   (Continued)

CHANGE MENU:

      MODIFY   —LINE-ITEM MODIFICATION MENU
      STATUS   —LINE-ITEM CONFIGURATION STATUS MENU
      EXIT   —RETURN TO MAIN MENU

CHANGE MENU OPTION [MODIFY]
66 ? exit _____

DO YOU WANT TO SAVE A RECORD OF THIS
CONFIGURATION [YES]
67 ? _____

      SAVING REVISION 1 OF OXKO.

DO YOU WANT TO VERIFY THIS CONFIGURATION [YES]
68 ? _____

      CONFIGURATION VERIFICATION IS A BACKGROUND
      TASK. USE THE QUEUE OPTION OF THE MAIN MENU TO
      SEE IF VERIFICATION HAS BEEN COMPLETED.

DO YOU WANT A MINIMUM FOOTPRINT FLOOR LAYOUT FOR
THIS CONFIGURATION [NO]
69 ? yes _____

ON A SCALE OF 1 TO 10 (10 HIGH), HOW WOULD YOU RATE
THIS SESSION [NO OPINION]
70 ? 9 _____

      THANK YOU.

In user response 25, the user used a special term: "ghost." This term tells XSEL that the equipment specification is already owned by the client, and the client wishes to consider this resource during the current configuration session.

Notice also that XSEL understands generic equipment nomenclature ("terminals"), partial component nomenclature ("VT220"), and complete component nomenclature ("VT220-F2").

To a user response that is not understood, XSEL responds, "I DO NOT KNOW WHAT YOU MEAN BY _____," followed by a repeat of the same question. The thirty-fourth XSEL communication is an example of this type of exchange.

XSEL can handle ambiguity in data. For example, look at XSEL's thirty-second communication. Here XSEL is telling the user that the TU80 specification can represent both a partial and a full component name and asks the user for the intended meaning of this nomenclature. With the receipt of the user's response, XSEL can continue.

When a user requests something that is in violation of an XSEL configuration rule, XSEL so notifies the user, as in XSEL's thirty-ninth communication, "THE TSVO5-BB CANNOT BE ORDERED FOR A VAX8600 RUN-NING UNDER VMS." XSEL, in this case, tries to satisfy the user's requirements with an alternative.

User response 42 indicates that the user is done presenting configuration requirements data to XSEL. XSEL responds with the Modify Menu, giving the user an opportunity to modify any line item data previously provided. The user here responded that no modifications were necessary.

XSEL indicates that it will now check the user's configuration as it now is specified for completeness.

XSEL finds some requisite items missing and so notifies the user. Through a dialogue between the user and XSEL, these items are specified. XSEL also adds requisite items using knowledge stored in the knowledge-base (for example, XSEL's sixty-fourth and sixty-fifth responses).

XSEL then provides the user with a Change Menu, and here the user responds with "exit"; in other words, the user has no changes to make at this time.

XSEL then asks if the user wishes to save a record of this consultation session, and the user responds affirmatively. XSEL saves the consultation record and asks if the user wishes to have the configuration verified and to have a minimum floor layout determined for this configuration. The user requests both.

The XSEL session is completed, but just before closing the session out, XSEL asks the user to rate the session, which the user does.

A lot went on in this session. This session is not unlike the thousands of sessions that DEC salespeople have with XSEL. At the time of writing XSEL was logged on to by DEC people over 18,000 times in one year, and this number is growing very rapidly.

Let us recapitulate some of the things XSEL did during our example session:

1. Provided a standard configuration process dialogue.

2. Prompted the user with easy-to-understand questions.

3. Provided the user with help in answering questions.

4. Allowed freedom in response format—the user was allowed to provide generic, partial, or full component names and nomenclatures.

5. Did not abort when the user provided incorrect responses; instead XSEL communicated the error to the user and allowed the user to continue with a new response.

6. Assisted the user by providing a list of valid responses when the user could not remember how to respond.

7. Helped the user with ambiguous specifications.

8. Guided the user to make the configuration correct by informing the user when certain combinations of components were not appropriate and helped the user to find effective substitutions.

9. Reminded the user of prerequisite components to support requested components.

10. Assisted the user with the selection of subcomponent options.

11. Added components to make the system configuration more complete.

12. Employed a dialogue form and language that is understandable to its intended users.

XSEL is an expert configuration system that supports the DEC sales force's selling function. XSEL provides DEC salespeople with an effective, integrated tool that provides DEC marketing, engineering, and manufacturing expertise together with up-to-date DEC product data.

XSEL is coded in OPS5 and uses the OPS5 MEA (means-ends analysis) conflict resolution strategy. XSEL code uses the standard OPS5 declaration section for describing data objects and user-defined functions and uses the production section for production rule specification. There are approximately 2800 OPS5 production rules in the XSEL knowledge base. Figure 13.3 gives examples of some XSEL rules from its production section.

The OPS5 production rule format requires the following items, in the following order:

1. Left parenthesis

2. The letter p (for production)

3. Rule name

4. A sequence of condition elements (the IF clauses)

5. The 3-byte symbol $\rightarrow$

6. A sequence of actions (the THEN clauses)

7. Right parenthesis

The context specifications included in the rules create element classes. Contexts can be used to group rules to act as procedures. The semicolon is used to mark comments. These comments are not read by the OPS5 language interpreter. They are provided by the programmer as documentation. The interpreter echoes the comments onto the source code listings without any other effect or use.

XSEL is integrated with other DEC expert systems like XCON and other data processing systems like the DEC product database system.

SYSTEM USE
TODAY
XSEL is available for use by all members of the DEC sales force as well as some other DEC personnel. It is accessible via DEC's internal computer network. XSEL runs on standard DEC VAX systems. XSEL is running on a BLISS version of OPS5 that is a DEC product. BLISS is a DEC computer programming

Figure 13.3   Examples of XSEL rules

```
;;  Context capacity-specified
;;
;;
;;  Description:
;;    This context was set up to handle capacity ordering, specifically for
;;    memory, but may be expanded later to handle disks and/or line-
;;    printers as well. The context will be entered in the case where the
;;    user entered a line-item in the form (nn megabytes / kilobytes [of
;;    memory]). Using the number of kilobytes / megabytes entered, the
;;    context fills the requirements with the appropriate quantity of an al-
;;    ready existing type or of a preferred type where appropriate.
;;
;;        Note:  due to the heavy usage of a local in this context and many
;;                 attributes of that local, a description of its usage follows:
;;             (local   ^type temporary ^context capacity-specified
;;                  ^class <valid-component-class>
;;                     >> exam: memory
;;                  ^information check-existing-controllers
;;                                  use-existing-controller
;;                                  use-pending-controller
;;                          or   set-aside
;;                     >> represents the mode for processing the local
;;                  ^status <status-of-controller>
;;                     >> nil if controller exists otherwise "pending"
;;                  ^name <valid-component-name>
;;                     >> exam: S780-FD, MS750-CA
;;                  ^quantity <number-of-kilobytes-each>
;;                     >> exam: 256, 1024—qty in kilobytes of each ^name
;;                  ^count <number-of-kilobytes-already-ordered>
;;                     >>exam: 1024,4096—already ordered for this ^name
;;                  ^number-required <number-of-bytes-to-add>
;;                     >> for the first local, this is the total requirement
;;                     >> for the set-aside local, this is the overage
;;                  ^remainder <space-remaining-for-a-controller>
;;                     >> exam: 15360, 12288—for controller of type ^name
;;                  ^value <divisor-for-display-quantity>
;;                     >>either 1 for kilobyte or 1024 for megabyte
;;                  ^meaning <meaning-of-display-quantity>
;;                     >> either the word "kilobyte" or "megabyte"
;;                  ^kilobytes-per-board <kilobytes-per-board>
;;                     >> exam: 256, 1024—density for type ^name
;;  Fragments:
;;
;;  Exit Conditions:
;;    exits immediately upon return from accept-line-item unless a combi-
;;    nation of controllers are to be used to fill the requirement in which
;;    case it exits immediately upon return of the last call to accept-line-
```

Figure 13.3 (Continued)

```
;;    item. Also exits immediately upon entry if the requirement is already
;;    met or exceeded.
;;
;; Assumptions:
;;    at least one completeness-data for the ^device-class memory exists
;;    upon entry (usually the case)
;;
;;    if this context aborts wo adding memory (or calling accept-line-item)
;;    and the line-item is still ^status input, then further-specify should be
;;    able to take over. However, if the ^status is generic, then it will
;;    cause problems for further specify later on.
;;
;; Modification history
;;      17-Oct-83 YURCHAK     Installed new
;;      5-Jan-84 YURCHAK      Extended capabilities to allow for system
;;                            with xx meg of memory' parse modified to
;;                            use bus network
;;      6-Sep-85 red          modified to remove dependancy upon bus-
;;                            node existing
;;      30-Oct-86 CORAK       Added 2bb, 5dd & 5ee to include sw-pro-
;;                            cessor-id in match call to prevent the
;;                            wrong software to be suggested for cer-
;;                            tain BI systems, eg: 8200, 8500, 8700
;;
(p capacity-specified:1:adjust-requirement
;        if memory capacity was ordered on the same line as the system
;        (e.g., system with 4 meg of memory), then assume the user
;        wants the requirement in total and not in addition to what is re-
;        turned as part of the system, therefore, adjust the requirement
;            (context ^status active ^cname capacity-specified)
;            (line-item ^status input ^class memory ^name nil ^units
;                    kilobytes ^kilobytes {<required>} > 0)
;                    ^token <token>)
;            (line-item ^status pending ^class system ^parse-token
;                    <token>)
;            (bus-node ^class memory ^name <device> ^ordered <count>)
;            - (local ^information count-memory-capacity ^source
;                    <device>)
;            (component ^status reference ^name <device> ^number-of-
;            kilobytes <kb>)
;         ->
;            (bind <ordered> (compute <count> * <kb>))
;            (bind <difference> (compute <required> - <ordered>))
;            (modify 2 ^kilobytes <difference>)
```

(Continued)

345

Figure 13.3   (Continued)

```
(make local ^type temporary ^context capacity-specified
        ^information count-memory-capacity ^source
        <device>))

(p capacity-specified:1a:implicit-memory
;       Some systems now have memory built into chips. If this is the
;       case a bus-node won't exist and we need to make up the info.
        (context     ^status active ^cname capacity-specified)
        (line-item   ^status input ^class memory ^name nil ^units
                     kilobytes ^kilobytes {<required> > 0} ^token
                     <token>)
        (line-item   ^status pending ^class system ^parse-token
                     <token>)
      - (bus-node  ^class memory)
        (component ^status reference ^name <device> ^class system
                     ^number-of-kilobytes { <kb> <=> 17 } )
      - (local     ^information count-memory-capacity ^source
                     <device>)
     →
        (bind <difference> (compute <required> - <kb>))
        (modify 2 ^kilobytes <difference>)
        (make local ^type temporary ^context capacity-specified
                ^information count-memory-capacity ^source <device>))

(p capacity-specified:1a:additional-requirement
;       if memory was ordered on the same line as the system and the
;       requirement is not fulfilled after adjustments, then make an
;       announcement and continue on
        (context ^status active ^cname capacity-specified)
        (line-item ^status input ^class memory ^name nil ^units
                kilobytes ^kilobytes >0 ^token <token>)
        (line-item ^status pending ^class system ^parse-token
                <token> ^name <system>)
     →
        (modify 2 ^token nil)
; text              | IN ADDITION TO THE MEMORY INCLUDED
;                   WITH THE |  <system>  | : |

        (call xselio_setup $1-to-1-var <system>)
        (call xselio_tty in-addition-to-memory))

(p capacity-specified:1b:no-additional-requirement
;       if memory was ordered on the same line as the system
;       and the system memory fulfills the total requirement, then
;           simply return (context ^status active ^cname capacity-specified)
        (line-item ^status input ^class memory ^name nil ^units
                kilobytes ^kilobytes 0 ^token <token>)
```

Figure 13.3   (Continued)

```
        (line-item ^status pending ^class system ^parse-token
                   <token>)
    →
        (remove 2))

(p capacity-specified:1c:requirement-exceeded
;           if memory was ordered on the same line as the system and the
;           system memory exceeds the total requirement, then let the user know
;           this and return.
        (context ^status active ^cname capacity-specified)
        (line-item ^status input ^class memory ^name nil ^units
                   kilobytes ^kilobytes < 0 ^token <token>)
        (line-item ^status pending ^class system ^parse-token
                   <token> ^name <system>)
    →
        (remove 2)
; text   | THE | <system> | CONTAINS MORE MEMORY THAN
;                          REQUESTED! |   | I'LL ASSUME THAT THIS IS OK
;                          AND CONTINUE. |
        (call xselio_setup $1-to-1-var <system>)
        (call xselio_tty more-memory-than-requested))

(p capacity-specified:2:check-existing-memory-controllers
;           look at an existing memory controller and save its information; note
;           that this rule will fire for each controller on the system
;        (context ^status active ^cname capacity-specified)
        (line-item ^status input ^class memory ^name nil ^units
                   kilobytes ^kilobytes {<required> > 0}
                   ^token nil)
        (bus-node ^class memory ^name <device> ^source <>
                  line-item ^ordered <count> ^unassigned 0)
        (bus-link ^bus-rider <device> ^seats reserved > 0
                  ^unreserved-seats <available>)
        (component ^status reference ^name <device> ^number-of-
                   kilobytes <kb> ^kilobytes-per-board
                   <kb-per-board>)
    →
        (bind <ordered> (compute <count> * <kb>))
        (bind <space-remaining> (compute <available> *<kb>))
        (make local ^type temporary ^context capacity-specified
                   ^class memory ^information check-existing-controllers
                   ^name <device> ^quantity <kb> ^count <ordered>
                   ^number-required <required> ^remainder <space-
                   remaining> ^kilobytes-per-board <kb-per-board>
                   ^token (genatom)))
```

(Continued)

347

Figure 13.3   (Continued)

```
(p capacity-specified:2a:check-pending-memory-controllers
;          look at a pending memory controller and save its information; note
;          that this rule will fire for each pending controller on the system
;          (context ^status active ^cname capacity-specified)
           (line-item ^status input ^class memory ^name nil ^units
                   kilobytes ^kilobytes {<required> > 0} ^token nil)
           (bus-node ^class memory ^name <device> ^source <>
                   line-item ^unassigned {<count> > 0}
           (bus-link ^bus-rider <device> ^seats-allowed-per-bus
                   <maximum>)
           (component ^status reference ^name <device> ^number-of-
                   kilobytes <kb> ^kilobytes-per-board <kb-per-
                   board>)
     →
           (bind <ordered> (compute <count> *<kb>))
           (bind <space-remaining> (compute (<maximum> − <count>) *
           <kb>))
           (make local ^type temporary ^context capacity-specified
                   ^class memory ^information check-existing-
                   controllers
                   ^status pending ^name <device> ^quantity <kb>
                   ^count <ordered>
                   ^number-required <required> ^remainder <space-
                   remaining>
                   ^kilobytes-per-board <kb-per-board> ^token
                   (genatom)))

(p capacity-specified:2b:check-implicit-memory-controllers
;          make this work even if the memory is a chip on processor board!
           (context ^status active ^cname capacity-specified)
           (line-item ^status input ^class memory ^name nil ^units
                   kilobytes {<required> > 0} ^token nil)
         - (bus-node ^class memory ^name <device> )
     →
           (make local ^type temporary ^context capacity-specified
                   ^class memory ^information set-aside
                   ^token (genatom)
           (make local ^type temporary ^context capacity-specified
                   ^class memory ^information use-pending-controller
                   ^status pending
                   ^number-required <required> ^token (genatom)))

(p capacity-specified:2d:check-deleted-memory-controllers
;          this is for the case when all memory has been deleted
           (context ^status active ^cname capacity-specified)
           (line-item ^status input ^class memory ^name nil ^units
                   kilobytes ^kilobytes {<required> > 0} ^token nil)
```

Figure 13.3   (Continued)

```
        (bus-node ^class memory ^name <device> ^source <> line-item
                    ^ordered 0 ^unassigned 0)
        (bus-link   ^bus-rider <device> ^seats-reserved 0
                    ^unreserved-seats <available>)
    →
        (make local ^type temporary ^context capacity-specified
                ^class memory ^information set-aside
                ^token (genatom))
                (make local ^type temporary ^context capacity-specified)
                ^class memory ^information use-pending-controller
                ^status pending
                ^number-required <required> ^token (genatom)))

(p capacity-specified:3:all-memory-controllers-checked
;       after all memory controllers have been noted, move on
                (context ^status active ^cname capacity-specified)
                (line-item ^status input ^class memory ^name nil ^units
                kilobytes ^kilobytes > 0)
        - (local ^information reset-status-of-line-items)
        →
                (make local ^type temporary ^context capacity-specified
                    ^information reset-status-of-line-item)
                (modify 2 ^status generic))

(p capacity-specified:4:narrowed-down-to-one
;       if there's only one controller left in consideration, move on
                (context ^status active ^cname capacity-specified)
                (line-item ^status generic ^class <class>)
                (local ^context capacity-specified ^class <class>
                        ^information check-existing-controllers
                        ^name <name>)
                        ^number-required <required> ^remainder
                        <space-remaining>
                        ^kilobytes-per-board <kb-per-board>)
        - (local ^context capacity-specified ^class <class>
                    ^information check-existing-controllers ^name <>
                    <name>)
        →
                (modify 3 ^information use-existing-controller))

(p capacity-specified:4a:choose-on-available-space
;       if a controller has enough space to fill the requirement and
;       a second controller doesn't, get rid of the latter
                (context ^status active ^cname capacity-specified)
                (line-item ^status generic ^class <class>)
```

(Continued)

Figure 13.3   *(Continued)*

```
(local ^context capacity-specified ^class <class>
       ^information check-existing-controllers
       ^name <name> ^number-required <required>
       ^remainder >= <required>)
(local ^context capacity-specified ^class <class>
       ^information check-existing-controllers
       ^name <> <name> ^remainder < <required>)
    →
    (remove 4))

(p capacity-specified:4b:choose-on-density
;        if it's not clear which controller to proceed with based on available
;        space, then set the one aside with the lesser capacity for the time
;        being
    (context ^status active ^cname capacity-specified)
    (line-item ^status generic ^class <class>)
    (local ^context capacity-specified ^class <class>
           ^information check-existing-controllers ^name
           <name> ^number-required <required> ^remainder
           <space-remaining>
           <kilobytes-per-board <kb-per-board>)
    (local ^context capacity-specified ^class <class>
           ^information check-existing-controllers
           ^name <> <name> ^kilobytes-per-board <=
           <kb-per-board>)
        →
        (bind <over> (compute <required> − <space-remaining>))
        (modify 4 ^information set-aside ^number-required
                  <over>))

(p capacity-specified:5:process-in-megabytes
;        if the capacity of the device type to be used is greater-than or equal
;        to 1024 kilobytes, then process requirements in megabytes
    (context ^status active ^cname capacity-specified)
    (line-item ^status generic ^class <class>)
    (local ^context capacity-specified ^class <class>
           ^information << use-existing-controller
                          use-pending controller>>
           ^quantity >= 1024 ^value nil)
        →
        (modify 3 ^value 1024 ^meaning megabyte))

(p capacity-specified:5a:process-in-kilobytes
;        if the capacity of the device type to be used is less-than 1024
;        kilobytes, then process requirements in kilobytes
    (context ^status active ^cname capacity-specified)
    (line-item ^status generic ^class <class>)
```

Figure 13.3   (Continued)

```
        (local ^context capacity-specified ^class <class>
               ^information << use-existing-controller
                               use-pending-controller >>
               ^quantity < 1024 ^value nil)
   →
        (modify 3 ^value 1 ^meaning kilobyte))

(p capacity-specified:6:use-existing-controller
;          as long as we have sufficient space remaining in an existing
;          controller, use it
           (context ^status active ^cname capacity-specified)
           (line-item ^status generic ^class <class>)
           (local ^context capacity-specified ^class <class>
                  ^information use-existing-controller
                  ^status nil ^name <name> ^quantity <kb>
                  ^number-required <required> ^remainder
                  {> 0 >= <required>}
                  ^value <divisor> ^meaning {<display-units> <>
                  nil})
   →
           (bind <mod> (compute <kb> − 1))
           (bind <quantity> (compute (<required> + <mod>) // <kb>))
           (bind <kilobytes> (compute <quantity> * <kb>))
           (bind <display-qty> (compute <kilobytes> // <divisor>))
           (remove 3)
; text      Adding <quantity> <name>
;           | ( | <display-qty> <display-units> | ) | to the
;           configuration to fill your memory requirements, pending re-
;           view.
           (call xselio_setup $1-to-1-var <quantity> <name>
                  <display-qty> <display-units>)
           (call xselio_tty adding-to-requirements)
           (make context ^status active ^cname accept-line-item)
           (modify 2 ^status possible ^name <name> ^quantity
                  <quantity> ^kilobytes <kilobytes>

(p capacity-specified:6a:use-multiple-controllers
;          if the combination of space remaining in two controllers can
;          fill the requirement, use them both
           (context ^status active ^cname capacity-specified)
           (line-item ^status generic ^class <class>)
           (local ^context capacity-specified ^class <class>
                  ^information use-existing-controller
                  ^number-required <required> ^remainder
                  < <required>)
```

(Continued)

Figure 13.3   (Continued)

```
      (local ^context capacity-specified ^class <class>
             ^information set-aside
             ^number-required <over> ^remainder >= <over>)
   →
      (modify 3 ^information use-pending-controller))

(p capacity-specified:6b:create-pending-controller
;        as long as we have to add another controller to support the new
;        requirements, use it up first before considering available space
;        still remaining on existing controllers
         (context ^status active ^cname capacity-specified)
         (line-item ^status generic ^class <class>)
         (local ^context capacity-specified ^class <class>
                ^information use-existing-controller
                ^number-required <required> ^remainder <
                <required>)
   →
      (modify 3 ^information set-aside ^number-required nil)
      (make local (substr 3 2 inf) ^information
             use-pending-controller
             ^name nil ^quantity nil ^count nil ^remainder nil
             ^value nil ^meaning nil ^kilobytes-per-board nil
             ^token (genatom)))

(p capacity-specified:6c:use-pending-controller
;        if we already have a pending controller and the requirement is
;        such that it does not exceed available space left on this control-
;        ler or the requirement exceeds the available space left on this
;        controller and any other existing controller(s), use it
         (context ^status active ^cname capacity-specified)
         (line-item ^status generic ^class <class>)
         (local ^context capacity-specified ^class <class>
                ^information use-existing-controller
                ^status pending)
   →
      (modify 3 ^information use-pending-controller))

(p capacity-specified:7:get-possible-memory-types
;        if we still have devices to add (capacity to fill) and no controller
;        to support them, then get all possible memory types for review
         (context ^status active ^cname capacity-specified)
         (line-item ^status generic ^class <class>)
         (local ^context capacity-specified ^class <class>
                ^information use-pending-controller
                ^token <token>)
       - (component ^status preferred ^class <class>)
         (interaction ^status closed ^keyword voltage
                ^response <voltage>)
```

Figure 13.3 (Continued)

```
    (interaction ^status closed ^keyword frequency
            ^response <frequency>)
→
    (call match_component $token <token> $search all
            $attributes name class kilobytes-per-board price
            $match class <class> kilobytes-per-board $not nil
                voltage $+ <voltage> universal nil +$
                frequency $+ <frequency> universal nil +$
                sales-category $+ new nil +$
                configurable yes
            $return status display-reference))

(p capacity-specified:8:discard-unwanted-memory-types
;       from the memory types just retrieved, throw away all but the one
;       with the most ^kilobytes-per-board, pick one with the greatest
;       density less than or equal to that desired.
        (context ^status active ^cname capacity-specified)
        (line-item ^status generic ^class <class>
                    ^kilobytes { <required> >0 } )
        (local ^context capacity-specified ^class <class>
                    ^information use-pending-controller ^token <token>)
    - (component ^status preferred ^class <class>)
        (component ^status display-reference ^name <name> ^token
                <token> ^kilobytes-per-board {<kb-per-board>
                <= <required> })
        (component ^status display-reference ^name <> <name>
                ^token <token> ^kilobytes-per-board
                <= <kb-per-board>)
→
        (remove 5))

(p capacity-specified:8a:discard-unwanted-memory-types-greater-
;       than get rid of all but the kind just greater than the amount
;       required
        (context ^status active ^cname capacity-specified)
        (line-item ^status generic ^class <class>
                    ^kilobytes { <required> > 0 } )
        (local ^context capacity-specified ^class <class>
                    ^information use-pending-controller ^token <token>)
    - (component ^status preferred ^class <class>)
        (component ^status display-reference ^name <name> ^token
                <token> ^kilobytes-per-board { <kb-per-board>
                > <required> } )
        (component ^status display-reference ^name <> <name>
                ^token <token> ^kilobytes-per-board >=
                <kb-per-board>)
→
        (remove 5))                                      (Continued)
```

Figure 13.3 (Continued)

(p capacity-specified:8b:discard-unwanted-memory-types-price
;   when we are down to two, then choose the lowest price assume
;   that zero price means that part is 'newer', and should therefore
;   be preferred
          (context ^status active ^cname capacity-specified)
          (line-item ^status generic ^class <class>
                     ^kilobytes { <required> > 0 })
          (local ^context capacity-specified ^class <class>
                 ^information use-pending-controller ^token <token>)
          − (component ^status preferred ^class <class>)
          (component ^status display-reference ^name <name> ^token
                     <token> ^price { <price> <=> 17 })
          (component ^status display-reference ^name { <name2> <>
                     <name> } ^token <token>
                     ^price { > <price> <=> 17 })
       - (component ^status display-reference ^name { <> <name>
                     <> <name2> } ^token <token>)
          →
          (remove 5))

(p capacity-specified:8c:discard-unwanted-memory-types-density
;   else, just choose on density.
          (context ^status active ^cname capacity-specified)
          (line-item ^status generic ^class <class>
                     ^kilobytes { <required> > 0 })
          (local ^context capacity-specified ^class <class>
                 ^information use-pending-controller ^token <token>)
       - (component ^status preferred ^class <class>)
          (component ^status display-reference ^name <name> ^token
                     <token> ^price { <price> <=> 17 }
                     ^kilobytes-per-board <kb-per-board>)
          (component ^status display-reference ^name { <name2> <>
                     <name> } ^token <token>
                     ^price <price> ^kilobytes-per-board <=<kb-
                     per-board>)
       - (component ^status display-reference ^name {<> <name>
                     <> <name2> } ^token <token>)
          →
          (remove 5))

(p capacity-specified:8d:discard-the eof-component
;   if retrieve_attributes sent back an end-of-file component
;   (i.e., ^status undefined), then pitch it
          (context ^status active ^cname capacity-specified)
          (local ^context capacity-specified ^class <class>
                 ^information use-pending-controller ^token <token>)

Figure 13.3   (Continued)

```
    - (component ˆstatus preferred ˆclass <class> )
      (component ˆstatus display-reference ˆtoken <token>)
      (component ˆstatus undefined ˆtoken <token>)
  →
      (remove 4 ))

(p capacity-specified:8e:prepared-to-abort
;        if we couldn't find anything, then let's get ready to quit the
;        context.
         (context ˆstatus active ˆcname capacity-specified
         (line-item ˆstatus generic ˆclass <class> )
         (local ˆcontext capacity-specified ˆclass <class> )
                 ˆinformation use-pending-controller ˆtoken <token>)
       - (component ˆstatus preferred ˆclass <class>)
       - (component ˆstatus display-reference ˆtoken <token>)
         (component ˆstatus undefined ˆtoken <token> )
       →
         (modify 3 ˆstatus input)
         (remove 4 ))

(p capacity-specified:9:get-preferred-memory-type
;        now that we have the best choice in ˆkilobytes-per-board, go get
;        the memory type with that value
         (context ˆstatus active ˆcname capacity-specified)
         (local ˆcontext capacity-specified ˆclass <class>
                 ˆinformation use-pending-controller ˆtoken <token>)
       - (component ˆstatus preferred ˆclass <class>)
         (component ˆstatus display-reference ˆname <name< ˆtoken
                     <token>)
       - (component ˆstatus display-reference ˆname <> <name>
                     ˆtoken <token> )
       →
         (remove 3)
         (call match_component
                 $return status preferred token <token>
                 $quantity 1 $match name <name>))

(p capacity-specified:9a:already-have-preferred-memory
;        now that we have the best choice in ˆkilobytes-per-board, if
;        there's already a preferred type in WM for this value, use it
         (context ˆstatus active ˆcname capacity-specified)
         (local ˆcontext capacity-specified ˆclass <class>
                 ˆinformation use-pending-controller ˆtoken <token>)
       - (component ˆstatus preferred ˆtoken <token>)
         (component ˆname <name> ˆtoken <token>)
         (component ˆstatus preferred ˆname <name>)
       →
         (remove 3))
```

(Continued)

Figure 13.3   (Continued)

```
(p capacity-specified:10:fill-in-memory-locals
 ;        after retrieving the preferred memory type, fill out all the
 ;        necessary local attributes
          (context ^status active ^cname capacity-specified)
          (line-item ^status generic ^class <class>)
          (local ^context capacity-specified ^class <class>
                          ^information use-pending-controller
                          ^number-required <required> ^remainder nil)
          (component ^status preferred ^class <class>
                          ^name <name> ^number-of-kilobytes <kb>
                          ^kilobytes-per-board <kb-per-board>
                          ^absolute-max-per-bus <maximum>)
          (local ^context capacity-specified ^class <class>
                          ^information set-aside)
      →
          (bind <available> (compute <kb> * <maximum>))
          (bind <over> (compute <required> – <available>))
          (modify 3 ^name <name> ^quantity <kb> ^count 0
                          ^remainder <available> ^kilobytes-per-board
                          <kb-per-board>)
          (remove 4)   (modify 5 ^number-required <over>))

(p capacity-specified:11:accept-total-or-remaining-requirement
 ;        once we have a device type which will fill the current
 ;        requirement, then go accept it.
          context ^status active ^cname capacity-specified)
          (line-item ^status generic ^class <class>)
          (local ^context capacity-specified ^class <class>
                          ^information use-pending-controller ^name <name>
                          ^quantity <kb> ^number-required <required>
                          ^remainder <> nil ^value <divisor> ^meaning
                          {<display-units> <> nil})
      →
          (bind <mod> (compute <kb> – 1))
          (bind <quantity> (compute (<required> + <mod>) // <kb>))
          (bind <kilobytes> (compute <quantity> * <kb>))
          (bind <display-qty> (compute <kilobytes> // <divisor>))
          (remove 3))
 ; text    Adding <quantity> <name>
 ;                  | ( | <display-qty> <display-units> | ( | to the
 ;                  configuration to fill your memory requirements,
 ;                                                   pending review.
 ;
          (call xselio_setup $1-to-1-var <quantity> <name>
                          <display-qty> <display-units>)
          (call xselio_tty adding-to-requirements)
          (modify 2 ^status possible ^name <name> ^quantity
                          <quantity> ^kilobytes <kilobytes>
          (make context ^status active ^cname accept-line-item))
```

Figure 13.3   (Continued)

```
(p capacity-specified:11a:partial-accept
;       if a combination of device types will fill the total requirement,
;       then go accept one portion of it. ˆThe remaining portion will be
;       filled on return from accept-line-item
            (context ˆstatus active ˆcname capacity-specified)
            (line-item ˆstatus generic ˆclass <class>)
            (local ˆcontext capacity-specified ˆclass <class>
                    ˆinformation use-pending-controller ˆname <name>
                    ˆquantity <kb> ˆnumber-required <required>
                    ˆremainder {<space-remaining> < <required> <>
                    nil} ˆvalue <divisor> ˆmeaning {<display-units>
                    <>nil})
            (local ˆcontext capacity-specified ˆclass <class>
                    ˆinformation set-aside ˆname {<> <name> <> nil }
                    ˆnumber-required <over> ˆremainder >= <over>)
    →
            (bind <mod> (compute <kb> − 1))
            (bind <quantity> (compute (<space-remaining> + <mod>) //
                    <kb> ))
            (bind <kilobytes> (compute <quantity> * <kb>))
            (bind <display-qty> (compute <kilobytes> // <divisor>))
            (remove 3))
; text    <quantity>   <name>   | ( |   <display-qty>   <display-units>
;         | ) |  along with
            (call xselio_setup $1-to-1-var <quantity> <name>
                    <display-qty> <display-units>)
            (call xselio_tty partial-requirement-accept)
            (modify 2 ˆstatus possible ˆname <name> ˆquantity
                    <quantity> ˆkilobytes <space-remaining>)
            (modify 4 ˆinformation use-pending-controller
                    ˆvalue nil ˆmeaning nil
            (make line-item (substr 2 2 inf) ˆkilobytes <over>)
            (make context ˆstatus active ˆcname accept-line-item))
```

language. The BLISS version of OPS5 runs approximately seven times faster than the LISP version of OPS5.

XSEL was beta-tested for ten months in selected areas. After the successful completion of the test phase, XSEL was made available to the entire DEC sales force in July 1985.

The DEC sales force makes heavy use of XSEL. It seems to be more popular in some parts of the company than other parts or regions. There is no obvious reason for this variation other than the usual situations that occur with the introduction of a new tool, especially one that is based on a new technology. To use XSEL, a DEC salesperson must have access to a VAX that runs it. The machine resource was sometimes a problem but is being rectified. A lack of sufficient terminals and network connections did slow down XSEL's company-wide introduction. XSEL is loaded onto DEC VAX machines that are regionally located. Individual access is through conventional DEC VT-2XX terminals that are connected to DEC's internal communications network. A region of approximately 400 people can receive XSEL support via a VAX-11/785 or a stand-alone VAX 8600.

DEC has learned that resource allocation planning and user training are very important to the introduction of a system as large and as important as XSEL. DEC has developed significant management planning procedures to cover these areas.

Knowledge-base breadth and system integration with related systems are also important to system acceptance and effectiveness.

DEC has learned that the XSEL knowledge-base must include a certain amount of knowledge before the user considers the tool worthy. The knowledge-base breadth has been found to be an important attribute in the mainstream tool. XSEL's knowledge-base today includes configuration knowledge on the entire VAX product line and the majority of the present PDP-11 product line. Therefore, the majority of sales proposals being developed can be supported by XSEL. XSEL supports its user through its own knowledge, the knowledge of related DEC expert systems, and the information contained in DEC databases like the DEC product database. XSEL provides the latter two through effective system integration.

Because XSEL is helpful and because DEC salespeople do compete, many salespeople are requesting XSEL training, which DEC provides via trainers.

To remain effective, XSEL must be updated and maintained. DEC schedules four major XSEL releases per year and, as needed, one upgrade for each release. Therefore, XSEL can see as many as eight updates per year.

XSEL's use helps salespeople with system configuration errors, omissions, and commissions. The error types XSEL looks for include configurations with too few components, too many components, or the wrong kinds of components. The user is assisted in rectifying the identified errors. If a particular "error" was intentional, XSEL allows the user to override its recommendations.

If XSEL has any weaknesses, it is probably its user-system interface. Its teletype (TTY)-style presentation is seldom seen these days. Although it is easy enough to follow, it could use some updating. XSEL's user-system interface does not include an explanation facility, common today in expert systems. An explanation facility would be quite helpful.

XSEL can be considered a front-end application to the noninteractive expert configurator system known as XCON. Salespeople can select line items (computer system components), including central processor units, memory, peripherals, and system software for a potential configuration with XSEL, get

Figure 13.4   Sample run of XCON using XSEL input

CONFIGURATION-ID OXKO CUSTOMER-NAME STEVE

XCON RELEASE AS OF V4.7-1
FULL SYSTEM CONFIGURATION
COMMENTS

4 2OMA CABLES WILL BE REQUIRED TO CONNECT THE TERMINALS TO THE
MULTIPLEXER PANELS
THE BC22E-25 IS INTENDED TO BE USED WITH THE DF112-AA
EACH DECSA-CA/DA REQUIRES A Q*726-UZ TERMINAL SERVER LICENSE
EACH ETHERNET INTERFACE OR SERVER REQUIRES A TRANSCEIVER OR
DELNI PORT CONNECTION
EACH ETHERNET INTERFACE OR SERVER REQUIRES A TRANSCEIVER CABLE
2 RT2XX KEYBOARD (S) ARE NEEDED FOR YOUR RT240 (S) IF TO
BE USED AS TERMINAL (S)

PASS 1

COMPONENTS ORDERED

LINE	QTY	NAME	DESCRIPTION	COMMENT
1	1	861AX-UA	861XA-UA IDTC UPGRADE VMS 120/6	
		KA86-AA	PROCESSOR	
			4096 KILOBYTES OF MEMORY	
2	1	MS86-BB	12MB ECC/MOS 860 EXP MEMORY	
3	2	RT240-EE	TERMINAL	
4	2	VT220-F2	TERMINAL	GHOST
5	1	RA81-AA	456MB 16B DISK,120V/60,NO CA	
6	1	UDA50-A	DSA UNIBUS DISK ADAPTER	
7	1	TU80-AA	1600BPI TAPE 25/100IPS 120V	
8	1	LA120-DA	LA120 UNIV PWR SUPPLY NUM PA	
9	1	TEU77-FB	1600/800 TAPE SYS 11/780 60H	
10	1	DELUA-M	UNIBUS ETHERNET ADAPTER	
11	1	TU81E-AA	TU81-PLUS, UNIBUS, 60HZ	
12	1	12-19321-02	CONN, POWER 4P5W RCPT 208V60	
13	1	QK001-HM	VAX/VMS UPD 16MT9	
14	1	DZ11-N	ASYNC-COMM	
15	1	DECSA-DA	32-LINE TERMINAL SERVER	GHOST
16	1	DFM04-AC	4LINE STAT MUX W/9600BPS MOD	
17	2	VT22K-AA	VT220 COUNTRY KIT US/CANADA	
18	1	QK726-UZ	TERMINAL SERVER LIC W/WARR	
19	1	DECSK-AA	COUNTRY KIT (USA, CAN-ENG) DECS	
20	1	CK-DELUA-KM	CABKIT FCC 8' CABLE	MUST HAVE CABINET KIT
21	1	CK-DZ11-HD	CAB KIT 20 MA GENERAL USE	MUST HAVE CABINET KIT
22	1	H9652-CA	8600 SBI EXP CAB SWHB 120V3P	NEEDED TO PROVIDE SPACE FOR ADAPTORS

(Continued)

Figure 13.4   (Continued)

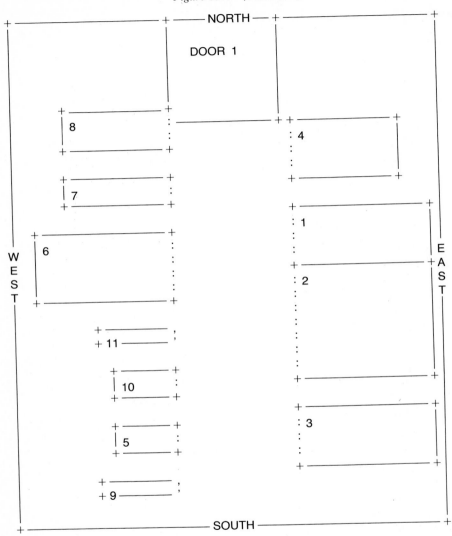

ROOM: COMPUTER-ROOM
| ——————— | = 2.5 FT.
THIS ROOM IS 14.6 FT. (NORTH) BY 16.9 FT. (WEST)

Figure 13.4   (Continued)

ROOM: COMPUTER-ROOM

QTY	DEVICE	PLUG(CAP)	PWR-REQ VAC	PH	PWR-CON WATTS	HEAT BTUS	WEIGHT POUNDS	H × W × D INCHES
1	70-19218-00	DF6516FP	120	3	6500	22191	850	60X28X30
1	70-19219-00	NO-DATA	120	0	0	0	850	60X52X30
1	H9652-CA*	NEMA-L21-30R	120	3	252	860	400	60X28X30
1	LA120-DA	NEMA-5-15P	120	1	153	522	102	33X28X24
2	RT240-EE	NEMA-5-15P	120	1	214	730	230	25X19X21
1	TU77-AF*	NEMA-L6-20P	120	1	1591	5431	500	58X36X32
1	TU80-AA**	NEMA-L5-30P	120	1	500	1707	500	41X21X30
1	TU81E-AA**	NEMA-L5-30P	120	1	550	1877	295	41X22X30
2	VT220-F2	NO-DATA	120	1	120	408	40	11X13X24
					9881	33726		

1	70-19218-00*	(FEC CABINET	)	WITHIN 70-19218-00*	ON OXKO
2	70-19219-00*	(CPU CABINET	)	WITHIN 70-19219-00*	ON OXKO
3	H9652-CA*	(CPUX CABINET	)	WITHIN H9652-CA*	ON OXKO
4	LA120-DA	(LA120 UNIV PWR SUPPLY NUM PAD)		WITHIN LA120-DA	ON OXKO
5	RT240-EE	(TERMINAL	)	WITHIN RT240-EE	ON OXKO
6	TU77-AF*	(TAPE	)	WITHIN TU77-AF*	ON OXKO
7	TU80-AA*	(TAPE	)	WITHIN TU80-AA*	ON OXKO
8	TU81E-AA	(TAPE	)	WITHIN TU81E-AA*	ON OXKO
9	VT220-F2	(TERMINAL	)	WITHIN VT220-F2	ON OXKO
10	RT240-EE	(TERMINAL	)	WITHIN RT240-EE	ON OXKO
11	VT220-F2	(TERMINAL	)	WITHIN VT220-F2	ON OXKO

THE FLOOR IN THE COMPUTER-ROOM MUST SUPPORT A DISTRIBUTED FLOORLOAD OF 15 POUNDS PER SQUARE FOOT, AND MUST SUPPORT A MAXIMUM FLOORLOAD OF 25 POUNDS PER SQUARE FOOT FROM COMPONENT 70-19218-00*.

ITEMS NOT CONFIGURED AND ARE TO BE USED AS SPARES, ON ANOTHER CONFIGURATION, OR FOR TESTING

6	17-00087-03	SBI-JUMPER CABLE
3	74-14103	BLANK-MODULE INTERCONNECT-HARDWARE
1	BC11A-15	EXTERNAL UNIVUS 15'
1	BC22E-25	25FT CABLE,ASYNC,15 WIRE SHLD
1	DF112-AA	DF112-AM MODEM-US/CAN HOUSING
6	G727	SHORT GRANT CONTINUITY
1	M9040	11780 CPU SBI TERMINATOR,HEX
1	M9202	M9192-M9292, 1"APART W/2'C

(Continued)

Figure 13.4 (Continued)

CABINET LAYOUT

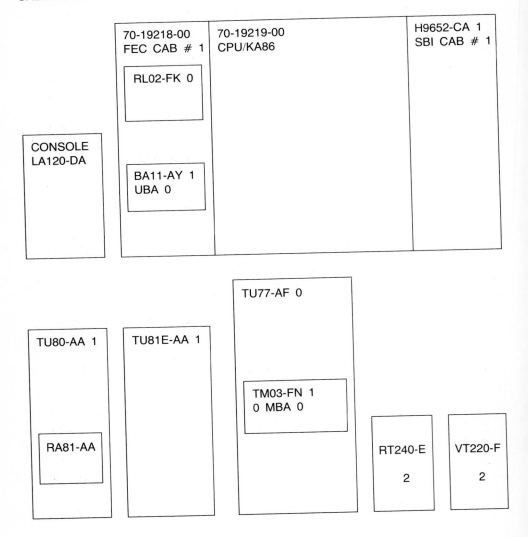

Figure 13.4 *(Continued)*

70-19218-00 # 1

RL02-FK 0 ON RLV12 1

RL02-FK 0 ON RLV12 1

BA11-AY BOX # 1 UBA # 0

BA11-AY BOX # 1 UBA # 0

C   1 2 3 4 5 6 7 8

B   1 2 3 4 5 6 7 8

A   1 2 3 4 5 6 7 8

(F R O N T)

(B A C K)

(Continued)

Figure 13.4 *(Continued)*

BA11-AY   BOX # 1 UBA # 0

OPTION	UNIT	ADDR	VECT
TU80	1	772520	224
DELUA-M	1	774510	120
DZ11-N	1	760100	300
UDA50-A " "	2	772150	154
RLV12	1	774400	160

```
                    A      B      C      D      E      F
DD11-DK          = = = | = = = = | = = = | = = = | = = = | = = =
              1  > - M9014 - <   > - - - - - M7454 - - - - - <
              2                        G727
              3  > - - - - - - - - - M7521 - - - - - - - - - <
              4  > - - - - - - - - - M7814 - - - - - - - - - <
              5                        G727
              6                        G727
              7  > - - - - - - - - - M7485 - - - - - - - - - <
              8  > - - - - - - - - - <7486 - - - - - - - - - <
              9  > - M9202 - <        G727
DD11-DK          = = = = | = = = = | = = = | = = = | = = = | = = =
             11  > - M9202 - <        G727
             12                       G727
             13                       G727
             14                       G727
             15                       G727
             16                       G727
             17                       G727
             18                       G727
             19  > - M9202 - <        G727
DD11-CK          = = = = | = = = = | = = = | = = = | = = = | = = =
             21  > - M9202 - <        G727
             22                       G727
             23                       G727
             24  > - M9302 - <        G727        M9049
DDV11-CK         = = = = | = = = = | = = = | = = = | = = = | = = =
             26  > - M9403 - <        >M8659<
             27                       > - - - - M8061 - - - - <
             28                       >M8659<
             29  >M9400 - YB<
                 = = = = | = = = = | = = = | = = = | = = = | = = =
                    A      B      C      D      E      F
```

F
R
O
N
T

Figure 13.4 (*Continued*)

70-19219-00 # 0

MEMORY	CPU	FPA	ABUS		I/O				
					POWER SUPPLIES				
			DB860	ABUS-TERM	DW7800	DW7802	UDA50-A1	TU811	M9302
MEMORY 16 MB	KA86-AA								
BBU									
H7231-A									

(F R O N T)

H9652-CA # 1

	I/O	I/O	I/O	I/O	
	RH7800 0	M9043			
	POWER SPACE	POWER SPACE			
COOLING					
POWER CONTROL					

(F R O N T)

(*Continued*)

Figure 13.4 *(Continued)*

LENGTH AND LOAD INFORMATION

	LENGTH	DC-LOAD	AC-LOAD
UNIBUS 0 SEGMENT 1	20	4	10
UNIBUS 2 SEGMENT 1	1	2	5

BOX POWER REMAINING (MILLIAMPS/MILLIWATTS)

	+15V-1ST	+15V-2ND	+5V	−15V
UNIBUS 0 FEC BOX 1	2830	5000	64700	3450

UNUSED CAPACITY

UDA50-A* 2 CAN SUPPORT 3 MORE DISK
UDA50-A* 1 IS UNUSED -- IT CAN SUPPORT 4 DISK
32 MEGABYTES MORE MEMORY COULD BE SUPPORTED
MBA 0 CAN SUPPORT 7 MORE CONTROLLERS
TM03-FN 1 CAN SUPPORT 3 MORE TAPE DRIVES

CABLING

1	BC22D-25	FROM THE CPU-CABINET TO THE CONSOLE-LA120-DA
		LENGTH: 25 FEET
		LENGTH-REQUIRED: 25 FEET
6	17-00087-04	FROM THE CPU CABINET TO CPUX CABINET 1
		LENGTH: 4 FEET
		LENGTH-REQUIRED: 4 FEET
1	70-20540-12	FROM UBA 0 TO BOX 1 ON UBA 0
		LENGTH: 12 FEET
		LENGTH-REQUIRED: 12 FEET
1	BC08S-10	FROM DZ11-N 1 TO PANEL INSERT A5-A8 IN CABINET 1—USING CK-DZ11-HD
		LENGTH: 10 FEET
		LENGTH-REQUIRED: 10 FEET
1	70-18798-08	FROM DELUA-M 1 TO PANEL INSERT A2-A3 IN CABINET 1
		LENGTH: 8 FEET
		LENGTH-REQUIRED: 4 FEET
1	70-19923-02	FROM TU80 1 TO PANEL INSERT A1 IN CABINET 1
		LENGTH: 10 FEET
		LENGTH-REQUIRED: 6 FEET
1	70-19922-02	FROM TU80 1 TO PANEL INSERT A1 IN CABINET 1
		LENGTH: 10 FEET
		LENGTH-REQUIRED: 6 FEET

Figure 13.4 *(Continued)*

1	70-18455-6K	FROM UDA50-A* 2 TO PANEL INSERT A4 IN CABINET 1 LENGTH: 6 FEET 9 INCHES LENGTH-REQUIRED: 6 FEET
1	70-19923-02	FROM TU81 1 TO PANEL INSERT A2 IN THE CPU CABINET LENGTH: 10 FEET LENGTH-REQUIRED: 6 FEET 9 INCHES
1	70-8455-6K	FROM UDA50-A* 1 TO PANEL INSERT A1 IN THE CPU CABINET LENGTH: 6 FEET 9 INCHES LENGTH-REQUIRED: 6 FEET 9 INCHES
1	BC17M-25	FROM MBA 0 TO TM03-FN 1 LENGTH: 25 FEET LENGTH-REQUIRED: 10 FEET
3	BC06R-06	FROM TM03-FN 1 ON MBA 0 TO TU77-AF* 0 LENGTH: 6 FEET LENGTH-REQUIRED: 5 FEET
1	BC26V-12	FROM UDA50-A* 2 TO RA81-AA* 1 IN TU80-AA* 1 LENGTH: 12 FEET LENGTH-REQUIRED: 12 FEET
1	BC80M-12	FROM RLV12* 1 TO RL02-FK 0 IN 70-19218-00* CABINET 1 LENGTH: 12 FEET LENGTH-REQUIRED: 10 FEET
2	BC17N-24	FROM TU80 1 TO TU80-AA* 0 LENGTH: 24 FEET LENGTH-REQUIRED: 8 FEET
1	BC17Y-20	FROM TU81 1 TO TU81E-AA* 0 LENGTH: 20 FEET LENGTH-REQUIRED: 8 FEET

ADDRESSES
LSI22   0

RLV12*   1   774400   M8061 WIRE WRAP PINS 12 13 14 15 16 17 18 19 20 21
FOR ADDRESS BITS   3   4   5   6   7   8   9 10 11 12
CONNECT TO PIN 22 FOR BITS: 8 11 12

UNIBUS   0

DZ11-N   1   760100   M7814 E72 SWITCHES 1 2 3 4 5 6 7   8   9 10
FOR ADDRESS BITS   3 4 5 6 7 8 9 10 11 12
CLOSE SWITCHES FOR BITS: 6

UDA50-A*2   772150   M7485 JMPR/SW W4 W5   1 2 3 4 5 6 7   8   9 10
FOR ADDR BITS A2=0 A2=1 3 4 5 6 7 8 9 10 11 12
CLOSE SW/INSTL JMPR FOR BITS: 3   5   6 10 12

TU80   1   772520   M7454 SWITCHPACK 20C SWITCHES 9 10=
ON ON FOR ADDR 772520 ON OFF FOR ADDR 772524
OFF ON FOR ADDR 772530 OFF OFF FOR ADDR 772534

(Continued)

Figure 13.4 (*Continued*)

```
DELUA-M    1    774510    M7521 E111 SWITCHES  1  2  3 4 5 6 7 8 9 10
                          FOR ADDRESS BITS     12 11 10 9 8 7 6 5 4  3
                          CLOSE SWITCHES FOR BITS: 2 4 5 7 9 10


UNIBUS 2
  UDA50-A*1    772150     M7485 JMPR/SW  W4  W5    1 2 3 4 5 6 7  8  9 10
                          FOR ADDR BITS A2=0 A2=1 3 4 5 6 7 8 9 10 11 12
                          CLOSE SW/INSTL JMPR FOR BITS: 3 5 6 10 12

  TU81      1  774500     M8739 E44 SWITCHES 10 9 8 7 6 5 4  3  2  1
                          FOR ADDRESS BITS      3 4 5 6 7 8 9 10 11 12

                          INSTALL JUMPER W2 FROM A-B IF ADDR = XXXXX0
                          INSTALL JUMPER W2 FROM B-C IF ADDR = XXXXX4

                          CLOSE SWITCHES FOR BITS: 6 8 11 12


VECTORS

LS122  0
  RLV12*    1   160       M8061 WIRE WRAP PINS 4 5 6 7 8 9 10
                          FOR VECTOR BITS        2 3 4 5 6 7  8
                          CONNECT TO PIN 3 FOR BITS: 4 5 6


UNIBUS 0
  DZ11-N    1   300       M7814 E81 SWITCHES 6 5 4 3 2 1
                          FOR VECTOR BITS      3 4 5 6 7 8
                          CLOSE SWITCHES FOR BITS: 2 3 4 5 8

  UDA50-A*2     154       VECTOR IS PROGRAMMABLE - NOT SWITCH
                          SELECTABLE

  TU80      1   224       M7454 20C SWITCHES 7 6 5 4 3 2 1
                          FOR VECTOR BITS      2 3 4 5 6 7 8
                          CLOSE SWITCHES FOR BITS: 3 5 6 8

  DELUA-M   1   120       M7521 E70 SWITCHES 4 5 6 7 8 9 10
                          FOR VECTOR BITS      8 7 6 5 4 3  2
                          CLOSE SWITCHES FOR BITS: 2 3 5 7 8

UNIBUS 2
  UDA50-A*1    154        VECTOR IS PROGRAMMABLE - NOT SWITCH
                          SELECTABLE

  TU81      1   260       VECTOR IS PROGRAMMABLE - NOT SWITCH
                          SELECTABLE
```

END OF FULL SYSTEM CONFIGURATION { XSEL }
END OF DEC-NUMBER 0XKO

assistance with the task, and ask XSEL to make sure the initial order is complete, consistent, and practical. Once an interactive XSEL session is completed, the XSEL-developed initial configuration file can be passed on to XCON for further checking, component list expansion, and configuring. Figure 13.4 provides an example of an XCON run. This run is in support of the XSEL run presented in Figure 13.2.

After the XCON run, the DEC salesperson has a complete, ready-to-present technical proposal including a complete and accurate component list, a computer room layout plan, a cabinet layout, and other pertinent information including cabling information.

The salespeople at DEC can quickly develop technical proposals that are totally informative, something DEC customers will appreciate, and are very accurate, something that generates confidence and assurance in the DEC sales staff.

CONCLUDING REMARKS

XSEL is an expert system that uses its knowledge about DEC computer system components, the relationships between them, the applications potential customers might have, and how to lead users through the component selection process in assisting DEC salespeople develop specific configurations for particular customers.

XSEL is easy to use; it responds to English verbs and adjectives as well as DEC jargon. XSEL has an online help facility to aid users in answering XSEL questions and to provide users with component information. XSEL provides links with other DEC data processing resources and information systems like the DEC product database and the XCON expert system. The links are, in some cases, transparent to XSEL users.

DEC can update its configuration data in a small number of databases and have its entire sales force in America be up-to-date. Time is saved, paper can be saved, and people can receive new information in a very timely fashion. Knowledge can be actively transferred from DEC configuration experts to its entire American sales force in a very short period of time. XSEL is an effective knowledge transfer vehicle.

XSEL can be used to prepare presales or sales proposals of any size quickly and accurately. Salespeople are capable of developing even the largest configurations in a short amount of time. Changes to proposals are inevitable, and XSEL assists the DEC salespeople with quick and accurate proposal changes.

Because XSEL saves time and costs less than the salaries of the people whose time is being saved, XSEL reduces the overall expense in proposal generation for DEC.

Because XSEL and XCON provide DEC salespeople with extensive, ac-

- Saves substantial salesman time.
- Leverages expertise.
- Decreases costs.
- Increases proposal consistency.
- Increases customer satisfaction.
- Demonstrates DEC's expert system expertise.

Figure 13.5   XSEL benefits

curate proposal documentation, DEC salespeople look very professional in the marketplace.

DEC customers should be satisfied that the systems they buy will be correct both from a system and an application perspective.

DEC sees many benefits developing from its use of XSEL. Figure 13.5 lists some of these benefits.

Both time and expertise are leveraged. The time it takes to develop proposals is decreased; more proposals can be accomplished in a shorter amount of time. Configuration and sales expertise are leveraged. The configuration experts use less of their time developing or repairing configurations for proposals. The salespeople use less of their time in developing configurations, giving them more time to be with additional potential clients.

Costs are decreased in the sales, order administration, and manufacturing areas. XSEL decreases the time needed to develop configuration proposals and change orders at a cost that is lower than the cost of the time that is saved. XSEL-generated configurations have fewer errors than manually generated configurations. Fewer errors save order administration and manufacturing costs.

XSEL provides configuration advice in a consistent manner. Therefore, configurations developed using XSEL are more consistent. If XSEL is used by the entire sales force or a large part of it, the proposals DEC develops will be more consistent. Customers can order à la carte, yet configuration proposals will be more consistent.

Because customers receive more accurate proposals more quickly that are supported with plenty of informative documentation, they are more satisfied with their dealings with DEC.

Through the use of XSEL, DEC's customers get to witness a product of DEC's expert system expertise and capability first hand. And since expert system technology is receiving a lot of press and market interest these days, it gives DEC a positive, forward-looking image.

Two of the keys to DEC's success with XSEL are as follows:

1. The effective integration of expert system technology with DEC's data processing resources, information systems, and business operations
2. The use of the right mix of expertise

As has already been stated, XSEL has been integrated into the mainstream operations of DEC in the area of sales. XSEL has also been integrated with other automated systems at DEC. In doing this, XSEL has not duplicated other DEC efforts; rather it has synergistically been developed and introduced into the DEC organization and its systems.

DEC has taken great steps to ensure that the right people participate in the development of expert systems. DEC brings together knowledgeable users, domain experts, and knowledge engineers to develop its systems. When starting out, DEC, which had little experience with knowledge engineering, obtained the requisite expertise from Carnegie-Mellon University until it could train and develop its own knowledge engineers. This effective teaming concept has ensured that DEC's expert systems are properly targeted at business requirements and are correct subjectively and technologically.

The XSEL project is continuing and expanding. It will be supporting more users with more information and knowledge in the future.

New work is going on at DEC in configuration, proposal, and quotation development under project names like R1 modularization, RIME, and AQS.

Additional work is going on at Carnegie-Mellon University. The XCALIBUR project is an example. The XCALIBUR project has an objective to provide flexible, natural-language access to XSEL in requests for order modification, task information, and component part database information. The XCALIBUR project's goal is to integrate the natural-language and expert system capabilities. This will make XSEL even easier to use. Training time spent prior to using XSEL should decrease.

The future for XSEL can go many ways. A great deal of development is going on at DEC. XSEL and XCON are going through changes. For example, the expert computer room planner in the XSEL and XCON systems used to be called XSITE; now it is called XFL. The name XSITE seems to be used in conjunction with a field service project. XSEL and XCON seem to be headed toward a marriage with an Automated Quotation System (AQS). In the future, there might be a tightly coupled XSEL-like system with a set of quotation programs. One could imagine a set of cooperating systems that develop initial configurations, make quotes, finish the sizing and pricing work, and finally develop complete proposals and orders with maximum automation support.

The future for the effective commercial use of large expert systems seems to be developing rapidly at Digital Equipment Corporation.

14 DEVELOPMENT OF A PERSONAL COMPUTER EXPERT SYSTEM

Personal-computer-based expert systems are being developed to support many subject domains. In this chapter, we present background and project development information about one personal-computer-based expert system that is in use today. This expert system aids users in the analysis of a small yet difficult problem. Through a simple, graphics-supported session, users can gain advice about their problem.

PROJECT INCEPTION

This expert system project began out of a need to detach a human development expert from the operations and maintenance phase of a manufacturing system that the expert helped to develop. The expert was being called on often to resolve operational problems or answer questions about the operation of the system. The expert wanted to move on to new work. The expert was very willing to transfer his knowledge to the knowledge-base of an expert system and made himself readily available.

Because both the organization and the expert could benefit from releasing the expert from this situation, a decision was made to develop an expert system that could provide the manufacturing system's operators with problem resolution and operations expertise and assistance.

The project started with the realization that the expert system to be built was primarily a diagnostic system. A secondary benefit from the expert system could be operational training assistance. In light of the diagnostic nature of the system, it was determined that a backward-chaining, goal-driven inference paradigm and a rule knowledge representation scheme would be appropriate to the task. It was also determined that other parts of the organization could supply an expert system development shell (that supported rules and backward chaining) and the computer hardware on which the shell and the resultant expert system would run. The software tools and the hardware were obtained, and the project began.

HOW THE PROJECT PROCEEDED

Using a chalkboard, the expert and a knowledge engineer defined the domain, developed the first set of rules, and discussed the results. This work took one week.

The system was developed by tracing through the various components of a manufacturing cell with a communications expert and discussing possible problems and solutions. The procedures the expert would go about in solving the problem were acquired and placed into the knowledge base of the expert system. The system was designed to offer simple solutions to the most common problems encountered.

The knowledge engineer spent three weeks developing and refining the rule knowledge base, consulting with the expert as needed. At the end of this three-week period, the expert system was ready for operational testing. Facilities like the user-system interface and explanation facility did not have to be developed; they were available from the shell software.

The expert system performed correctly. It asked appropriate questions and, after receiving user inputs, provided useful recommendations. However, the operational test was not considered a success because the users did not accept the expert system. This initial system test and evaluation took approximately one week.

The next step was to add graphics to the expert system. Using a personal computer–based graphics development tool, color graphics depictions of the subject system and its components were developed. The expert system was modified so that when the expert system asked a question about a component, it would also present a picture of the component. The graphics work and integration with the expert system took approximately three weeks.

The resulting expert diagnostic system was tested and was better received. This expert system is being used in the operational environment. Through its use, experience is being gained. When appropriate, the system is being enhanced to handle more operational and maintenance cases.

FMS COMMUNICATIONS DIAGNOSTIC SYSTEM

The developed expert system is called the FMS Communications Diagnostic System. It helps identify and correct computer communications problems in the Flexible Manufacturing System (FMS) running at Texas Instruments' Trinity Mills facility.

The Trinity Mills FMS is an automated manufacturing system capable of machining, deburring, and cleaning raw aluminum castings without human intervention. The FMS cell consists of a part input queue, four numerically controlled machine tools, a part transfer robot, a deburring robot, and an automatic wash station. A typical part processing cycle starts at the gravity-fed part input queue, where the raw casting is picked up by the transfer robot and carried to one of four machine tools. After machining, the part is picked up by the transfer robot and taken to the deburring robot, where sharp edges and metal burrs are removed. The transfer robot transports the deburred part to the wash station, where dirt, aluminum dust, and machining oil are removed. Finally, the part exits the FMS manufacturing cell.

The operation of these machines is coordinated by a distributed computer control system. Included in this control system is a Digital Equipment Corporation PDP-11/24 minicomputer. This computer is responsible for determining the tasks to be performed. This determination is based on consideration of human safety, availability of resources, efficiency of competing tasks, and avoidance of robot collisions. Implementation of tasks is primarily performed by a programmable controller and individual robot and machine controllers. Information about the current state of the FMS cell is passed to the computer through a factory communications network. The PDP-11/24 computer makes decisions based on this information as to which tasks need to be performed. Task commands are passed back to the manufacturing cell controllers for implementation. If the action is to transfer a part from one station to another, a command will be sent to the Cincinnati Milacron robot controller. If the action is to deburr a part, the GMF robot controller is sent the command. The Texas Instruments 530 programmable controller is notified if the action is to machine a casting.

When a controller receives a command from the PDP-11/24, the command is acknowledged and control is passed to the controller. For example, if a part is ready to be transferred from the cell input queue to a machine tool, the computer will issue a command to the Milacron robot. The robot will acknowledge the command and be passed control to carry out the task. The robot will work with the programmable controller to execute the task. The computer is not involved in the decision making pertaining to performing the transfer. When the task is complete, the robot will communicate with the PDP-11/24 that it is available for another part transfer. The same distributed control philosophy is used for the machining and deburring operations.

Smooth operation of the FMS cell is dependent on timely and accurate passage of information across the FMS communications network.

QUICK AND ACCURATE DIAGNOSIS

The FMS Diagnostic System was developed to help ensure that problems with FMS cell communications would be diagnosed and corrected quickly and accurately. Help is always available from this diagnostic system. The system was developed using the Personal Consultant expert system shell. It runs on a Texas Instruments Professional Computer. Knowledge about diagnosing the communications in the Trinity Mills FMS cell was acquired from a human expert and is represented in the diagnostic system's knowledge base. The knowledge-base is composed of 55 rules. These rules are presented in Figure 14.1 in two forms: first in an English, easy-to-read format and then in a LISP format. A logic tree representation of these rules is presented in Figure 14.2.

Figure 14.1 Communications rule base

RULE001 [COMMUNICATIONSRULES]

If determines if the HA is receiving the signal if OFF,
Then 1) BLINK 138 204 208 170 204 240 1 1, and
　　　2) it is definite (100%) that no signal to HA, and
　　　3) Inform the user of the decision, and
　　　4) DOGRAPH PROB-COM, and
　　　5) BLINK 138 204 240 170 204 8 30.

PREMISE:　($AND (SAME ONTXT HA-TRANS OFF))
ACTION:　 (DO-ALL (BLINK 138 204 208 170 204 240 1 1)
　　　　　　　 (CONCLUDE CNTXT NO-TRANS YES TALLY 1000)
　　　　　　　 (SPRINTT "The Host Adapter is not receiving any signal
　　　　　　　 so the problem is probably in the computer room.")
　　　　　　　 (DOGRAPH "PROB-COM")
　　　　　　　 (BLINK 138 204 240 170 204 240 8 30))

RULE002 [COMMUNICATIONSRULES]

If 1) no signal to HA, and
　 2) status of the HA is BLINKING/OFF, and
　 3) checking the power connections is POWER-NOT-OK,
Then it is definite (100%) that the following is one of recommended
　　　action : Reattach the Host Adapter Power connections.
　　　　　　You may also want to check the wall power connection with
　　　　　　a device you know is working.

PREMISE:　($AND (SAME CNTXT NO-TRANS)
　　　　　　　 (SAME CNTXT HA-GOOD BLINKING/OFF)
　　　　　　　 (SAME CNTXT CHECK-POWER POWER-NOT-OK))
ACTION:　 (DO-ALL
　　　　　　　 (CONCLUDE CNTXT SOLVE-IT "Reattach the Host
　　　　　　　 Adapter Power connections. You may also want to check
　　　　　　　 the wall power connection with a device you know is
　　　　　　　 working." TALLY 1000))

Figure 14.1   (Continued)

RULE004 [COMMUNICATIONSRULES]

If 1) no signal to HA, and
   2) status of the HA is STEADY, and
   3) determines if the HA is online or offline is
      SWITCH-DOWN,
Then it is definite (100%) that the following is one of
      recommended action : The Host Adapter is offline. Put it
      back online by putting the third switch back up.

PREMISE: ($AND (SAME CNTXT NO-TRANS)
                 (SAME CNTXT HA-GOOD STEADY)
                 (SAME CNTXT HA-ONLINE SWITCH-DOWN))
ACTION: (DO-ALL
                 (CONCLUDE CNTXT SOLVE-IT "The Host Adapter is
                 offline.
                 Put it back online by putting the third switch
                 back up." TALLY 1000))

RULE005 [COMMUNICATIONSRULES]

If 1) no signal to HA, and
   2) status of the HA is BLINKING/OFF, and
   3) checking the power connections is POWER-OK,
Then it is definite (100%) that section HA-1 is ok.

PREMISE: ($AND (SAME CNTXT NO-TRANS)
                 (SAME CNTXT HA-GOOD BLINKING/OFF)
                 (SAME CNTXT CHECK-POWER POWER-OK))
ACTION: (DO-ALL (CONCLUDE CNTXT HA-1 YES TALLY 1000))

RULE006 [COMMUNICATIONSRULES]

If 1) the Host Adapter is ok, and
   2) diagnostics on the Host Adapter is PROBLEM,
Then it is definite (100%) that the following is one of
      recommended action : There is probably a problem with the
      Host Adapter. You may want to replace it with another
      one.

PREMISE: ($AND (SAME CNTXT HA-OK)
                 (SAME CNTXT RUN-DIAG PROBLEM))
ACTION: (DO-ALL (CONCLUDE CNTXT HA-1 YES TALLY 1000))

(Continued)

Figure 14.1   (Continued)

RULE007 [COMMUNICATIONSRULES]

If 1) no signal to HA, and
   2) status of the HA is STEADY, and
   3) determines if the HA is online or offline is SWITCH-UP, and
   4) checks the communication cables is COMM-NO,
Then it is definite (100%) that the following is one of
       recommended action : The communication cables are not
       hooked up properly and need to be reattached.

PREMISE: ($AND (SAME CNTXT NO-TRANS)
                  (SAME CNTXT HA-GOOD STEADY)
                  (SAME CNTXT HA-ONLINE SWITCH-UP)
                  (SAME CNTXT CHECK-COMM COMM-NO))
ACTION: (DO-ALL
                  (CONCLUDE CNTXT SOLVE-IT "The communication
                  cables are not hooked up properly and need to be
                  reattached." TALLY 1000))

RULE008 [COMMUNICATIONSRULES]

If 1) no signal to HA, and
   2) status of the HA is STEADY, and
   3) determines if the HA is online or offline is SWITCH-UP, and
   4) checks the communication cables is COMM-OK,
Then it is definite (100%) that the Host Adapter is ok.

PREMISE: ($AND (SAME CNTXT NO-TRANS)
                  (SAME CNTXT HA-GOOD STEADY)
                  (SAME CNTXT HA-ONLINE SWITCH-UP)
                  (SAME CNTXT CHECK-COMM COMM-OK))
ACTION: (DO-ALL (CONCLUDE CNTXT HA-OK YES TALLY 1000))

RULE009 [COMMUNICATIONSRULES]

If 1) the Host Adapter is ok, and
   2) diagnostics on the Host Adapter is OK, and
   3) checks the PDP to see if it is working is NOT-ACTIVE,
Then it is definite (100%) that the following is one of recommended
       action : There may be a problem with the PDP-11 computer. Call
       the Trinity Mills computer operator at 555-1111 for assistance.

Figure 14.1 *(Continued)*

PREMISE: ($AND (SAME CNTXT HA-OK) (SAME CNTXT RUN-DIAG OK)
(SAME CNTXT CHECK-PDP-STATUS NOT-ACTIVE))
ACTION: (DO-ALL
(CONCLUDE CNTXT SOLVE-IT "There may be a problem
with the PDP-11 computer. Call the Trinity Mills
computer operator at 555-1111 for
assistance." TALLY 1000))

RULE010 [COMMUNICATIONSRULES]

If 1) the Host Adapter is ok, and
2) diagnostics on the Host Adapter is OK, and
3) checks the PDP to see if it is working is ACTIVE, and
4) this checks to see how many secondaries are attached
is 0,
Then it is definite (100%) that the following is one of
recommended action : The NIM is not attached to the
network. Reattach the secondary by using the ACTIVATE
command. After typing in the ACTIVATE command, a prompt
for the secondary you wish to activate will appear.
Type #0101 here, then hit the RETURN key. This should
activate the secondary.

PREMISE: ($AND (SAME CNTXT HA-OK) (SAME CNTXT RUN-DIAG OK)
(SAME CNTXT CHECK-PDP-STATUS ACTIVE)
(SAME CNTXT CHECK-SECONDARY 0))
ACTION: (DO-ALL
(CONCLUDE CNTXT SOLVE-IT "The NIM is not attached
to the network. Reattach the secondary by using
the ACTIVATE command. After typing in the
ACTIVATE command, a prompt for the secondary you
wish to activate will appear. Type #0101 here,
then hit the RETURN key. This should activate
the secondary." TALLY 1000))

RULE011 [COMMUNICATIONSRULES]

If 1) the Host Adapter is ok, and
2) diagnostics on the Host Adapter is OK, and
3) checks the PDP to see if it is working is ACTIVE, and
4) this checks to see how many secondaries are attached
is 1, and
5) checks to see if the POL530 software is running is
SHORT-RESP,

(Continued)

Figure 14.1 (Continued)

Then it is definite (100%) that the following is one of
    recommended action : The POL530 software is not active.
    Go to the PDP-11 console and start the POL530 software
    by typing: RUN POL530 and then hitting the RETURN key.

PREMISE: ($AND (SAME CNTXT HA-OK) (SAME CNTXT RUN-DIAG OK)
            (SAME CNTXT CHECK-PDP-STATUS ACTIVE)
            (SAME CNTXT CHECK-SECONDARY 1)
            (SAME CNTXT CHECK-POL530 SHORT-RESP))
ACTION: (DO-ALL
            (CONCLUDE CNTXT SOLVE-IT "The POL530 software is
            not active. Go to the PDP-11 console and start
            the POL530 software by typing: RUN POL530 and
            then hitting the RETURN key." TALLY 1000))

RULE012 [COMMUNICATIONSRULES]

If 1) diagnostics on the Host Adapter is OK, and
   2) checks the PDP to see if it is working is ACTIVE, and
   3) this checks to see how many secondaries are attached
      is 1, and
   4) checks to see if the POL530 software is running is
      LONG-RESPONSE,
Then it is definite (100%) that ok so far.

PREMISE: ($AND (SAME CNTXT RUN-DIAG OK)
            (SAME CNTXT CHECK-PDP-STATUS ACTIVE)
            (SAME CNTXT CHECK-SECONDARY 1)
            (SAME CNTXT CHECK-POL530 LONG-RESPONSE))
ACTION: (DO-ALL (CONCLUDE CNTXT OK-3 YES TALLY 1000))

RULE013 [COMMUNICATIONSRULES]

If 1) the Host Adapter is ok, and
   2) ok so far, and
   3) checking to see if the PDP connections are secure is
      NOT-ATTACHED,
Then it is definite (100%) that the following is one of
    recommended action : The PDP-11 communication cables are
    not hooked up properly. Reconnect them.

PREMISE: ($AND (SAME CNTXT HA-OK) (SAME CNTXT OK-3)
            (SAME CNTXT CHECK-PDP-COMM NOT-ATTACHED))
ACTION: (DO-ALL
            (CONCLUDE CNTXT SOLVE-IT "The PDP-11
            communication cables are not hooked up properly.
            Reconnect them." TALLY 1000))

Figure 14.1 *(Continued)*

RULE014 [COMMUNICATIONSRULES]

If 1) no signal to HA, and
  2) status of the HA is STEADY, and
  3) determines if the HA is online or offline is SWITCH-UP,
     and
  4) checks the communication cables is COMM-OK, and
  5) diagnostics on the Host Adapter is OK, and
  6) checks the PDP to see if it is working is ACTIVE, and
  7) this checks to see how many secondaries are attached
     is 1, and
  8) checks to see if the POL530 software is running is
     LONG-RESPONSE, and
  9) checking to see if the PDP connections are secure is
     ATTACHED, and
  10) checks for error message is NO-MSG,
Then 1) it is definite (100%) that the following is one of
       recommended action: You need the help of a human
       expert. Call Mr. Smith for help. Print out this
       report for reference by pressing the ALT PRINT keys,
       and
    2) DOGRAPH PROB-5.

PREMISE: ($AND (SAME CNTXT NO-TRANS)
              (SAME CNTXT HA-GOOD STEADY)
              (SAME CNTXT HA-ONLINE SWITCH-UP)
              (SAME CNTXT CHECK-COMM COMM-OK)
              (SAME CNTXT RUN-DIAG OK)
              (SAME CNTXT CHECK-PDP-STATUS ACTIVE)
              (SAME CNTXT CHECK-SECONDARY 1)
              (SAME CNTXT CHECK-POL530 LONG-RESPONSE)
              (SAME CNTXT CHECK-PDP-COMM ATTACHED)
              (SAME CNTXT CHECK-ERROR-MSG NO-MSG))
ACTION: (DO-ALL
              (CONCLUDE CNTXT SOLVE-IT "You need the help of a
              human expert. Call Mr. Smith
              at 555-1111. Print out this report for
              reference by pressing the ALT PRINT keys."
              TALLY 1000)
              (DO-GRAPH "PROB-5"))

(Continued)

Figure 14.1   *(Continued)*

RULE015 [COMMUNICATIONSRULES]

If 1) no signal to HA, and
   2) status of the HA is STEADY, and
   3) determines if the HA is online or offline is SWITCH-UP, and
   4) checks the communication cables is COMM-OK, and
   5) ok so far, and
   6) checking to see if the PDP connections are secure is ATTACHED, and
   7) checks for error message is MSG,
Then 1) it is definite (100%) that the following is one of recommended action : Refer to the Reference Guide for the meaning of the error message. Call Mr. Smith 555-1111 for help and print this report using the ALT and PRINT keys, and
   2) DOGRAPH PROB-MG5.

PREMISE: ($AND (SAME CNTXT NO-TRANS)
           (SAME CNTXT HA-GOOD STEADY)
           (SAME CNTXT HA-ONLINE SWITCH-UP)
           (SAME CNTXT CHECK-COMM COMM-OK)
           (SAME CNTXT OK-3)
           (SAME CNTXT CHECK-PDP-COMM ATTACHED)
           (SAME CNTXT CHECK-ERROR-MSG MSG))
ACTION: (DO-ALL
           (CONCLUDE CNTXT SOLVE-IT "Refer to the Reference Guide for the meaning of the error message. Call Mr. Smith at 555-1111 for help and print this report using the ALT and PRINT keys." TALLY 1000) (DOGRAPH "PROB-MG5"))

RULE017 [COMMUNICATIONSRULES]

If section HA-1 is ok,
Then it is definite (100%) that the Host Adapter is ok.

PREMISE: ($AND (SAME CNTXT HA-1))
ACTION: (DO-ALL (CONCLUDE CNTXT HA-OK YES TALLY 1000))

RULE018 [COMMUNICATIONSRULES]

If determines if the HA is receiving the signal is BLINKING,
Then 1) BLINK 138 204 208 170 236 208 1 1, and
      2) it is definite (100%) that problem is in the machine-room, and

Figure 14.1 (Continued)

3) Inform the user of this decision, and
4) DOGRAPH PROB-FMS, and
5) BLINK 170 236 208 170 204 208 8 30.

PREMISE: ($AND (SAME CNTXT HA-TRANS BLINKING))
ACTION: (DO-ALL (BLINK 138 204 208 170 236 208 1 1)
              (CONCLUDE CNTXT YES-TRANS YES TALLY 1000)
              (SPRINTT "Since the Host Adapter is receiving the
              communications signal the problem is probably in
              the machine room.") (DOGRAPH "PROB-FMS")
              (BLINK 170 236 208 170 204 208 8 30))

RULE019 [COMMUNICATIONSRULES]

If 1) PASTE, and
  2) checks to see if the TI530 is functioning or not is
     NON-ACTIVE,
Then it is definite (100%) that the following is one of
     recommended action : Activate the TI530.

PREMISE: ($AND (SAME CNTXT NIM-10)
              (SAME CNTXT PC-STATUS NOT-ACTIVE))
ACTION: (DO-ALL
              (CONCLUDE CNTXT SOLVE-IT "Activate the TI530."
              TALLY 1000))

RULE021 [COMMUNICATIONSRULES]

If 1) PASTE, and
  2) checks to see if the TI530 is functioning or not is
     ACTIVE, and
  3) checks to see if the NIM is secure in the I/O rack of
     the 530 is SECURE,
Then it is definite (100%) that ok so far.

PREMISE: ($AND (SAME CNTXT NIM-10)
              (SAME CNTXT PC-STATUS ACTIVE)
              (SAME CNTXT CHECK-NIM-INSERT SECURE))
ACTION: (DO-ALL (CONCLUDE CNTXT NIM-1 YES TALLY 1000))

RULE022 [COMMUNICATIONSRULES]

If 1) PASTE, and
  2) checks to see if the TI530 is functioning or not is
     ACTIVE, and
  3) checks to see if the NIM is secure in the I/O rack of
     the 530 is NOT-SECURE,

(Continued)

Figure 14.1 *(Continued)*

Then it is definite (100%) that the following is one of
recommended action : The NIM is not properly inserted in
the I/O rack of the TI530. Insert it properly.

PREMISE: ($AND (SAME CNTXT NIM-10)
          (SAME CNTXT PC-STATUS ACTIVE)
          (SAME CNTXT CHECK-NIM-INSERT SECURE))
ACTION: (DO-ALL
          (CONCLUDE CNTXT SOLVE-IT "The NIM is not properly
          inserted in the I/O rack of the TI530. Insert
          it properly." TALLY 1000))

RULE023 [COMMUNICATIONSRULES]

If 1) ok so far, and
   2) perform diagnostics on the NIMbox is TEST-FAIL,
Then it is definite (100%) that the following is one of
          recommended action : There is probably a problem with the
          NIM. You may want to replace it.

PREMISE: ($AND (SAME CNTXT NIM-1)
          (SAME CNTXT DIAGNOSTICS-NIM TEST-FAIL))
ACTION: (DO-ALL
          (CONCLUDE CNTXT SOLVE-IT "There is probably a
          problem with the NIM. You may want to replace
          it." TALLY 1000))

RULE024 [COMMUNICATIONSRULES]

If 1) problem is in the machine-room, and
   2) checks to see if the NIM is receiving the signal or
      not is OFF, and
   3) checks to see if the TI530 is functioning or not is
      ACTIVE, and
   4) checks to see if the NIM is secure in the I/O rack of
      the 530 is SECURE, and
   5) perform diagnostics on the NIMbox is TEST-OK,
Then 1) it is definite (100%) that the following is one of
          recommended action : You need the help of a human
          expert. Call Mr. Smith at 555-1111.
          Print out this report for reference by pressing the ALT PRINT
          keys, and
   2) DOGRAPH PROB-1.

PREMISE: ($AND (SAME CNTXT YES-TRANS)
          (SAME CNTXT NIM-RECEIVE OFF)
          (SAME CNTXT PC-STATUS ACTIVE)

Figure 14.1   (Continued)

```
            (SAME CNTXT CHECK-NIM-INSERT SECURE)
            (SAME CNTXT DIAGNOSTICS-NIM TEST-OK))
ACTION:   (DO-ALL
            (CONCLUDE CNTXT SOLVE-IT "You need the help of a
            human expert. Call Mr. Smith at 555-1111.
            Print out this report for reference by pressing
            the ALT PRINT keys." TALLY 1000)
            (DOGRAPH "PROB-1"))
```

RULE025 [COMMUNICATIONSRULES]

If 1) problem is in the machine-room, and
   2) checks to see if the NIM is receiving the signal or
      not is BLINKING, and
   3) checks the NIM GOOD light is BLINKING/OFF,
Then it is definite (100%) that merger between two paths.

```
PREMISE:   ($AND (SAME CNTXT YES-TRANS)
            (SAME CNTXT NIM-RECEIVE BLINKING)
            (SAME CNTXT NIM-GOOD BLINKING/OFF))
ACTION:   (DO-ALL (CONCLUDE CNTXT NIM YES TALLY 1000))
```

RULE026 [COMMUNICATIONSRULES]

If 1) problem is in the machine-room, and
   2) checks to see if the NIM is receiving the signal or
      not is BLINKING, and
   3) checks the NIM GOOD light is STEADY, and
   4) checks to see if the NIM is online is NIM-OFFLINE,
Then it is definite (100%) that the following is one of
      recommended action : The NIM is offline. Put it back
      online by flipping the third toggle into the upright
      position.

```
PREMISE:   ($AND (SAME CNTXT YES-TRANS)
            (SAME CNTXT NIM-RECEIVE BLINKING)
            (SAME CNTXT NIM-GOOD STEADY)
            (SAME CNTXT NIM-ONLINE-STATUS NIM-OFFLINE))
ACTION:   (DO-ALL
            (CONCLUDE CNTXT SOLVE-IT "The NIM is offline. Put
            it back online by flipping the third toggle into
            the upright position." TALLY 1000))
```

(Continued)

Figure 14.1 (Continued)

RULE027 [COMMUNICATIONSRULES]

If 1) problem is in the machine-room, and
  2) checks to see if the NIM is receiving the signal or
     not is BLINKING, and
  3) checks the NIM GOOD light is STEADY, and
  4) checks to see if the NIM is online is NIM-ONLINE,
Then it is definite (100%) that ok so far.

PREMISE: ($AND (SAME CNTXT YES-TRANS)
              (SAME CNTXT NIM-RECEIVE BLINKING)
              (SAME CNTXT NIM-GOOD STEADY)
              (SAME CNTXT NIM-ONLINE-STATUS NIM-ONLINE))
ACTION: (DO-ALL (CONCLUDE CNTXT NIM-2 YES TALLY 1000))

RULE028 [COMMUNICATIONSRULES]

If 1) ok so far, and
  2) check the NIM communication lines is
     NIM-COMM-DISCONNECTED,
Then it is definite (100%) that the following is one of
     recommended action : The NIM communication cables are not
     attached properly. Reconnect them.

PREMISE: ($AND (SAME CNTXT NIM-2)
              (SAME CNTXT NIM-COMM NIM-COMM-DISCONNECTED))
ACTION: (DO-ALL
              (CONCLUDE CNTXT SOLVE-IT "The NIM communication
              cables are not attached properly. Reconnect
              them." TALLY 1000))

RULE029 [COMMUNICATIONSRULES]

If 1) ok so far, and
  2) check the NIM communication lines is
     NIM-COMM-CONNECTED, and
  3) perform diagnostics on the NIMbox is TEST-FAIL,
Then it is definite (100%) that the following is one of
     recommended action : There is probably a problem with the
     NIM. You may want to replace it.

PREMISE: ($AND (SAME CNTXT NIM-2)
              (SAME CNTXT NIM-COMM NIM-COMM-CONNECTED)
              (SAME CNTXT DIAGNOSTICS-NIM TEST-FAIL))

Figure 14.1   (Continued)

ACTION: (DO-ALL
              (CONCLUDE CNTXT SOLVE-IT "There is probably a
              problem with the NIM. You may want to replace it."
              TALLY 1000))

RULE030 [COMMUNICATIONSRULES]

If 1) ok so far, and
   2) check the NIM communication lines is
      NIM-COMM-CONNECTED, and
   3) perform diagnostics on the NIMbox is TEST-OK,
Then 1) it is definite (100%) that the following is one of
        recommended action : You need the help of a human
        expert. Call Mr. Smith at 555-1111.
        Print out this report for reference by pressing the
        ALT and PRINT keys, and
     2) DOGRAPH PROB-3.

PREMISE: ($AND (SAME CNTXT NIM-2)
              (SAME CNTXT NIM-COMM NIM-COMM-CONNECTED)
              (SAME CNTXT DIAGNOSTICS-NIM TEST-OK))
ACTION: (DO-ALL
              (CONCLUDE CNTXT SOLVE-IT "You need the help of a
              human expert. Call Mr. Smith at 555-1111.
              Print out this report for reference by pressing
              the ALT and PRINT keys." TALLY 1000)
              (DOGRAPH "PROB-3"))

RULE031 [COMMUNICATIONSRULES]

If 1) problem is in the machine-room, and
   2) checks to see if the NIM is receiving the signal or
      not is OFF,
Then it is definite (100%) that PASTE.

PREMISE: ($AND (SAME CNTXT YES-TRANS)
              (SAME CNTXT NIM-RECEIVE OFF))
ACTION: (DO-ALL (CONCLUDE CNTXT NIM-10 YES TALLY 1000))

RULE032 [COMMUNICATIONSRULES]

If merger between two paths,
Then it is definite (100%) that PASTE.

(Continued)

Figure 14.1 *(Continued)*

PREMISE: ($AND (SAME CNTXT NIM))
ACTION: (DO-ALL (CONCLUDE CNTXT NIM-10 YES TALLY 1000))

RULE033 [COMMUNICATIONSRULES/antecedent]

If there is an determines if the HA is receiving the signal,
Then GCLEAR 0.

PREMISE: ($AND (ONCEKNOWN CNTXT HA-TRANS))
ACTION: (DO-ALL (GCLEAR 0))
ANTECEDENT: T

RULE034 [COMMUNICATIONSRULES/antecedent]

If there is an status of the HS,
Then 1) GCLEAR 0, and
      2) BLINK 138 204 208 170 204 240 1 1.

PREMISE: ($AND (ONCEKNOWN CNTXT HA-GOOD))
ACTION: (DO-ALL (GCLEAR 0
                (BLINK 138 204 208 170 204 240 1 1))
ANTECEDENT: T

RULE035 [COMMUNICATIONSRULES/antecedent]

If there is an checking the power connections,
Then GCLEAR 0.

PREMISE: ($AND (ONCEKNOWN CNTXT CHECK-POWER))
ACTION: (DO-ALL (GCLEAR 0))
ANTECEDENT: T

RULE036 [COMMUNICATIONSRULES/antecedent]

If there is an determines if the HA is online or offline,
Then GCLEAR 0.

PREMISE: ($AND (ONCEKNOWN CNTXT HA-ONLINE))
ACTION: (DO-ALL (GCLEAR 0))
ANTECEDENT: T

RULE037 [COMMUNICATIONSRULES/antecedent]

If there is an diagnostics on the Host Adapter,
Then GCLEAR 0.

Figure 14.1   (Continued)

PREMISE: ($AND (ONCEKNOWN CNTXT RUN-DIAG))
ACTION: (DO-ALL (GCLEAR 0))
ANTECEDENT: T

RULE038 [COMMUNICATIONSRULES/antecedent]

If there is an checks the communication cables,
Then GCLEAR 0.

PREMISE: ($AND (ONCEKNOWN CNTXT CHECK-COMM))
ACTION: (DO-ALL (GCLEAR 0))
ANTECEDENT: T

RULE039 [COMMUNICATIONSRULES/antecedent]

If there is an checking to see if the PDP connections are
   secure,
Then GCLEAR 0.

PREMISE: ($AND (ONCEKNOWN CNTXT CHECK-PDP-COMM))
ACTION: (DO-ALL (GCLEAR 0))
ANTECEDENT: T

RULE040 [COMMUNICATIONSRULES/antecedent]

If there is an checks to see if the TI530 is functioning or
   not,
Then GCLEAR 0.

PREMISE: ($AND (ONCEKNOWN CNTXT PC-STATUS))
ACTION: (DO-ALL (GCLEAR 0))
ANTECEDENT: T

RULE041 [COMMUNICATIONSRULES/antecedent]

If there is an checks to see if the NIM is receiving the
   signal or not,
Then 1) GCLEAR 0, and
     2) BLINK 138 204 208 170 204 240 1 1.

PREMISE: ($AND (ONCEKNOWN CNTXT NIM-RECEIVE))
ACTION: (DO-ALL (GCLEAR 0)
            (BLINK 138 204 208 170 204 240 1 1))
ANTECEDENT: T

(Continued)

Figure 14.1 (Continued)

RULE042 [COMMUNICATIONSRULES/antecedent]

If there is an checks to see if the NIM is secure in the I/O
  rack of the 530,
Then GCLEAR 0.

PREMISE: ($AND (ONCEKNOWN CNTXT CHECK-NIM-INSERT))
ACTION: (DO-ALL (GCLEAR 0))
ANTECEDENT: T

RULE043 [COMMUNICATIONSRULES/antecedent]

If there is an perform diagnostics on the NIMbox,
then GCLEAR 0.

PREMISE: ($AND (ONCEKNOWN CNTXT DIAGNOSTICS-NIM))
ACTION: (DO-ALL (GCLEAR 0))
ANTECEDENT: T

RULE044 [COMMUNICATIONSRULES/antecedent]

If there is an checks the NIM GOOD light,
Then 1) GCLEAR 0, and
     2) BLINK 138 204 208 170 204 240 1 1.

PREMISE: ($AND (ONCEKNOWN CNTXT NIM-GOOD))
ACTION: (DO-ALL (GCLEAR 0)
              (BLINK 138 204 208 170 204 240 1 1))
ANTECEDENT: T

RULE045 [COMMUNICATIONSRULES/antecedent]

If there is an checks to see if the NIM is online,
Then GCLEAR 0.

PREMISE: ($AND (ONCEKNOWN CNTXT NIM-ONLINE-STATUS))
ACTION: (DO-ALL (GCLEAR 0))
ANTECEDENT: T

RULE046 [COMMUNICATIONSRULES/antecedent]

If there is an check the NIM communication lines,
Then GCLEAR 0.

Figure 14.1 *(Continued)*

PREMISE: ($AND (ONCEKNOWN CNTXT NIM-COMM))
ACTION: (DO-ALL (GCLEAR 0))
ANTECEDENT: T

RULE048 [COMMUNICATIONSRULES/antecedent]

If recommended action is,
Then GCLEAR 0.

PREMISE: ($AND (SAME CNTXT SOLVE-IT))
ACTION: (DO-ALL (GCLEAR 0))
ANTECEDENT: T

RULE049 [COMMUNICATIONSRULES/antecedent]

If there is an checks the PDP to see if it is working,
Then GCLEAR 0.

PREMISE: ($AND (ONCEKNOWN CNTXT CHECK-PDP-STATUS))
ACTION: (DO-ALL (GCLEAR 0))
ANTECEDENT: T

RULE050 [COMMUNICATIONSRULES/antecedent]

If there is an this checks to see how many secondaries are
    attached,
Then GCLEAR 0.

PREMISE: ($AND (ONCEKNOWN CNTXT CHECK-SECONDARY))
ACTION: (DO-ALL (GCLEAR 0))
ANTECEDENT: T

RULE051 [COMMUNICATIONSRULES/antecedent]

If there is an checks to see if the POL 530 software is
    running,
Then GCLEAR 0.

PREMISE: ($AND (ONCEKNOWN CNTXT CHECK-POL530))
ACTION: (DO-ALL (GCLEAR 0))
ANTECEDENT: T

(Continued)

Figure 14.1   (Continued)

RULE052 [COMMUNICATIONSRULES]

If 1) no signal to HA, and
  2) status of the HA is BLINKING/OFF, and
  3) checking the power connections is POWER-OK, and
  4) diagnostics on the Host Adapter is OK, and
  5) checks the PDP to see if it is working is ACTIVE, and
  6) this checks to see how many secondaries are attached
    is 1, and
  7) checks to see if the POL530 software is running is
    LONG-RESPONSE, and
  8) checking to see if the PDP connections are secure is
    ATTACHED, and
  9) checks for error message is NO-MSG,
Then 1) it is definite (100%) that the following is one of
      recommended action : You need the help of a human
      expert. Call Mr. Smith at 555-1111.
      Print out this report for reference by pressing the
      ALT and PRINT keys, and
  2) DOGRAPH PROB-4.

PREMISE: ($AND (SAME CNTXT NO-TRANS)
          (SAME CNTXT HA-GOOD BLINKING/OFF)
          (SAME CNTXT CHECK-POWER POWER-OK)
          (SAME CNTXT RUN-DIAG OK)
          (SAME CNTXT CHECK-PDP-STATUS ACTIVE)
          (SAME CNTXT CHECK-SECONDARY 1)
          (SAME CNTXT CHECK-POL530 LONG-RESPONSE)
          (SAME CNTXT CHECK-PDP-COMM ATTACHED)
          (SAME CNTXT CHECK-ERROR-MSG NO-MSG))
ACTION: (DO-ALL
          (CONCLUDE CNTXT SOLVE-IT "You need the help of a
          human expert. Call Mr. Smith at 555-1111.
          Print out this report for reference by pressing
          the ALT and PRINT keys." TALLY 1000)
          (DOGRAPH "PROB-4"))

RULE053 [COMMUNICATIONSRULES]

If 1) problem is in the machine-room, and
  2) checks to see if the NIM is receiving the signal or
    not is BLINKING, and
  3) checks the NIM GOOD light is BLINKING/OFF, and
  4) checks to see if the TI530 is functioning or not is
    ACTIVE, and

Figure 14.1 *(Continued)*

5) checks to see if the NIM is secure in the I/O rack of the 530 is SECURE, and

6) perform diagnostics on the NIMbox is TEST-OK,

Then 1) it is definite (100%) that the following is one of recommended action : You need the help of a human expert. Call Mr. Smith at 555-1111. Print out this report for reference by pressing the ALT and PRINT keys, and

     2) DOGRAPH PROB-2.

PREMISE: ($AND (SAME CNTXT YES-TRANS)
                (SAME CNTXT NIM-RECEIVE BLINKING)
                (SAME CNTXT NIM-GOOD BLINKING/OFF)
                (SAME CNTXT PC-STATUS ACTIVE)
                (SAME CNTXT CHECK-NIM-INSERT SECURE)
                (SAME CNTXT DIAGNOSTICS-NIM TEXT-OK))

ACTION: (DO-ALL
                (CONCLUDE CNTXT SOLVE-IT "You need the help of a human expert. Call Mr. Smith at 555-1111. Print out this report for reference by pressing the ALT and PRINT keys."
                TALLY 1000)
                (DOGRAPH "PROB-2"))

RULE054 [COMMUNICATIONSRULES/antecedent]

If there is an checks for error message,
Then GCLEAR 0.

PREMISE: ($AND (ONCEKNOWN CNTXT CHECK-ERROR-MSG))
ACTION: (DO-ALL (GCLEAR 0))
ANTECEDENT: T

RULE055 [COMMUNICATIONSRULES]

If 1) no signal to HA, and

  2) status of the HA is BLINKING/OFF, and

  3) checking the power connections is POWER-OK, and

  4) ok so far, and

  5) checking to see if the PDP connections are secure is ATTACHED, and

  6) checks for error message is MSG,

(Continued)

Figure 14.1 (*Continued*)

Then 1) it is definite (100%) that the following is one of
recommended action : Refer to the Reference Guide for
the meaning of the error message. Call Mr. Smith
555-1111 for help and print this report using the ALT
and PRINT keys, and
2) DOGRAPH PROB-MG4.

PREMISE: ($AND (SAME CNTXT NO-TRANS)
            (SAME CNTXT HA-GOOD BLINKING/OFF)
            (SAME CNTXT CHECK-POWER POWER-OK)
            (SAME CNTXT OK-3)
            (SAME CNTXT CHECK-PDP-COMM ATTACHED)
            (SAME CNTXT CHECK-ERROR-MSG MSG))

ACTION: (DO-ALL
         (CONCLUDE CNTXT SOLVE-IT "Refer to the Reference
Guide for the meaning of the error message. Call Mr.
Smith at 555-1111 for help and print this report using the
ALT and PRINT keys." TALLY 1000) (DOGRAPH "PROB-
MG4"))

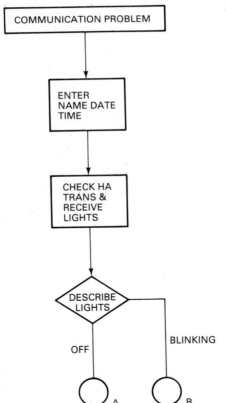

Figure 14.2 Logic tree

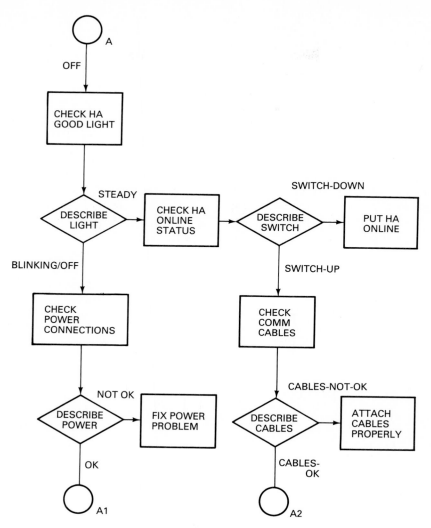

Figure 14.2   (Continued)

(Continued)

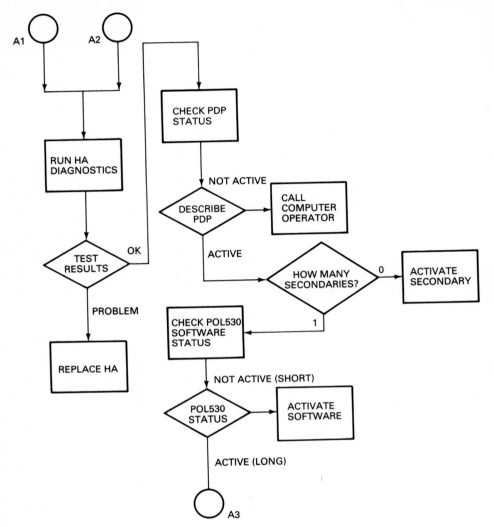

Figure 14.2 (Continued)

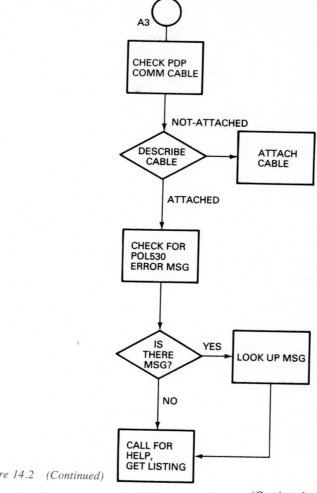

Figure 14.2 *(Continued)*

(Continued)

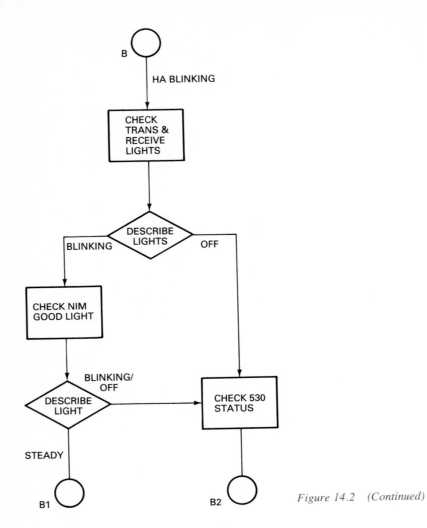

B — HA BLINKING

CHECK
TRANS &
RECEIVE
LIGHTS

DESCRIBE
LIGHTS

BLINKING

OFF

CHECK NIM
GOOD LIGHT

BLINKING/
OFF

DESCRIBE
LIGHT

CHECK 530
STATUS

STEADY

B1

B2

Figure 14.2   (Continued)

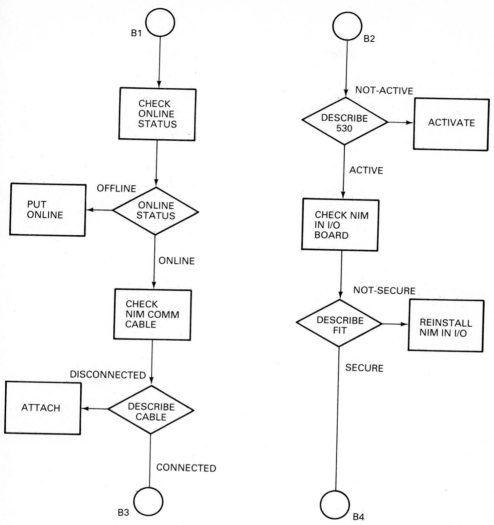

Figure 14.2   (Continued)

(Continued)

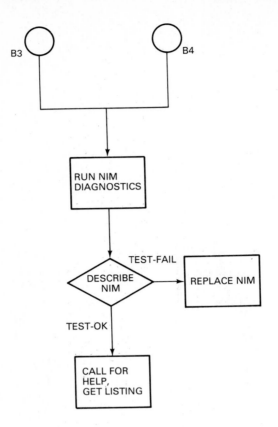

Figure 14.2   (Continued)

When a problem with the FMS cell communications between the PDP-11/24 and the TI530 is announced by a POL530 software error message (see Figure 14.3) or is observed by an FMS operator, the operator will run the FMS Diagnostic System. The operator will be asked questions pertaining to the state of various elements in the communications network. Each question is based on answers to previous questions and the communications expertise stored in the knowledge base. The operator is provided with online help information and is shown color graphics of the communications equipment to clarify the questions and help the operator choose the appropriate answers. The system will prompt the user for information regarding the current status of the cell and its components. From the responses, it attempts to determine what the problem is. The user will sometimes have to go back to the computer room or out into the shop to obtain the necessary information. When the system has collected enough information to come to a conclusion, it will inform the user of the cause of the communications breakdown and will make recommendations about how to correct the problem. In cases where the system cannot reach a conclusion, the

Figure 14.3 POL530 software error messages

FACILITY 1,<TIWAY> ; ASCII level errors

These errors are detected by TIWAY subroutines or other routines. They generally represent levels of inconsistent segments.

MESSAGE 1,	<No such function for disputed argument>
MESSAGE 2,	<Not enough arguments for specified function>
MESSAGE 3,	<Too many arguments for specified function>
MESSAGE 4,	<Wrong INITes state for specified function>
MESSAGE 5,	<Wrong length response for queue>
MESSAGE 6,	<Highway number out of range>
MESSAGE 7,	<Bad ASCII tag specification>
MESSAGE 8,	<Tag not found>
MESSAGE 9,	<User supplied buffer too small for request>
MESSAGE 10,	<Unexpected response length from NIM>
MESSAGE 11,	<Invalid CIM memory or image register data type>
MESSAGE 12,	<Illegal number of blocks defined>
MESSAGE 13,	<Illegal data type TTI, M or C>

FACILITY 2,<NETEXCEPT> ; Host adapter - Return exception

These errors are detected by the host adapter and pertain to the TIWAY communications.

MESSAGE 0,	<Undefined network problem>
MESSAGE 1,	<Lost DCD on receive>
MESSAGE 2,	<Lost CTS on receive>
MESSAGE 3,	<Secondary timeout>
MESSAGE 4,	<Secondary will not correct to return>
MESSAGE 5,	<Miscellaneous secondary protocol errors>
MESSAGE 6,	<FRMP received>
MESSAGE 7,	<REJ received>
MESSAGE 8,	<Secondary in RMF state longer than 2 seconds>
MESSAGE 9,	<Secondary Send and/or Receive count test>
MESSAGE 10,	<Bad CRT or receive from secondary>
MESSAGE 11,	<Secondary starts frame>
MESSAGE 12,	<Frame too long>
MESSAGE 13,	<Frames too short>
MESSAGE 14,	<Wrong secondary responded>

FACILITY 3,<INTERMEXCP> ; Host adapter exception

These errors are errors detected by the host adapter and pertain to inconsistencies or other internal errors.

MESSAGE 0,	<Undefined adapter problem>
MESSAGE 1,	<Memory management error>
MESSAGE 2,	<Receiver overrun>

(Continued)

Figure 14.3 *(Continued)*

MESSAGE 3,   \<Transmitter overrun>
MESSAGE 4,   \<No network media card installed>
MESSAGE 5,   \<System stack management error>
MESSAGE 6,   \<System queue management error>

FACILITY 4,\<HOSTEXCEPT> ; Host adapter - Host exception

These errors are detected by the host adapter and pertain to host communications errors or errors detected while trying to process a host adapter case code command.

MESSAGE 0,   \<Problem undefined on host>
MESSAGE 1,   \<Lost DCD on host receive>
MESSAGE 2,   \<Lost CTS on transmit to host>
MESSAGE 3,   \<Communications timed out>
MESSAGE 4,   \<Unrecognized command code>
MESSAGE 5,   \<Invalid field received with command code>
MESSAGE 6,   \<Host frame of excessive length>
MESSAGE 7,   \<Host frame too short>
MESSAGE 8,   \<Secondary not connected to network>
MESSAGE 9,   \<Missed start of message delimiter>
MESSAGE 10,   \<Missed end of message delimiter>
MESSAGE 11,   \<Message length count error>
MESSAGE 12,   \<Message checksum bad>

FACILITY 5,\<PRIMITIVE> ; TIWAY1 primitive errors

These errors are detected by KIM-based secondaries while processing a KIM primitive.

MESSAGE 0,   \<Primitive is not implemented>
MESSAGE 1,   \<Data type (TT) is not defined on device>
MESSAGE 2,   \<Data element location (TT) is out of range>
MESSAGE 3,   \<Primitive has excess data unit bytes>
MESSAGE 4,   \<Primitive has insufficient data unit bytes>
MESSAGE 5,   \<Number of bytes rcvd does not match length>
MESSAGE 6,   \<Device in wrong mode for primitive execution>
MESSAGE 7,   \<User program has communications disabled>
MESSAGE 8,   \<Written data type location (TT) did not verify>
MESSAGE 9,   \<Data type location (TT) is write protected>
MESSAGE 10,   \<Device fails to respond>
MESSAGE 11,   \<Primitive aborted due to a fatal error in device>
MESSAGE 12,   \<Invalid data type value due to primitive execution>
MESSAGE 13,   \<Error was encountered while executing primitive>
MESSAGE 14,   \<Primitive not valid for specified data type>
MESSAGE 15,   \<Data pattern requested was not found>
MESSAGE 16,   \<Number of locations exceeds the maximum
                           allowed>

Figure 14.3 *(Continued)*

MESSAGE 17,   <Daq block number exceeds the maximum allowed>

MESSAGE 18,   <The block number requested has not been defined>

MESSAGE 19,   <Number of data bytes in requested block too big>

MESSAGE 20,   <Report by condition data type location too big>

MESSAGE 21,   <Primitive not allowed in local mode>

MESSAGE 22,   <Data type not allowed in specified device>

MESSAGE 23,   <Error in attached device communications>

MESSAGE 24,   <Data type not implemented in KIM, is in device>

MESSAGE 25,   <Data element location out of range>

MESSAGE 26,   <Attached device communications is not established>

MESSAGE 27,   <Store and forward buffer full, message discarded>

MESSAGE 28,   <Data element field improperly formatted>

MESSAGE 29,   <Number of locations to access is zero>

MESSAGE 221,   <Attached device exception not identified>

FACILITY 6,<$DSW> ; System service errors ($DSW)

These are directive errors detected while issuing system service directives. The error messages are those reported by the $DSW after an attempt to process the request.

.RADIX 8   ; System reports errors in octal

MESSAGE 377,   <Insufficient dynamic storage>

MESSAGE 373,   <Unassigned LUX>

MESSAGE 372,   <Driver not resident>

MESSAGE 360,   <Privilege violation>

MESSAGE 257,   <Illegal mapping specified>

MESSAGE 255,   <Window has I/O in progress>

MESSAGE 254,   <Alignment error>

MESSAGE 253,   <Address window allocation overflow>

MESSAGE 252,   <Invalid region ID>

MESSAGE 251,   <Invalid address window ID>

MESSAGE 250,   <Invalid TI parameter>

MESSAGE 244,   <Invalid device or unit>

MESSAGE 242,   <Partition/region not in system>

MESSAGE 240,   <Invalid LUX>

MESSAGE 237,   <Invalid event flag>

MESSAGE 236,   <Part of DPB out of users space>

MESSAGE 235,   <DIO or DPB size invalid>

FACILITY 7,<I/O STATUS> ; I/O status errors (HADRU detected)

These are I/O errors, reported by the I/O status block, that are detected either by the SDRQIO directive processing routine for QIO system services or by HADRU, the host adapter device driver. They represent

(Continued)

403

Figure 14.3 *(Continued)*

I/O errors pertaining to the general I/O request or link-level errors detected by the device driver.

.RADIX 8	; QIO reports errors in octal
MESSAGE 377,	\<Bad parameters\>
MESSAGE 376,	\<Invalid function code\>
MESSAGE 375,	\<Device not ready\>
MESSAGE 374,	\<Parity error on device\>
MESSAGE 373,	\<Hardware option not present\>
MESSAGE 372,	\<Illegal user buffer\>
MESSAGE 371,	\<Device not attached\>
MESSAGE 370,	\<Device already attached\>
MESSAGE 367,	\<Device not attachable\>
MESSAGE 366,	\<End-of-file detected\>
MESSAGE 363,	\<Data overrun\>
MESSAGE 361,	\<Request terminated\>
MESSAGE 360,	\<Privilege violation\>
MESSAGE 277,	\<Device offline\>
MESSAGE 276,	\<Block check, CRC, or framing error\>
MESSAGE 275,	\<Device online\>
MESSAGE 241,	\<Timeout on request\>

FACILITY 8,\<CIM EXCEPT\> ; CIM functional command errors

These are errors reported by CIM-based secondaries while processing a CIM functional command.

.RADIX 10	; CIM errors are in decimal
MESSAGE 80,	\<Invalid memory specified\>
MESSAGE 81,	\<Invalid loop number specified\>
MESSAGE 82,	\<Loop not defined\>
MESSAGE 83,	\<Error number greater than 46 in clearing error number\>
MESSAGE 84,	\<Invalid command code or illegal CCU task code\>
MESSAGE 85,	\<Bad block table\>
MESSAGE 86,	\<Ignore this message\>
MESSAGE 87,	\<N not specified or bad data for READ/WRITE Memory/IR\>
MESSAGE 88,	\<Ignore this message\>
MESSAGE 89,	\<Read after write check error\>
MESSAGE 90,	\<Download error - invalid use, illegal character, not 8 char\>
MESSAGE 91,	\<Upload error - invalid use, illegal character, not 8 char\>
MESSAGE 92,	\<Attempt to send less than 2 or over 32 characters to CCU\>
MESSAGE 93,	\<Not used\>

Figure 14.3 (Continued)

MESSAGE 94,	\<Wrong amount of data with specified command function\>
MESSAGE 95,	\<CCU communications error\>
MESSAGE 96,	\<Data link fatal error\>
MESSAGE 100,	\<Not enough data in download, expected 8 + 512 characters\>
MESSAGE 101,	\<L or C in ROM — attempt to download to ROM\>
MESSAGE 102,	\<CCU in run state, invalid for download\>
MESSAGE 103,	\<Invalid download sequence\>
MESSAGE 104,	\<MM is incorrect for downloading\>
MESSAGE 105,	\<Non-ASCII character in input buffer\>
MESSAGE 106,	\<Download active, other commands invalid\>
MESSAGE 108,	\<Upload active, other commands invalid\>
MESSAGE 109,	\<Invalid upload sequence\>
MESSAGE 110,	\<MM is incorrect for upload\>
MESSAGE 111,	\<CCU put non-ASCII characters in output buffer\>

results of all the problem determination activities performed are presented and can be printed. The printed report can be taken to a human expert for consultation.

As characteristics of the FMS cell communications are studied further, rules can be easily edited or added to the knowledge-base to increase its effectiveness and broaden its scope of expertise. The FMS Diagnostic System is a prototype and is currently being tested and, when appropriate, expanded on the shop floor at TI's Trinity Mills facility.

The FMS Communications Diagnostic System will decrease downtime by allowing the FMS operators quickly to identify and solve communications problems without requiring an expert to be on hand at all times. The system provides diagnostics on the communications link between the PDP-11/24 and the TI530. The communications involves five components, the PDP-11/24, the TI530, a TIWAY local area network, a host adapter, and a network interface module.

The PDP-11/24 is a 16-bit minicomputer. It has 512K words of memory and two 10-megabyte cartridge disk drives. It acts as a supervisor that sends instructions to the TI530 Programmable Controller. The PDP-11/24 is located in a computer room. The TI530 is located in the FMS manufacturing cell. The TI530 monitors the state of the equipment in the cell and relays this information to the PDP-11/24.

The programs to control the robots and the controllable machine tools are stored in the PDP-11/24 host computer. The PDP-11/24 determines the tasks to be performed. The microprocessor-based TI530 implements the tasks. The PDP-11/24 communicates with the TI530 over the Texas Instruments TIWAY local area network (LAN). This LAN was developed by Texas Instruments for industrial applications like this FMS application. A host adapter (HA) provides the interface between the PDP-11/24 host computer and the LAN. The host adapter provides the necessary services to allow the host computer to communicate over the TIWAY network. A network interface module (NIM) provides the interface between the TI530 and the LAN. The NIM translates the incoming TIWAY signal into standard command codes used by the programmable controller. The NIM handles all the data communication exchanges between the programmable controller and the TIWAY network.

The PDP-11/24 transmits instructions to the TI530. However, the two machines use different protocols. The PDP-11/24 communicates mostly by sending messages, while the TI530 communicates by toggling flags. An interpreter is therefore needed to translate between the two protocols. The POL530 software provides the means to do this. POL530 stands for "poll the 530." The POL530 software is written in Pascal and resides on the PDP-11/24. When an event occurs in the manufacturing cell, flags in the TI530's memory change. The POL530 software senses the change and reports what is happening. New instructions are developed by other software modules in the PDP-11/24 in the form of intertask messages. These messages are handed off to the POL530 software module, which translates this information and sends it to the TI530 programmable controller. When the POL530 software senses problems in the operation, it provides an error message, which is presented on the computer operator console. Figure 14.3 lists the error messages that the POL530 software can present.

A RUN EXAMPLE   To run the system, insert an FMS diskette in disk drive A and type "COMMLINK" in response to the DOS "A>" prompt. A screen message declaring that IQLISP is loading will appear and stay on the screen for approximately 20 seconds. This will be followed by a screen message declaring that Personal Consultant is loading. The FMS diagnostic expert system title screen will then appear approximately 20 seconds later. Replace the FMS diskette in drive A with the FMS graphics diskette. To continue, press any key on the keyboard.

During consultations, there will be times when the message "Memory Recovery in Progress" appears on the screen and "busy" appears blinking at the bottom of the screen. This means that the system is doing a LISP garbage collection—a memory reallocation. The procedure takes about 40 seconds. This procedure will not cause the system to lose any active data. When the procedure is completed, the system will continue from where it was interrupted.

Once Personal Consultant is loaded and after the title screen disappears, the screen shown in Figure 14.4 appears.

This expert system was developed with graphics-generated pictures to provide the user with a better understanding of the procedure to be followed. This first picture is an overall look at part of the manufacturing cell. It shows the

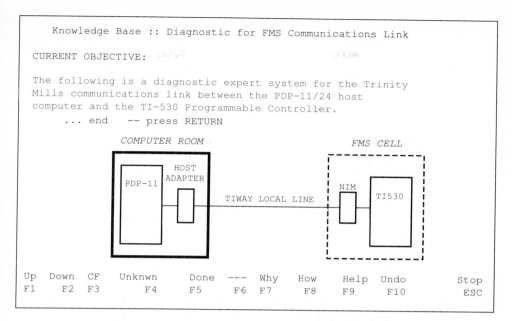

```
    Knowledge Base :: Diagnostic for FMS Communications Link

 CURRENT OBJECTIVE:

 The following is a diagnostic expert system for the Trinity
 Mills communications link between the PDP-11/24 host
 computer and the TI-530 Programmable Controller.
    ... end   -- press RETURN
```

Figure 14.4 FMS Expert System Example Run (1 of 10)

components in the computer room and the machine room (the FMS cell) with which the FMS expert system is concerned.

At the bottom of the screen is a list of the functions available to the user. The F7 function key can be pressed to obtain information on why a specific question is being asked. The F8 key will present information on how a particular result was developed. For the FMS diagnostic system, all of the responses given will be inferred from information given by a user (with 100 percent certainty). If the F8 key is pressed after the F7 key, a list of the parameters (values being searched for) will appear. Selection of any of these parameters is possible by positioning the cursor over the parameter name by means of the cursor control keys and pressing the RETURN key. The messages that appear for each parameter will tell the user how the system derived its value. The F9 key will provide more information about the question. The F10 key allows the user to go back a step. To stop the program, press the ESC key.

By hitting the RETURN key, the next screen will appear and will prompt for the user's name, the date, and the current time. After answering this query, hit the RETURN key again, and the screen in Figure 14.5 will appear.

By hitting the F9 key, additional information about the question can be obtained. The following HELP screen in Figure 14.6 will appear to give additional, more detailed information. The screen will flash once to alert you that you are looking at a HELP screen.

Choose OFF by using the arrow keys to place the cursor over the word

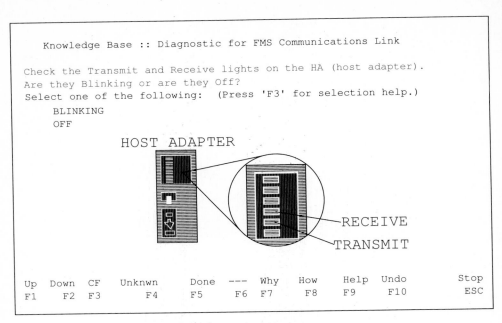

```
    Knowledge Base :: Diagnostic for FMS Communications Link

Check the Transmit and Receive lights on the HA (host adapter).
Are they Blinking or are they Off?
Select one of the following:  (Press 'F3' for selection help.)
      BLINKING
      OFF

              HOST ADAPTER


                                                 ──RECEIVE
                                                 ─TRANSMIT



Up   Down  CF   Unknwn      Done   ───  Why   How    Help  Undo          Stop
F1     F2  F3        F4      F5    F6   F7    F8     F9    F10           ESC
```

Figure 14.5   FMS Expert System Example Run (2 of 10)

```
       Knowledge Base :: Diagnostic for FMS Communications Link

  The Transmit and Receive lights are located on the front
  panel of the HA box, and are the fourth and fifth lights
  down on the box.
  Select one of the following:  (Press 'F3' for selection help.)
          BLINKING
          OFF




















Up   Down  CF   Unknwn      Done   ───  Why   How    Help  Undo          Stop
F1     F2  F3        F4      F5    F6   F7    F8     F9    F10           ESC
```

Figure 14.6   FMS Expert System Example Run (3 of 10)

and hitting RETURN. The system now comes up with an intermediate conclusion that indicates that the problem is probably in the computer room (see Figure 14.7). After reading the intermediate conclusion, hitting the RETURN key brings up the next screen (Figure 14.8) with a new question. The new question considers the status of the GOOD light on the host adapter. By hitting the F7 key, the WHY function is activated (Figure 14.9a).

This screen provides the premise (the IF part of the rule) and the action (the THEN part of the rule) used to diagnose the problem for this particular situation. The premise specifies that this question is necessary to determine if the action specified in the rule is appropriate to this situation. Since the rule is too large to be displayed on the screen altogether, you must hit the RETURN key to view the part of the rule that is not shown at first (Figure 14.9b).

Hitting the RETURN key once after looking at the rule will again present the current question asking the status of the host adapter. Answering STEADY to the current question will bring up the display in Figure 14.10.

If you make an error and want to go back, hitting the F10 function key will send the system back to the previous step and will erase the previous answer. The previous screen will reappear. Selecting the "BLINKING/OFF" response will cause the screen in Figure 14.11 to appear.

Select the POWER-NOT-OK answer to the next question, which asks about the power connections. The screen in Figure 14.12 will appear.

```
     Knowledge Base :: Diagnostic for FMS Communications Link

  The Host Adapter is not receiving any signal so the problem is
  probably in the computer room.
       ... end    -- press RETURN




















  Up   Down   CF    Unknwn     Done   ---   Why   How   Help   Undo          Stop
  F1     F2   F3       F4      F5     F6    F7    F8    F9    F10           ESC
```

Figure 14.7   FMS Expert System Example Run (4 of 10)

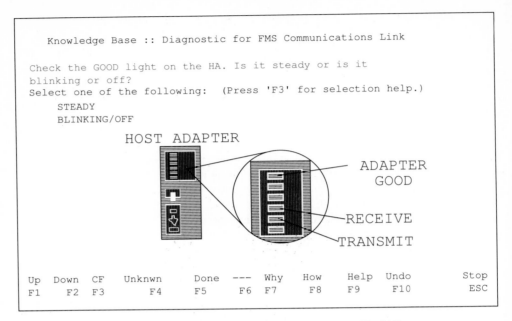

Knowledge Base :: Diagnostic for FMS Communications Link

Check the GOOD light on the HA. Is it steady or is it
blinking or off?
Select one of the following: (Press 'F3' for selection help.)
    STEADY
    BLINKING/OFF

HOST ADAPTER

ADAPTER
GOOD

RECEIVE

TRANSMIT

| Up | Down | CF | Unknwn | | Done | --- | Why | How | Help | Undo | | Stop |
| F1 | F2 | F3 | F4 | | F5 | F6 | F7 | F8 | F9 | F10 | | ESC |

Figure 14.8   FMS Expert System Example Run (5 of 10)

The system believes this is the solution to the problem at hand. After reading the recommendation, press the RETURN key. The screen in Figure 14.13 appears.

You are given the opportunity to save the recommendation for future reference (New file name). You can place the recommendation into a file (New file name), print the recommendation (Printer), or exit the program (Exit) without saving the recommendation. Choosing one of these options will activate the system, which will then present the activity menu. You can start another session (GO) or terminate the consultation (QUIT). Selecting QUIT exits the program and returns the computer to DOS.

CONCLUDING REMARKS

The FMS Communications Diagnostic System is a small yet helpful expert system that assists FMS operators in the identification and correction of certain computer communications problems in a manufacturing cell. This system ties together important information that is usually obtained from technical manuals and human experts. The system is easier to use than the technical manuals. This is particularly true with the graphics support. The system is always available to the manufacturing people, whereas the human experts often are not.

This system includes two kinds of rules: diagnostic rules, such as rules 5 and 8, and prescription rules, such as rules 10 and 11.

```
  Knowledge Base :: Diagnostic for FMS Communications Link

Check the GOOD light on the HA. Is it steady or is it
blinking or off?
Why this question is needed:

Status of the HA is needed to determine recommended action

RULE014
If 1) no signal to HA, and
   2) status of the HA is STEADY, and
   3) determines if the HA is online or offline is SWITCH-UP, and
   4) checks the communication cables is COMM-OK, and
   5) diagnostics on the Host Adapter is OK, and
   6) checks the PDP to see if it is working is ACTIVE, and
   7) this checks to see how many secondaries are attached is 1, and
   8) checks to see if the POL530 software is running is
      LONG-RESPONSE, and
            more ...   -- press RETURN

Up   Down  CF   Unknwn     Done   ---  Why   How    Help  Undo         Stop
F1     F2  F3       F4      F5    F6  F7    F8     F9    F10          ESC
```
(a)

```
   Knowledge Base :: Diagnostic for FMS Communications Link

Check the GOOD light on the HA. Is it steady or is it
blinking or off?
Why this question is needed:
   5) diagnostics on the Host Adapter is OK, and
   6) checks the PDP to see if it is working is ACTIVE, and
   7) this checks to see how many secondaries are attached is 1, and
   8) checks to see if the POL530 software is running is
      LONG-RESPONSE, and
   9) checking to see if the PDP connections are secure is ATTACHED, and
   10) checks for error message is NO-MSG,
Then 1) it is definite (100%) that the following is one of
        recommended action : You need the help of a human expert.
        Call Bill Rogers for help. Print out this report for
        reference by pressing the ALT PRINT keys, and
     2) DOGRAPH PROB-5.
     ... end    -- press RETURN

Up   Down  CF   Unknwn     Done   ---  Why   How    Help  Undo         Stop
F1     F2  F3       F4      F5    F6  F7    F8     F9    F10          ESC
```
(b)

Figure 14.9   FMS Expert System Example Run (6 of 10)

411

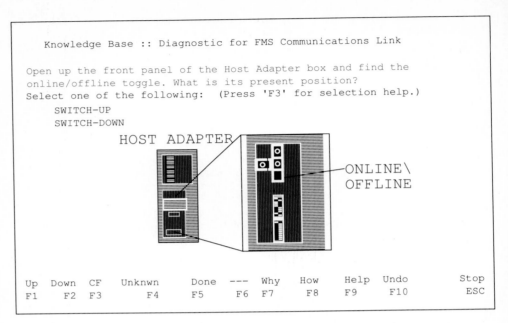

Figure 14.10   FMS Expert System Example Run (7 of 10)

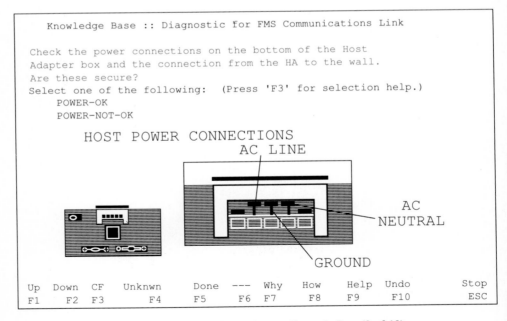

Figure 14.11   FMS Expert System Example Run (8 of 10)

```
Knowledge Base :: Diagnostic for FMS Communications Link

Recommended action is as follows: Reattach the Host Adapter
Power connections. You may also want to check the wall power
connection with a device you know is working.

   ... end   --  press RETURN




Up  Down  CF   Unknwn      Done   ---  Why   How    Help  Undo          Stop
F1    F2  F3        F4      F5    F6  F7     F8     F9    F10           ESC
```

Figure 14.12   FMS Expert System Example Run (9 of 10)

```
    Knowledge Base :: Diagnostic for FMS Communications Link

  Save Recommendations and Rationale (extension .REC assumed):

  Select one of the following:
          Exit
          Printer
          New file name




Up  Down  CF   Unknwn      Done   ---  Why   How    Help  Undo          Stop
F1    F2  F3        F4      F5    F6  F7     F8     F9    F10           ESC
```

Figure 14.13   FMS Expert System Example Run (10 of 10)

This expert diagnostic system is very small; 55 rules make up its entire knowledge-base. Yet notice that the material presented in Figures 14.1 and 14.2 is rather bulky. Imagine a similar but bigger knowledge-base. The task of managing the rules and the logic will quickly become overwhelming if performed manually. This small system well illustrates the need for automated knowledge engineering tools like knowledge editors, logic and network diagrammers, and knowledge consistency checkers.

This system illustrates that relatively small expert systems that run on microcomputer systems can be useful and do have their place in industry.

Small expert systems like this one will most likely become commonplace in the next few years. These systems will have new names, such as technician systems, training systems, or monitoring systems. Their artificial intelligence foundations will be played down and their utility and cost effectiveness will be played up.

15 HOW TO SELECT THE RIGHT TOOLS

In selecting the right tools with which to develop expert systems, three main concepts should be considered. The first has to do with the subject domain requirements versus the capabilities of expert system construction tools. The expert system tools should provide the requisite knowledge representation, reasoning strategies, and tool functionality that is required for a particular problem to be codified and supported by an expert system. The second concept is interoperability. The selected tools should be able to operate with other development tools like graphics packages. The tools should also assist in the construction of an expert system that will interoperate with other automated systems (such as database management systems). The third concept is selection criteria. Today many expert system building tools are available. To pick the most effective tools for a particular project for an organization, the person in charge of selecting them should draw up a list of selection criteria. This list should help in the identification of tools that best fit the needs of the particular project and organization. The expert system building tools on the market should be evaluated against this list of selection criteria.

KNOWLEDGE REPRESENTATIONS AND REASONING STRATEGIES

The requirements of a particular problem will dictate what knowledge representation and reasoning strategy or inferencing scheme should be used to support a particular problem. Today, there are two available techniques for choosing the most appropriate knowledge representation and reasoning strategy schemes. The first is to use schemes that have been used for a similar project in the past. The second technique is trial and error, whereby more than one of each scheme is tried against a particular problem.

Where experimentation is not desired, adopting schemes that have been used in the past is the dominant technique for selecting expert system building tools. Let us look at some examples of expert systems that have been built and then look at the knowledge representation and reasoning strategy schemes that were used in the development of these systems.

The expert system XCON from the Digital Equipment Corporation configures DEC minicomputers. The system matches up DEC minicomputers with specific customer requirements. XCON accepts inputs on subcomponents a customer would like and provides as output a fully configured DEC minicomputer that will support that customer's requirements. It is an expert configuration system. XCON uses the *rule knowledge representation* scheme and the *forward-chaining* reasoning strategy or inferencing scheme.

MYCIN accepts information about the medical history of a patient and provides the system user, a doctor, with a diagnosis of the patient's problem and makes recommendations. It is a medical diagnosis and prescription expert system. It uses the *rule knowledge representation* scheme and the *backward-chaining* reasoning strategy.

The Ventilator Manager expert system was designed to monitor and interpret real-time data. This expert system is used specifically for the interpretation of the clinical significance of data from a monitoring system for patient breathing. Knowledge representation is *rule-based;* the reasoning strategy includes an *event-driven control scheme* and an *exhaustive-search* algorithm.

The EL expert system was developed to analyze the steady state of resistor-diode-transistor circuits to determine voltages and currents. Its knowledge representation is *rule-based,* and its reasoning strategy is predominantly *forward chaining* with some *backward-chaining* support.

General Electric developed a system known as CATS-1. It is an expert system to assist maintenance personnel with the maintenance of diesel-electric locomotives. This expert maintenance system uses the *rule knowledge representation* scheme. The reasoning strategy is a *hybrid forward- and backward-chaining* inference strategy. Backward chaining is used predominantly for troubleshooting tasks, and forward chaining is used for the help facility provided to the maintenance staff.

The French gas and petrochemical company known as ELF had an expert system developed for the purpose of diagnosing drilling problems, particularly in the environment of offshore drilling rigs. This expert diagnosis system accepts information about situations where the drill is stuck in the well and drilling has stopped. The Drilling Advisor expert system diagnoses the situation and suggests solutions. It also tells how to avoid the same situation in the future. This expert system is *rule-based* and uses the *backward-chaining* reasoning strategy.

The Tele-Fincor-Motor expert system was developed for Baker Brothers/Systems. This expert system is used to diagnose problems with the hoist movement control of a plating line. The system asks for the facts of a particular problem situation, infers and explains the possible problem, and recommends action to be taken. This expert system uses the *rule knowledge representation* scheme and the *backward-chaining* reasoning strategy for most of its reasoning. However, at the beginning of a session, the system uses one small piece of *forward-chaining* logic in order to allow the user to prune the knowledge-base and provide the expert system with a starting point for a particular session. The user has the capability of using this forward-chaining capability to identify the specific area of interest and thereby decrease the amount of interaction required between the user and the system during a session. If the user is unable to provide information during this forward-chaining session, the expert system will apply its total knowledge to solving the problem.

The XSEL expert system assists DEC salespeople in the selection of DEC minicomputer components to be offered to a potential customer. XSEL is an interactive system that allows the salesperson to ask questions of the potential customer and to provide this information to the expert system. The expert system will then provide the salesperson with an initial system configuration and an initial floor layout for a system. XSEL is a planning and configuring system. It uses *rule-based knowledge representation* and a *forward-chaining* reasoning strategy.

The YES/MVS expert system was built to assist computer operators with the monitoring and controlling functions of the MVS operating system used on IBM mainframe computers. This system uses the *rule knowledge representation* scheme and a *forward-chaining* reasoning and control strategy.

The FOLIO expert system assists portfolio managers in the determination of client investment goals and assists in the selection of portfolios that will meet the client's goals. This system determines the needs of a particular client through an interactive session and then recommends the action that the portfolio manager should take. This expert system is *rule-based* and uses the *forward-chaining* control strategy for its reasoning.

The SAL expert system assists claims adjustors with the evaluation of claims related to asbestos exposure. This system uses knowledge about damages, plaintiff responsibility, and case characteristics, such as type of litigants, to assist in determining an appropriate claim adjustment. This expert system is *rule-based* and uses *forward chaining*.

The expert system known as ISIS assists factory managers with the development of job shop schedules. It is an expert planning system that acts as an intelligent assistant to factory managers. The system features a *hybrid knowledge representation* scheme that uses *both frames and rules*. The *control strategy is also a hybrid*.

The PTRANS expert system assists Digital Equipment Corporation with controlling the manufacture and distribution of its minicomputer systems. It uses customer orders and information about plant activity to develop a plan for the assembly of ordered computer systems. PTRANS also monitors the progress of the plan, diagnoses any problems that might be occurring on the manufacturing floor, and suggests solutions to the problems. PTRANS is designed to work with the XSEL expert system so that once an order is made through XSEL, a delivery date can be determined. PTRANS is a *rule-based, forward-chaining* expert system.

The WILLARD expert system is used by meteorologists in the diagnosis of meteorological conditions in the central United States. This system was developed specifically to determine the likelihood of severe thunderstorms that might occur in this region. The system obtains information from meteorologists on pertinent weather conditions for a particular area and then forecasts the likelihood of severe thunderstorms for that area. The *knowledge is represented in rules,* and the control strategy is *backward chaining.*

The FALCON expert system assists in the identification of probable causes of process disturbances in chemical process plants. It interprets numeric data from gauges, alarms, and switches in these plants by applying its knowledge of the process and of disturbances. The knowledge is represented in *both rule and semantic network* form. The inferencing used by FALCON includes *forward chaining* and a *causal model* paradigm.

The expert system known as ECESIS provides autonomous control for the environmental support system aboard a space station. This system will monitor events occurring in the space station and trigger necessary actions to keep the environment within certain parameters. This expert system uses a hybrid knowledge representation scheme that is based on *rules and semantic networks.* It uses a *hybrid reasoning* strategy.

The NAVEX expert system monitors radar data used to estimate the velocity and position of a space shuttle as it is getting ready to land. This expert system uses a hybrid knowledge representation scheme based on *rules and frames.* The inferencing performed includes *forward and backward chaining.* This system is interesting in that it runs in real time, processing information about the landing of a space shuttle and presenting this information to experts on the ground as the space shuttle is actually going through its landing phases.

FOSSIL is an expert system that supports the paleontology subject domain. FOSSIL assists nonexpert collectors in the identification of fossil specimens. It is written in PROLOG. FOSSIL's knowledge is represented in PROLOG assertions and is arranged in a taxonomy. FOSSIL uses a *logic knowledge representation.* Inferencing is based on a technique of *tracing inference paths via a polyclave algorithm.* FOSSIL's architecture is well suited for domains whose entities naturally fit into taxonomic structures. A FOSSIL-type architecture, for example, could be used for a spare parts expert system.

The expert system known as SYN is a *rule-based* system that uses *forward chaining* for its reasoning strategy. This expert system is used to synthesize new circuits. It does this by determining the values for components that are required in electrical circuits. This system uses some of the ideas that were developed for the EL expert system.

As we can see, systems that have been built to date use a variety of schemes and strategies to represent domain knowledge and provide support to their users. The expert system development tool that a knowledge engineer uses must provide the knowledge representation and reasoning strategy paradigms that are required for a particular problem. It is impossible to state exactly which schemes are best for each problem. The examples provided should, however, assist a new knowledge engineer in determining which might be effective for a similar problem.

If the problem a knowledge engineer wants to work on is not among the examples given, the engineer must research whether this particular type of problem has been supported with an expert system. The engineer should study projects that were successful and ones that were not, noting the knowledge representation and reasoning strategies used. The engineer should try to ascertain why some of the projects failed and why others succeeded. From this research and analysis, the knowledge engineer should be able to determine which knowledge representation schemes and reasoning strategies will best fit the problem at hand.

REQUISITE TOOL FUNCTIONALITY

The functional requirements of an expert system tool go beyond being able to represent domain expertise and knowledge and provide that information to the user when necessary. For many expert system applications to be effective for organizations, these tools will have to tie in to other automated systems in the organizations.

For example, where an expert system is going to provide information about the financial position of an organization, the expert system is going to have to be able to obtain knowledge base data from the knowledge base and corporate business data from the corporate database. This means that the expert system development tool should be able to help develop an interface between the expert system knowledge base and the corporate information system database. Expert system tools that provide this interface will be beneficial to the expert system developer insofar as this interface will not have to be custom-coded. Being able to connect the expert system to the corporate information system database is a function that some organizations will need from their expert system development tools.

Other users will require the capability of connecting the expert system to graphics systems. The graphics capabilities might be for input or output. More commonly, the need for graphics capability will be for graphics output. This output will often be used to represent graphically the meaning of some knowledge that the expert system is trying to communicate to its user. For example, if an expert maintenance system has just told its user that the user must repair an engine, some of the parts of the procedure of repairing the engine could be presented graphically. If a particular piece of the engine must be dismantled, the expert system could present graphics of the engine before it is dismantled, the access points for the particular parts that have to be dismantled, and the engine after it is dismantled. The expert system could also graphically show how to put the engine back together. Sometimes the adage "a picture is worth a thousand words" is very true. For some users, a picture is a lot easier to comprehend than any number of words. In places where graphical presentations are needed, it is important that the chosen expert system development tool have either graphic capabilities or the ability to connect to an effective graphics software system.

Other requisite tool functionalities that might be required for a particular application include the ability to connect to real-time processes, the ability to communicate with other automated systems through telecommunications assets, and the ability for expert systems to provide outputs other than text or graphics on a screen (for example, providing process control data directly to a process).

INTEROPERABILITY   Expert systems that will be most effective in the field in the future will most likely be those that have the ability to interoperate with other systems. There are two interoperability issues that a knowledge engineer should take into consideration when selecting an expert system development tool or expert system shell.

The first interoperability issue is that the tool, as a component of a development environment, should be able to interoperate with other software development tools. This has already been mentioned for tools found in database management systems and graphics systems. It is also important that the expert system tool be able to work with other automated system tools, such as language compilers. Many shells available today will work with various programming languages including C, Pascal, LISP, and PROLOG.

The second issue related to interoperability is that developed expert systems be able to cooperate with other automated systems. What we are talking about is the ability for developed, delivered expert systems to cooperate with other information systems and other automated systems within organizations. For example, if a company is in the business of processing chemicals, it might already have an automated control system for chemical processing. Such automated control systems are algorithmic, developed with programming languages like C and Pascal. Expert monitoring systems might assist these process control systems from the viewpoint of safety or efficiency.

From the viewpoint of safety, an expert system could be developed to observe various process attributes and correlate them in such a way as to be sensitive to the potential of a hazard or safety-related situation that might be developing. The potential hazard might be determined through the correlation of many other process control variables or through the history of a few variables as they change over time. If the expert monitoring system notices that a potential hazard is developing, it could warn the process control operators.

From an efficiency standpoint, an expert system could monitor a process and use the expert system's heuristics to determine if the process is being run at its most efficient potential. If it is, the system can communicate this fact to the operator. If it is not, the system can recommend process changes to the operator so that the process can run more efficiently.

Expert monitoring systems will need to interoperate with process control systems, directly, to get the real-time input data that they will require. They will also have to interoperate with whatever systems serve as user-system interfaces.

Another dimension in the use of expert systems in the process control environment is intelligent process control systems. These systems are hybrids. Parts of the systems are developed in a language like Pascal or C and provide algorithmic control data for the process. The other parts are expert systems that provide control information and data through heuristic knowledge and inferencing. The process control systems' algorithms accept input information and develop outputs. These outputs are usually acted on by the process systems.

The expert subsystem in an intelligent process control system would check the algorithms' outputs versus the system's state at the particular time that a control piece of information is to be sent back to the process system. If the expert control system has a heuristic that would modify the algorithmic control data, this modification would be performed prior to the sending of the process control data back to the process system. In the case of intelligent process control systems, the expert system would have to be able to interoperate with the control system both from the standpoint of input and output process data and from the standpoint of being able to communicate what the process control system is doing to the process operator. Therefore, the interoperability of an intelligent process control system includes inputs from the process system and outputs to the process system as well as inputs from and outputs to the human operator via a user-system interface.

Expert system building tools that assist knowledge engineers in the interoperability issue decrease the workload of the knowledge engineer and other computer developers. If a system to be developed is to interoperate with other automated systems and the expert system building tool does not provide for this interoperability, the software for this interoperability will have to be developed by the knowledge engineer or by others. Therefore, the knowledge engineer should ascertain the interoperability requirements for a particular expert system project and try to match them with the capabilities of the candidate expert system building tools.

SELECTION CRITERIA

The final subject in selecting the right expert system development tool that we will discuss is selection criteria. Choosing the right expert system development tool is similar to selecting other software products like database management systems. If an organization already has standard procedures for selecting software products, the selection of an expert system shell could use the same or similar procedures. The development of an expert system is the development of a software system. The selection of an expert system development tool is similar to the selection of any other software development tool.

In the development of an expert system, certain technical points must be addressed. These technical points should also be addressed during the tool selection process. We have already discussed domain requirements that must be fulfilled through effective knowledge representation schemes, reasoning strategies, and requisite tool functionality. We have also discussed interoperability requirements. Beyond these requirements, other technical issues that should be considered include the user-system interface and the knowledge acquisition facility.

Selection criteria should cover not only technical issues like what knowledge representation scheme is necessary to do the job but also business issues related to the purchase and use of expert system building tools. The company that the expert system building tool is being purchased from should be taken into consideration. Does this vendor support the tool? Does the vendor provide training with the tool? Is the training available at the vendor's site, or on-site at the customer's location, or both? Does the vendor provide knowledge engineering support and consulting support if necessary? What is the availability of documentation from the vendor? Is it only development documentation, or is run-time documentation also available?

Other important selection considerations include the price of the product, the cost of maintenance of the product, and the costs related to training, documentation, installation, and distribution of the developed expert system. If an organization produces an expert system that it wants to provide to many users in the field, the cost of run-time software packages must be taken into account. Most of the time, the expert system shell vendors require users to have at least a run-time copy of the shell software. This run-time copy must be purchased from the vendor. Some vendors allow organizations to have an organizationwide license. Other vendors require run-time licenses to be purchased on an as-needed basis.

If an organization already has a major investment in hardware, this hardware might need to be taken into consideration. If a particular shell does not run on any of the hardware already in the organization and the organization does not wish to invest in any new hardware, this shell will not be right for this organization. It is better first to select the problem, then the proper expert system building tools that will effectively support the problem, and finally the hardware on which the expert system building tools will be run.

Another consideration is vendors' long-term commitment to support their tools. The number of years vendors have been in business and their financial status are indicators of the likelihood that they will be available to support the tools in the future. The number of copies of the tools in use is also an indicator of acceptance and hence success. A rule of thumb is that a tool that has many users will most likely be around a long time and will receive vendor attention and support, while a product that has few users has a higher likelihood of not being around in the future.

A benefit of a large user base is that the tools are well tested by the user base, and often large user bases develop user groups. These user groups provide opportunities for users to come together and provide information to each other on how to use a particular tool more effectively. The information gained in user groups is often very beneficial to developers.

Besides the technical attributes and the business and vendor attributes, another area to consider is utility programs that are available either from the vendor of the expert system development tool or from third-party vendors that are also supporting the tool.

Often the existence of third-party support vendors shows a strong acceptance of a particular tool in the marketplace. In the area of expert system shells, third-party vendors might be providing knowledge acquisition facilities, knowledge acquisition editors, rule consistency checkers, graphic rule editors, and other facilities to make the development and maintenance of expert systems with a particular tool more efficient. These third-party vendors often are users of the particular tool and see a business opportunity to develop and sell a capability to make a popular expert system tool product more effective. In this area, the expert system tool market resembles the database management system market, where third-party vendors have developed performance and maintenance adjunct tools for popular DBMS products.

The process used to select an expert system tool should be thought out and documented beforehand. Figure 15.1 provides a picture of a possible selection process.

The first six selection steps should be taken sequentially:

1. Define the objectives.
2. Determine the constraints.
3. List the assumptions.
4. Obtain user requirements.
5. Assess the environment.
6. Research available tools.

Defining the objectives involves identifying what the expert system is going to do for the organization.

Determining the constraints involves exploring the limits and restrictions of this project. For instance, if the organization has determined that this expert system will run on an IBM PC or compatible, then one constraint is that the expert system tool or shell, or at least the run-time system, must run on an IBM PC or compatible.

Listing the assumptions makes sure that the knowledge engineer's assump-

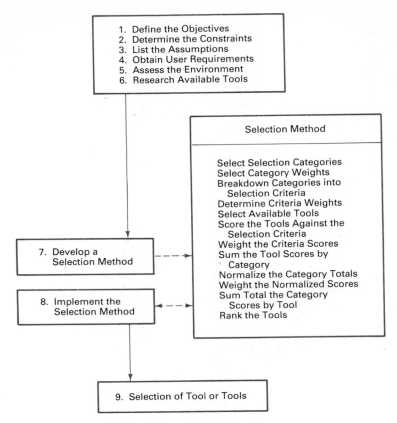

1. Define the Objectives
2. Determine the Constraints
3. List the Assumptions
4. Obtain User Requirements
5. Assess the Environment
6. Research Available Tools

Selection Method

Select Selection Categories
Select Category Weights
Breakdown Categories into
  Selection Criteria
Determine Criteria Weights
Select Available Tools
Score the Tools Against the
  Selection Criteria
Weight the Criteria Scores
Sum the Tool Scores by
  Category
Normalize the Category Totals
Weight the Normalized Scores
Sum Total the Category
  Scores by Tool
Rank the Tools

7. Develop a
   Selection Method

8. Implement the
   Selection Method

9. Selection of Tool or Tools

Figure 15.1   The selection process

tions about the project are recorded. For example, one assumption might be that the user would like to have the expert system's output in both text and graphical format.

The next step is to obtain specific requirements from the user. The user must tell the knowledge engineer what is needed to help the user get his or her job done. The knowledge engineer can also present the user with the constraints and the assumptions as the knowledge engineer understands them and obtain feedback from the user.

The next step is to assess the environment in which the expert system is going to run. The environment is assessed by looking at how the expert system can fit into the existing organization and its operations. Special interface requirements to existing manual and automated procedures and systems must be determined.

The sixth step in the selection process is to research the available tools. The knowledge engineer should either do this personally or engage a knowledge engineering consultant to help. All available tools that might meet the requirements of the particular project should be investigated and considered.

The next two steps in the selection process are to construct and implement a selection methodology. We present one methodology for the selection process (as illustrated in Figure 15.1 and discussed here). If this process does not fit the standard operating procedures of a particular organization, a different one can be substituted.

The final step is tool selection. The information garnered in the two selection methodology steps is used to assist in selecting the appropriate tool or tools for the expert system project. The selected tools are purchased, and expert system construction may begin.

The selection method should take into account the project to be supported and the organization's selection and procurement procedures. One selection method that might be used entails 12 steps, as shown in Figure 15.1:

1. Select selection categories.
2. Select category weights.
3. Break down categories into selection criteria.
4. Determine criteria weights.
5. Select available tools.
6. Score tools against the criteria.
7. Weight the criteria scores.
8. Sum the tool scores by category.
9. Normalize the category totals.
10. Weight the normalized scores.
11. Sum the category scores by tool.
12. Rank the tools.

The first selection task is to determine selection categories. A list of categories of selection criteria is developed. For instance, one category might be knowledge representation; another might be reasoning strategies (control mechanisms or inferencing techniques); a third might be interoperability with other software development tools; another might be interoperability of the developed expert system with other automated systems; another might be cost elements related to the purchase of the expert system; yet another might be attributes that have to do with support of the tool.

Each category must be weighted in terms of importance; therefore, the next step is to determine category weights. Technical issues like knowledge representation and reasoning strategies should be given a lot of weight since the success of the project will, to a great extent, depend on the selected tools' capabilities in these areas.

Category: Vendor/Business Data — Raw Data — Tools/Products Being Scored

Selection Criteria	Weight Factor	Score Range*	ART	KEE	KC	Super Expert	Knowledge Pro or KP	I2+	EXSYS	PC Easy	PC+	KES	N EXPERT	EXPERT 1	Gold Works	ESE	Intelligence Compiler or IC	GURU	SAGE	TIMM	First Class	VP EXPERT
Vendor: Years in business		0–5																				
Vendor: Financial status		0–5																				
Product: Number of copies sold		0–5																				
Vendor support available		0/5																				
Vendor training available		0/5																				
On-site training available		0/5																				
Vendor knowledge engineering available		0/5																				

Vendor hotline available	0/5									
Product documentation	0–5									
Price	0–5									
Annual maintenance costs	0–5									
Documentation costs	0–5									
Run-time license costs	0–5									
Third-party add-on tools available	0/5									
Third-party training available	0/5									
Third-party knowledge engineering available	0/5									

*0/5 denotes a binary where 0 stands for "capability does not exist" and 5 stands for "capability does exist." 0–5 denotes a continuum with 5 a high score and 0 a low score.

Figure 15.2 Category score sheet

Tabulated Data

Category: Vendor/Business Data

Tools/Products Being Scored

Selection Criteria	ART	KEE	KC	S1	IKE	12+	EXSYS	PC Easy	PC+	KES	N EXPERT	EXPERT 1	ACORN	ESE	M1	GURU	SAGE	TIMM	First Class	VP EXPERT
Vendor: Years in business																				
Vendor: Financial status																				
Product: Number of copies sold																				
Vendor support available																				
Vendor training available																				
On-site training available																				
Vendor knowledge engineering available																				

Vendor hotline available												
Product documentation												
Price												
Annual maintenance costs												
Documentation costs												
Run-time license costs												
Third-party add-on tools available												
Third-party training available												
Third-party knowledge engineering available												
Category totals:												
Normalized results (percentage):												

Figure 15.3   Category worksheet

Category Totals | **Final Results**

Tools/Products Being Scored

Category	Weight Factor	ART	KEE	KC	S1	iKE	I2+	EXSYS	PC Easy	PC+	KES	N EXPERT	EXPERT 1	ACORN	ESE	M1	GURU	SAGE	TIMM	First Class	VP EXPERT
Knowledge representation																					
Reasoning strategy																					
Interoperability: Tools																					
Interoperability: Systems																					
OEM-system interface																					
Knowledge acquisition tools																					
Vendor/business																					
Final totals:																					
Ranking:																					

Figure 15.4 Final results worksheet

The next step in the selection methodology is to break down categories into specific selection criteria. For example, the knowledge representation category can be broken down into the different knowledge representation schemes that are available (for example, rules, frames, semantic networks, and logic). This breakdown will form the basis for the actual analysis between the available tools and how well they support project requirements.

Determining criteria weights for each criterion is the next selection step. Each of the criteria is important to investigate. However, for a specific set of project requirements, some criteria are more important than others. Therefore, weights are attached to each of the criteria to reflect its estimated importance to the project.

The next step is to select available tools, the ones that will be used for the actual scoring. If some of the products that are available in the marketplace are totally out of scope for a project, they can be dropped from consideration. For example, if total project funds available are $50,000, a tool that costs $75,000 is beyond the scope of the project.

Once the products to be scored are selected, scoring is performed. For each selection criterion, a score is given to each tool. This process will take a lot of time and investigation. It will show where the tools support and do not support the project requirements.

The next step is to weight the criteria scores using the weights developed previously. After the criteria scores are weighted, the product scores are summed by category. After the category scores are summed, the category totals are normalized. The normalized scores are then weighted. Next, totals of the category scores by tool are calculated. The tools now are ranked from highest to lowest. This information plus the raw scores are used by the project manager or knowledge engineer to select the tool or tools that will be used for the project.

To apply the selection methodology effectively, score sheets should be designed and used. Figure 15.2 provides an example of a category score sheet. Notice that this score sheet is broken down into the selection criteria for the category. Each category should have a similar sheet.

Figure 15.3 presents another category worksheet. This worksheet shows tabulated data (versus raw data shown in Figure 15.2). The raw scores derived as shown in Figure 15.2 are multiplied by their appropriate weighting factors to calculate the tabulated data scores. These scores are totaled by tool. The tool scores are then normalized.

Figure 15.4 is a category total score worksheet. Totals are calculated by tool. The weighting factors for the categories are provided on this worksheet. When this sheet is entirely filled in, the final totals and ranking are available.

This selection methodology should assist the knowledge engineer in selecting the most effective expert system building tool or tools for an organization's needs for a particular project. It should be remembered that the development of a selection methodology and the use of this methodology, if used in as consistent and accurate a manner as possible, should provide the organization with a realistic assessment of the expert system building tools available and their applicability to the project.

SUMMARY   The selection of the right expert system building tools involves three major concepts:

1. Problem domain requirements versus expert system tool capabilities
2. Interoperability of the expert system development tools with other development tools, as well as interoperability of the completed expert systems with other automated systems
3. Specific selection criteria used in selecting expert system building tools for specific projects

The first concept, domain requirements versus expert system tool capabilities, is specific to expert system technology. This concept includes such areas as knowledge representation, reasoning strategy, and tool functionality. The second concept, interoperability, is becoming important to expert system developers, as to software developers of all automated technologies, and its importance will continue to grow. The third concept involves defining and applying selection criteria to select appropriate expert system building tools. If consistent selection techniques are used, the tools selected should effectively support an organization's expert system building projects.

16 THE FUTURE OF EXPERT SYSTEM TECHNOLOGY

Expert system technology is gaining wide commercial acceptance. Firms are talking about their expert system project successes. Many other firms are studying and experimenting with the technology. This interest has generated a demand for expert system development tools. Companies have emerged to meet the demand. To improve their expert system products and to develop product differentiation, these expert system tool vendors are performing research and will be developing new tools. Some vendors and government agencies are sponsoring research at universities.

In the future, watch for improvements in five expert system technology areas:

1. Knowledge representation
2. Knowledge acquisition
3. Expert system tools
4. Expert system design
5. Expert system programming

KNOWLEDGE REPRESENTATION

Knowledge representation is key to the development of effective expert systems. Figure 16.1 lists areas of research interest for knowledge representation. Products of this research will be visible in new methodologies and tools in the future.

Existing knowledge representation schemes will be extended. For example, the rule knowledge representation scheme might be extended to handle inheritance directly.

Presently, we do not know the theoretical limitations of the knowledge representation schemes that we are using. Research will continue to seek out

- Improvement to existing knowledge representations
- Integration of existing knowledge representations
- Development of new knowledge representation schemes

Figure 16.1   The future for knowledge representation

and understand the bounds. At the same time, we will try to extend the bounds. If our present rule systems can effectively handle 10,000 rules, we would like to be able to extend this limitation to 100,000.

Where extended knowledge representation schemes are sought for particular requirements and the extensions are not immediately available, engineers will integrate knowledge representation schemes. These integrations will ensure that each piece of knowledge is codified once, in one representation scheme (the one that most easily and completely can provide an effective representation of the knowledge entity) and that the integrated schemes will work together to provide the desired consultations.

New knowledge representation schemes will be developed and provided in new expert system tools or new releases of existing tool products. Two knowledge representation schemes to look for in the future are the model-based knowledge representation scheme and the script knowledge representation scheme. Model-based systems are developed through the specification of an analog model of the original problem. Scripts are frames that include a single dimension of time that includes such specifications as done-before and done-after.

KNOWLEDGE ACQUISITION

Knowledge acquisition is an important research area. Effective knowledge acquisition is key to the realization of useful, cost-effective expert systems. Expert systems are useful only after the requisite subject domain knowledge is acquired, codified, and applied.

The majority of the time spent in developing an expert system, when using an expert system shell, is with knowledge acquisition activities. Decreasing costs related to knowledge acquisition would significantly decrease expert system development costs. Decreasing knowledge acquisition costs can be achieved in several ways:

1. Decrease the amount of time required to acquire the knowledge

2. Decrease the skill requirements of the person acquiring the knowledge

3. Automate some aspects of knowledge acquisition

4. Enable users and domain experts to add to the knowledge

5. Sell packaged knowledge where appropriate (e.g., textbook knowledge or static knowledge)

Knowledge acquisition research is in progress in industrial and university laboratories. Figure 16.2 lists some of the areas of research and development interest. This research and its results will determine the future for knowledge acquisition.

Automated knowledge acquisition tools should be able to support all three knowledge acquisition cost reduction activities. These tools should be able to decrease the amount of time required to acquire knowledge in at least two ways. First, they might be able to extract domain knowledge from other automated resources (such as databases). Second, some automated knowledge acquisition tools will assist the knowledge engineer by performing some of the knowledge acquisition tasks (for example, isolating the appropriate subset of subject domain concepts and facts that properly characterize the task to be supported with an expert system).

Automated knowledge acquisition tools will allow more people to acquire knowledge for expert system knowledge bases. Effective knowledge acquisition presently requires extensive training and experience. With better tools, these requirements should be relaxed. For example, a lot of skill is required when an expert provides a knowledge engineer with domain knowledge data that does not neatly fit any of the knowledge representation schemes supported by the expert system shells that the knowledge engineer has access to or that exist commercially. The knowledge engineer must handle the mismatch between the expert's knowledge data form and the forms supported by the available expert system shells. If a tool can be developed to solve this knowledge acquisition problem, the knowledge engineer will not need to know how to handle it.

Automating the knowledge acquisition tasks is a central theme with automated knowledge acquisition tools. We have referred to automated methods to assist with goals like decreasing the amount of time required of a knowledge engineer or domain expert in developing an expert system. Here we are now explicitly thinking about the goal of shifting knowledge acquisition tasks from people to the computer. If the cost of developing these automation tools plus

- Automated knowledge acquisition tools
- Automated knowledge consistency tools and editors
- Self-learning systems

Figure 16.2   The future for knowledge acquisition

the cost of using them is less than the cost of manual knowledge acquisition, these tools would decrease the cost of knowledge acquisition. The construction of generalized knowledge acquisition tools that are cost-effective to build and use should be feasible. Knowledge acquisition tools that automate knowledge acquisition tasks (such as knowledge data management) should become available in the future.

Automated knowledge consistency tools and editors are being developed in research laboratories. Knowledge consistency tools and knowledge editors will most likely be expert systems in their own right. These tools and editors will assist expert system builders in three important ways. First, they will help the expert system builder develop a knowledge base that represents its knowledge in a consistent manner. This might be achieved through knowledge templates. The builder would provide the knowledge to the tool through a builder- or tool-defined template form, and the tool would then apply the knowledge to the knowledge-base accordingly.

The second service these tools will provide the expert system builder is to ensure consistency of knowledge data entities in the knowledge base. This will often be accomplished by comparing the new knowledge data entities an expert system builder is applying against the current knowledge data in the expert system's knowledge-base. If a consistency checking tool identifies a potential inconsistency between some knowledge data in the knowledge-base and knowledge being applied by the expert system builder, the tool will notify the builder prior to applying the knowledge data to the knowledge-base. For example, a rule in the knowledge-base might read

> IF power light is lit
> THEN power is being supplied.

If the following rule is provided to the tool, the tool would notify the builder of a potential inconsistency:

> IF NOT power light is lit
> THEN power is being supplied.

In this case where the NOT is a keyword of the particular expert system shell, this consistency check is easy. However, consider the following rule:

> IF power light is not lit
> THEN power is being supplied.

This rule would be more difficult to check against the rule in the knowledge-base. Now the consistency checker must have some knowledge of the English-language components of the rule IF and THEN clauses. However, with the use of the natural-language and expert system technologies, such consistency checking is feasible.

Sometime consistency checkers will either have to have subject domain expertise or have to work with the expert system builder. Look at the following two rules:

```
IF the color of the sky at sunset is red
THEN it will be nice in the morning.

IF the color of the sky at sunset is blue
THEN it will be nice in the morning.
```

It is possible that both rules are correct. Even though these rules conclude the same fact from different conditions, they both might be valid. Some shells let us write this same knowledge in the following shorter form:

```
IF the color of the sky at sunset is red
OR the color of the sky at sunset is blue
THEN it will be nice in the morning.
```

Using this form would assist a consistency checker by explicitly stating that both conditions are valid for the same conclusion.

What if the two rules are not consistent? In this case, when the consistency checker informs the expert system builder of the potential consistency problem, the builder can modify the new rule, forget applying the new rule, modify the rule in the knowledge base that is in conflict with the new rule, or delete the rule in the knowledge base.

The consistency checking capability will become available in an evolutionary manner. Expert system development product vendors will provide this capability either as part of their knowledge editors or as a separate tool that is used in a cooperative manner with their editors. As knowledge consistency is better understood, as a result of research, consistency checking capabilities will evolve from simple pattern matchers to expert knowledge consistency checking systems.

The last service the automated knowledge consistency tools and editors will help to provide is a uniform, consistent knowledge presentation to the expert system user.

Self-learning systems are truly the hope of the future. With self-learning systems, knowledge acquisition could be accomplished much more quickly. However, research in this area has yet to produce effective tools. The only tools that have been produced so far are induction tools.

Human experts gain a lot of their expertise from experience. Each related event helps an expert by providing new data about the subject domain. The expert stores this data. As a person experiences more events, a person finds meaningful, useful causal relationships between the various pieces of data. Often the person who is the expert is the person with the most data points and the ability to develop these causal associations. Attempts have been made to develop knowledge acquisition tools based on this inductive process. Limited success has been realized so far. Effective self-learning induction programs will most likely be available in the future.

The greatest potential users of these induction systems will be organizations that have large databases. The induction systems will read these databases, look for meaningful causal relationships, and develop knowledge-base entities. For example, a large retail merchandising organization might have large historical databases of merchandise sales. Relationships among the data might allow an induction system to develop rules like these:

> IF the item is a dress
> AND the item comes in light and dark colors
> AND the season is winter
> THEN ship the light-colored dresses to Florida
> AND ship the dark-colored dresses to New England.

Another area of interest in self-learning research is tied to another knowledge source that human experts use, textbooks and subject-specific magazines and journals. It is hoped that someday we will use electronic text scanners to read this material and then use an intelligent knowledge acquisition program to derive domain knowledge from this material and load it into our knowledge bases.

Other self-learning ideas are being researched. One other self-learning area of interest is dynamic knowledge-base extension and modification. Here the self-learning capability is integrated with the user-system interface of an operational expert system. As the user interacts with the system, the self-learning module monitors user-system communications. One way the self-learning module can derive new knowledge is through the archiving of user responses, building a database of this information, and then applying induction techniques, looking for information relationships that will point to new domain knowledge. Another self-learning technique could be developed whereby, after the expert system provides the user with a recommendation, the user is asked a few pertinent questions about the recommendation. The user's responses are stored in a database. Again, an induction algorithm could be used. The result is an extension or modification of the expert system's knowledge-base.

Knowledge acquisition will continue to be an important area of research. Cost-effective, time-efficient knowledge acquisition techniques and tools are needed if we are to realize our dreams of supporting the many subject areas that could benefit from this technology.

EXPERT SYSTEM TOOLS

The first expert systems were built without the benefit of expert system tools or shells. These first expert systems required hundreds of thousands of worker-hours for their development. The second and current generation of expert systems use the first generation of expert system shells. Second-generation expert systems are being built in thousands to tens of thousands of worker-hours. The next generation of expert systems will be built with the second generation of expert system shells. These expert systems should be more capable yet take less time to develop. Significant systems should take less than one worker-year to develop.

The second generation of expert system shells should be built in a modular fashion. The basic shell product will be a structural module (see Figure 16.3). This module will provide some basic development capabilities, such as general knowledge data management and a knowledge-engineer expert-system-building tool interface. This module will be built in such a manner as to allow it to accept other, more specific function modules. These function modules will plug into the structural module and provide the expert system shell with requisite functions like inferencing and with nonrequisite but useful functions like graphics (see Figure 16.3). These function modules will provide various functional capabilities; for example, there might be two inference engine modules available, one for backward chaining and one for forward chaining. Although these mod-

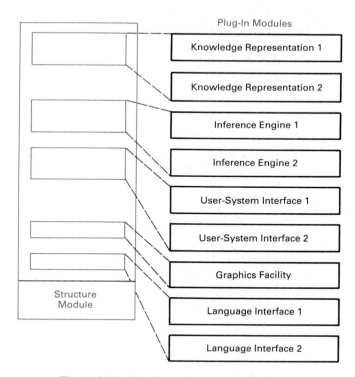

Figure 16.3   The future for expert system tools

ules provide different functions, the structural module provides them in a consistent way. The builder only has to learn one development environment.

The structural module will provide one additional and valuable service: the capability to use more than one type of functional module simultaneously. This will give, for example, the ability to use more than one inference scheme through an effective integration of the capabilities of the various functional modules.

The second generation of expert systems will also bring other advances. For example, generic and task-specific shell components should become available. Generic shell components will be designed to provide support to a specific general problem domain. Examples of generic problems include maintenance, configuration, and proposal generation.

Designing an expert system involves studying the subject domain, matching effective knowledge representation schemes and inferencing schemes to the needs of the domain problem, studying the intended users, and matching an effective user-system interface to the needs and abilities of the intended users. Included in the design task area is the selection of the expert system building tools. These tasks are presently performed manually. In the future, automated design aids will be available. Figure 16.4 lists some of the possibilities.

Intelligent design tools will be developed to assist the knowledge engineer with many design tasks. Expert-system-based tools will be developed to assist in the following areas:

- Determining problem domain characteristics
- Making sure all important attributes of a problem are studied
- Determining which knowledge representation scheme(s) to use
- Determining which inference mechanism(s) to use
- Determining user capabilities
- Selecting effective user-system interface designs

> - Intelligent design tools
>   — Automatic selection of knowledge representation
>   — Automatic selection of inference mechanism(s)
> - Automated design tools
>   — Graphics and icons
>   — CAD-like design

Figure 16.4   The future for expert system design

- Selecting expert system building tools that will support the requirements of the system

- Determining if other software needs to be designed and, if it does, do that software design work

Automated design tools using graphics, icons, CAD-like tools, and expert system modules will be available. Expert system builders will be able to use these aids to determine quickly what the design of a particular expert system will be and what expert system building tools are most appropriate.

EXPERT SYSTEM PROGRAMMING

Expert system programming today is a tedious manual task. There is a lot of potential for providing automated support for this work. Figure 16.5 lists some of the aids we will be seeing.

Acquired knowledge needs to be encoded in the language of the chosen shell. The user-system interface must be coded. If needed, other software programming must be performed and interface modules coded.

Expert programming assistants will help the knowledge engineer with many of these programming steps. For example, an expert programming assistant could help codify acquired subject domain knowledge in the syntax of the chosen shell. Automated programming systems, CAM-tools, and tools that use graphics and icons will provide the knowledge engineer with automated aids to speed up the programming tasks. Some of these kinds of programming tools are already starting to make their way into other computer programming arenas.

EXPERT SYSTEM INTERFACING

Expert systems started as separate, autonomous systems. Expert systems were originally developed to provide a single-user, consultation-type interface. The system would ask questions, the user would respond, and the system would offer its consultation advice when it could. Expert systems were developed ei-

- Expert programming assistance systems
- Automated programming systems
- CAM-like programming tools
- Use of graphics and icons

Figure 16.5   The future for expert system programming

- Hardware to connect LISP-machine-based expert systems to traditional computer systems
- Hardware that will accept LISP-machine-based software and software based on traditional computer systems simultaneously
- Software that will port LISP-machine-based expert systems over to traditional computer systems
- Software that will port expert systems to special-purpose hardware like ROM-based microprocessor systems, industrial controllers, and military systems
- Software to allow intercommunication between expert systems and other computer-based systems
- Software to allow expert systems the ability to receive real-world data and information and to send their results to other systems and machines

Figure 16.6   Interface products for expert system technology

ther on single-user systems like LISP machines or as stand-alone, single-user programs on multiuser systems like the DEC-10.

With the increase in interest in expert system technology and its applicability, expert systems are now starting to be interfaced with other computer systems and machines. Products that will interface expert system technology with other systems and machines will be appearing on the market. Figure 16.6 provides ideas of the services some of these products will provide.

Expert systems that are used as direct consultation systems for users will also see new system designs and new integration designs with other automated systems. For example, user-system interfaces of future expert systems will be integrated with speech recognition and synthesis systems. Users will be able to vocalize their queries and responses, and expert systems will provide questions and consultations to the user verbally. These speech interfaces will be helpful to users such as machinists who have their hands full. Other interface system possibilities include vision and advanced graphics.

EXPERT SYSTEM APPLICATIONS

Expert system technology is going to be applied to many different application areas. Figure 16.7 provides one view of how these systems can be classified. As can be deduced from the figure, expert system technology will be used to develop a large number of new products and new configurations of established products. When established products are modified to include an expert system

Product-Specific Systems

- Commodity-based
- Systems developed from a single design to be embedded in a mass-marketed product
- Examples include vehicles, home appliances, instruments, and office machines.

Service-Specific Systems

- Generic-task-based
- Systems designed to be employed by many users doing the same task
- Examples include computer system use adviser and database access assistant.

Organization-Specific Systems

- Corporate-goal-based
- Systems designed for a single organization's use
- Examples include intelligent customer services assistant, expert configuration system, and intelligent proposal-generation assistant.

Task-Specific Systems

- Personal workstation
- Systems developed to assist a single, key knowledge worker
- Examples include an intelligent assistant for job shop scheduling, an intelligent sales manager's assistant, and an intelligent assistant for the system programmer.

Figure 16.7 The application of expert systems

as a component or when an established product item is replaced with an expert system, the expert-system-supported entity will often be described as "intelligent." Figure 16.8 lists some of the expert-system-based products that will be appearing on the market.

Where an expert system is going to be integrated into a product that is not computer-based, a computer system architecture will have to be included in the expert system design. Some of these designs will use minicomputers, workstations, or personal computers. However, where space is an issue, these computing resources will not offer viable solutions. AT&T has already announced a solution. Bell Laboratories has announced that they have produced an inference

- Intelligent technical manuals
- Intelligent repair manuals
- Intelligent process controllers
- Intelligent monitoring systems
- Intelligent training systems

Figure 16.8 New product lines: Expert-system-based products

engine and a knowledge-base on a custom CMOS chip. They claim that this expert system chip can perform 80,000 fuzzy logical inferences per second. We can expect to see more chip-based expert systems and components on the market in the future. These chips will certainly make it easy to deliver expert system components to commodity items like digitally controlled microwave ovens.

SUMMARY

The future of expert system technology looks exciting. The successes already experienced with the technology, though modest, have generated great interest, research support, and business development. The research should provide us with more capable systems that can be developed with fewer resources, particularly human resources. This should result in generating even more interest.

Businesses are developing to support the technology. Some of these new businesses are chartered to develop tools to build expert systems. Other businesses are chartered to assist organizations in the development of expert systems.

With the products and services of these firms, organizations should find it relatively easy to introduce expert system technology into their operations.

Some of the expert systems already developed are affecting corporate operations in positive ways. Systems help with organizational plan development, project management, product concept formulation, product design, equipment maintenance, data analysis, and process monitoring, among others. Expert systems now exist or are being developed to deal with virtually all of the analytic problems that organizations must deal with today.

It is now clear that there are vast numbers of applications of expert systems in business, many of which can add to the profits of a business. Some of these systems will become relatively easy to build. Some specific types of expert systems are needed by businesses everywhere, for example, expert systems that guide in equipment maintenance and diagnostics, expert systems for generating sales proposals, expert systems for software development, and expert systems for customer service hotlines. Packages are likely to be available for these and other mass-market applications.

We can expect to see the number of expert systems developed and the intelligence and capability of these systems increase dramatically. As the knowledge engineering discipline moves on and improves, expert systems will be developed with the ability to deal with more and more complex problems whose solutions elude numeric analysis techniques. Expert systems will move from the role of assistant to the role of adviser and from the role of monitor to the role of controller.

As the expert system technology is integrated with other advanced technologies like the vision and speech technologies, computer systems nearing the capabilities of *2001's* HAL 9000 computer will probably be here by 2001.

INDEX

Index

TEAR OUT THIS PAGE TO ORDER OTHER TITLES BY JAMES MARTIN

THE JAMES MARTIN BOOKS

Quantity	Title	Title Code	Price	Total $
_____	Action Diagrams: Clearly Structured Program Design	00330–1	$42.00	_____
_____	Application Development Without Programmers	03894–3	$59.00	
	A Breakthrough In Making Computers Friendly:			
_____	The Macintosh Computer (paper)	08157–0	$26.95	_____
_____	(case)	08158–8	$35.00	_____
_____	Building Expert Systems: A Tutorial	08624–9	$48.00	_____
_____	Communications Satellite Systems	15316–3	$64.00	_____
_____	Computer Data-Base Organization, 2nd Edition	16542–3	$59.00	_____
_____	The Computerized Society	16597–7	$28.67	_____
_____	Computer Networks and Distributed Processing:	16525–8	$59.00	_____
	Software, Techniques and Architecture			
_____	Data Communication Technology	19664–2	$49.00	
_____	Design and Strategy of Distributed Data Processing	20165–7	$62.00	
_____	Design of Man-Computer Dialogues	20125–1	$60.00	
_____	Design of Real-Time Computer Systems	20140–0	$60.00	
_____	Diagramming Techniques for Analysts and	20879–3	$55.00	_____
	Programmers			
_____	An End User's Guide to Data Base	27712–9	$46.00	_____
_____	Fourth-Generation Languages, Vol. I: Principles	32967–2	$46.00	_____
_____	Fourth-Generation Languages, Vol. II:	32974–8	$46.00	_____
	Representative 4GLs			
_____	Fourth-Generation Languages, Vol. III:	32976–3	$46.00	_____
	4GLs from IBM			
_____	Future Developments in Telecommunications,	34585–0	$61.00	_____
	2nd Edition			
_____	An Information Systems Manifesto	46476–8	$54.00	_____
_____	Introduction to Teleprocessing	49981–4	$48.00	_____
_____	Managing the Data-Base Environment	55058–2	$62.00	_____
_____	Principles of Data-Base Management	70891–7	$48.00	_____
_____	Principles of Data Communication	70989–9	$44.00	_____
_____	Recommended Diagramming Standards for Analysts	76737–6	$48.00	_____
	and Programmers			
_____	Security, Accuracy, and Privacy in Computer	79899–1	$62.00	_____
	Systems			
_____	SNA: IBM's Networking Solution	81514–2	$48.00	_____
_____	Software Maintenance: The Problem and Its	82236–1	$54.00	_____
	Solutions			
_____	Strategic Data Planning Methodologies	85111–3	$48.00	_____
_____	Structured Techniques: The Basis for CASE, Revised	85493–5	$52.00	_____
	Edition			
_____	Systems Analysis for Data Transmission	88130–0	$64.00	_____
_____	System Design from Provably Correct Constructs	88148–2	$53.33	_____
_____	Technology's Crucible (paper)	90202–3	$15.95	_____
_____	Telecommunications and the Computer, 2nd Edition	90249–4	$59.00	_____

(over)

_____	Telematic Society: A Challenge for Tomorrow	90246–0	$31.95	_____
_____	Teleprocessing Network Organization	90245–2	$38.00	_____
	VSAM: Access Method Services and Programming		
_____	Techniques	94417–3	$48.00	_____

Total: _____

-discount (if appropriate) _____

New Total: _____

AND TAKE ADVANTAGE OF THESE SPECIAL OFFERS!

When ordering 3 or 4 copies (of the same or different titles) take 10% off the total list price.

When ordering 5 to 20 (of the same or different titles) take 15% off the total list price.

To receive a greater discount when ordering more than 20 copies, call or write:

Special Sales Department
College Marketing
Prentice Hall
Englewood Cliffs, NJ 07632
(201)592–2046

SAVE!

If payment accompanies order, plus your state's sales tax where applicable, Prentice Hall pays postage and handling charges. Same return privilege refund guarantee. Please do not mail cash.

☐ **PAYMENT ENCLOSED**—shipping and handling to be paid by publisher (please include your state's tax where applicable).

☐ **SEND BOOKS ON 15-DAY TRIAL BASIS** and bill me (with small charge for shipping and handling).

Name _____

Address _____

City _____ State _____ Zip _____

I prefer to charge my   ☐ Visa   ☐ MasterCard

Card Number _____ Expiration Date _____

Signature _____

All prices listed are subject to change without notice.
This offer not valid outside U.S.

Mail your order to: Prentice Hall Book Distribution Center
Route 59 at Brook Hill Drive
West Nyack, NY 10994

Dept. 1: D-JMAR-NK(4)

THE COMPUTERIZED SOCIETY	INFORMATION ENGINEERING (Volume I: Introduction and Strategy)	APPLICATION DEVELOPMENT WITHOUT PROGRAMMERS	DIAGRAMMING TECHNIQ ANALYSTS AND PROGRA
TELEMATIC SOCIETY: A CHALLENGE FOR TOMORROW		ACTION DIAGRAMS: CLEARLY STRUCTURED PROGRAM DESIGN	
TECHNOLOGY'S CRUCIBLE			
SECURITY, ACCURACY, AND PRIVACY IN COMPUTER SYSTEMS	INFORMATION ENGINEERING (Volume II: Analysis, Design, and Construction)	PROGRAMMING REAL-TIME COMPUTER SYSTEMS	RECOMMENDED DIAGRA STANDARDS FOR ANALYSTS AND PROGRA
	STRATEGIC DATA-PLANNING METHODOLOGIES (second edition)	FOURTH-GENERATION LANGUAGES (Volume I: Principles)	STRUCTURED TECHNI A BASIS FOR CAS
	SOFTWARE MAINTENANCE: THE PROBLEM AND ITS SOLUTIONS	FOURTH-GENERATION LANGUAGES (Volume II: Representative 4G Ls)	ACTION DIAGRAM CLEARLY STRUCTU PROGRAM DESIG
	DESIGN AND STRATEGY FOR DISTRIBUTED DATA PROCESSING	FOURTH-GENERATION LANGUAGES (Volume III: 4G Ls from IBM)	DATABASE ANALY AND DESIGN
	CORPORATE COMMUNICATIONS NETWORKS		DATA COMMUNICA DESIGN TECHNIQ
			SOFTWARE MAINTENAN PROBLEM AND ITS SOL
			SYSTEM DESIGN FROM PROVABLY CORRECT CONSTRU
			EXPERT SYSTEMS: DE AND CONSTRUCTI